This is the last page.

BEASTARS reads from right to left to preserve the orientation of the original Japanese artwork.

Cats of the Louvre

by TAIYO MATSUMOTO

A surreal tale of the secret world of the cats of the Louvre,
told by Eisner Award winner Taiyo Matsumoto.

The world-renowned Louvre museum in Paris contains more than
just the most famous works of art in history. At night, within its
darkened galleries, an unseen and surreal world comes alive—
a world witnessed only by the small family of cats that lives in
the attic. Until now…

Translated by *Tekkonkinkreet* film director Michael Arias.

The Way of the House Husband

It's a day in the life of your average househusband—if your average househusband is the legendary yakuza "the Immortal Dragon"!

Story and Art by
Kousuke Oono

A former yakuza legend leaves it all behind to become your everyday househusband. But it's not easy to walk away from the gangster life, and what should be mundane household tasks are anything but!

CHILDREN OF THE WHALES

In this postapocalyptic fantasy, a sea of sand swallows everything but the past.

In an endless sea of sand drifts the Mud Whale, a floating island city of clay and magic. In its chambers a small community clings to survival, cut off from its own history by the shadows of the past.

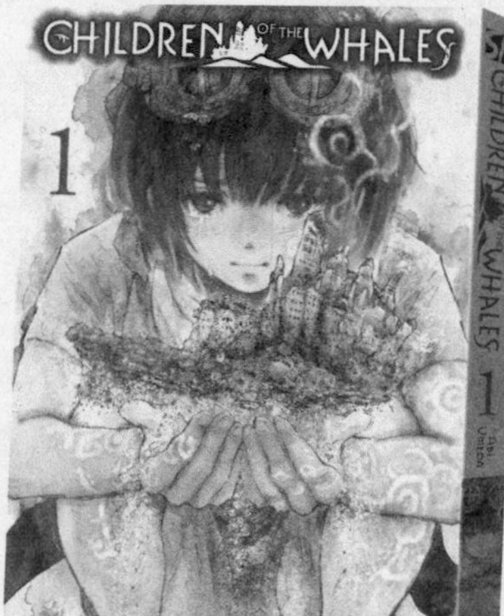
CHILDREN OF THE WHALES
1
ABI UMEDA
CHILDREN OF THE WHALES
1
VIZ

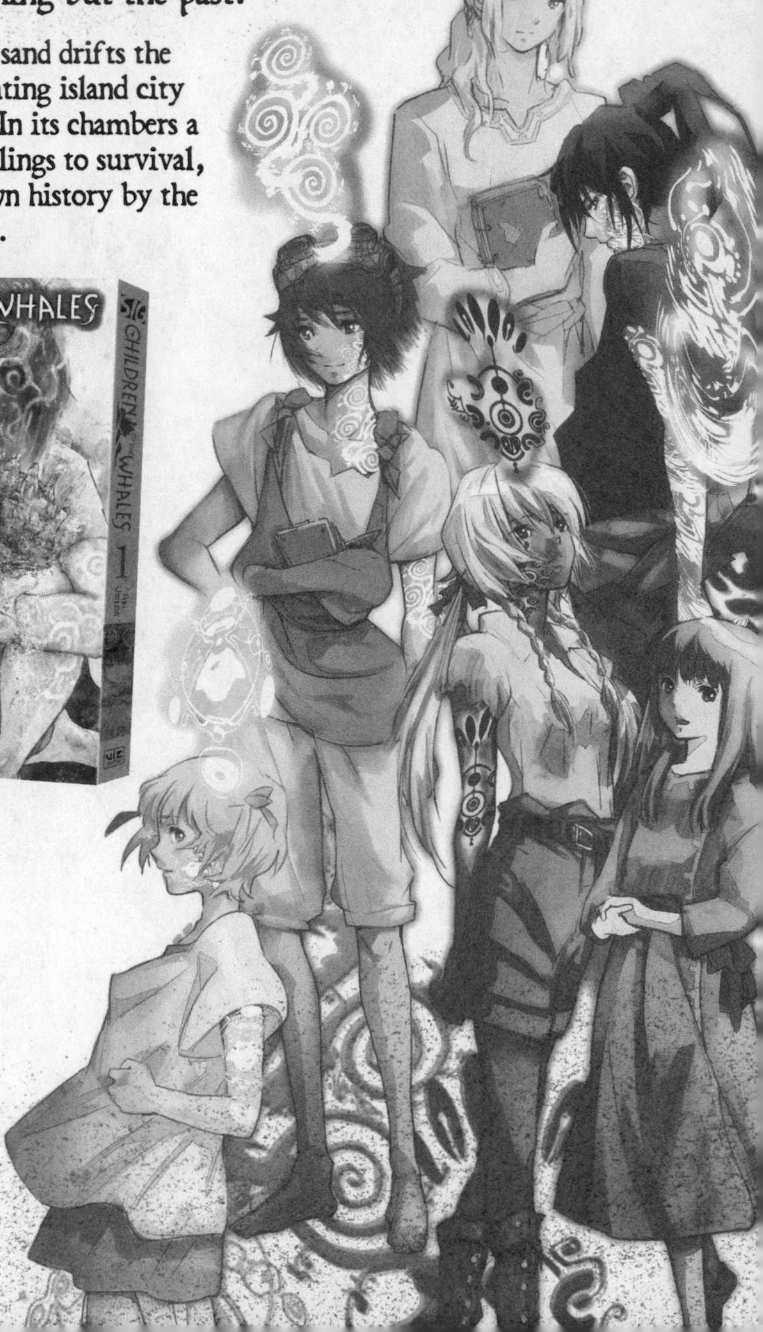

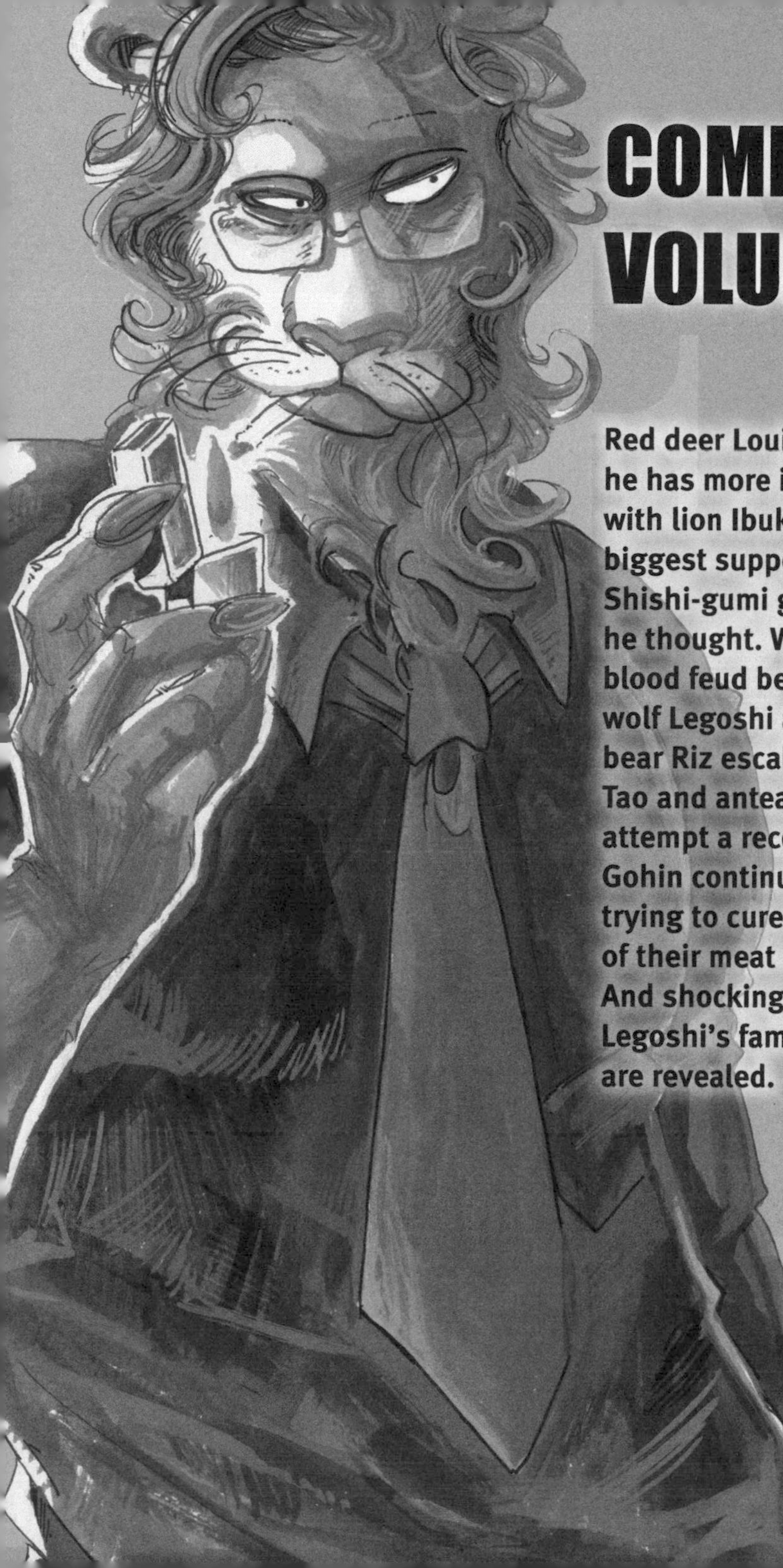

COMING IN VOLUME 10...

Red deer Louis learns he has more in common with lion Ibuki, his biggest supporter in the Shishi-gumi gang, than he thought. While the blood feud between gray wolf Legoshi and brown bear Riz escalates, puma Tao and anteater Kibi attempt a reconciliation. Gohin continues his work trying to cure carnivores of their meat addiction. And shocking secrets of Legoshi's family and past are revealed.

BEASTARS
VOL. 9
VIZ Signature Edition

Story & Art by
Paru Itagaki

Translation/Tomo Kimura
English Adaptation/Annette Roman
Touch-Up Art & Lettering/Susan Daigle-Leach
Cover & Interior Design/Yukiko Whitley
Editor/Annette Roman

BEASTARS Volume 9
© 2018 PARU ITAGAKI
All rights reserved.
First published in 2018 by Akita Publishing Co., Ltd., Tokyo
English translation rights arranged with Akita Publishing Co., Ltd., through
Tuttle-Mori Agency, Inc., Tokyo

The stories, characters and incidents mentioned in this publication are entirely
fictional.

Printed in the U.S.A.

Published by VIZ Media, LLC
P.O. Box 77010
San Francisco, CA 94107

10 9 8 7 6 5 4 3 2 1
First printing, November 2020

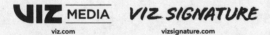

viz.com   vizsignature.com

BEASTARS

Volume 9

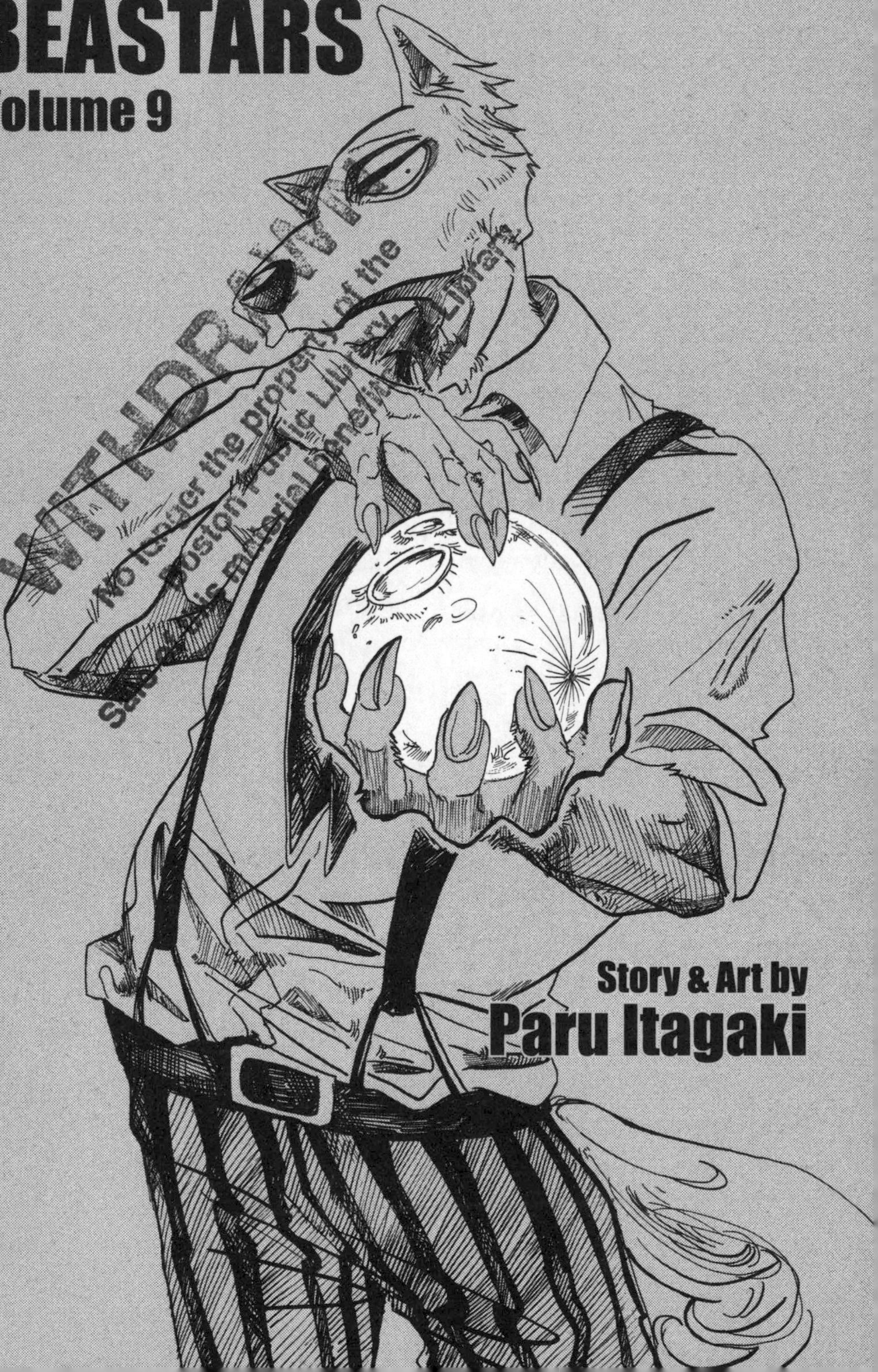

Story & Art by
Paru Itagaki

STORY & CAST OF CHARACTERS

Plot Treatment...

Cherryton Academy is an integrated boarding school for a diverse group of carnivores and herbivores. Recently Tem, an alpaca member of the Drama Club, was slain and devoured on campus. The murderer has yet to be identified, and tensions between predators and prey are running high.

After telling a group of carnivore students that he is trying to find his friend Tem's killer, gray wolf Legoshi is viciously attacked by a mysterious beast. Legoshi then begins training under giant panda Gohin to learn to better defend himself and his loved ones. With the help of a meditation practice, Legoshi manages to overcome his innate desire to eat meat, but as a consequence, his jaws grow weak. As he helps Gohin capture meat-addicted carnivores, Legoshi develops his own fighting style employing his arms and legs instead of his teeth.

Meanwhile, red deer Louis's father Oguma refuses to allow his son to withdraw from Cherryton Academy. When Louis passes through the black market, he is disheartened to see Legoshi with a large sack of meat. Louis doesn't know the meat is intended for Legoshi's meditation practice, not consumption.

BEASTARS

Dwarf rabbit Haru catches Legoshi napping in Cherryton's study hall. She is angry because Legoshi has been cold towards her lately. Legoshi doesn't fully comprehend her reaction and, in a moment of panic, attempts to repair things by asking her to marry him. Haru turns him down hard...

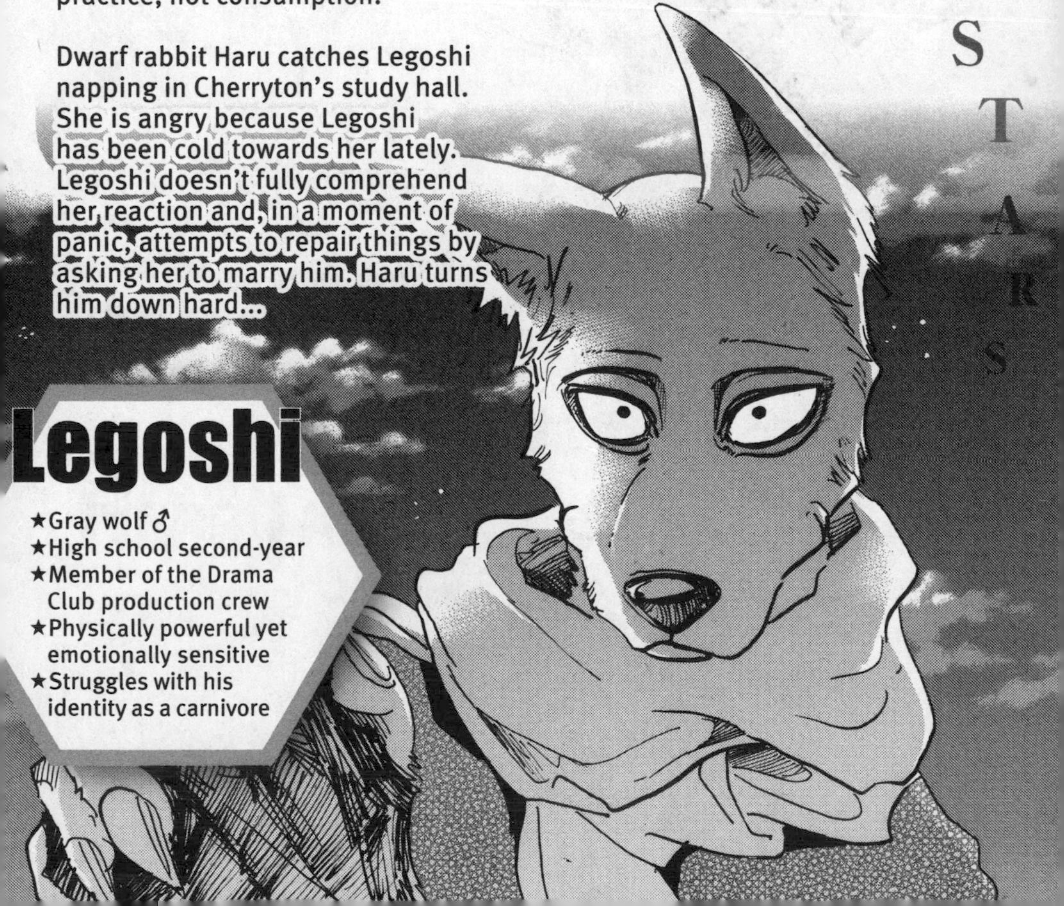

Legoshi

- ★Gray wolf ♂
- ★High school second-year
- ★Member of the Drama Club production crew
- ★Physically powerful yet emotionally sensitive
- ★Struggles with his identity as a carnivore

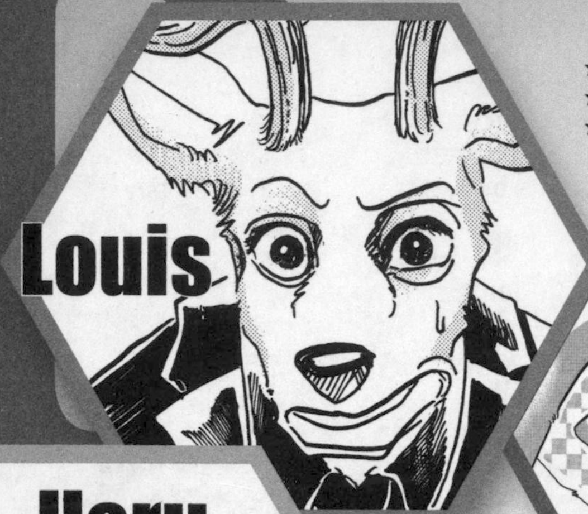
Louis

★Red deer ♂
★High school third-year
★Former leader of the Drama Club actors pool, but now leader of the Shishi-gumi

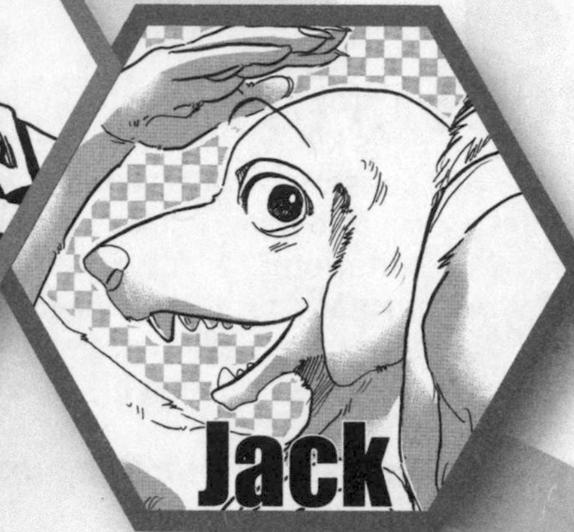
Jack

★Labrador retriever ♂
★High school second-yea
★Legoshi's best friend

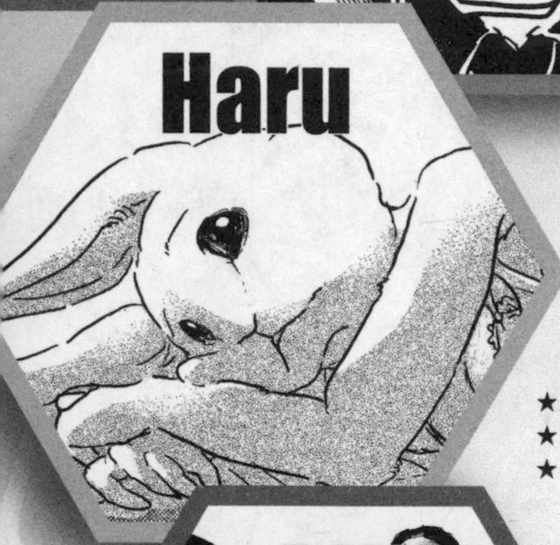
Haru

★Netherland dwarf rabbit ♀
★High school third-year
★Member of the Gardening Club

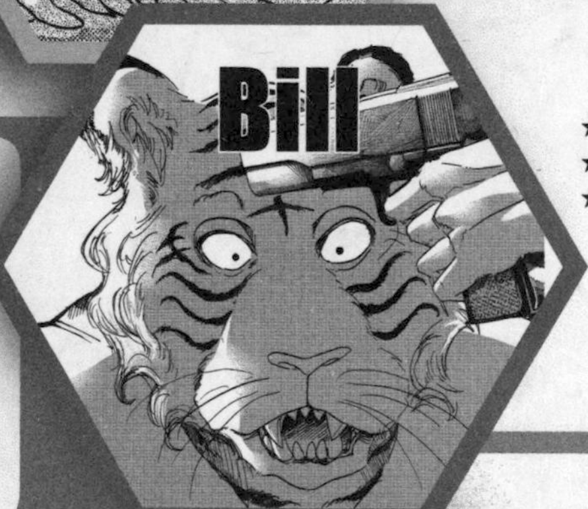
Bill

★Bengal tiger ♂
★High school second-year
★Member of the Drama Club actors pool

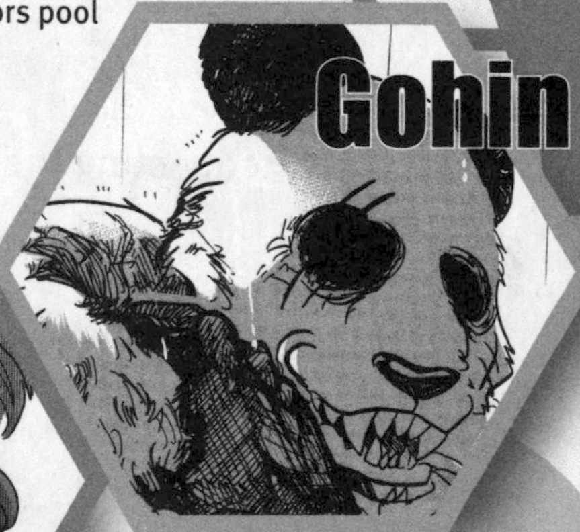
Gohin

★Giant panda ♂
★Psychologist who runs a clinic at the black market

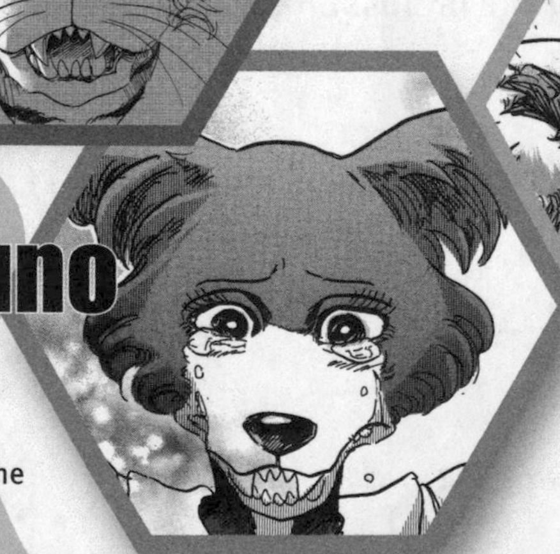
Juno

★Gray wolf ♀
★High school first-year
★Member of the Drama Club actors pool

BEASTARS
Volume 9

CONTENTS

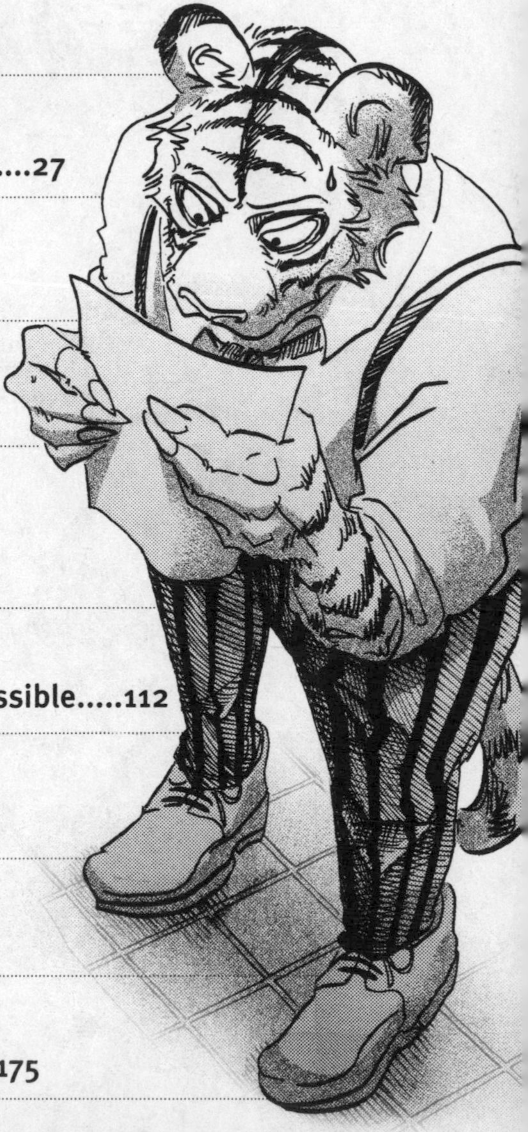

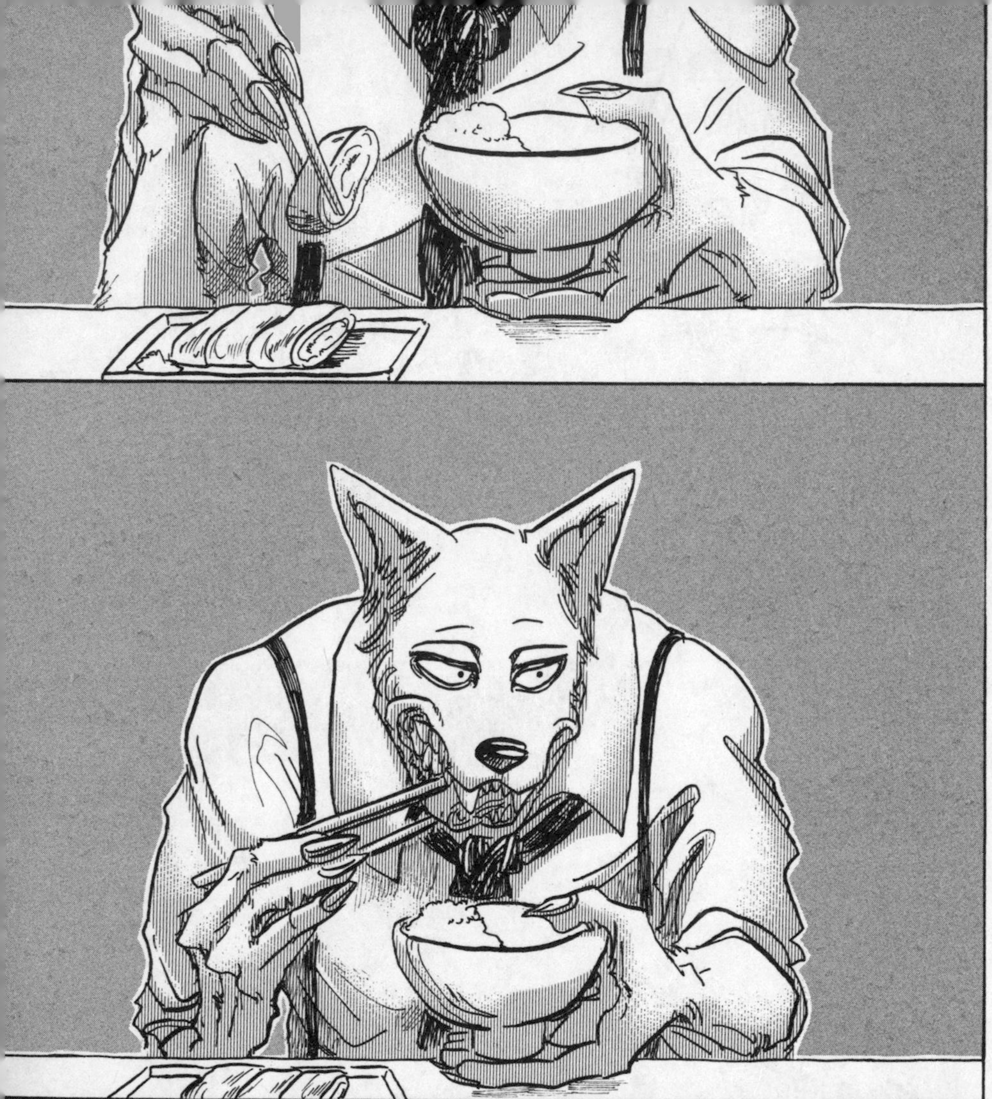

Chapter 71: A Day Among Many

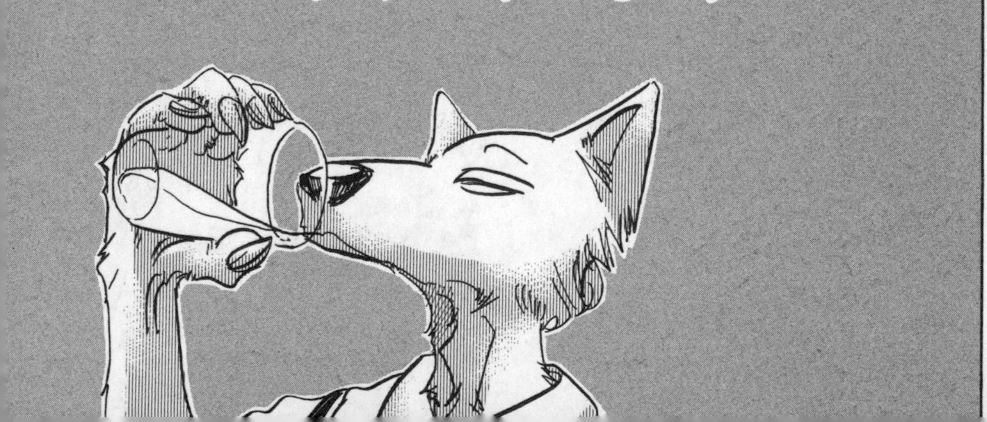

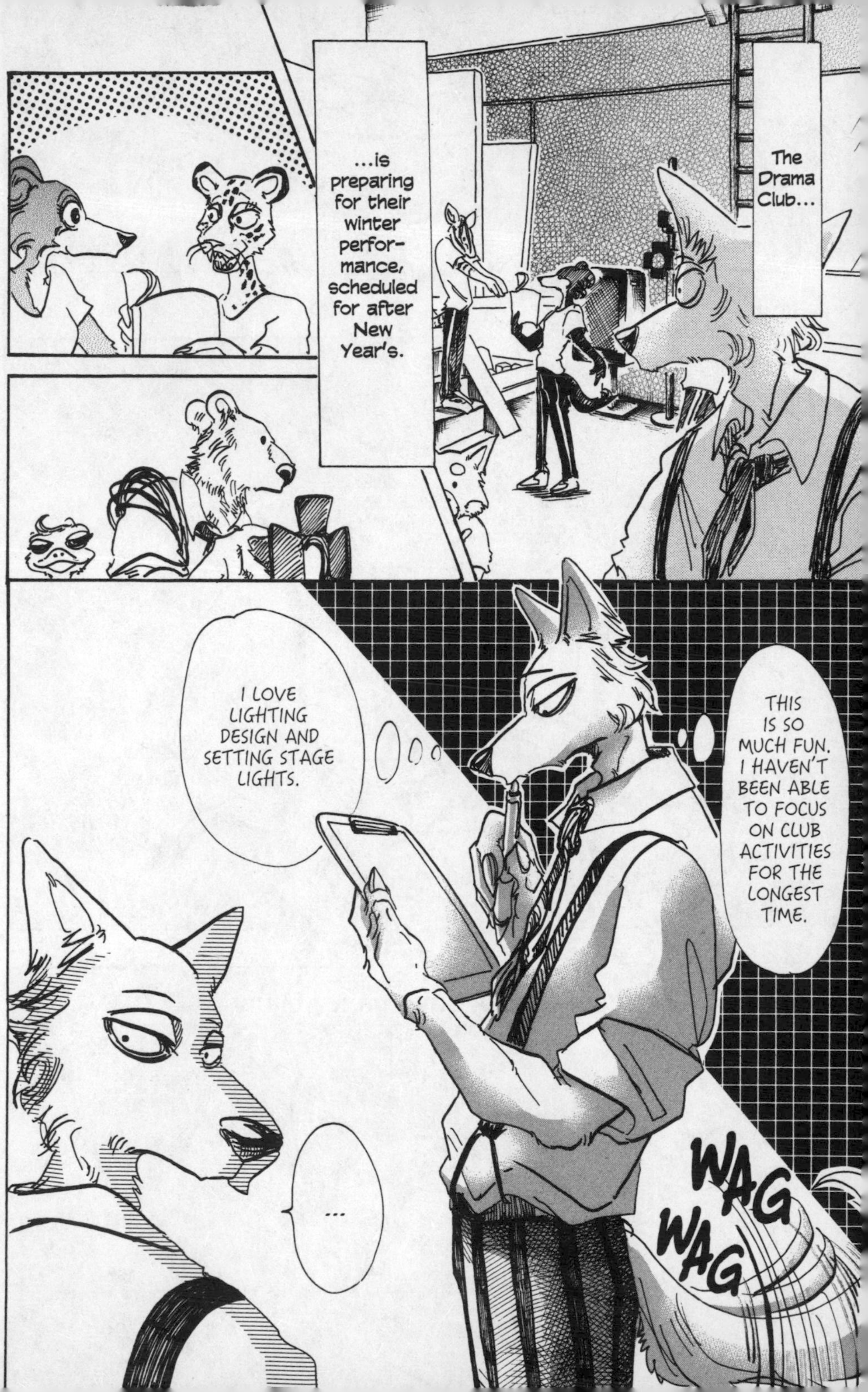
The Drama Club...
...is preparing for their winter perfor-mance, scheduled for after New Year's.
THIS IS SO MUCH FUN. I HAVEN'T BEEN ABLE TO FOCUS ON CLUB ACTIVITIES FOR THE LONGEST TIME.
I LOVE LIGHTING DESIGN AND SETTING STAGE LIGHTS.
WAG WAG
...

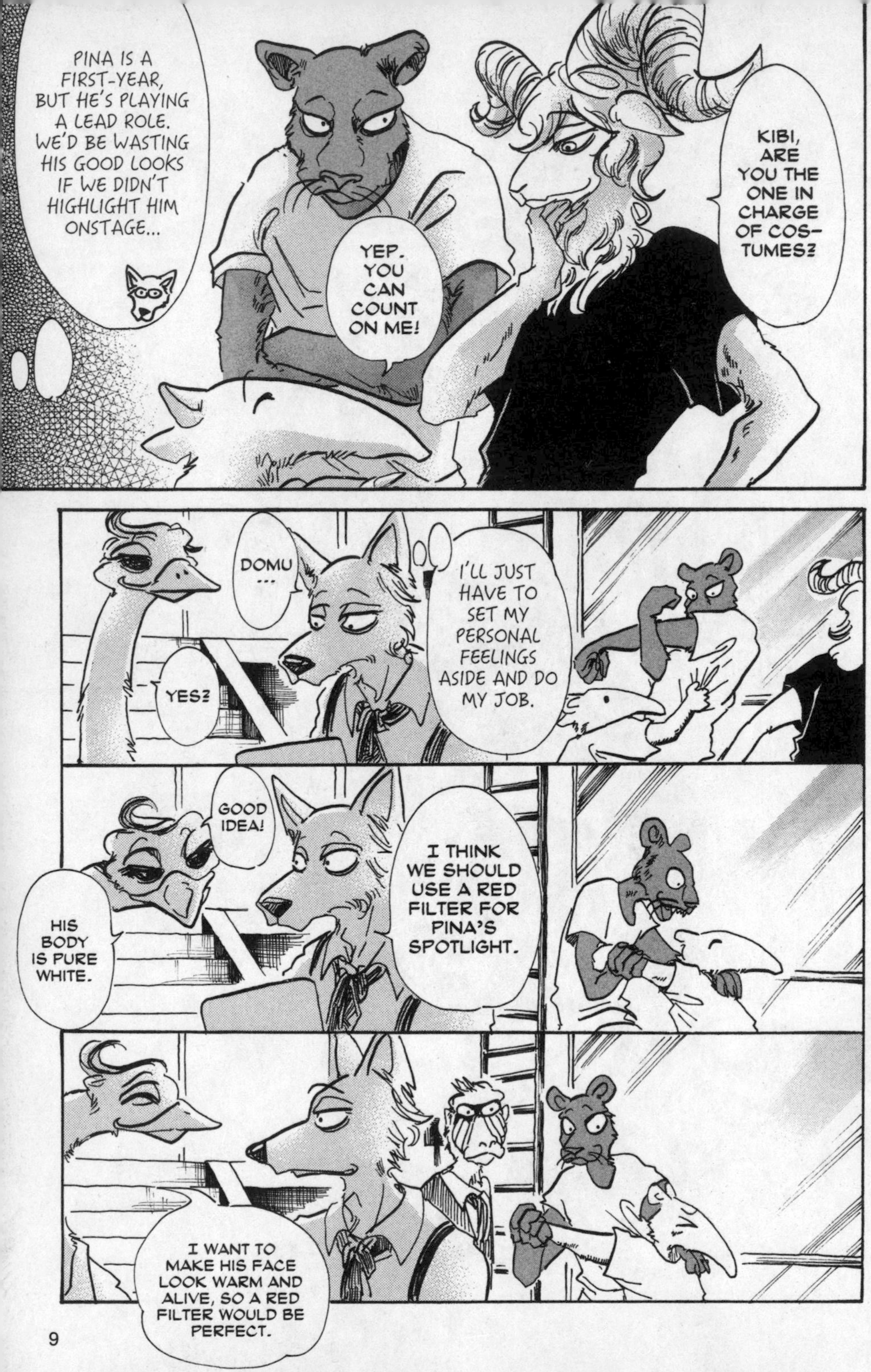
KIBI, ARE YOU THE ONE IN CHARGE OF COS-TUMES?
YEP. YOU CAN COUNT ON ME!
PINA IS A FIRST-YEAR, BUT HE'S PLAYING A LEAD ROLE. WE'D BE WASTING HIS GOOD LOOKS IF WE DIDN'T HIGHLIGHT HIM ONSTAGE...
I'LL JUST HAVE TO SET MY PERSONAL FEELINGS ASIDE AND DO MY JOB.
DOMU...
YES?
I THINK WE SHOULD USE A RED FILTER FOR PINA'S SPOTLIGHT.
GOOD IDEA!
HIS BODY IS PURE WHITE.
I WANT TO MAKE HIS FACE LOOK WARM AND ALIVE, SO A RED FILTER WOULD BE PERFECT.

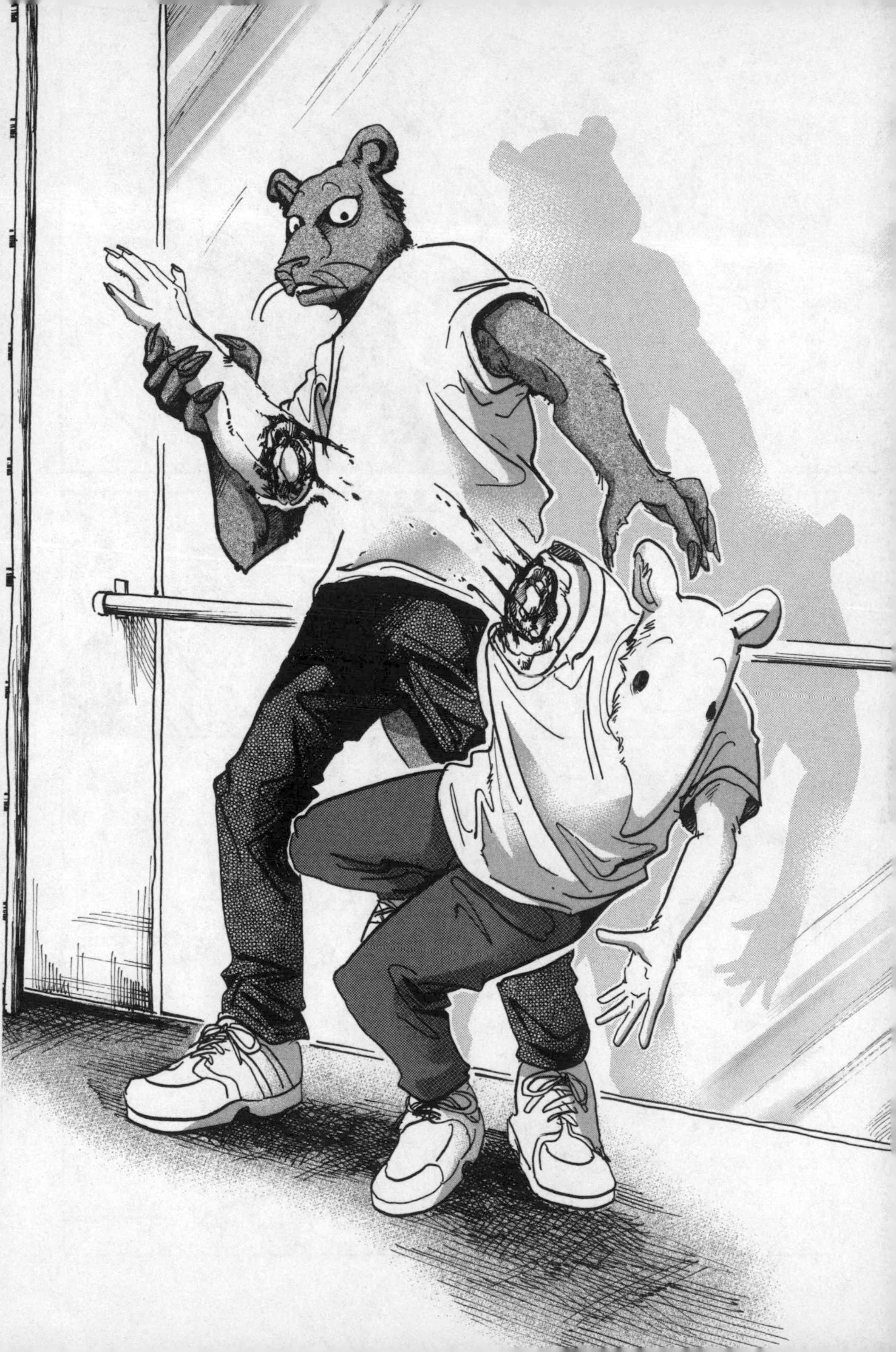

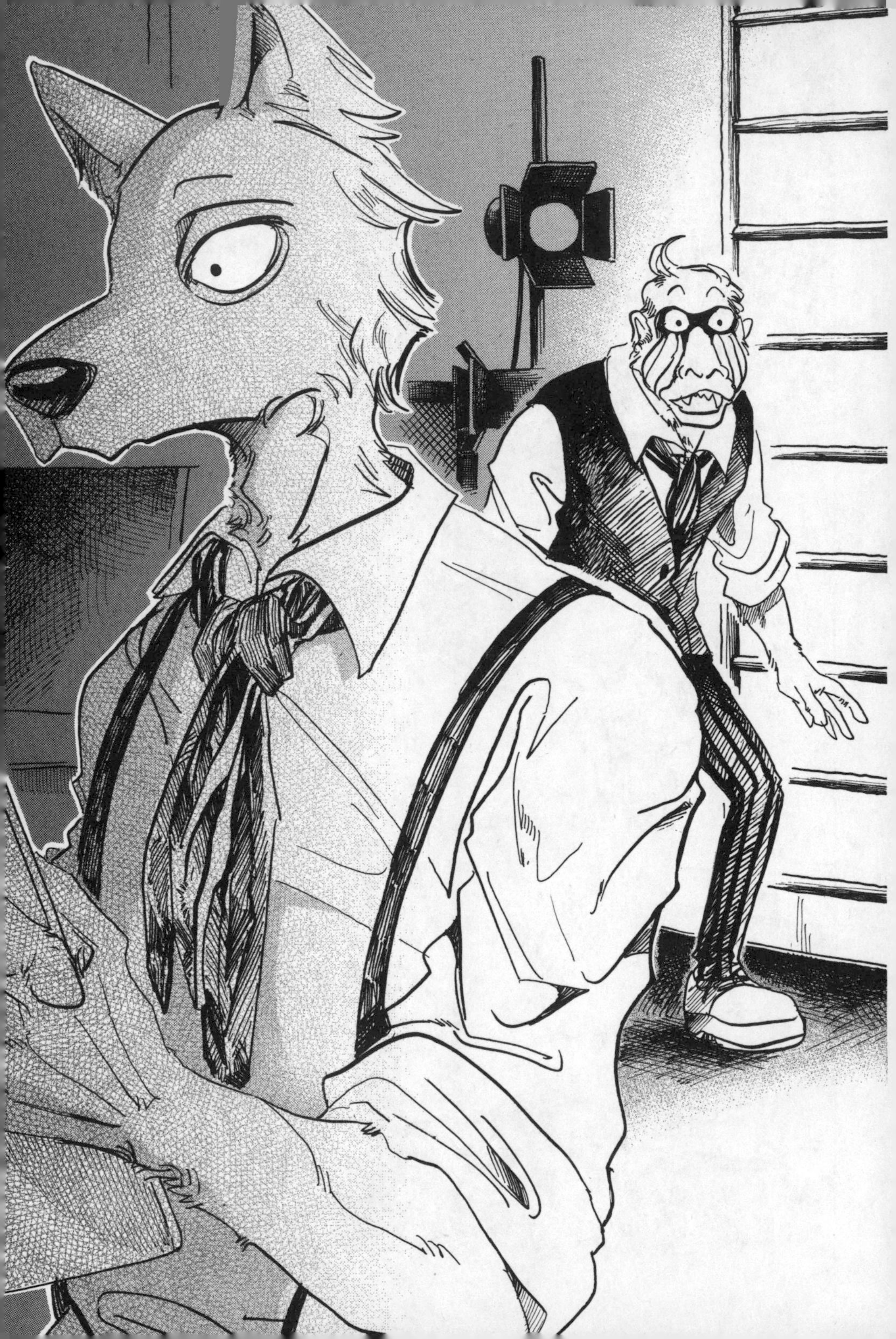

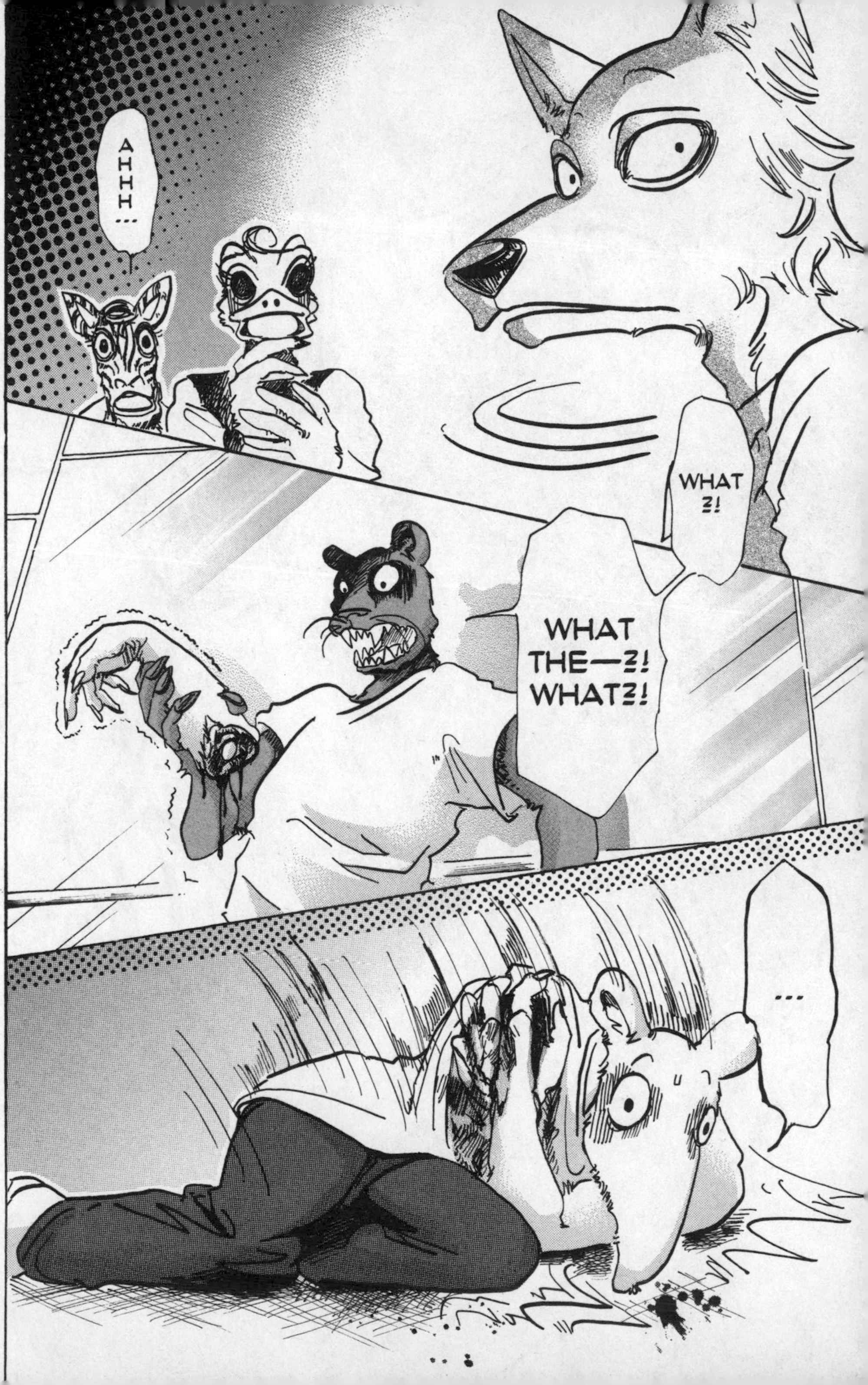
AHHH...
WHAT?!
WHAT THE—?! WHAT?!
...

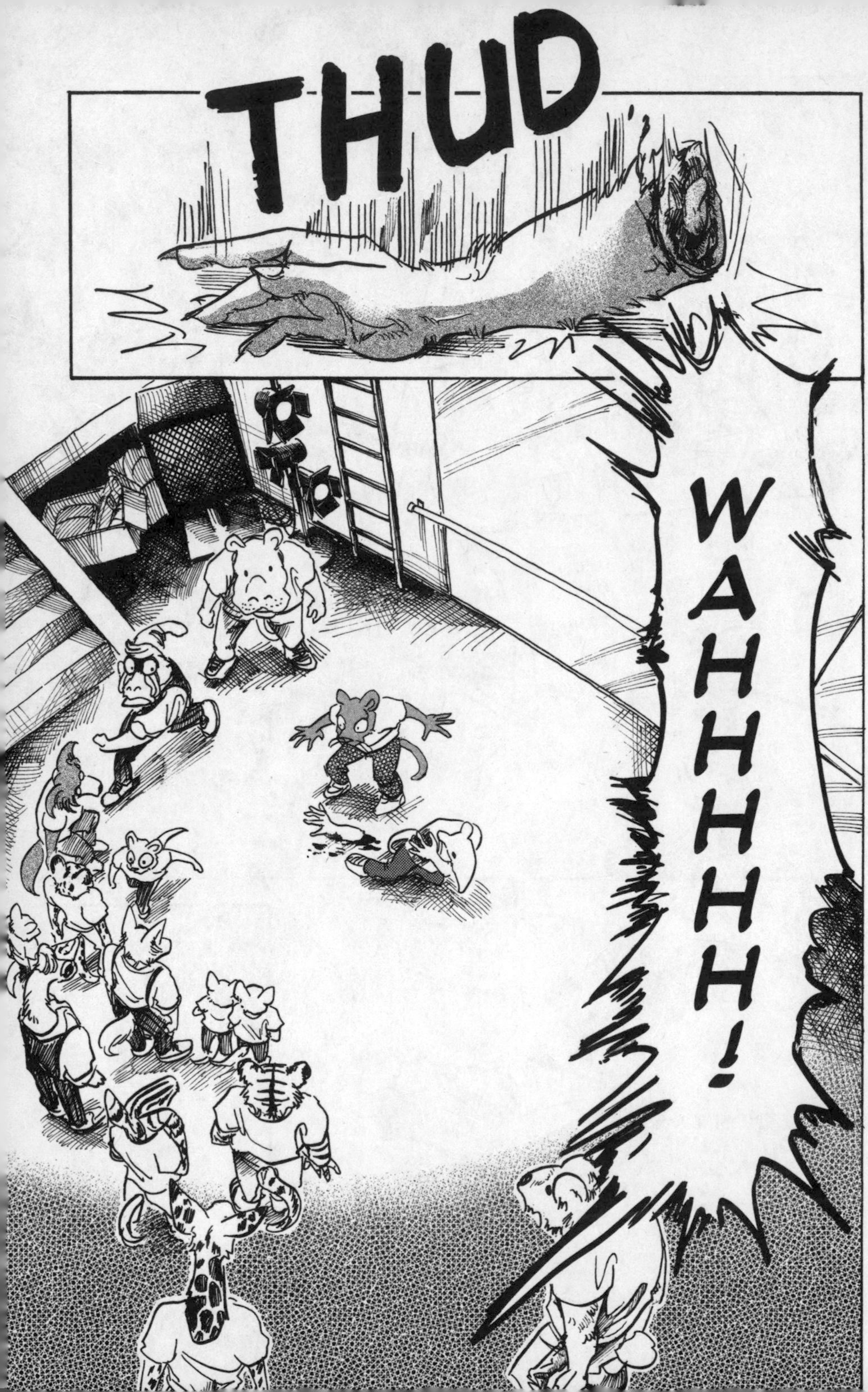
THUD
WAHHHHH!

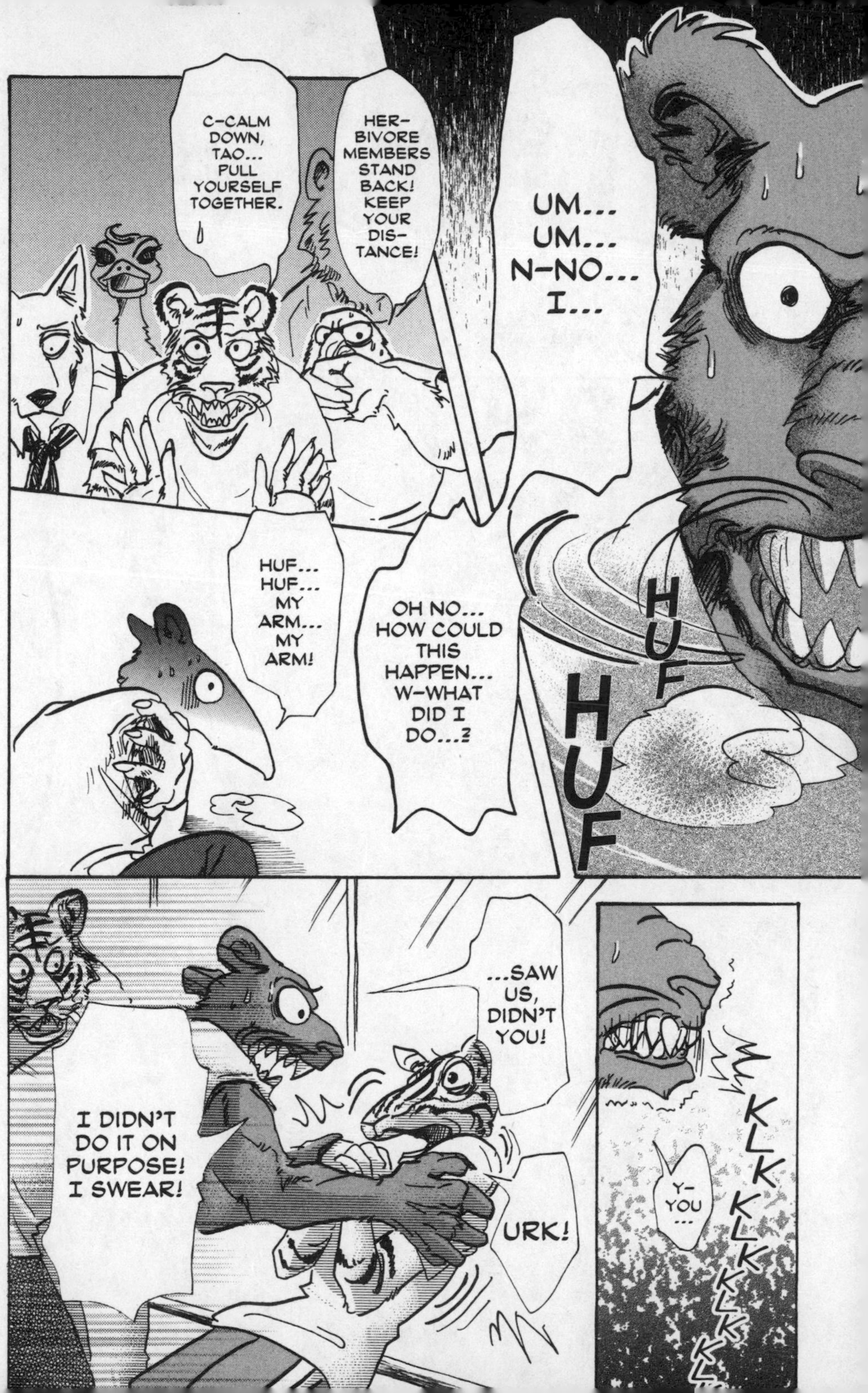
UM... UM... N-NO... I...
HUF HUF
HER-BIVORE MEMBERS STAND BACK! KEEP YOUR DIS-TANCE!
C-CALM DOWN, TAO... PULL YOURSELF TOGETHER.
OH NO... HOW COULD THIS HAPPEN... W-WHAT DID I DO...?
HUF... HUF... MY ARM... MY ARM!
Y-YOU...
KLK KLK KLK KLK
...SAW US, DIDN'T YOU!
URK!
I DIDN'T DO IT ON PURPOSE! I SWEAR!

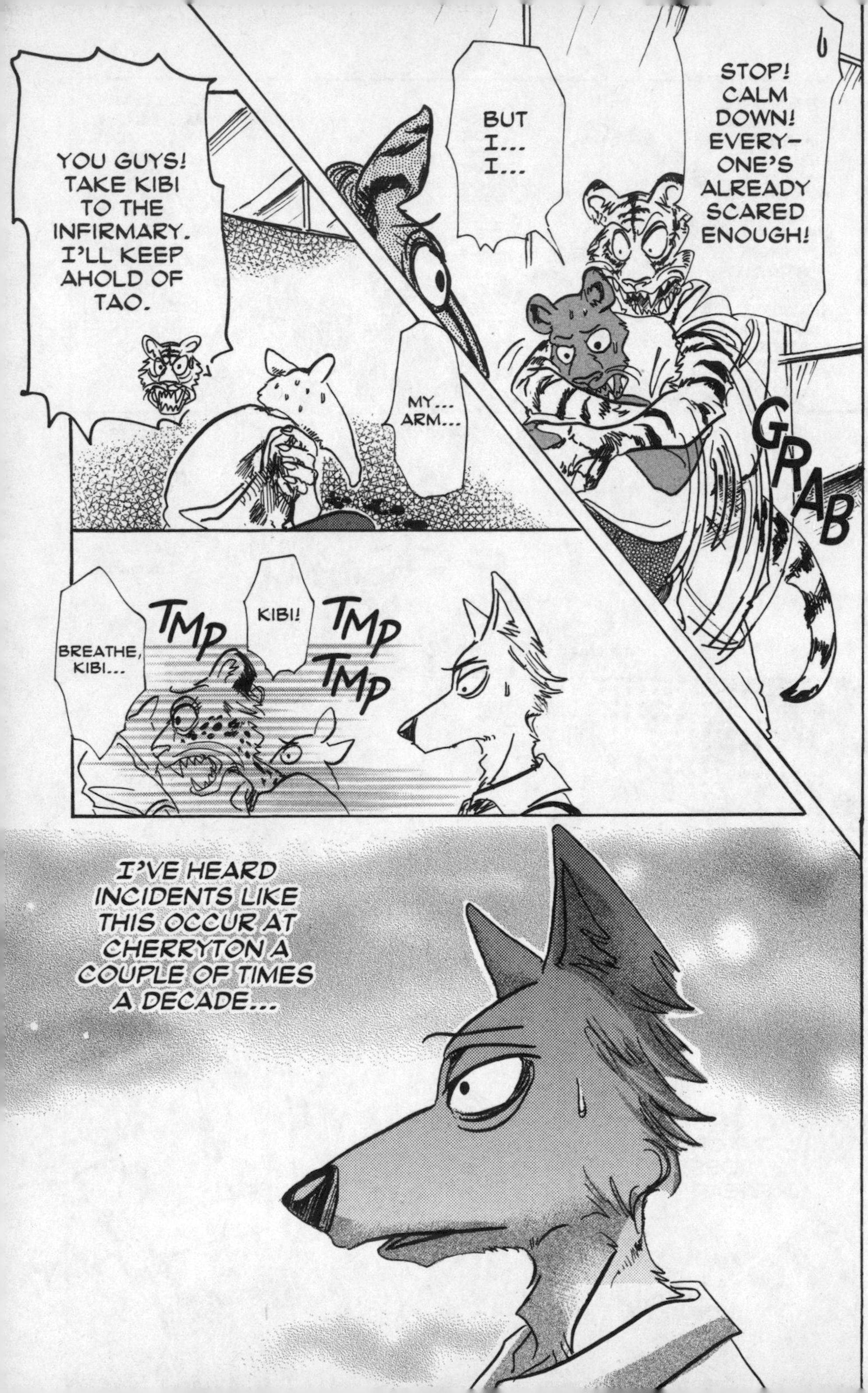
STOP! CALM DOWN! EVERY-ONE'S ALREADY SCARED ENOUGH!
BUT I... I...
GRAB
YOU GUYS! TAKE KIBI TO THE INFIRMARY. I'LL KEEP AHOLD OF TAO.
MY... ARM...
TMP TMP
KIBI!
TMP
BREATHE, KIBI...
I'VE HEARD INCIDENTS LIKE THIS OCCUR AT CHERRYTON A COUPLE OF TIMES A DECADE...

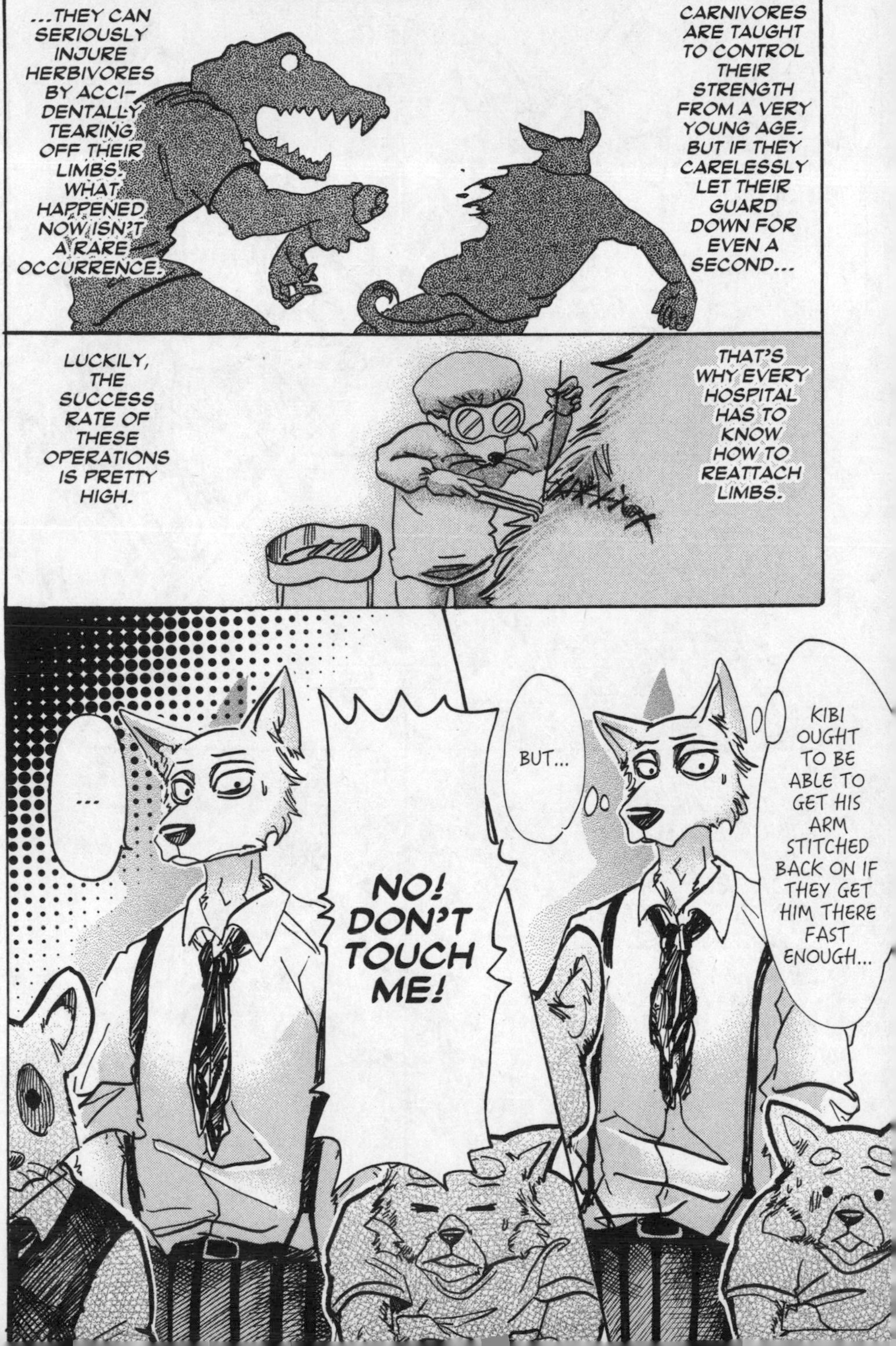
CARNIVORES ARE TAUGHT TO CONTROL THEIR STRENGTH FROM A VERY YOUNG AGE. BUT IF THEY CARELESSLY LET THEIR GUARD DOWN FOR EVEN A SECOND...
...THEY CAN SERIOUSLY INJURE HERBIVORES BY ACCI-DENTALLY TEARING OFF THEIR LIMBS. WHAT HAPPENED NOW ISN'T A RARE OCCURRENCE.
THAT'S WHY EVERY HOSPITAL HAS TO KNOW HOW TO REATTACH LIMBS.
LUCKILY, THE SUCCESS RATE OF THESE OPERATIONS IS PRETTY HIGH.
KIBI OUGHT TO BE ABLE TO GET HIS ARM STITCHED BACK ON IF THEY GET HIM THERE FAST ENOUGH...
BUT...
NO! DON'T TOUCH ME!
...

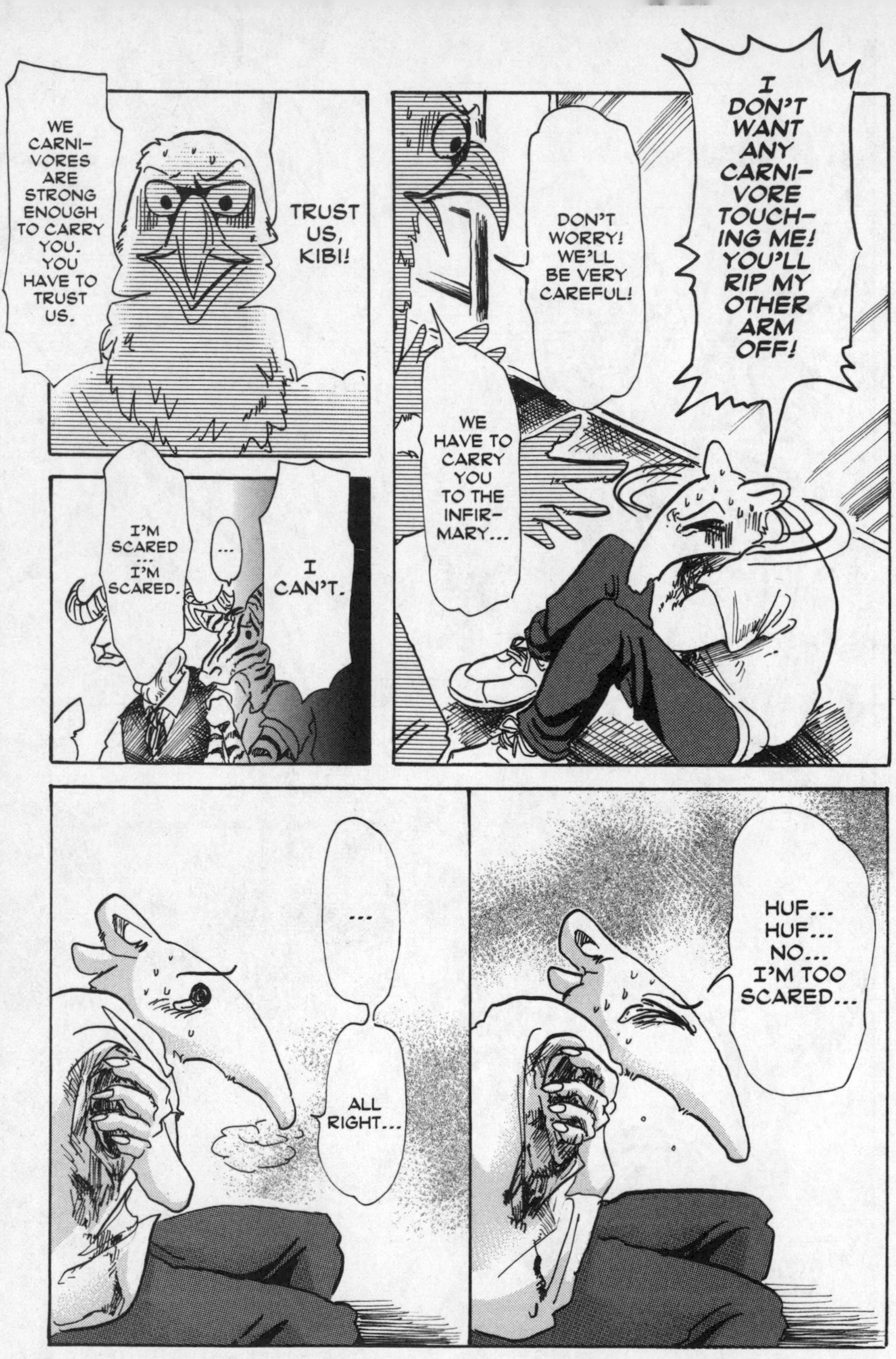
I DON'T WANT ANY CARNIVORE TOUCHING ME! YOU'LL RIP MY OTHER ARM OFF!
DON'T WORRY! WE'LL BE VERY CAREFUL!
WE HAVE TO CARRY YOU TO THE INFIRMARY...
TRUST US, KIBI!
WE CARNIVORES ARE STRONG ENOUGH TO CARRY YOU. YOU HAVE TO TRUST US.
I CAN'T.
...
I'M SCARED... I'M SCARED.
HUF... HUF... NO... I'M TOO SCARED...
...
ALL RIGHT...

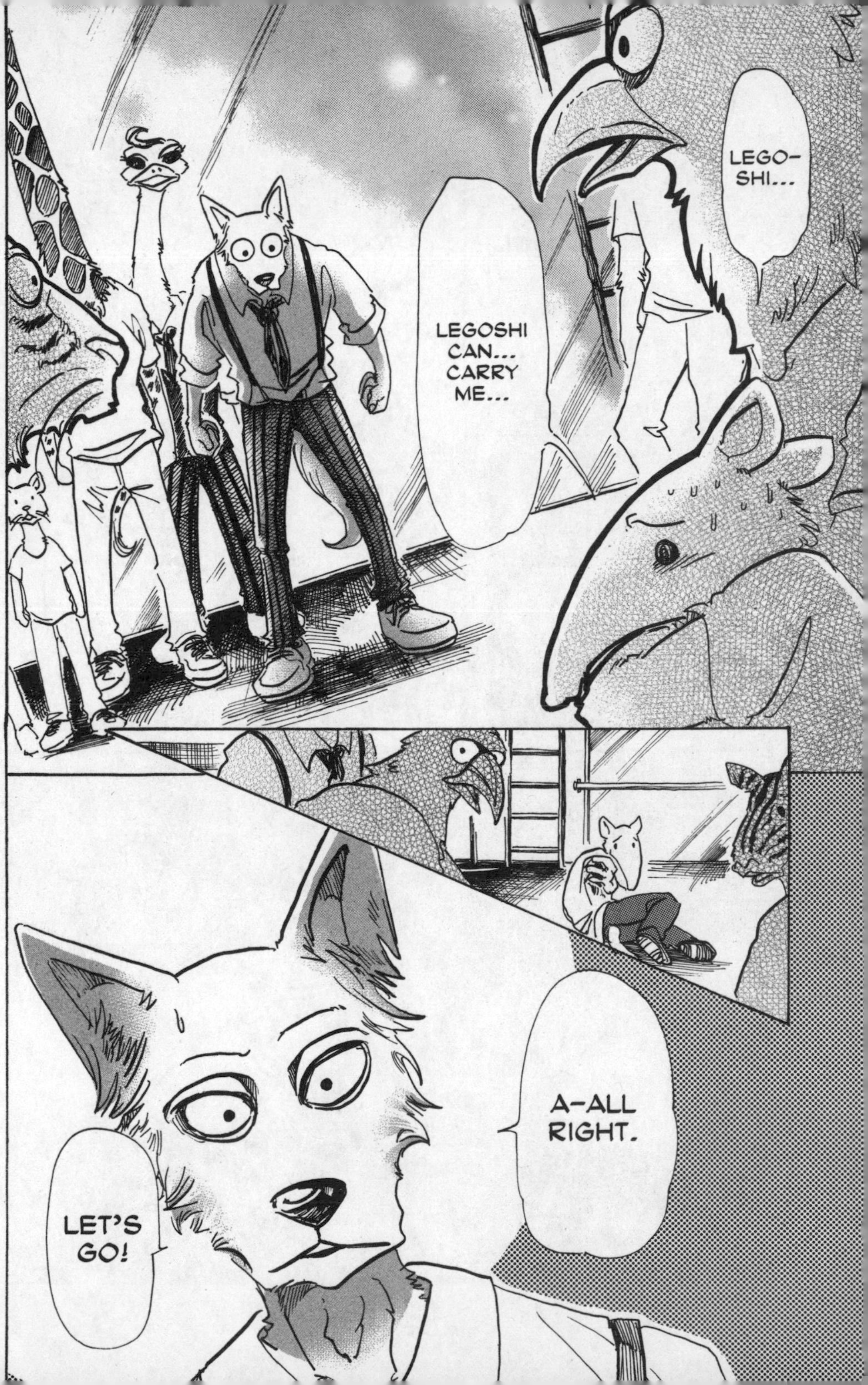
LEGO-SHI...
LEGOSHI CAN... CARRY ME...
A-ALL RIGHT.
LET'S GO!

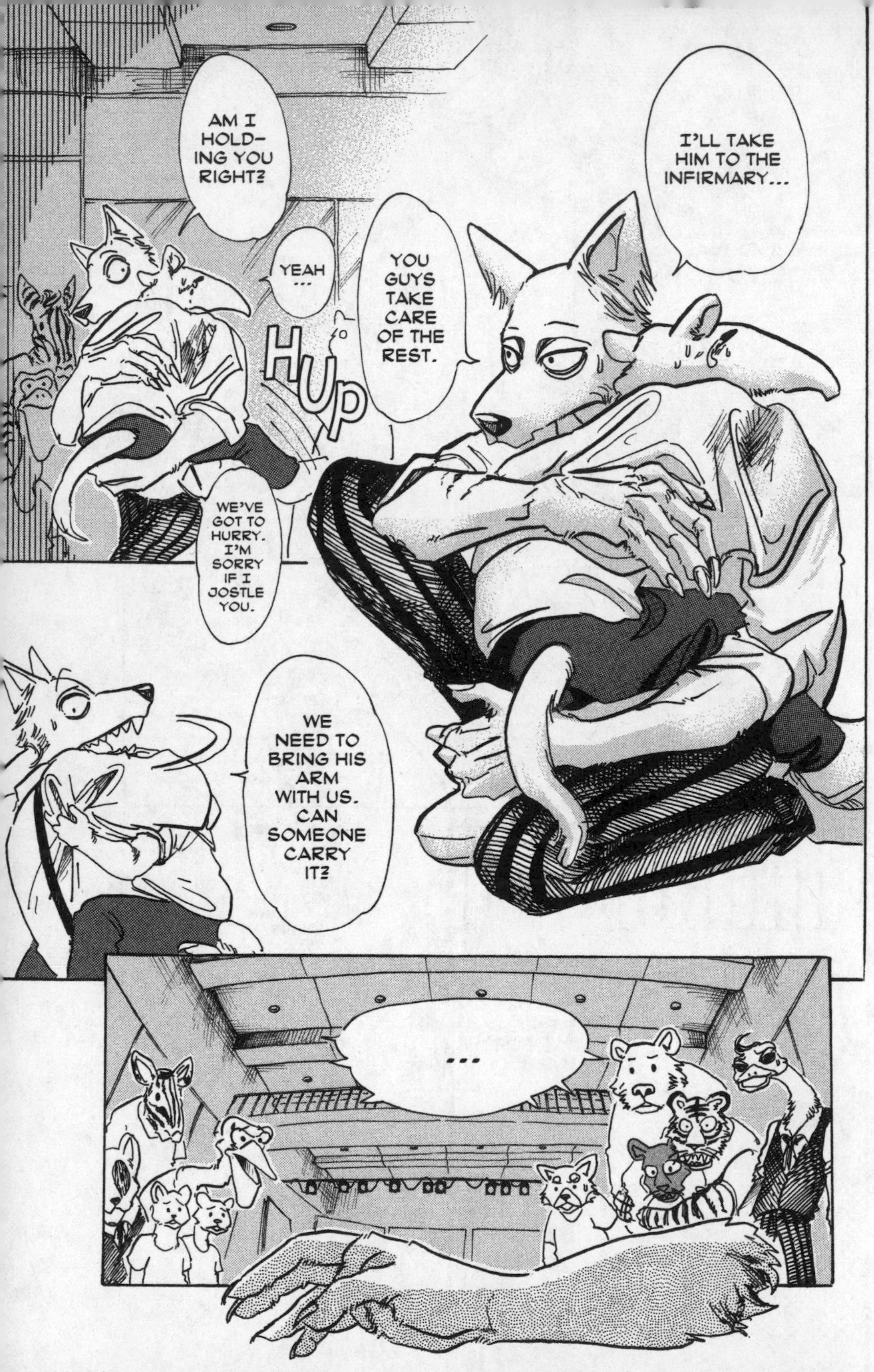

I'LL TAKE HIM TO THE INFIRMARY...
YOU GUYS TAKE CARE OF THE REST.
HUP
AM I HOLDING YOU RIGHT?
YEAH...
WE'VE GOT TO HURRY. I'M SORRY IF I JOSTLE YOU.
WE NEED TO BRING HIS ARM WITH US. CAN SOMEONE CARRY IT?
...

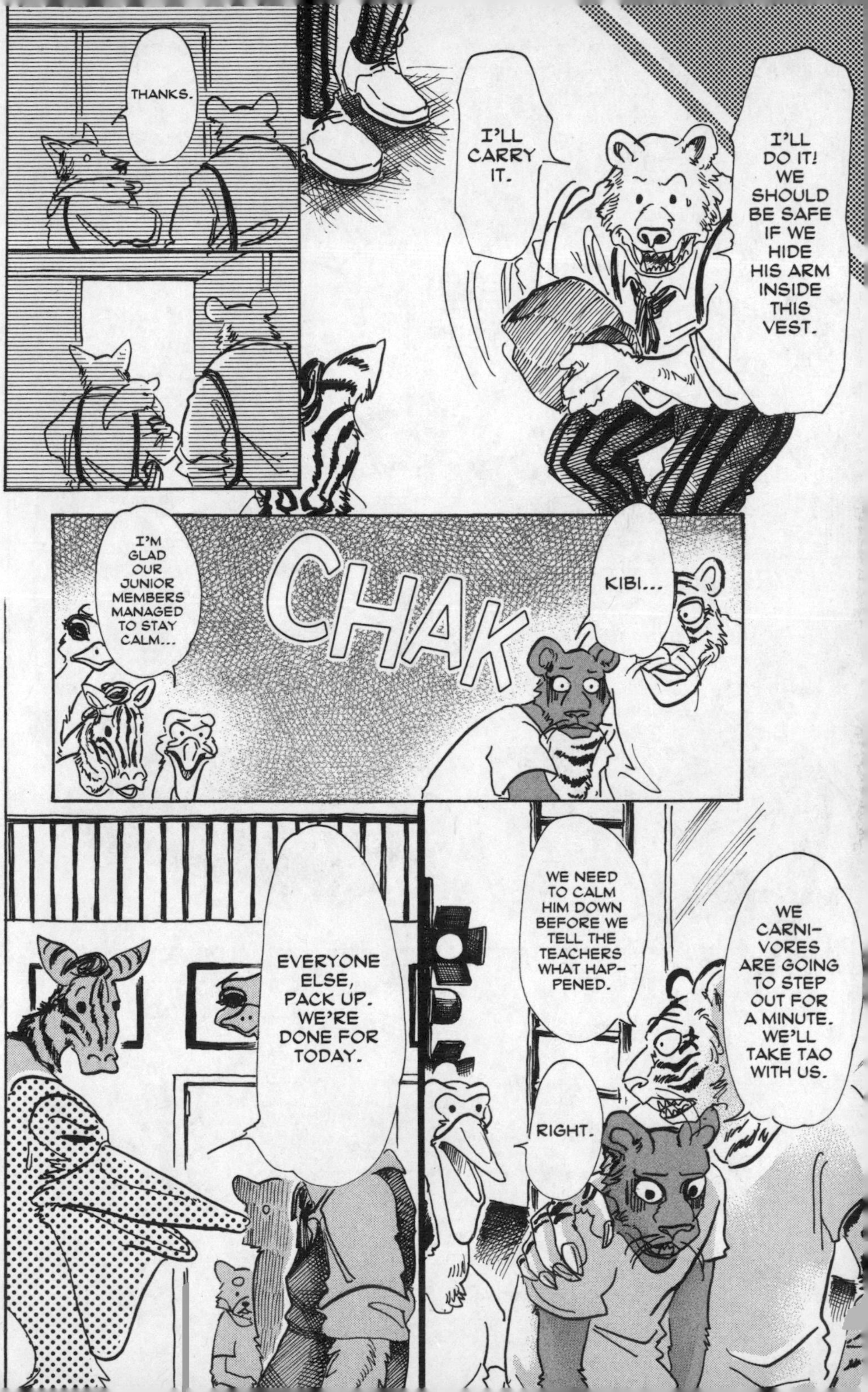
I'LL DO IT! WE SHOULD BE SAFE IF WE HIDE HIS ARM INSIDE THIS VEST.
I'LL CARRY IT.
THANKS.
KIBI...
CHAK
I'M GLAD OUR JUNIOR MEMBERS MANAGED TO STAY CALM...
WE CARNI-VORES ARE GOING TO STEP OUT FOR A MINUTE. WE'LL TAKE TAO WITH US.
WE NEED TO CALM HIM DOWN BEFORE WE TELL THE TEACHERS WHAT HAP-PENED.
RIGHT.
EVERYONE ELSE, PACK UP. WE'RE DONE FOR TODAY.

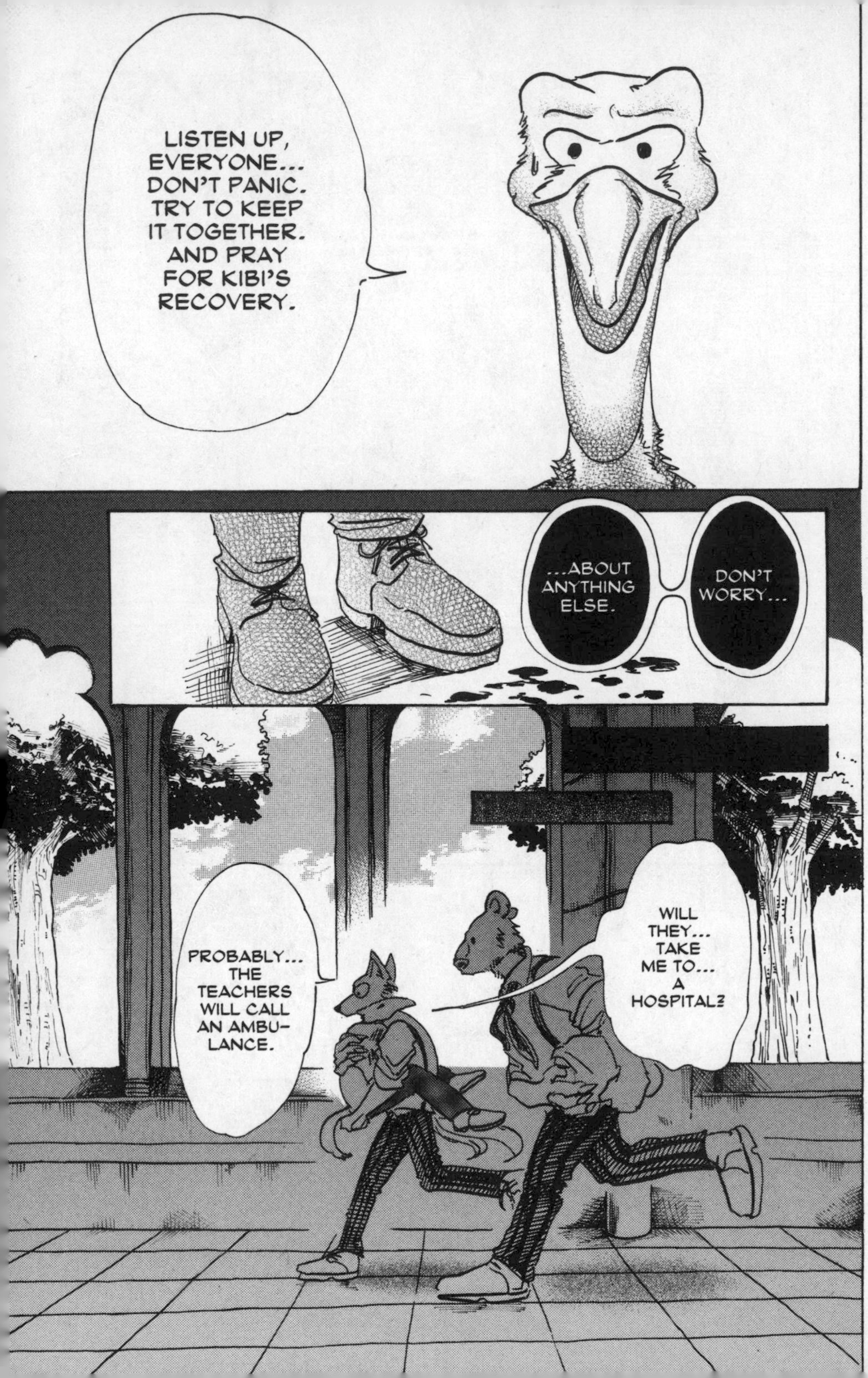
LISTEN UP, EVERYONE... DON'T PANIC. TRY TO KEEP IT TOGETHER. AND PRAY FOR KIBI'S RECOVERY.
DON'T WORRY...
...ABOUT ANYTHING ELSE.
WILL THEY... TAKE ME TO... A HOSPITAL?
PROBABLY... THE TEACHERS WILL CALL AN AMBU-LANCE.

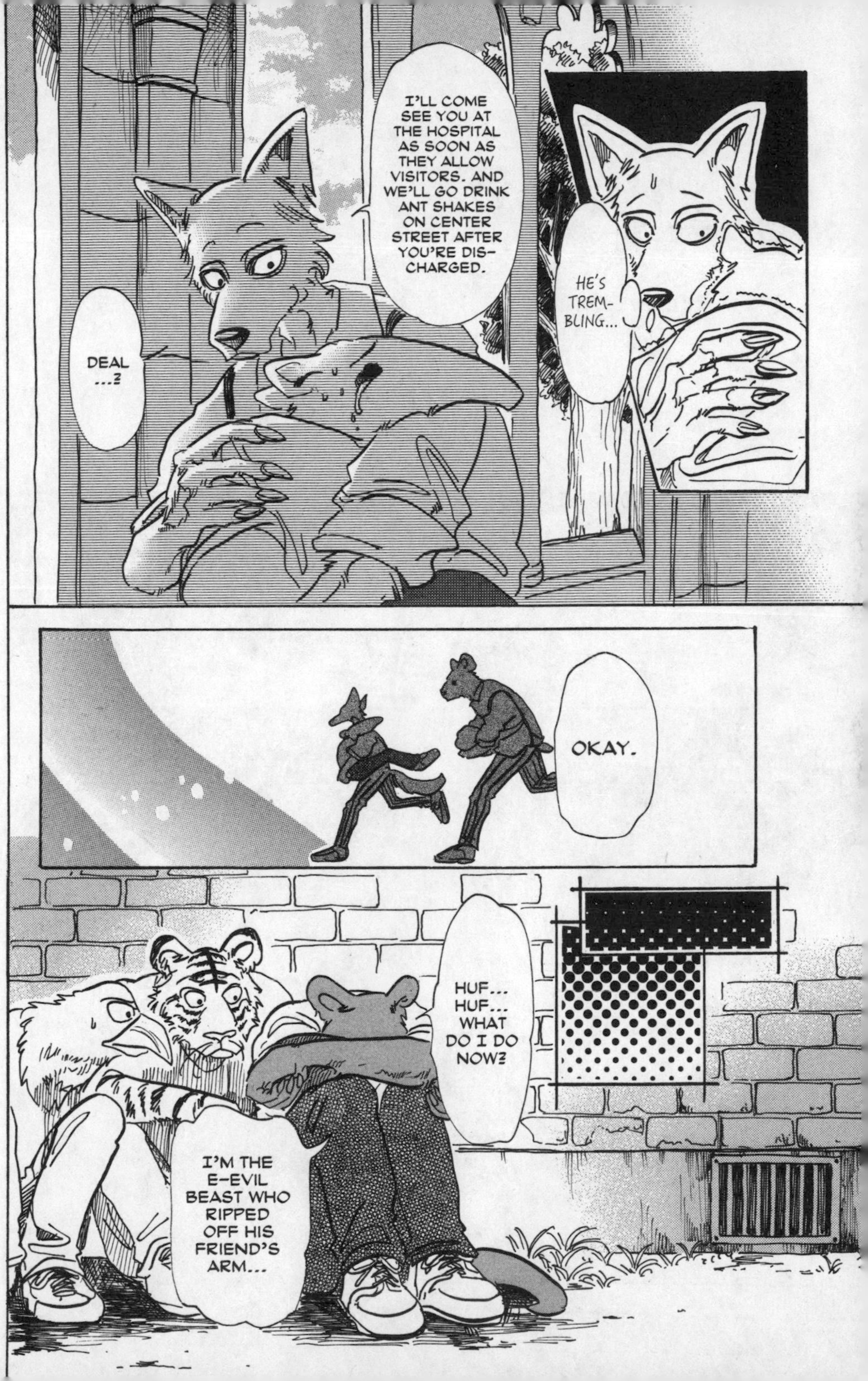
HE'S TREMBLING...
I'LL COME SEE YOU AT THE HOSPITAL AS SOON AS THEY ALLOW VISITORS. AND WE'LL GO DRINK ANT SHAKES ON CENTER STREET AFTER YOU'RE DISCHARGED.
DEAL...?
OKAY.
HUF... HUF... WHAT DO I DO NOW?
I'M THE E-EVIL BEAST WHO RIPPED OFF HIS FRIEND'S ARM...

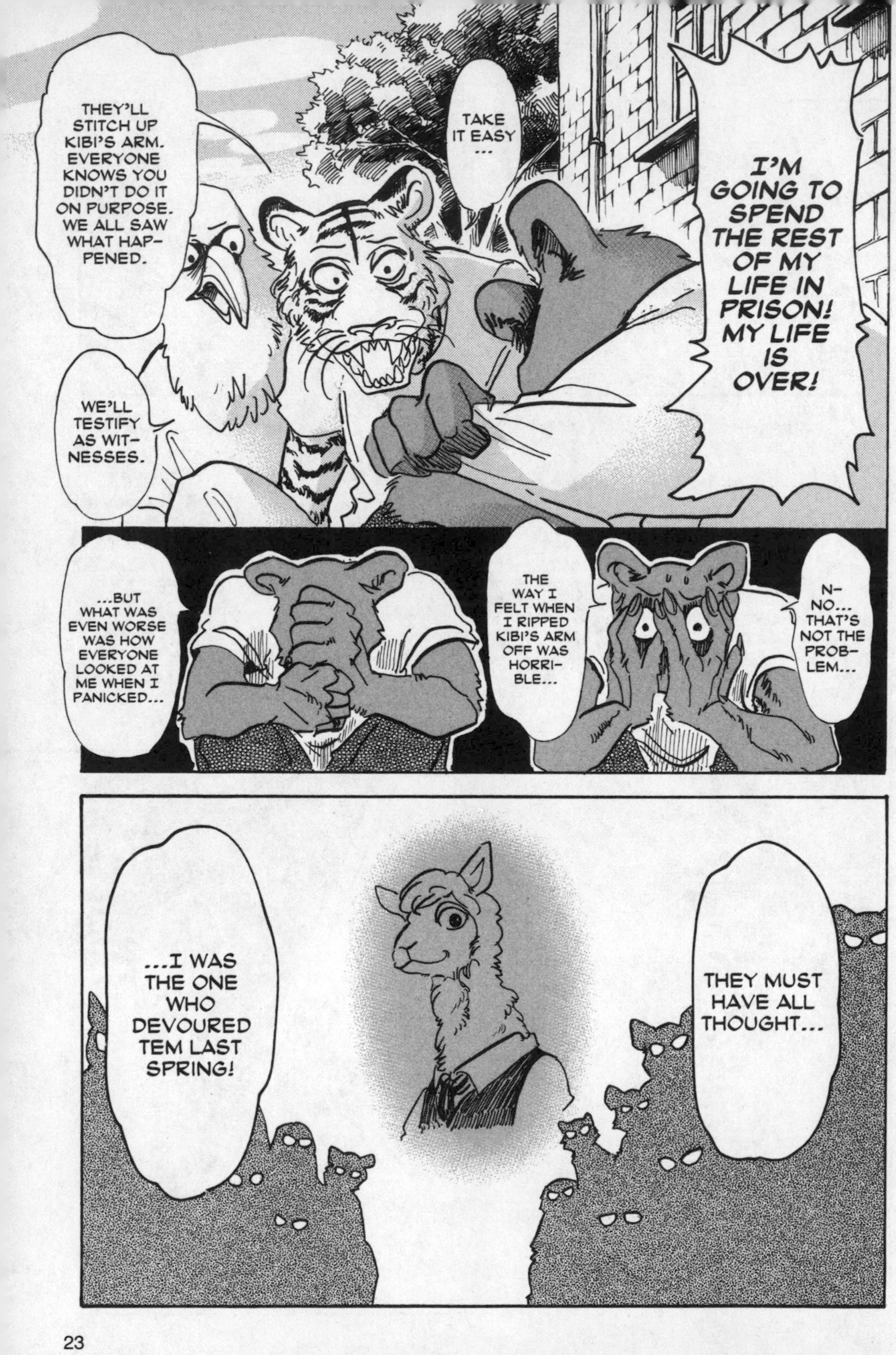
I'M GOING TO SPEND THE REST OF MY LIFE IN PRISON! MY LIFE IS OVER!
TAKE IT EASY...
THEY'LL STITCH UP KIBI'S ARM. EVERYONE KNOWS YOU DIDN'T DO IT ON PURPOSE. WE ALL SAW WHAT HAPPENED.
WE'LL TESTIFY AS WITNESSES.
N-NO... THAT'S NOT THE PROBLEM...
THE WAY I FELT WHEN I RIPPED KIBI'S ARM OFF WAS HORRIBLE...
...BUT WHAT WAS EVEN WORSE WAS HOW EVERYONE LOOKED AT ME WHEN I PANICKED...
THEY MUST HAVE ALL THOUGHT...
...I WAS THE ONE WHO DEVOURED TEM LAST SPRING!

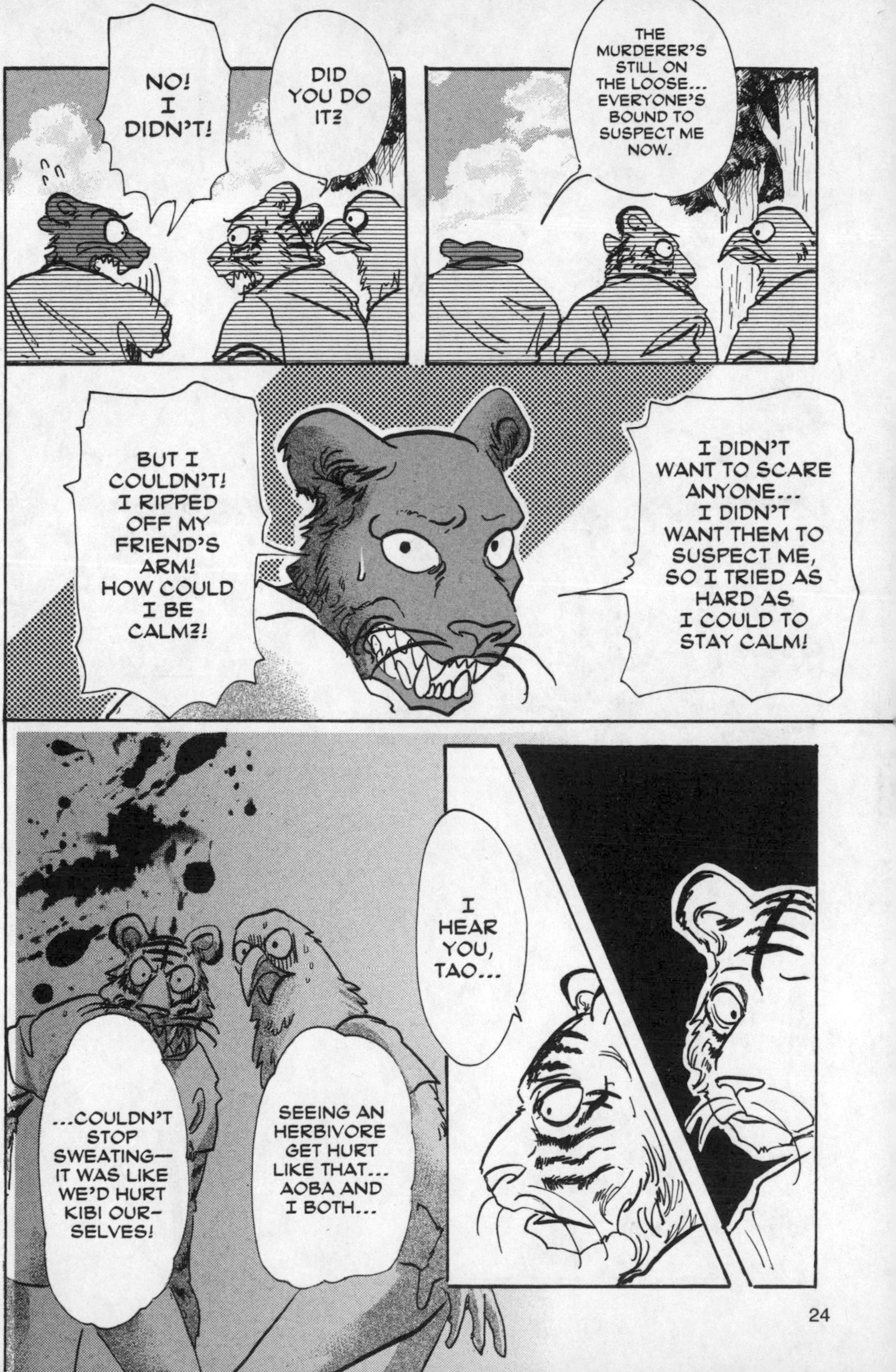
THE MURDERER'S STILL ON THE LOOSE... EVERYONE'S BOUND TO SUSPECT ME NOW.
DID YOU DO IT?
NO! I DIDN'T!
I DIDN'T WANT TO SCARE ANYONE... I DIDN'T WANT THEM TO SUSPECT ME, SO I TRIED AS HARD AS I COULD TO STAY CALM!
BUT I COULDN'T! I RIPPED OFF MY FRIEND'S ARM! HOW COULD I BE CALM?!
I HEAR YOU, TAO...
SEEING AN HERBIVORE GET HURT LIKE THAT... AOBA AND I BOTH...
...COULDN'T STOP SWEATING— IT WAS LIKE WE'D HURT KIBI OUR-SELVES!

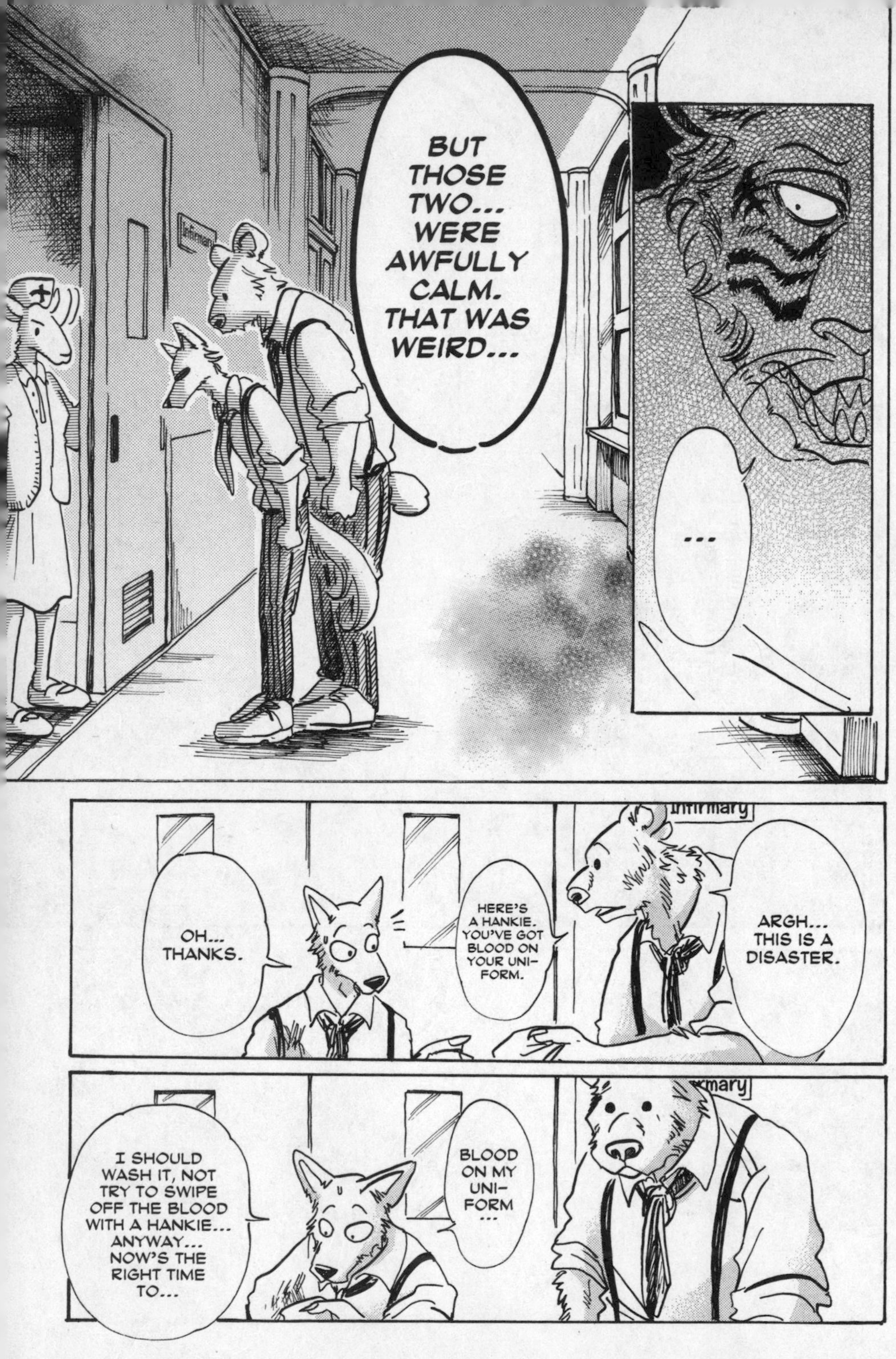
...
BUT THOSE TWO... WERE AWFULLY CALM. THAT WAS WEIRD...
Infirmary
ARGH... THIS IS A DISASTER.
HERE'S A HANKIE. YOU'VE GOT BLOOD ON YOUR UNI-FORM.
OH... THANKS.
BLOOD ON MY UNI-FORM ...
I SHOULD WASH IT, NOT TRY TO SWIPE OFF THE BLOOD WITH A HANKIE... ANYWAY... NOW'S THE RIGHT TIME TO...

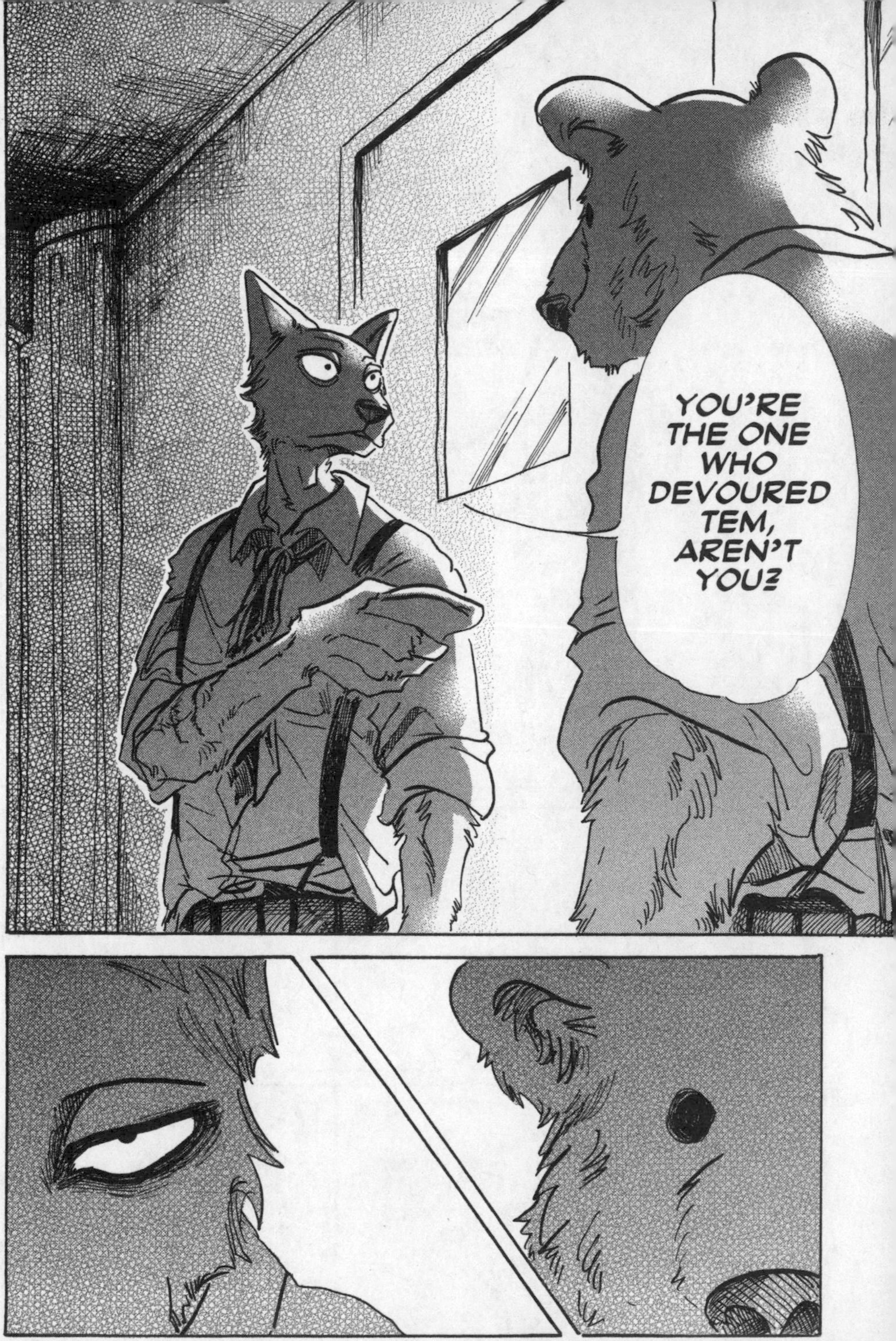
YOU'RE THE ONE WHO DEVOURED TEM, AREN'T YOU?

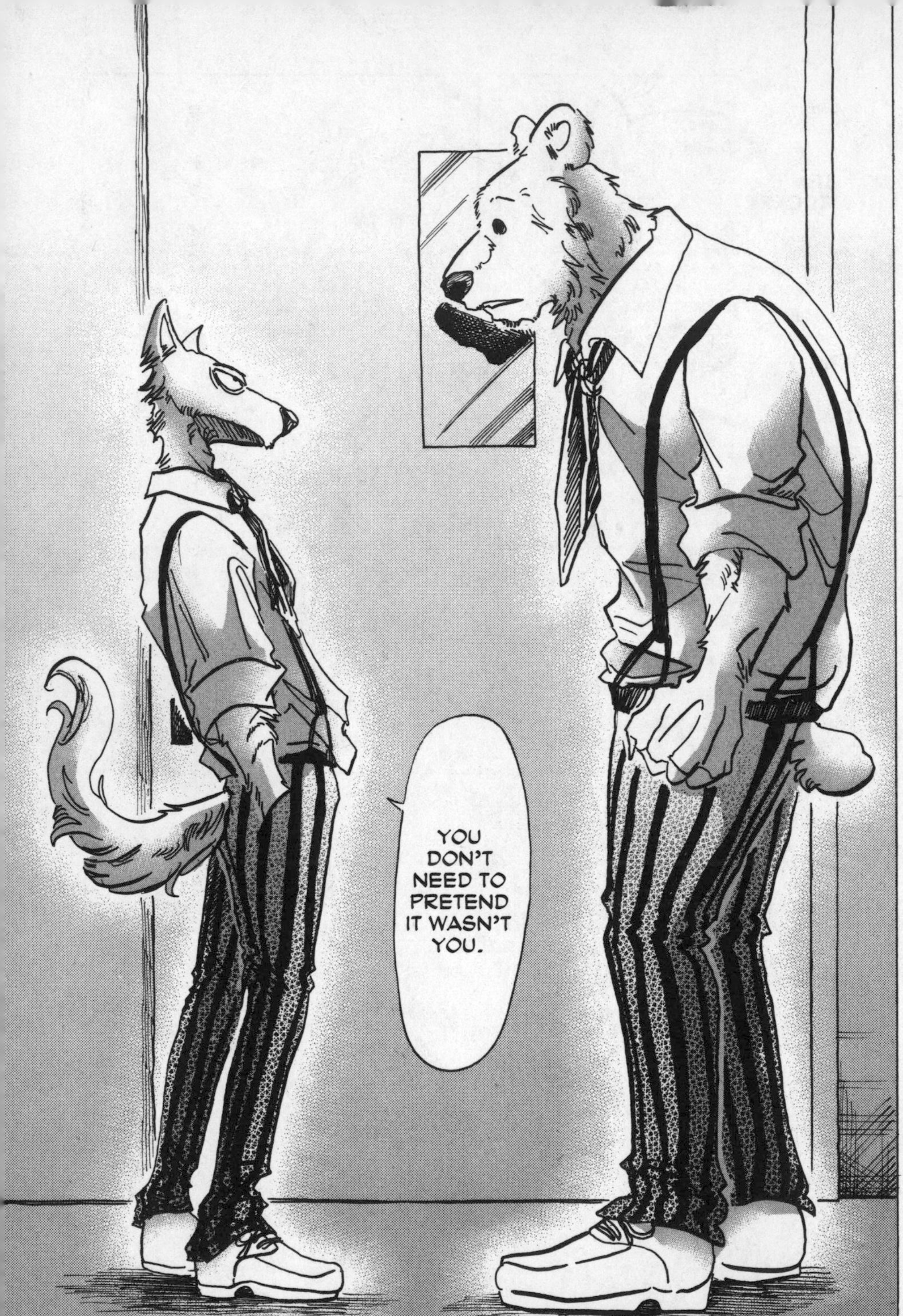
YOU DON'T NEED TO PRETEND IT WASN'T YOU.

Chapter 72: You'll Be Burned by White Flames

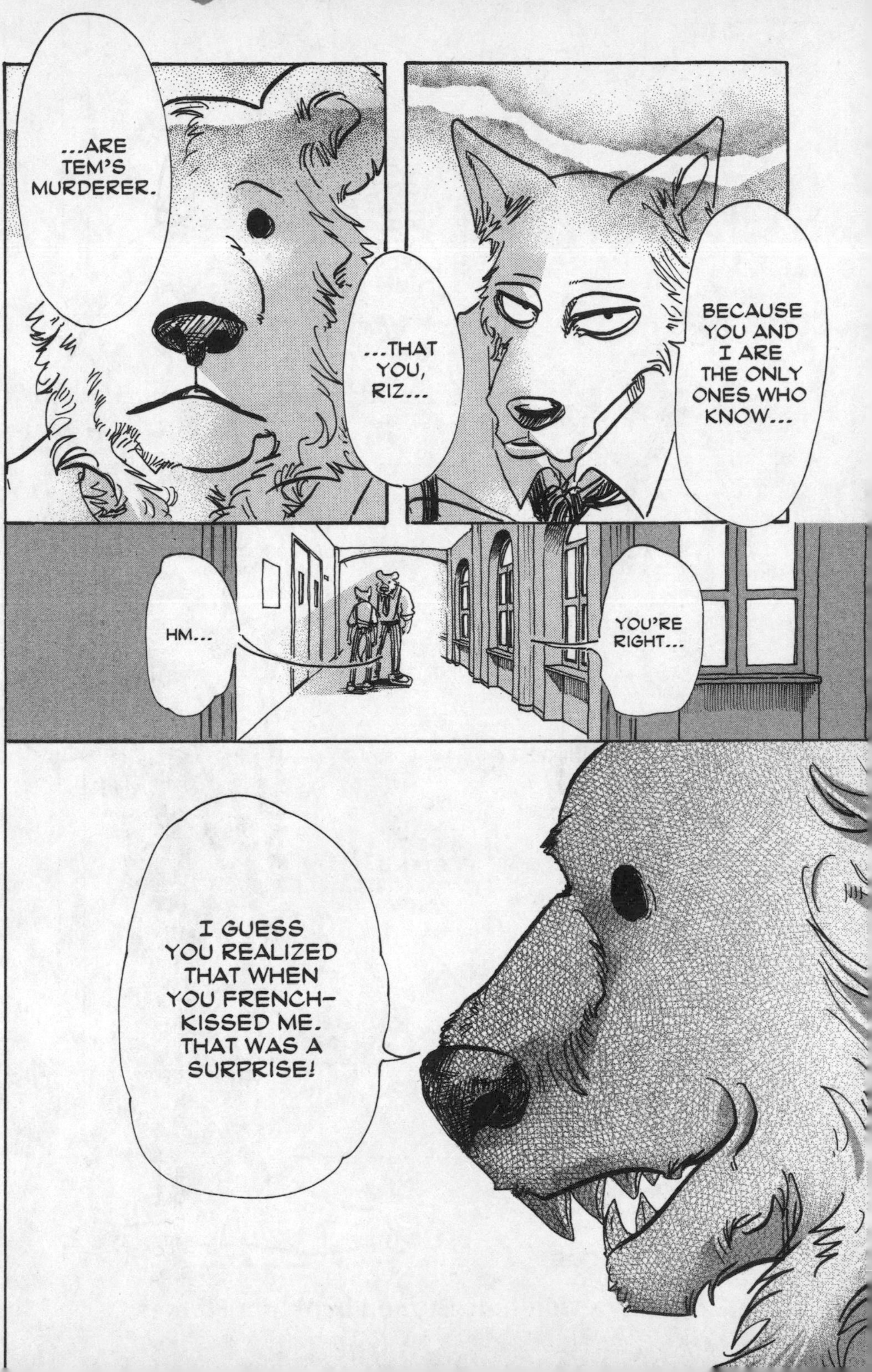
BECAUSE YOU AND I ARE THE ONLY ONES WHO KNOW...
...THAT YOU, RIZ...
...ARE TEM'S MURDERER.
YOU'RE RIGHT...
HM...
I GUESS YOU REALIZED THAT WHEN YOU FRENCH-KISSED ME. THAT WAS A SURPRISE!

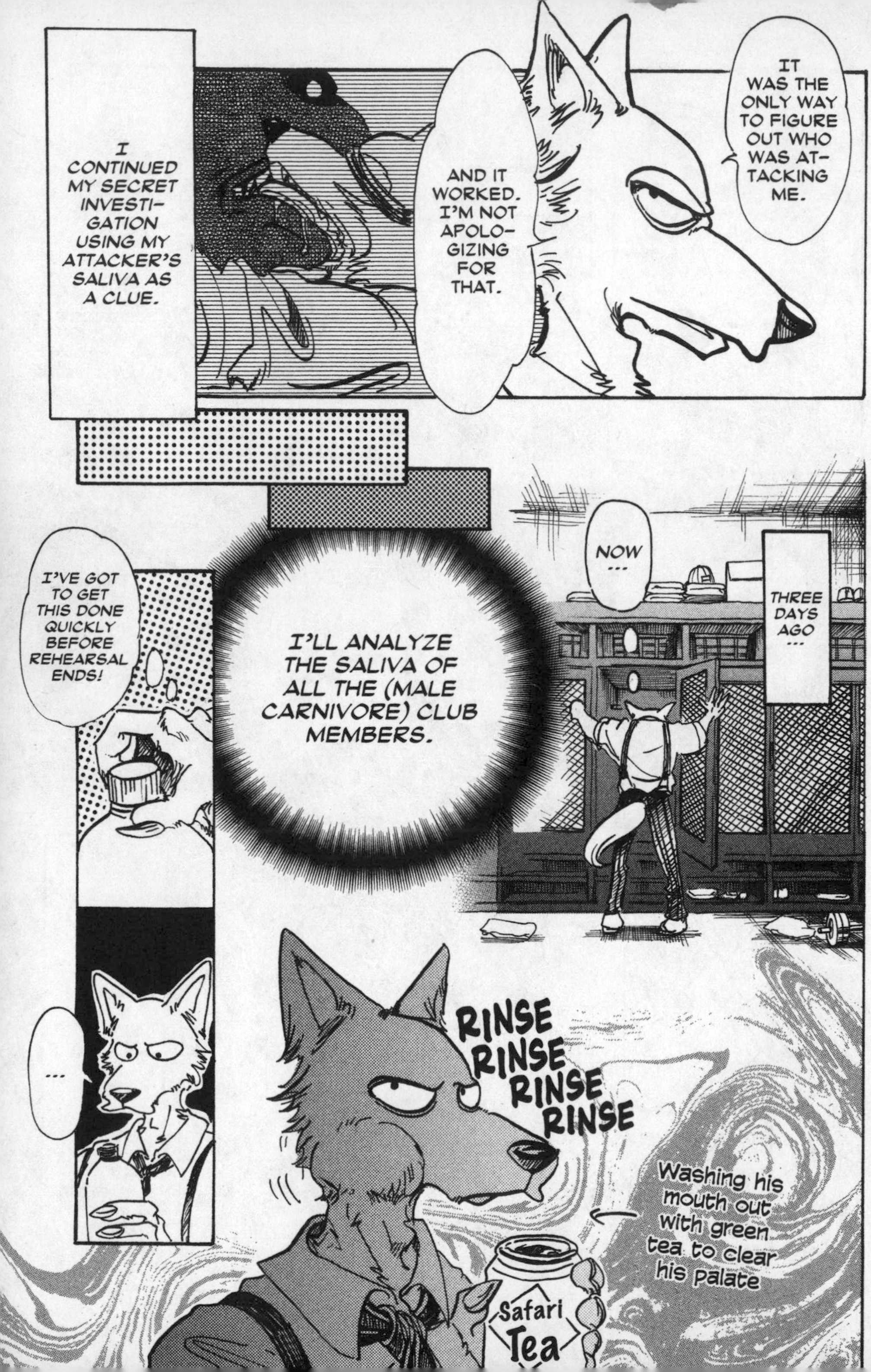
IT WAS THE ONLY WAY TO FIGURE OUT WHO WAS ATTACKING ME.
AND IT WORKED. I'M NOT APOLOGIZING FOR THAT.
I CONTINUED MY SECRET INVESTIGATION USING MY ATTACKER'S SALIVA AS A CLUE.
THREE DAYS AGO ...
NOW ...
I'LL ANALYZE THE SALIVA OF ALL THE (MALE CARNIVORE) CLUB MEMBERS.
I'VE GOT TO GET THIS DONE QUICKLY BEFORE REHEARSAL ENDS!
RINSE RINSE RINSE RINSE
Washing his mouth out with green tea to clear his palate
Safari Tea
...

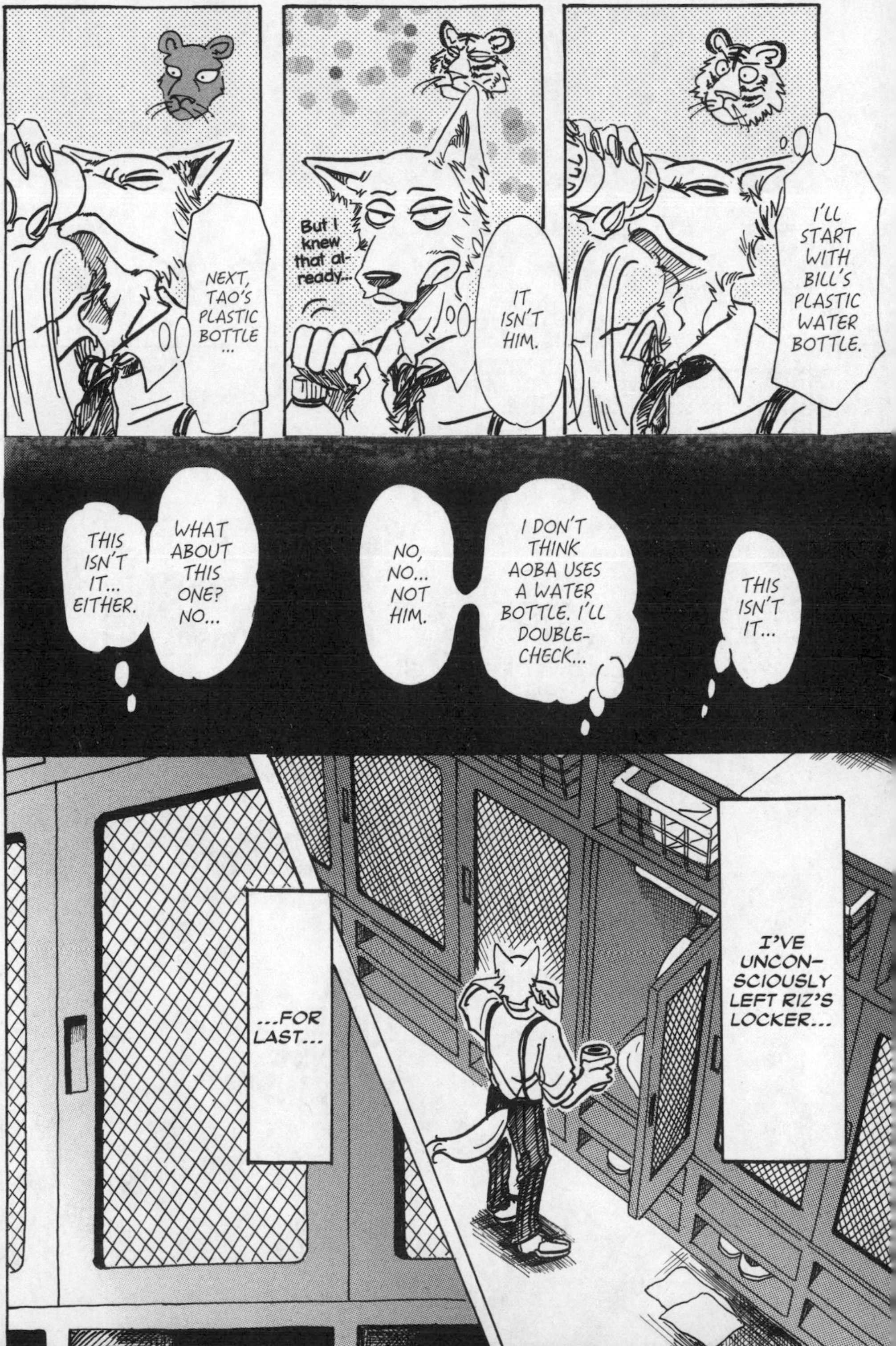
I'LL START WITH BILL'S PLASTIC WATER BOTTLE.
IT ISN'T HIM.
But I knew that already...
NEXT, TAO'S PLASTIC BOTTLE ...
THIS ISN'T IT...
I DON'T THINK AOBA USES A WATER BOTTLE. I'LL DOUBLE-CHECK...
NO, NO... NOT HIM.
WHAT ABOUT THIS ONE? NO...
THIS ISN'T IT... EITHER.
I'VE UNCONSCIOUSLY LEFT RIZ'S LOCKER...
...FOR LAST...

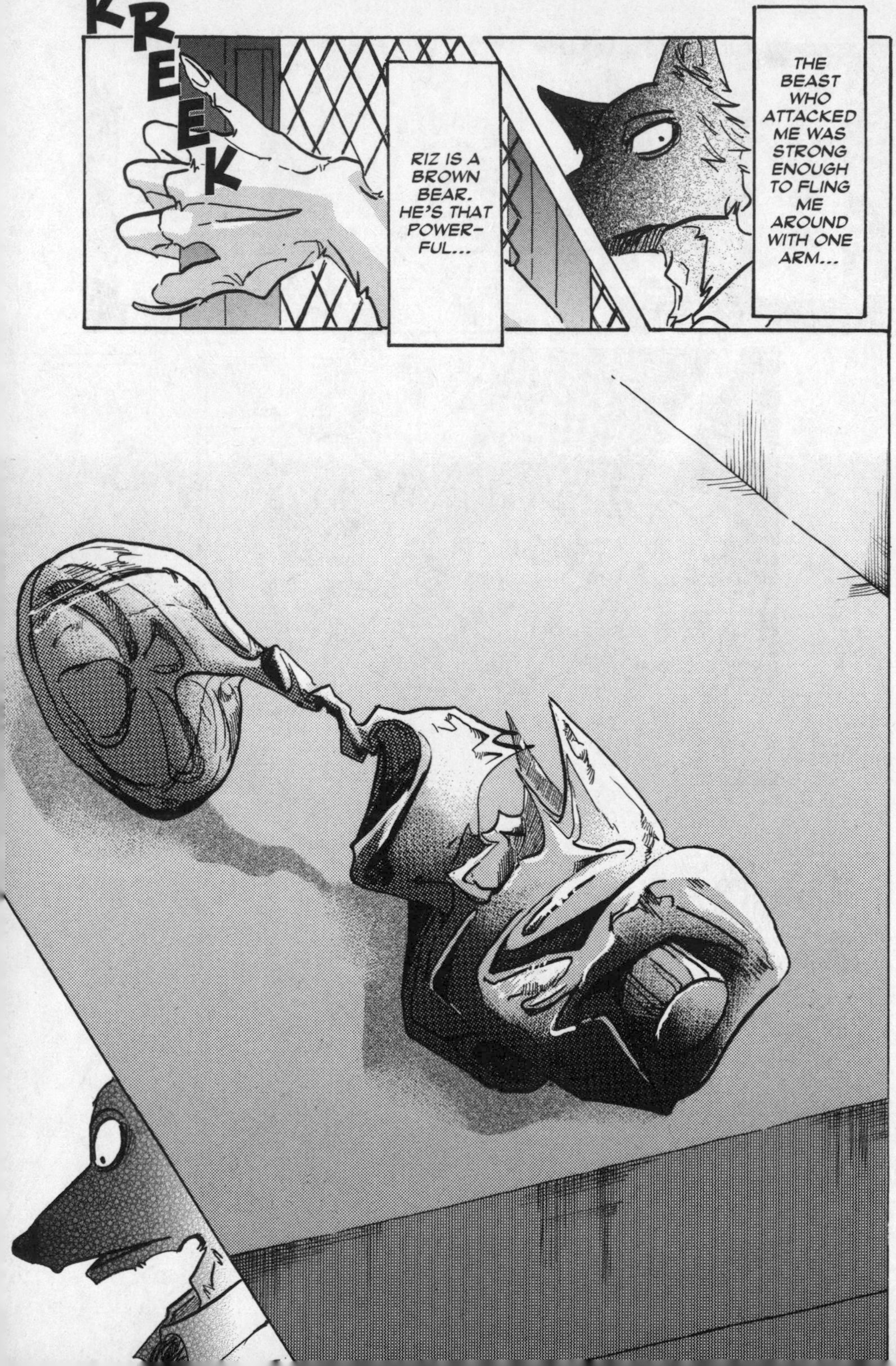
THE BEAST WHO ATTACKED ME WAS STRONG ENOUGH TO FLING ME AROUND WITH ONE ARM...
RIZ IS A BROWN BEAR. HE'S THAT POWER-FUL...
KREEK

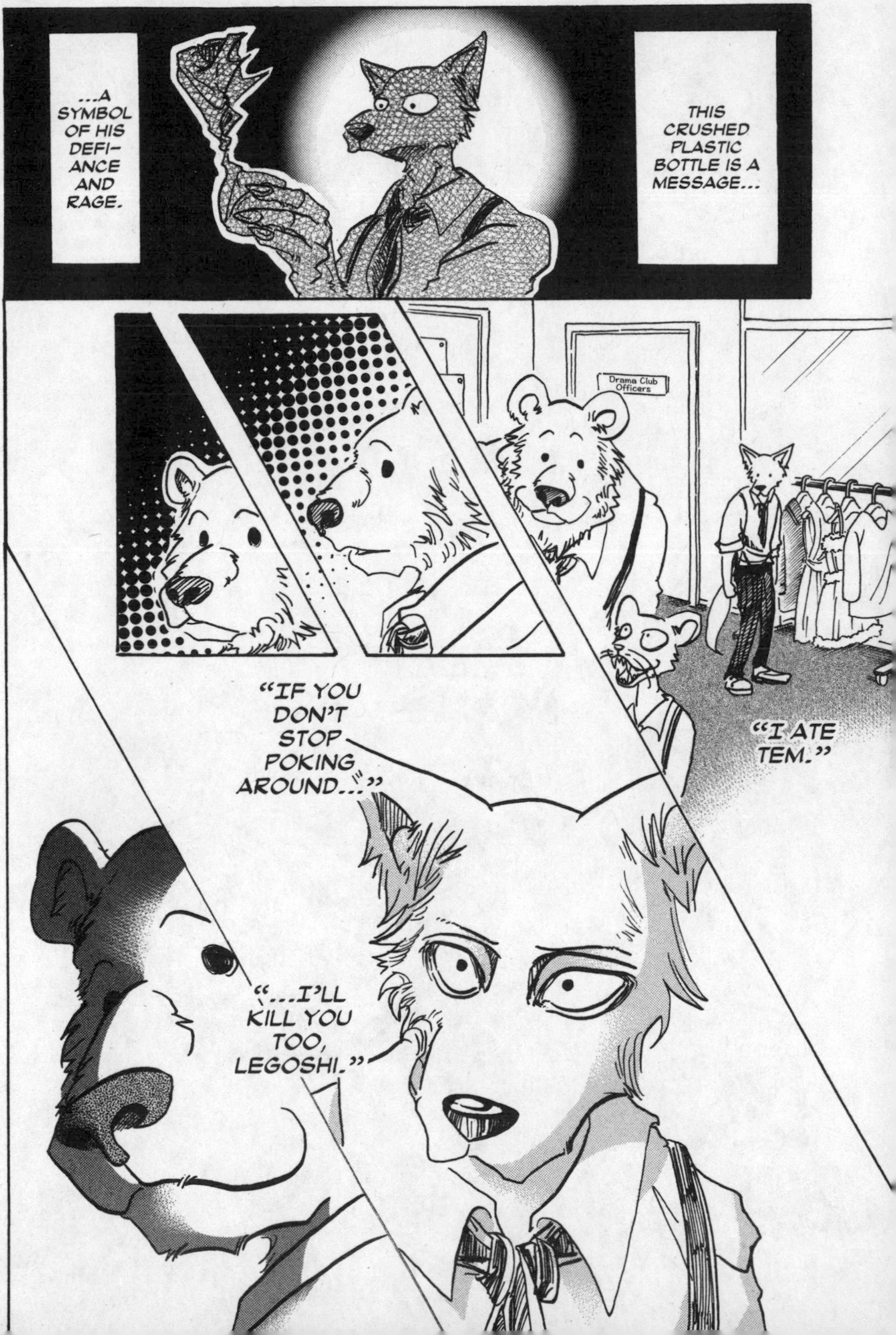
THIS CRUSHED PLASTIC BOTTLE IS A MESSAGE...
...A SYMBOL OF HIS DEFI-ANCE AND RAGE.
Drama Club Officers
"I ATE TEM."
"IF YOU DON'T STOP POKING AROUND...!"
"...I'LL KILL YOU TOO, LEGOSHI."

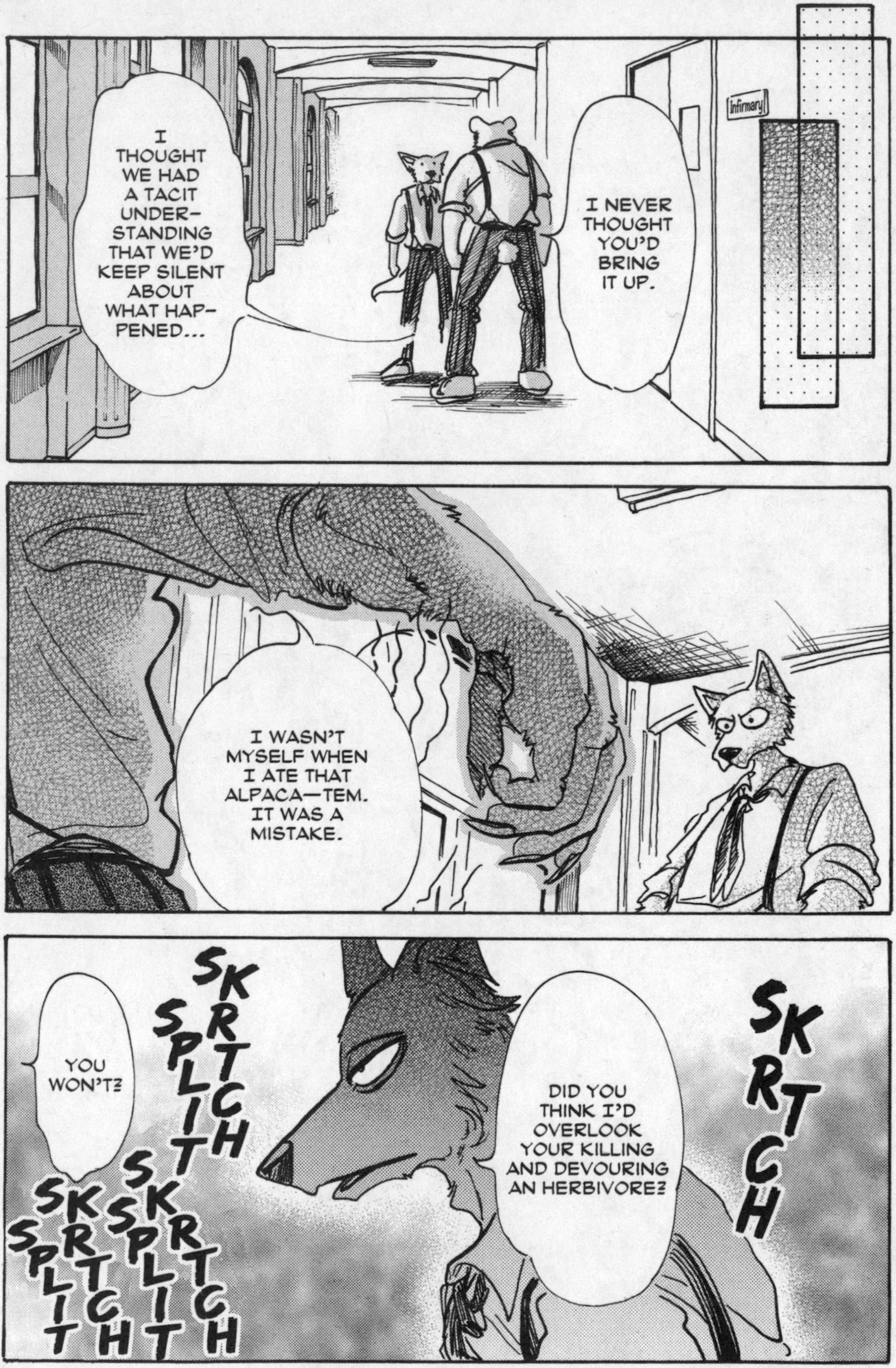
Infirmary
I NEVER THOUGHT YOU'D BRING IT UP.
I THOUGHT WE HAD A TACIT UNDER-STANDING THAT WE'D KEEP SILENT ABOUT WHAT HAP-PENED...
I WASN'T MYSELF WHEN I ATE THAT ALPACA—TEM. IT WAS A MISTAKE.
SKRTCH
DID YOU THINK I'D OVERLOOK YOUR KILLING AND DEVOURING AN HERBIVORE?
SKRTCH
SPLIT
YOU WON'T?
SKRTCH
SPLIT
SKRTCH
SPLIT

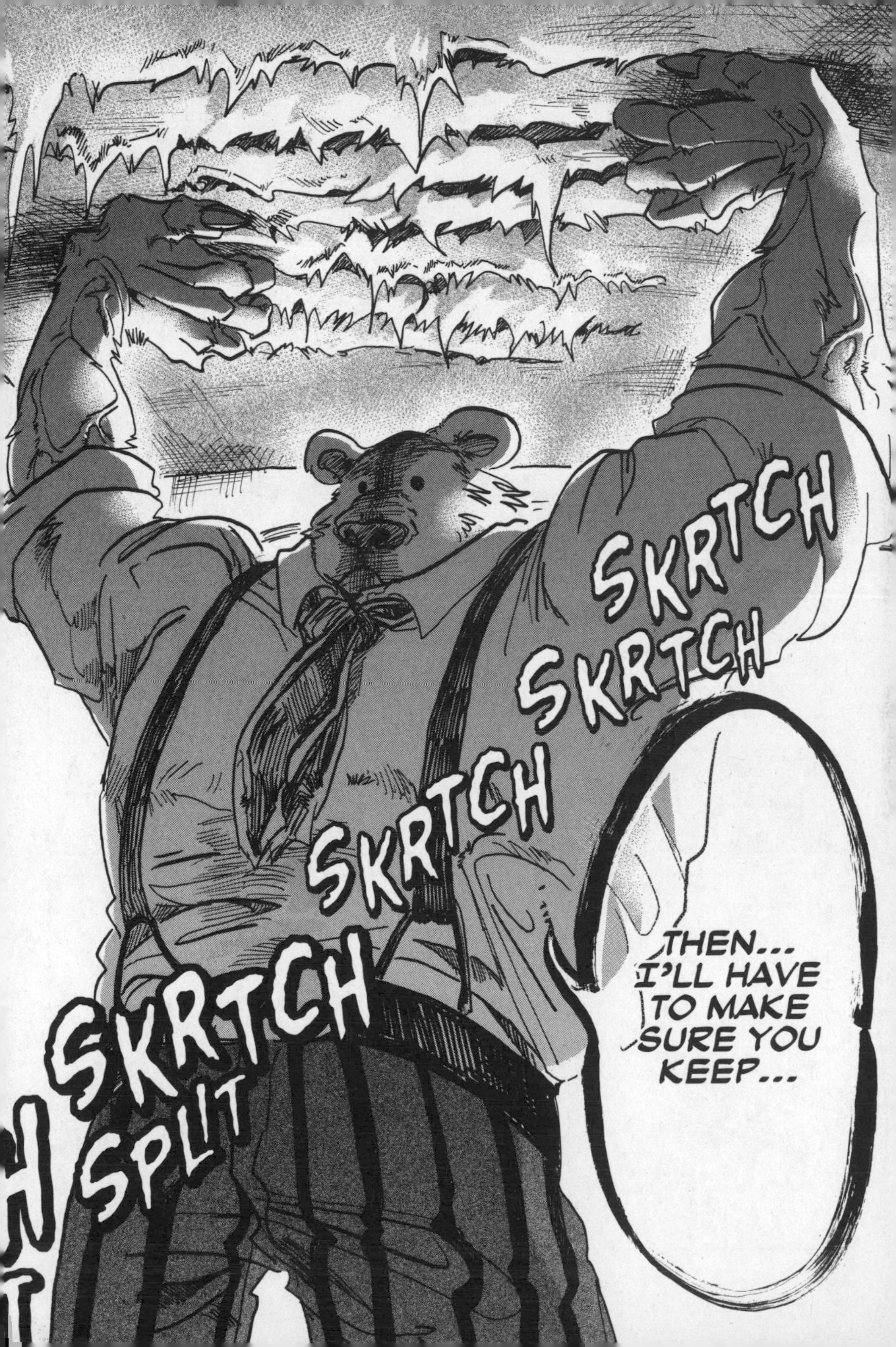
SKRTCH
SKRTCH
SKRTCH
THEN... I'LL HAVE TO MAKE SURE YOU KEEP...
SKRTCH
SPLIT

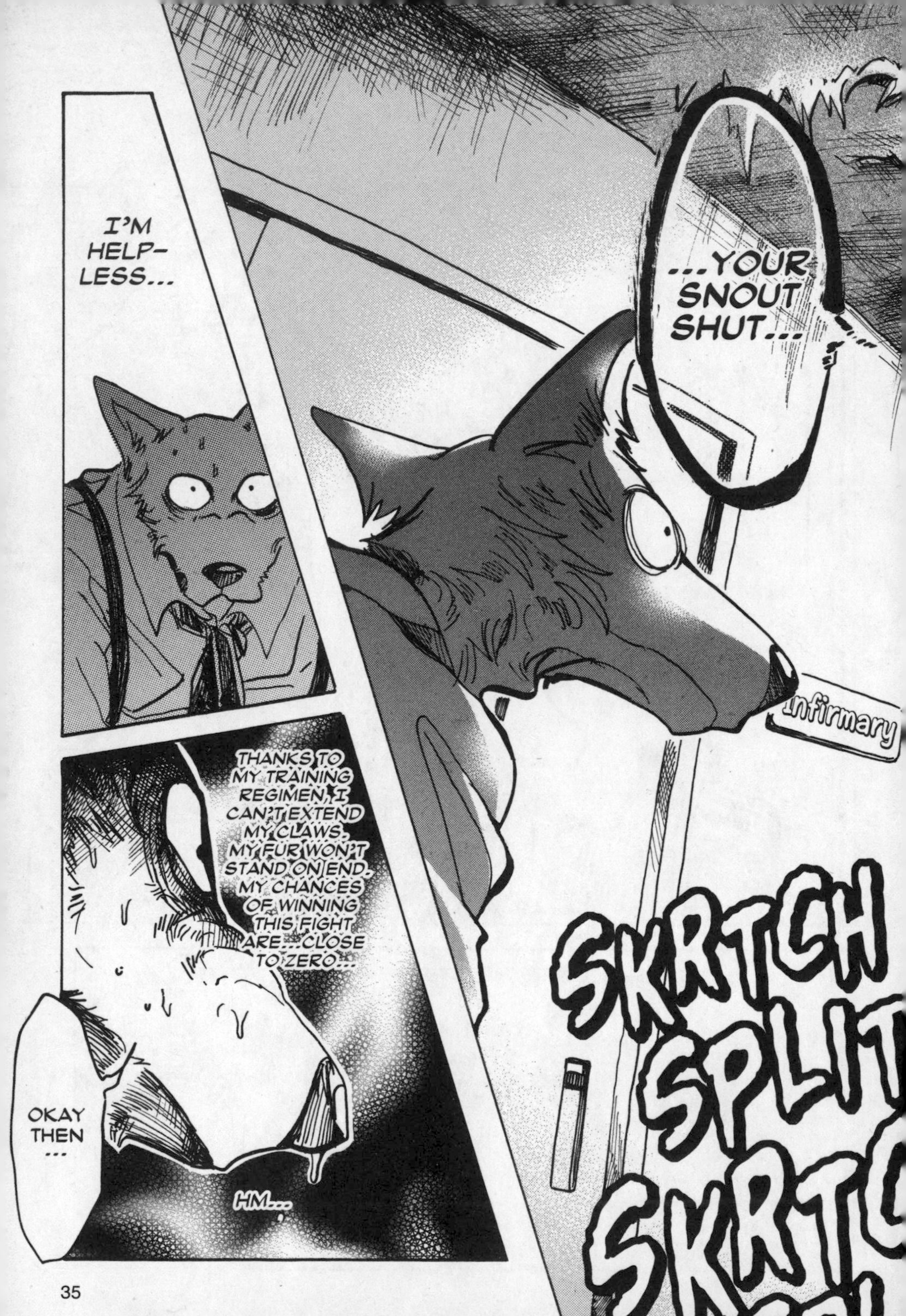
...YOUR SNOUT SHUT...
Infirmary
SKRTCH
SPLIT
SKRTC
I'M HELP-LESS...
THANKS TO MY TRAINING REGIMEN, I CAN'T EXTEND MY CLAWS. MY FUR WON'T STAND ON END. MY CHANCES OF WINNING THIS FIGHT ARE... CLOSE TO ZERO...
OKAY THEN ...
HM...

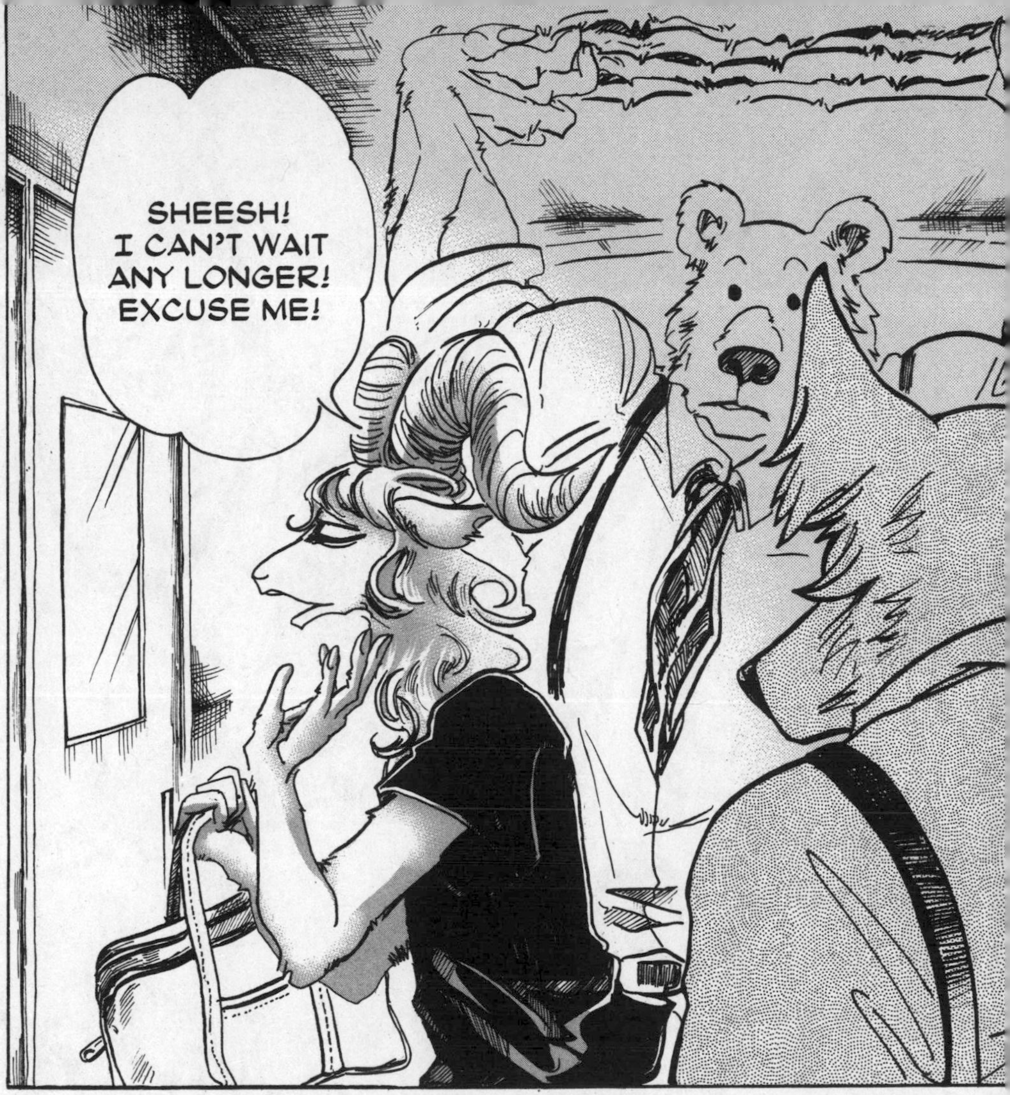
SHEESH! I CAN'T WAIT ANY LONGER! EXCUSE ME!
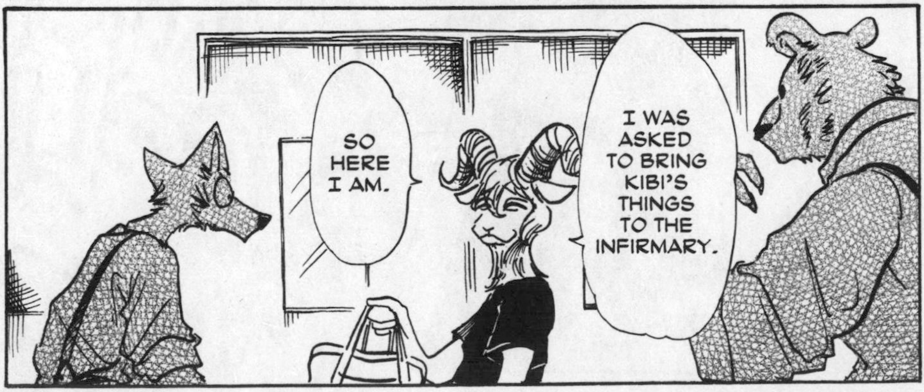
I WAS ASKED TO BRING KIBI'S THINGS TO THE INFIRMARY.
SO HERE I AM.

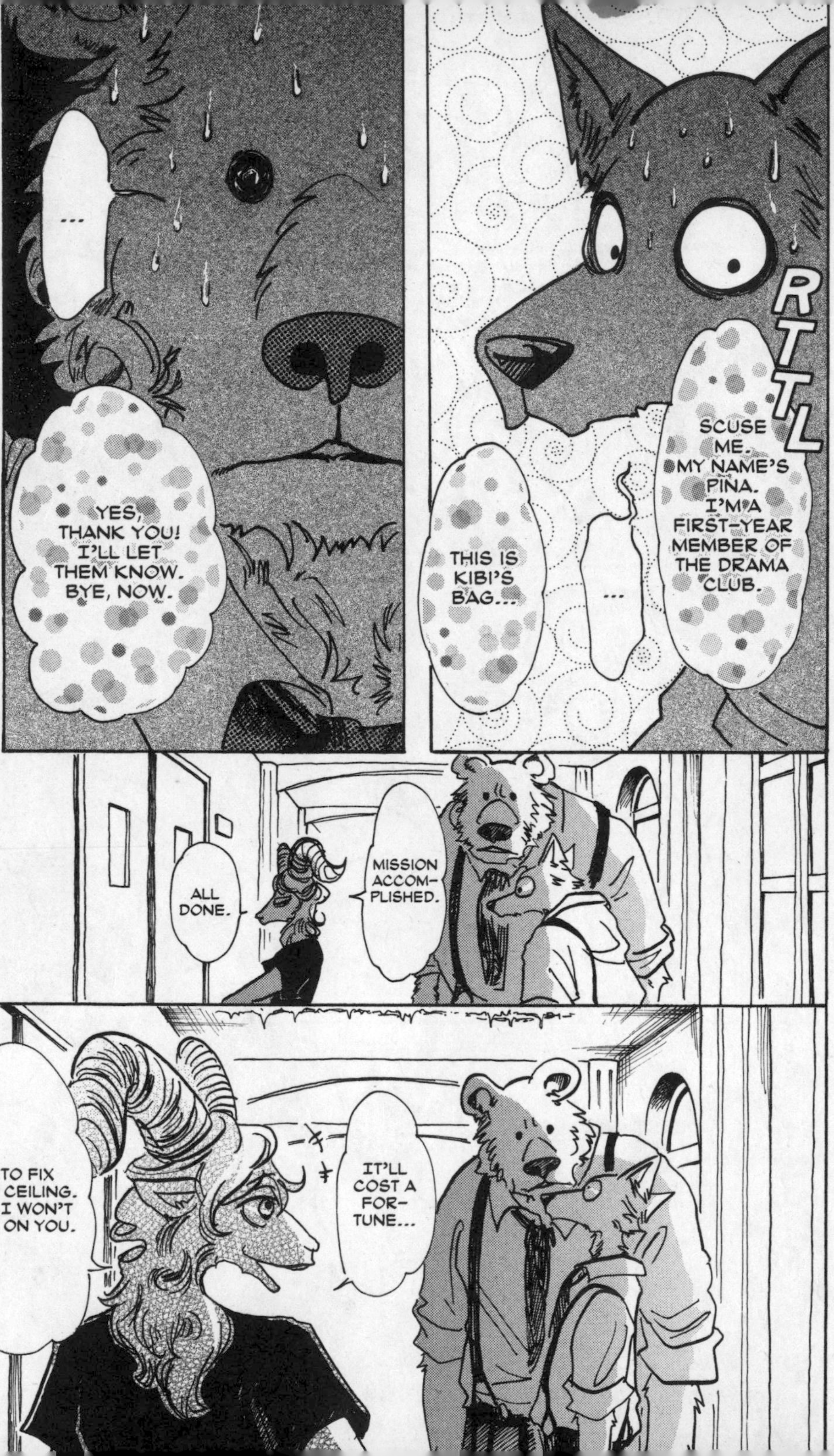
RTTL
SCUSE ME. MY NAME'S PINA. I'M A FIRST-YEAR MEMBER OF THE DRAMA CLUB.
...
THIS IS KIBI'S BAG...
...
YES, THANK YOU! I'LL LET THEM KNOW. BYE, NOW.
MISSION ACCOMPLISHED.
ALL DONE.
IT'LL COST A FORTUNE...
...TO FIX THAT CEILING. BUT I WON'T TELL ON YOU.

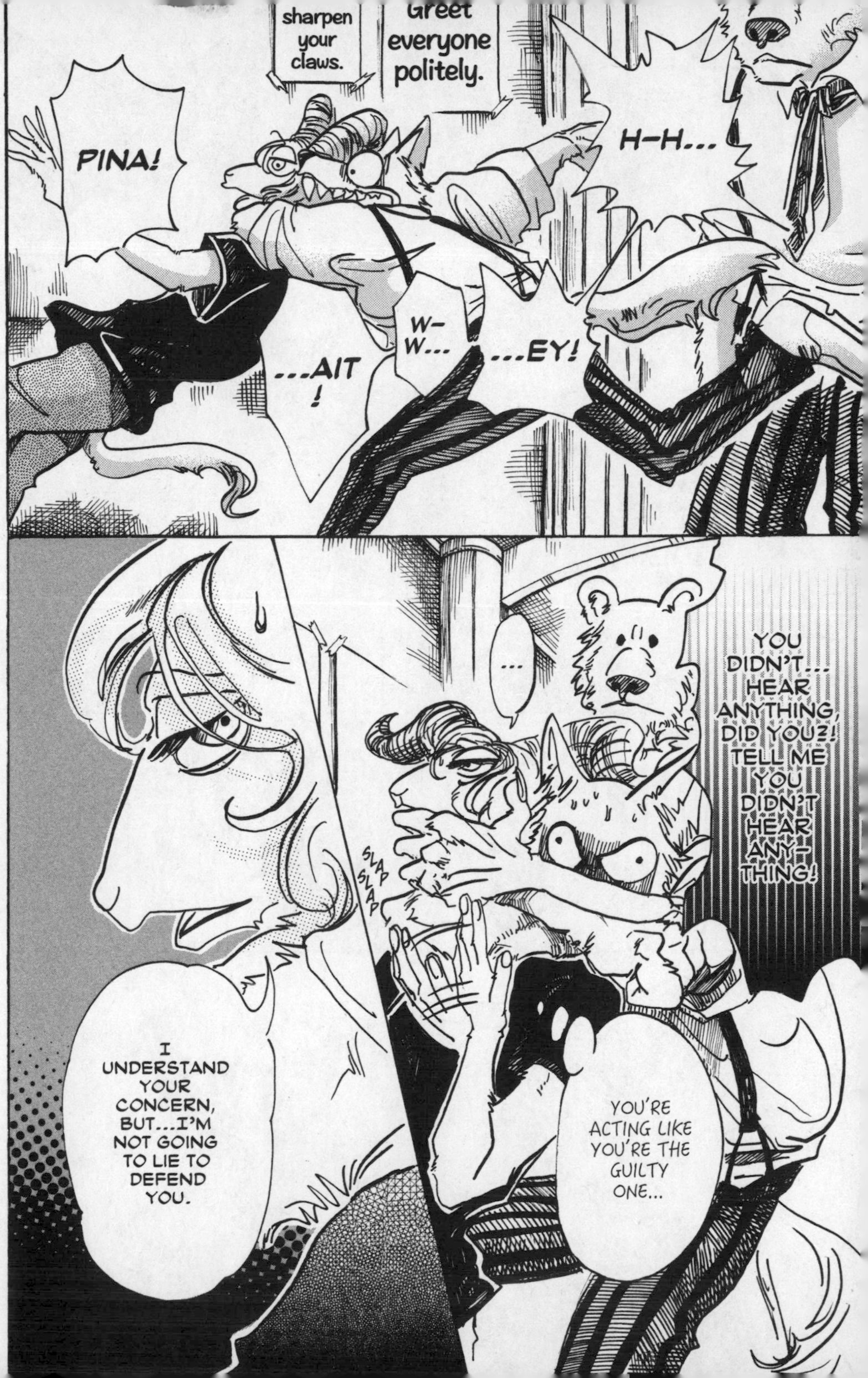

Greet everyone politely.
sharpen your claws.
H-H...
...EY!
W-W...
...AIT!
PINA!
YOU DIDN'T... HEAR ANYTHING, DID YOU?! TELL ME YOU DIDN'T HEAR ANYTHING!
...
SLAP SLAP SLAP
YOU'RE ACTING LIKE YOU'RE THE GUILTY ONE...
I UNDERSTAND YOUR CONCERN, BUT...I'M NOT GOING TO LIE TO DEFEND YOU.

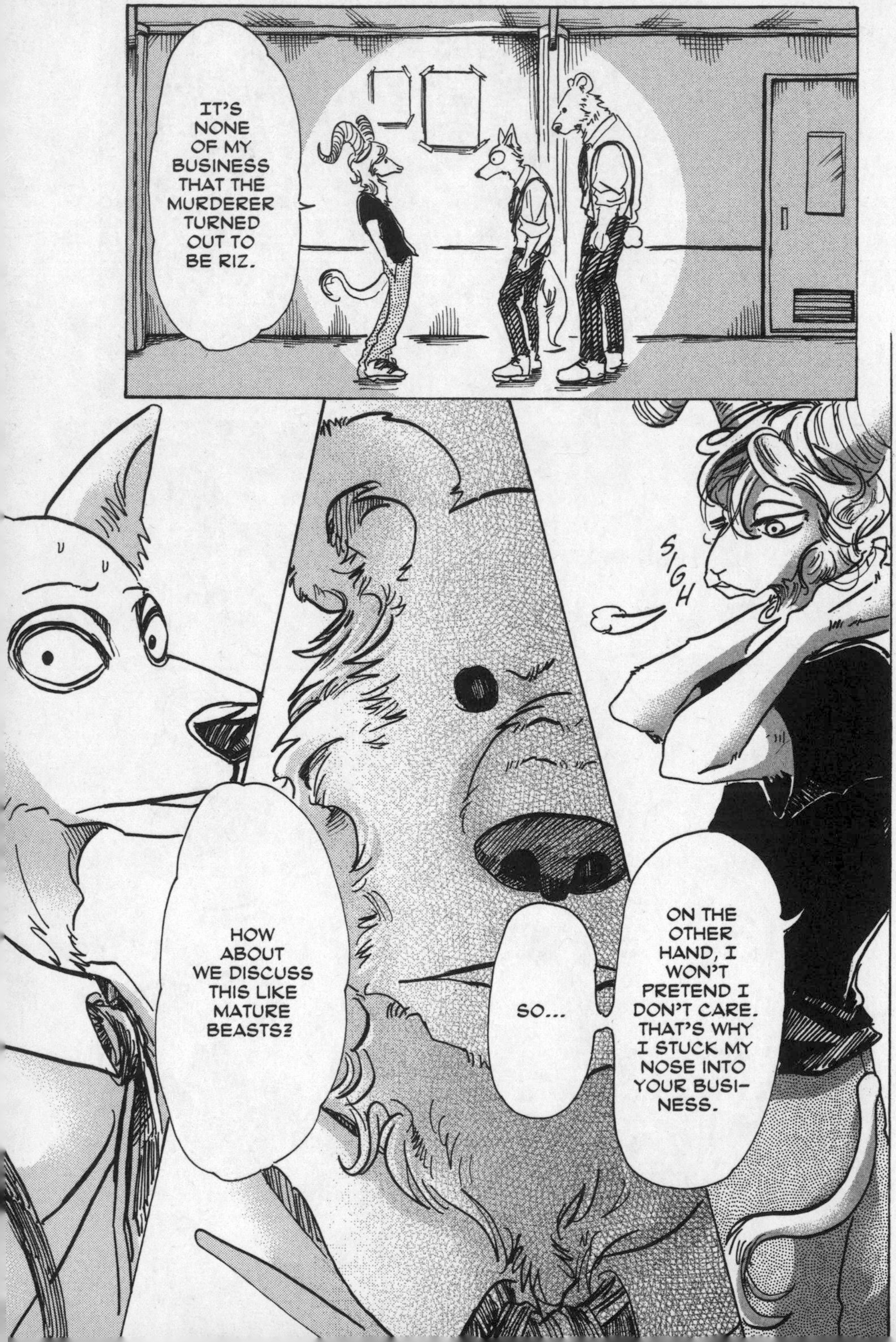
IT'S NONE OF MY BUSINESS THAT THE MURDERER TURNED OUT TO BE RIZ.
SIGH
ON THE OTHER HAND, I WON'T PRETEND I DON'T CARE. THAT'S WHY I STUCK MY NOSE INTO YOUR BUSINESS.
SO...
HOW ABOUT WE DISCUSS THIS LIKE MATURE BEASTS?

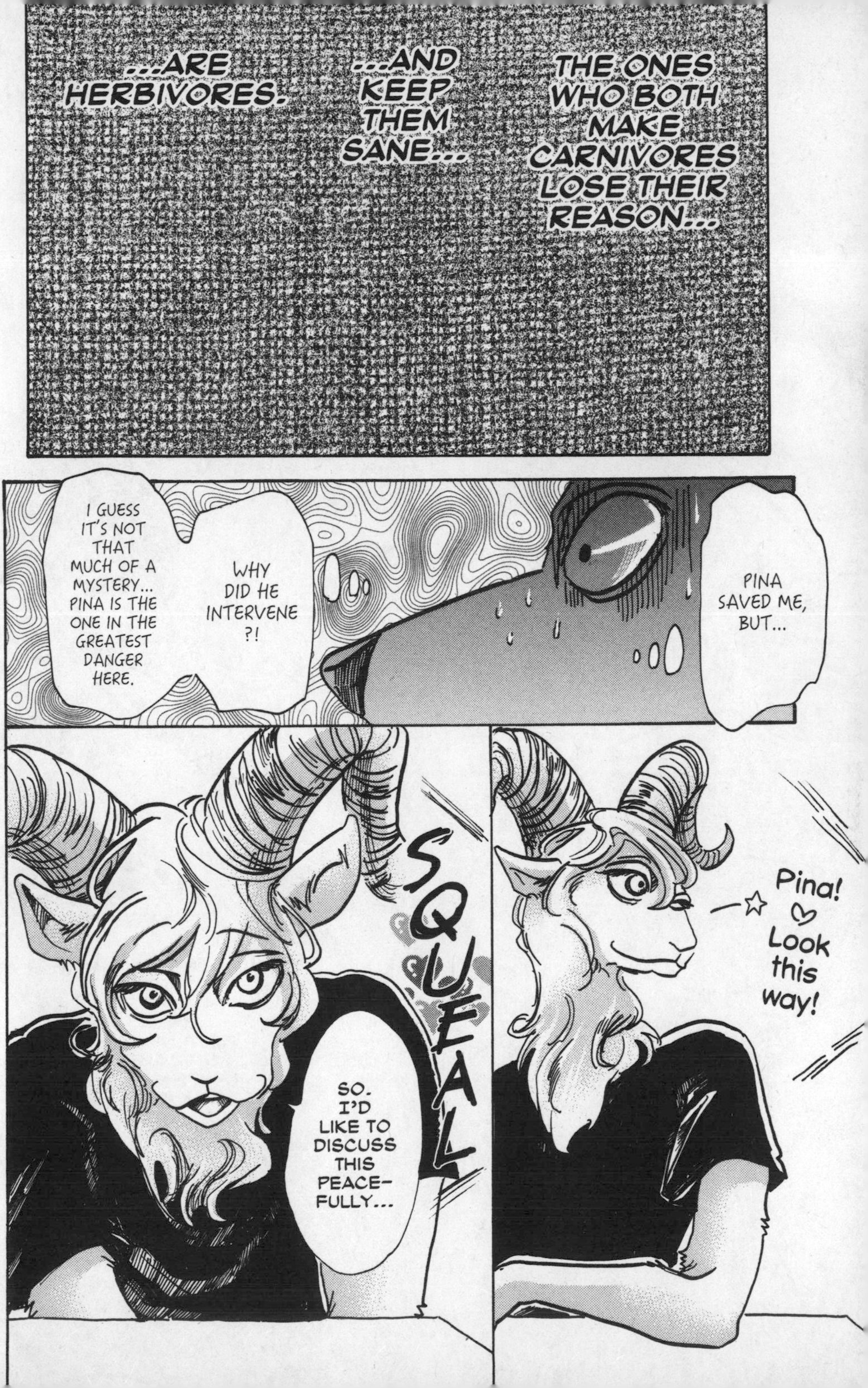
THE ONES WHO BOTH MAKE CARNIVORES LOSE THEIR REASON...
...AND KEEP THEM SANE...
...ARE HERBIVORES.
PINA SAVED ME, BUT...
WHY DID HE INTERVENE?!
I GUESS IT'S NOT THAT MUCH OF A MYSTERY... PINA IS THE ONE IN THE GREATEST DANGER HERE.
Pina! ♡ Look this way!
SQUEAL
SO. I'D LIKE TO DISCUSS THIS PEACEFULLY...

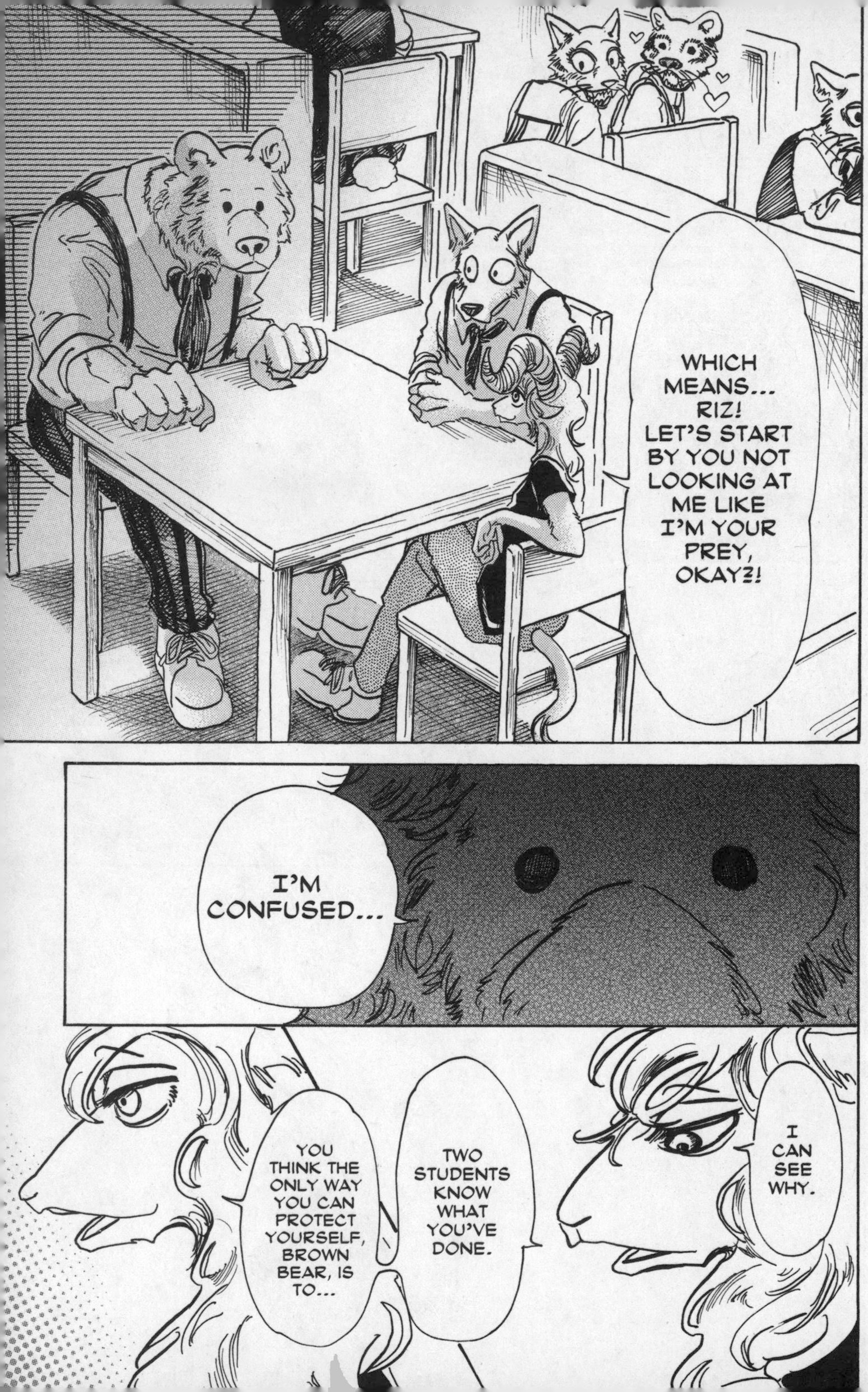
WHICH MEANS... RIZ! LET'S START BY YOU NOT LOOKING AT ME LIKE I'M YOUR PREY, OKAY?!
I'M CONFUSED...
I CAN SEE WHY.
TWO STUDENTS KNOW WHAT YOU'VE DONE.
YOU THINK THE ONLY WAY YOU CAN PROTECT YOURSELF, BROWN BEAR, IS TO...

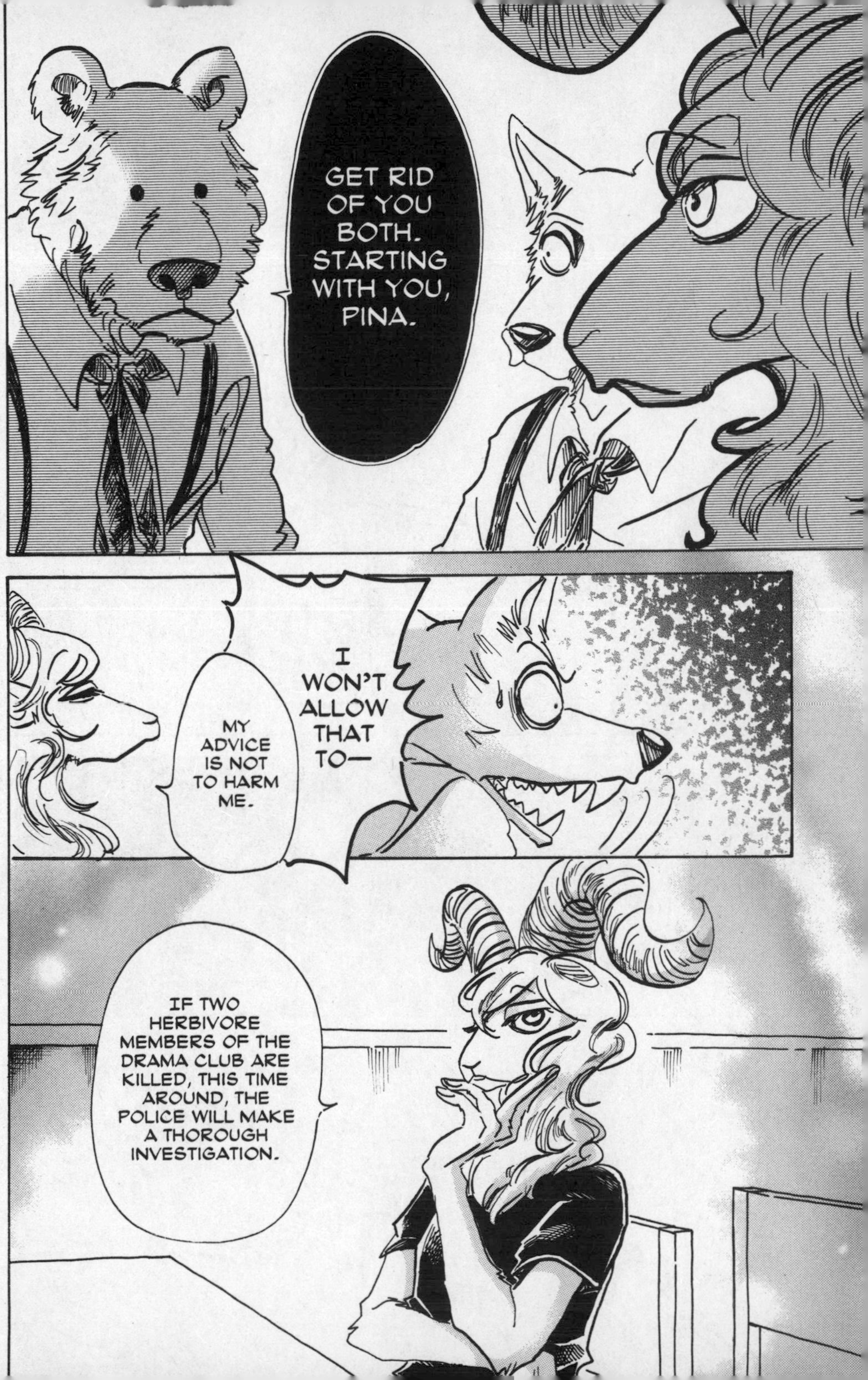
GET RID OF YOU BOTH. STARTING WITH YOU, PINA.
I WON'T ALLOW THAT TO—
MY ADVICE IS NOT TO HARM ME.
IF TWO HERBIVORE MEMBERS OF THE DRAMA CLUB ARE KILLED, THIS TIME AROUND, THE POLICE WILL MAKE A THOROUGH INVESTIGATION.

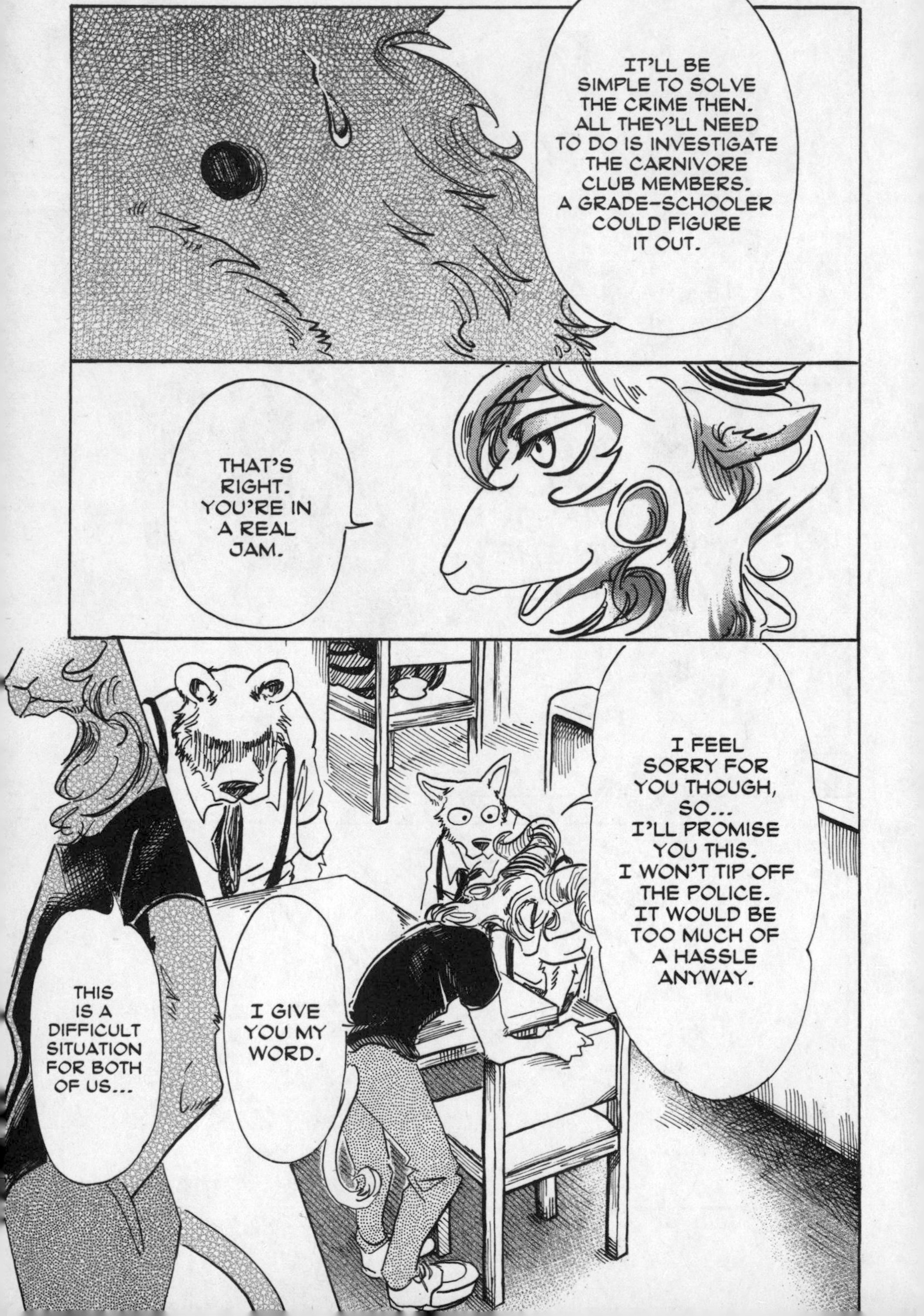
IT'LL BE SIMPLE TO SOLVE THE CRIME THEN. ALL THEY'LL NEED TO DO IS INVESTIGATE THE CARNIVORE CLUB MEMBERS. A GRADE-SCHOOLER COULD FIGURE IT OUT.
THAT'S RIGHT. YOU'RE IN A REAL JAM.
I FEEL SORRY FOR YOU THOUGH, SO... I'LL PROMISE YOU THIS. I WON'T TIP OFF THE POLICE. IT WOULD BE TOO MUCH OF A HASSLE ANYWAY.
I GIVE YOU MY WORD.
THIS IS A DIFFICULT SITUATION FOR BOTH OF US...

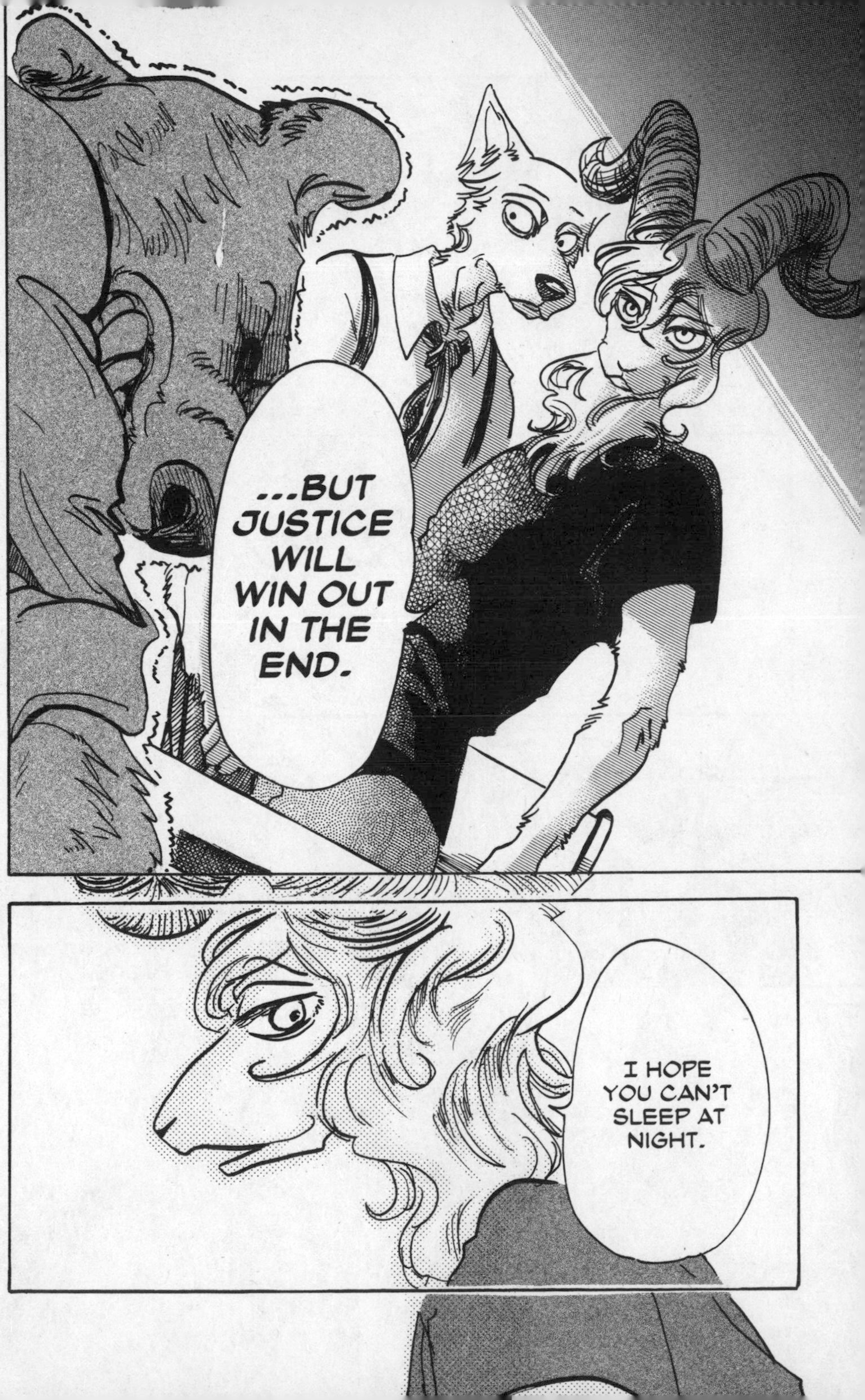
...BUT JUSTICE WILL WIN OUT IN THE END.
I HOPE YOU CAN'T SLEEP AT NIGHT.

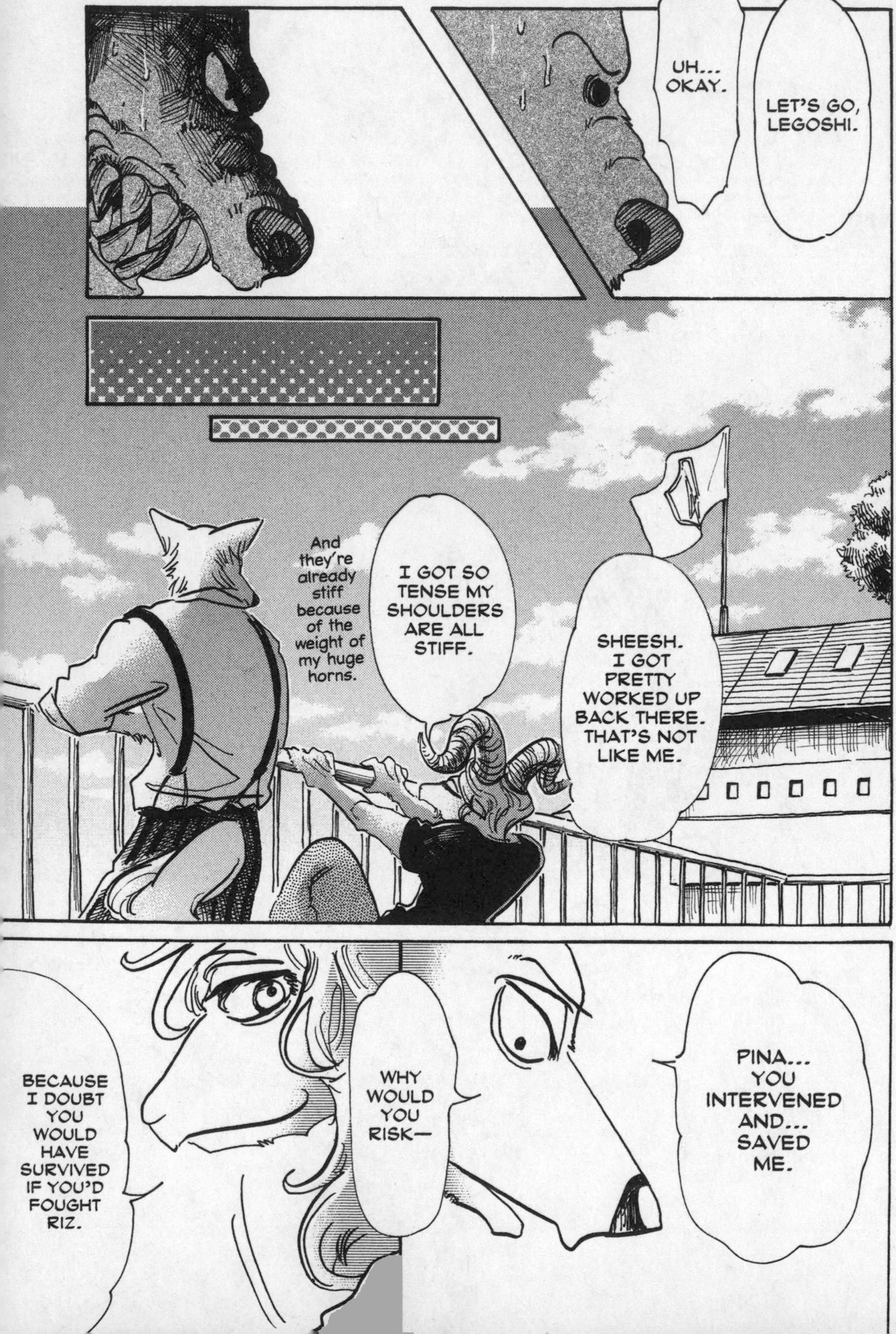
LET'S GO, LEGOSHI.
UH... OKAY.
SHEESH. I GOT PRETTY WORKED UP BACK THERE. THAT'S NOT LIKE ME.
I GOT SO TENSE MY SHOULDERS ARE ALL STIFF.
And they're already stiff because of the weight of my huge horns.
PINA... YOU INTERVENED AND... SAVED ME.
WHY WOULD YOU RISK—
BECAUSE I DOUBT YOU WOULD HAVE SURVIVED IF YOU'D FOUGHT RIZ.

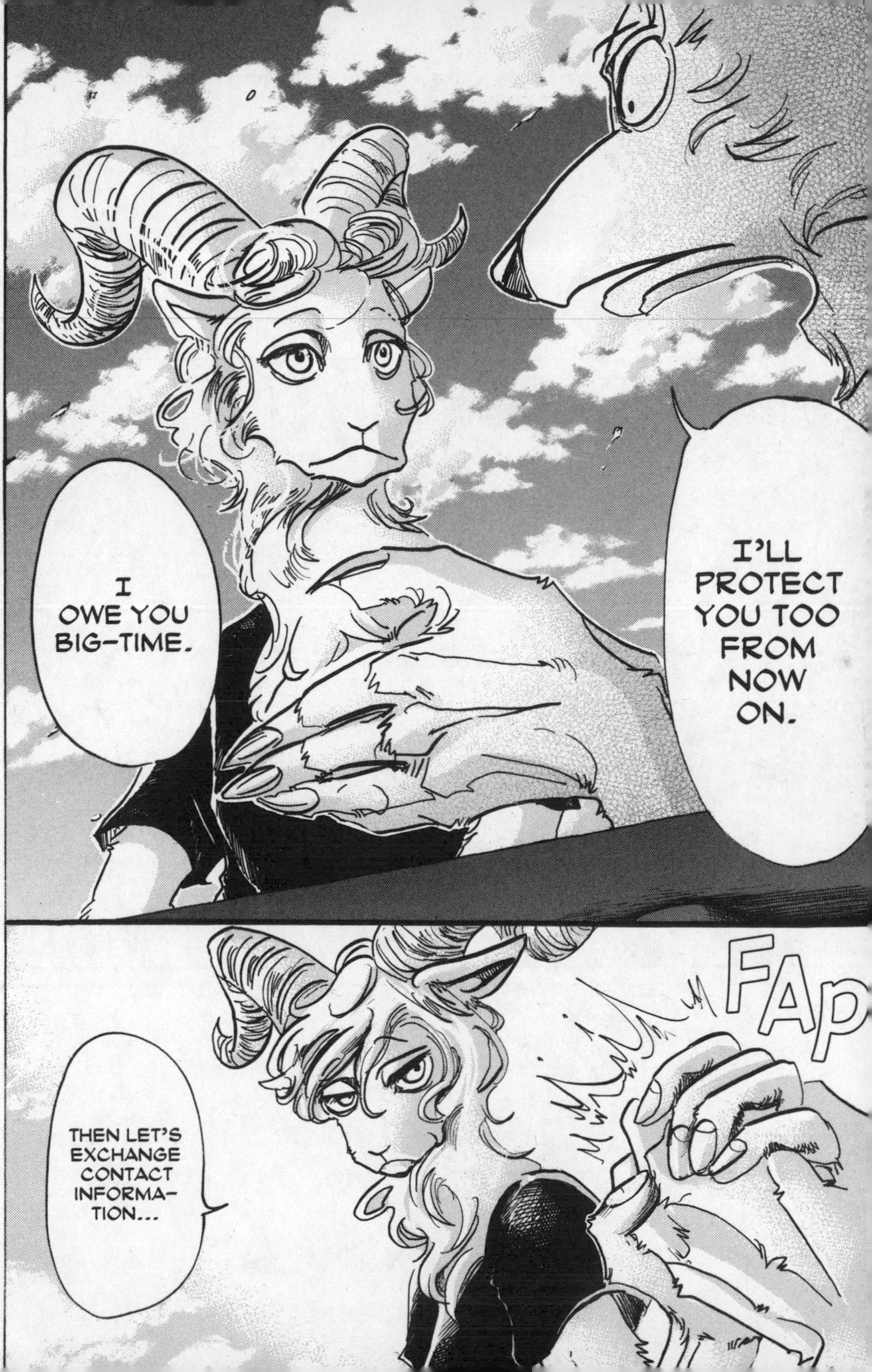
I'LL PROTECT YOU TOO FROM NOW ON.
I OWE YOU BIG-TIME.
FAP
THEN LET'S EXCHANGE CONTACT INFORMATION...

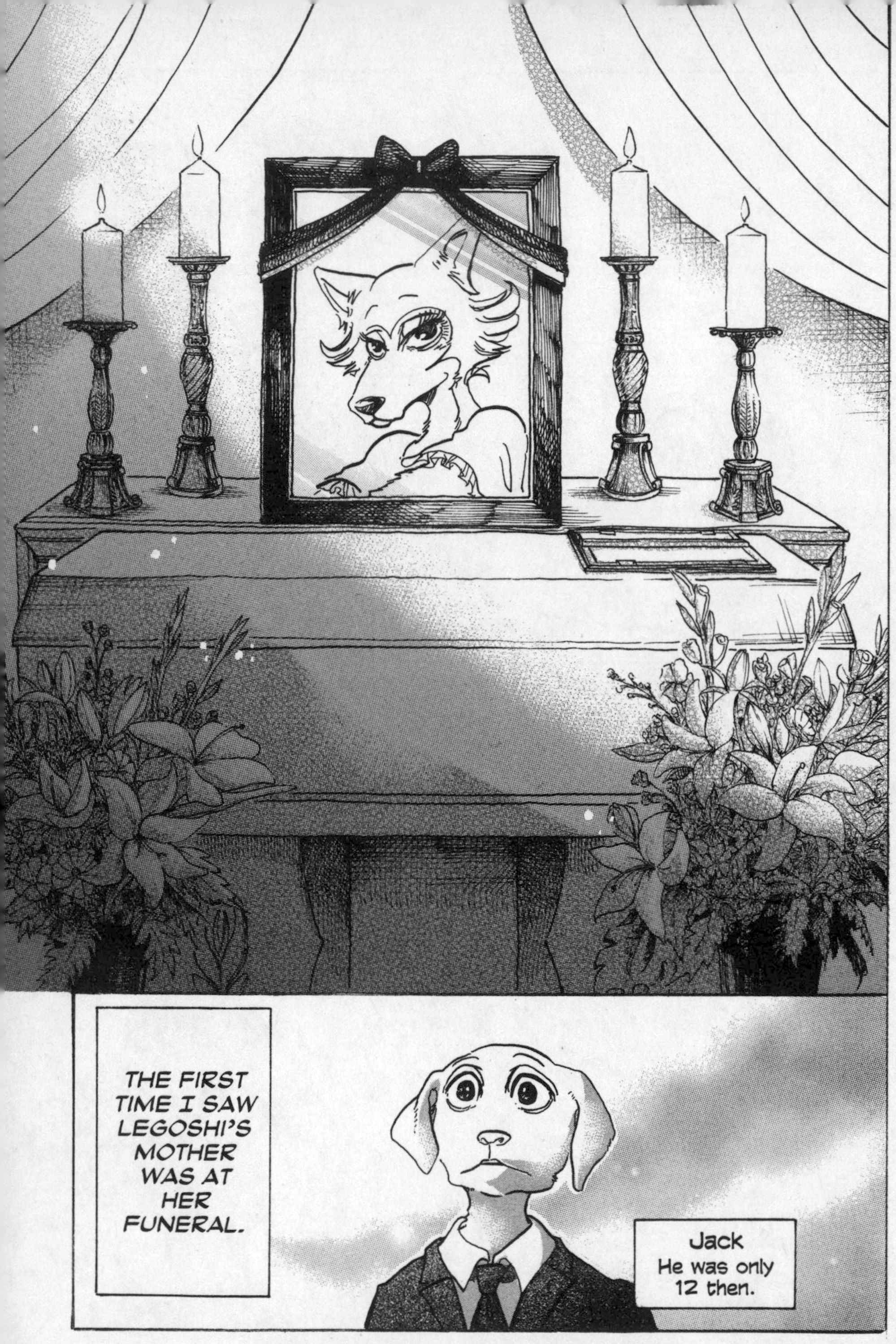
THE FIRST TIME I SAW LEGOSHI'S MOTHER WAS AT HER FUNERAL.
Jack
He was only 12 then.

Chapter 73: A Well-Bred "Wolf"

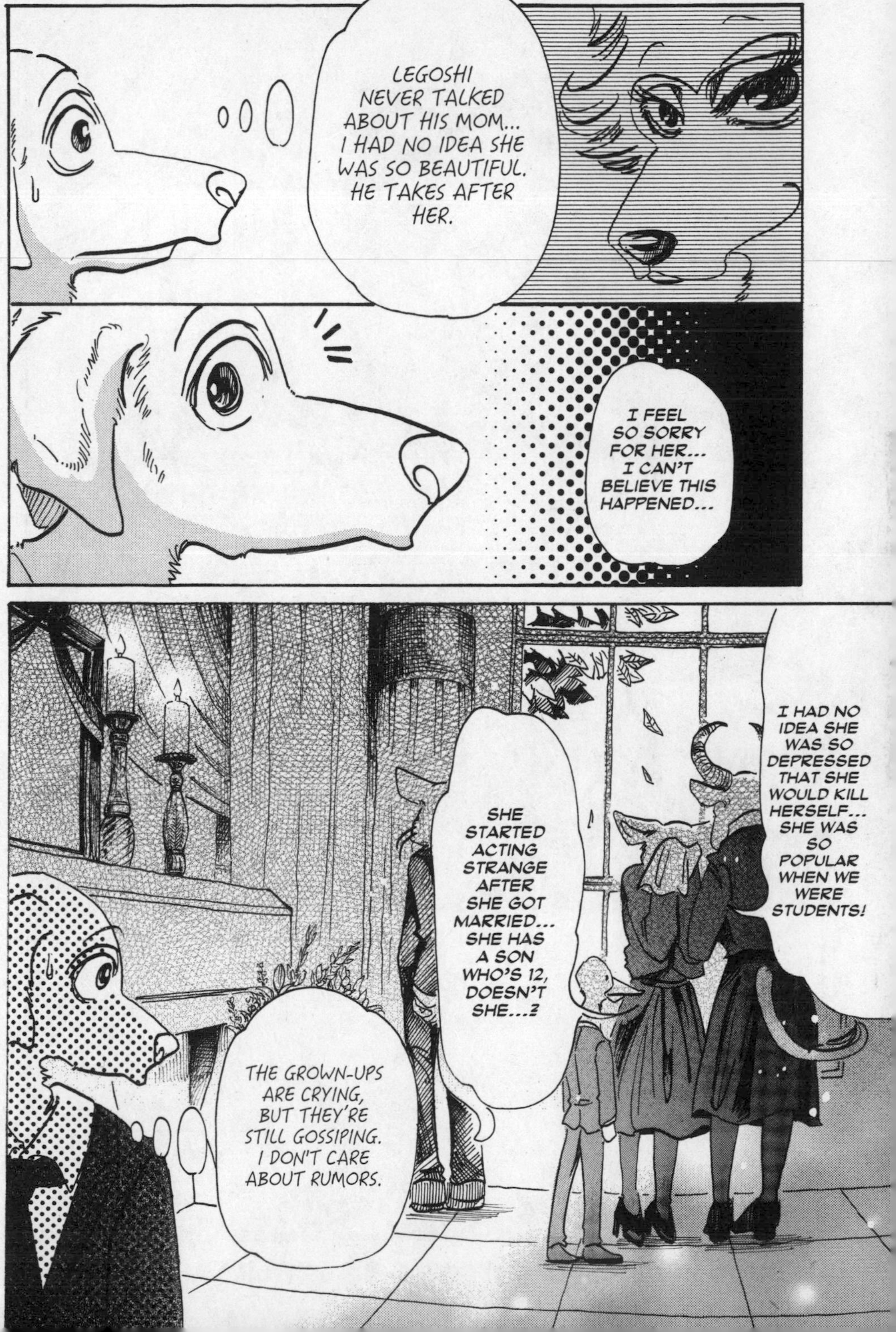

LEGOSHI NEVER TALKED ABOUT HIS MOM... I HAD NO IDEA SHE WAS SO BEAUTIFUL. HE TAKES AFTER HER.
I FEEL SO SORRY FOR HER... I CAN'T BELIEVE THIS HAPPENED...
I HAD NO IDEA SHE WAS SO DEPRESSED THAT SHE WOULD KILL HERSELF... SHE WAS SO POPULAR WHEN WE WERE STUDENTS!
SHE STARTED ACTING STRANGE AFTER SHE GOT MARRIED... SHE HAS A SON WHO'S 12, DOESN'T SHE...?
THE GROWN-UPS ARE CRYING, BUT THEY'RE STILL GOSSIPING. I DON'T CARE ABOUT RUMORS.

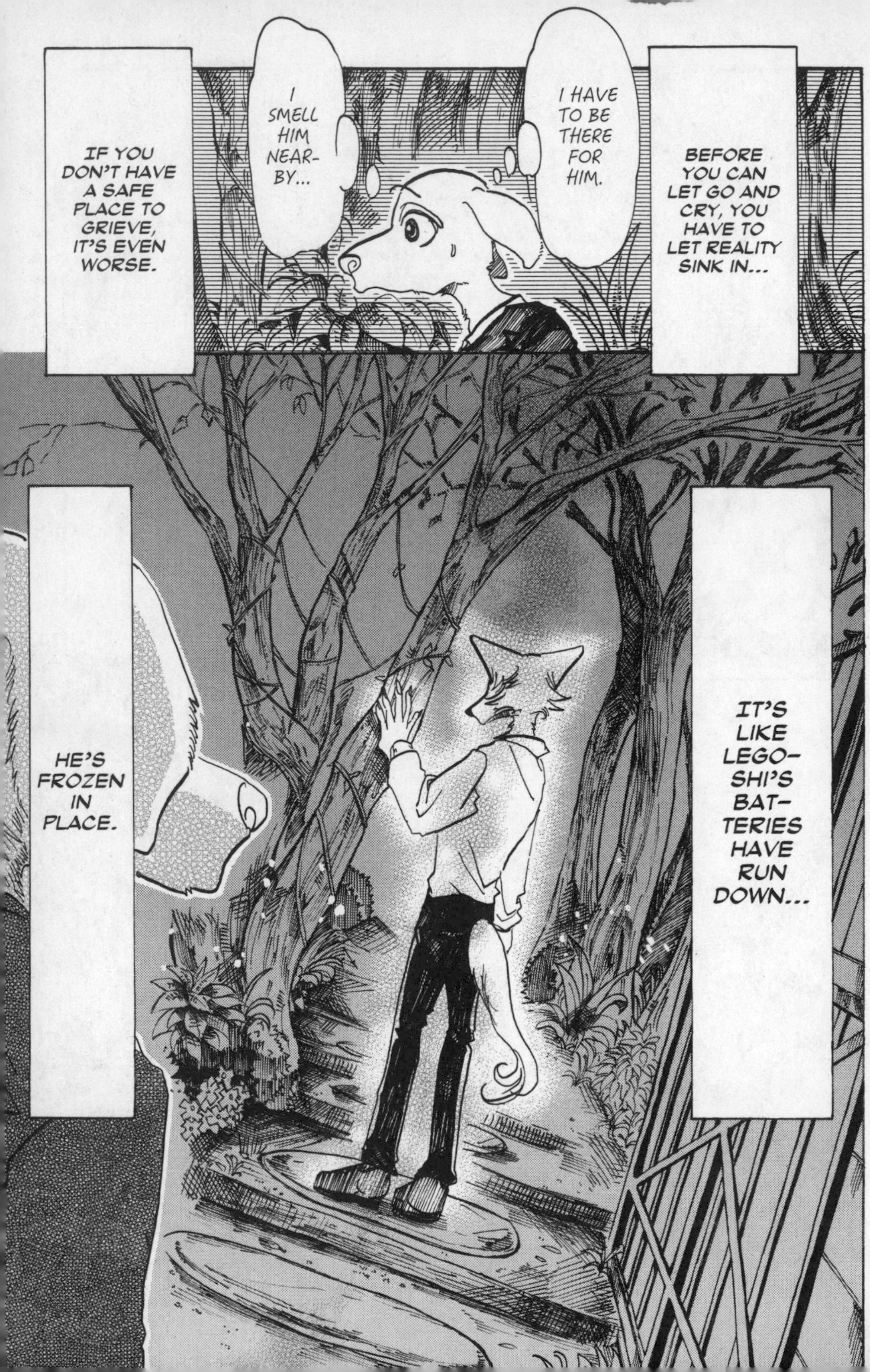
BEFORE YOU CAN LET GO AND CRY, YOU HAVE TO LET REALITY SINK IN...
I HAVE TO BE THERE FOR HIM.
I SMELL HIM NEAR-BY...
IF YOU DON'T HAVE A SAFE PLACE TO GRIEVE, IT'S EVEN WORSE.
IT'S LIKE LEGO-SHI'S BAT-TERIES HAVE RUN DOWN...
HE'S FROZEN IN PLACE.

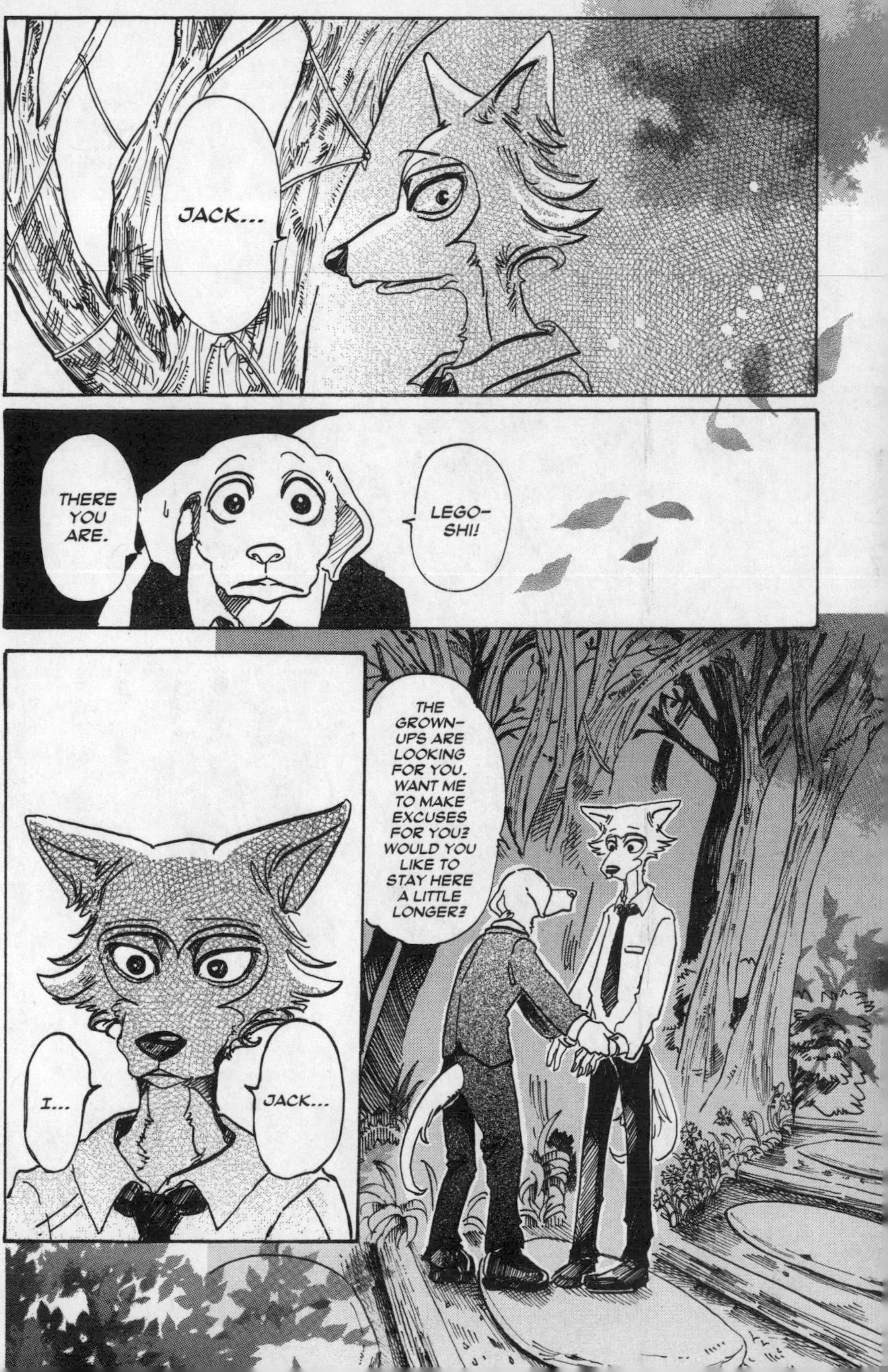
JACK...
LEGO-SHI!
THERE YOU ARE.
THE GROWN-UPS ARE LOOKING FOR YOU. WANT ME TO MAKE EXCUSES FOR YOU? WOULD YOU LIKE TO STAY HERE A LITTLE LONGER?
JACK...
I...

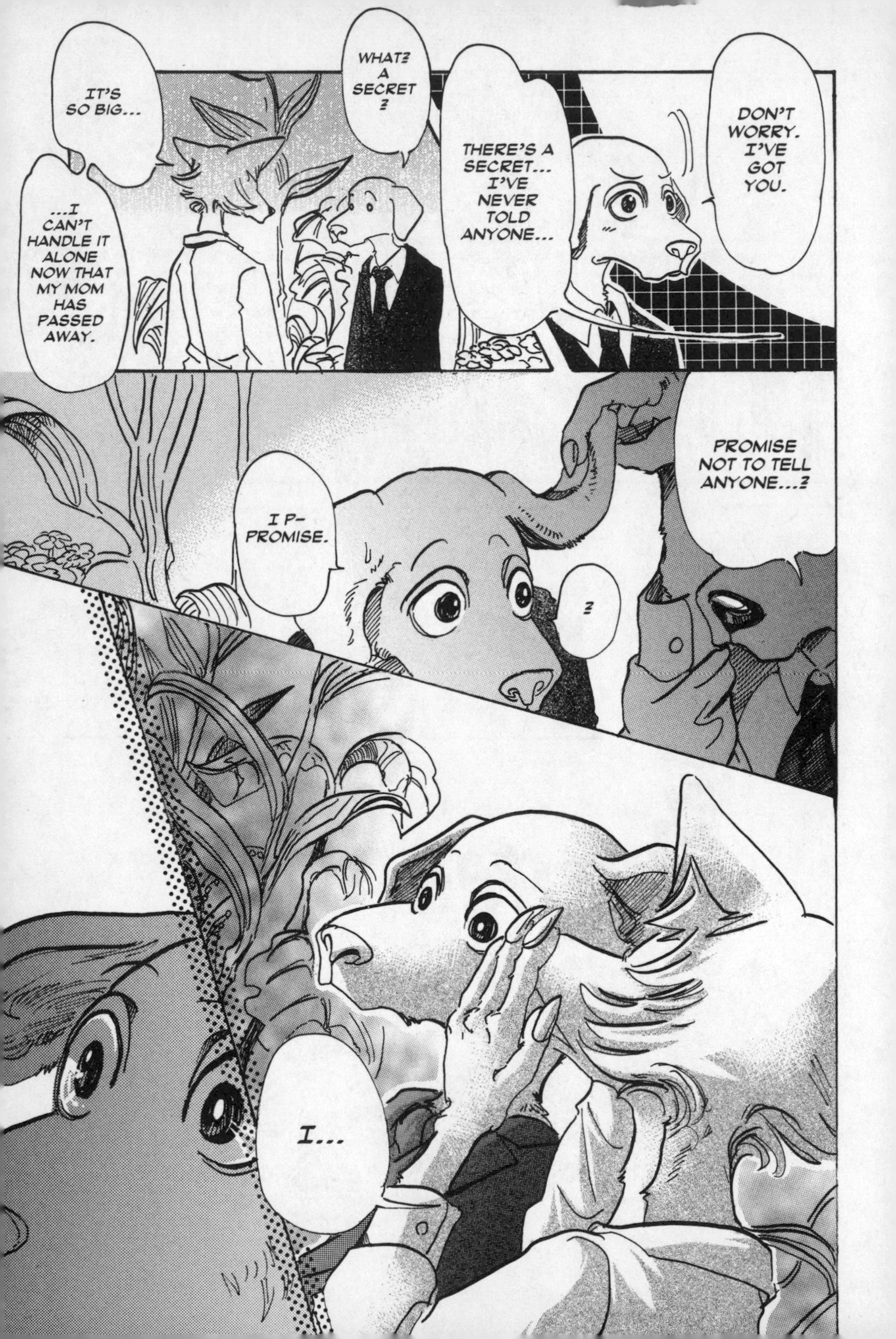
DON'T WORRY. I'VE GOT YOU.
THERE'S A SECRET... I'VE NEVER TOLD ANYONE...
WHAT? A SECRET?
IT'S SO BIG...
...I CAN'T HANDLE IT ALONE NOW THAT MY MOM HAS PASSED AWAY.
PROMISE NOT TO TELL ANYONE...?
?
I P-PROMISE.
I...

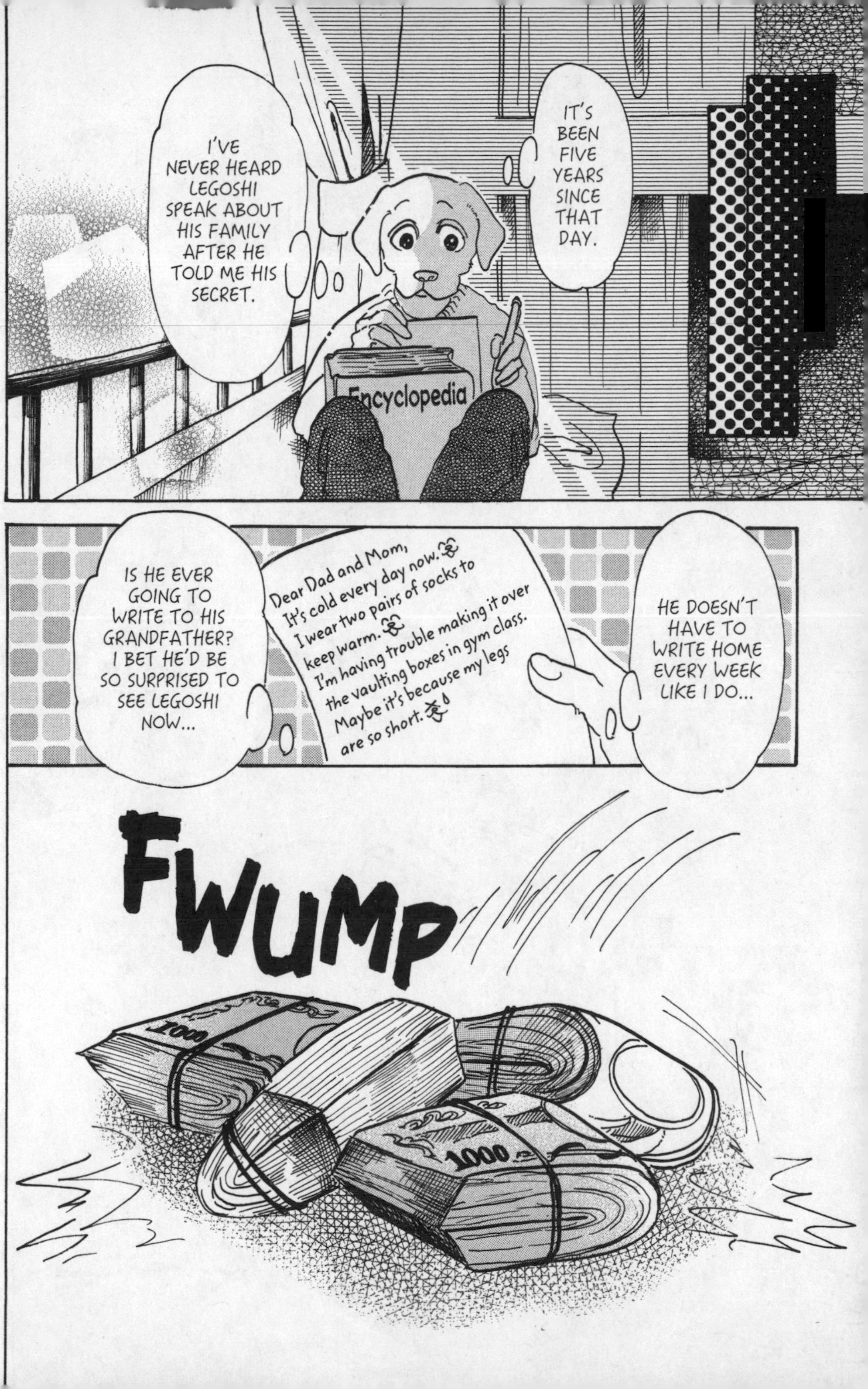
IT'S BEEN FIVE YEARS SINCE THAT DAY.
I'VE NEVER HEARD LEGOSHI SPEAK ABOUT HIS FAMILY AFTER HE TOLD ME HIS SECRET.
Encyclopedia
HE DOESN'T HAVE TO WRITE HOME EVERY WEEK LIKE I DO...
Dear Dad and Mom,
It's cold every day now.
I wear two pairs of socks to keep warm.
I'm having trouble making it over the vaulting boxes in gym class.
Maybe it's because my legs are so short.
IS HE EVER GOING TO WRITE TO HIS GRANDFATHER? I BET HE'D BE SO SURPRISED TO SEE LEGOSHI NOW...
FWUMP
1000
1000

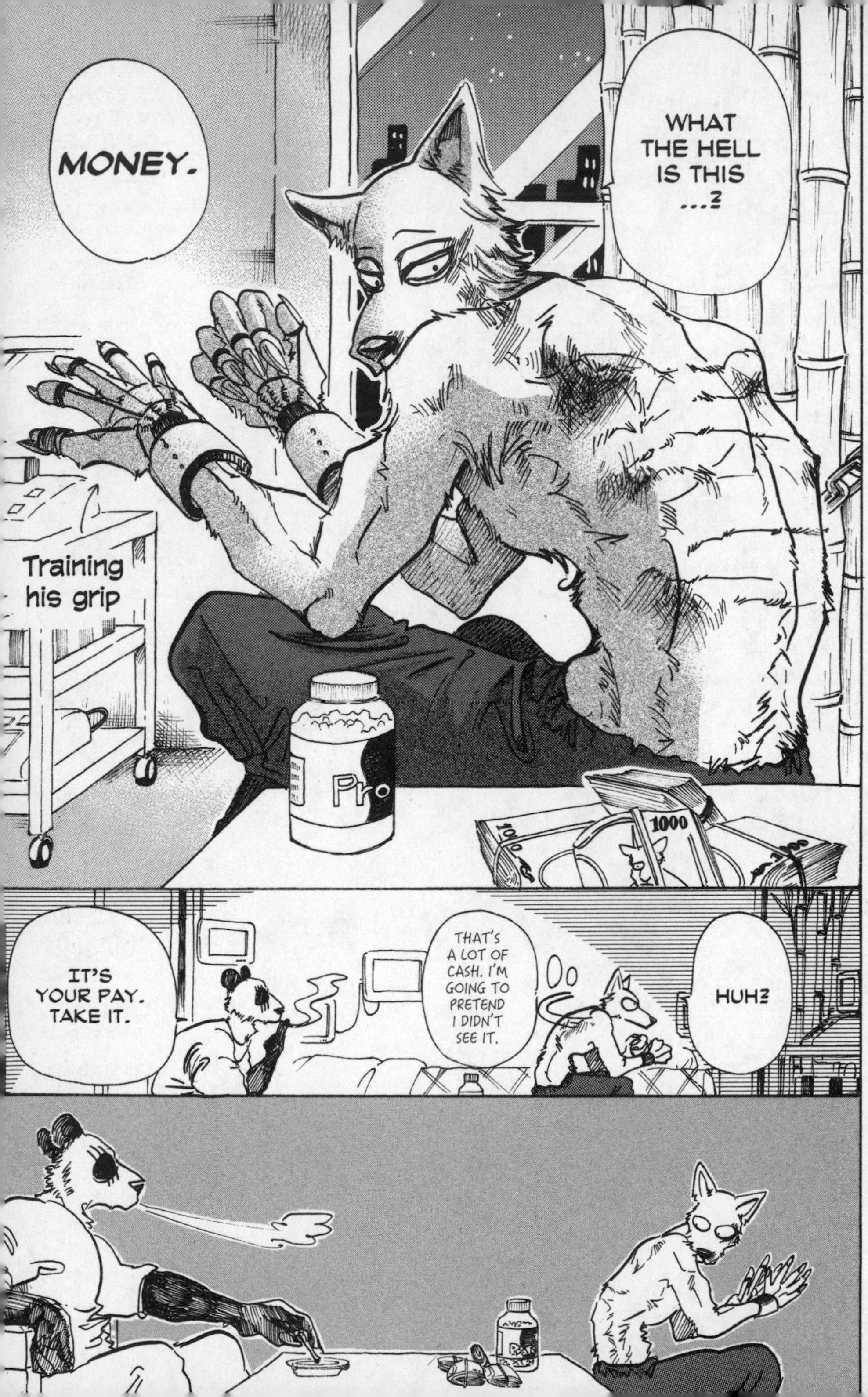
WHAT THE HELL IS THIS ...?
MONEY.
Training his grip
Pro
1000
HUH?
THAT'S A LOT OF CASH. I'M GOING TO PRETEND I DIDN'T SEE IT.
IT'S YOUR PAY. TAKE IT.

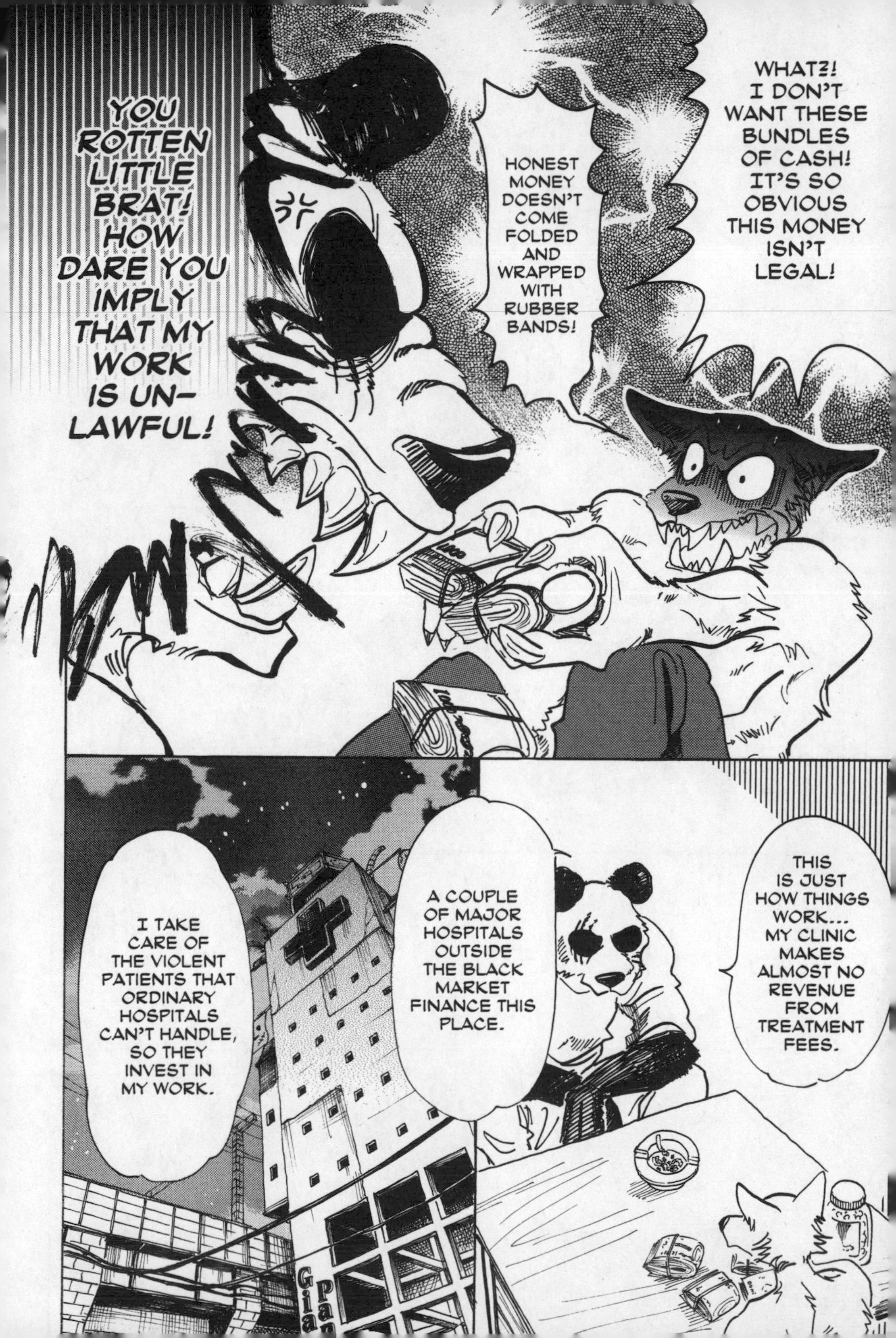
WHAT?! I DON'T WANT THESE BUNDLES OF CASH! IT'S SO OBVIOUS THIS MONEY ISN'T LEGAL!
HONEST MONEY DOESN'T COME FOLDED AND WRAPPED WITH RUBBER BANDS!
YOU ROTTEN LITTLE BRAT! HOW DARE YOU IMPLY THAT MY WORK IS UN-LAWFUL!
THIS IS JUST HOW THINGS WORK... MY CLINIC MAKES ALMOST NO REVENUE FROM TREATMENT FEES.
A COUPLE OF MAJOR HOSPITALS OUTSIDE THE BLACK MARKET FINANCE THIS PLACE.
I TAKE CARE OF THE VIOLENT PATIENTS THAT ORDINARY HOSPITALS CAN'T HANDLE, SO THEY INVEST IN MY WORK.

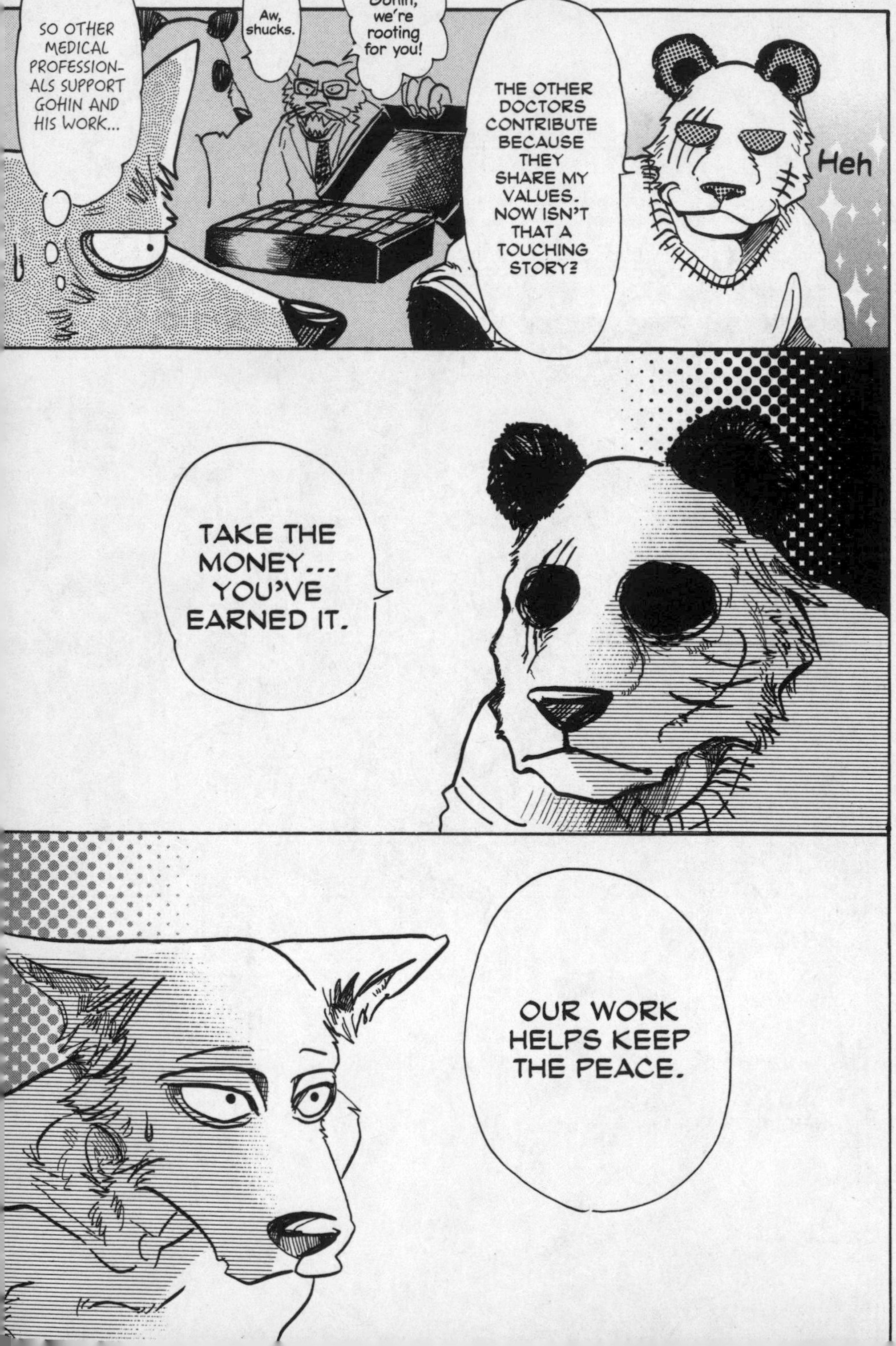
Heh
THE OTHER DOCTORS CONTRIBUTE BECAUSE THEY SHARE MY VALUES. NOW ISN'T THAT A TOUCHING STORY?
Dr. Gohin, we're rooting for you!
Aw, shucks.
SO OTHER MEDICAL PROFESSION-ALS SUPPORT GOHIN AND HIS WORK...
TAKE THE MONEY... YOU'VE EARNED IT.
OUR WORK HELPS KEEP THE PEACE.

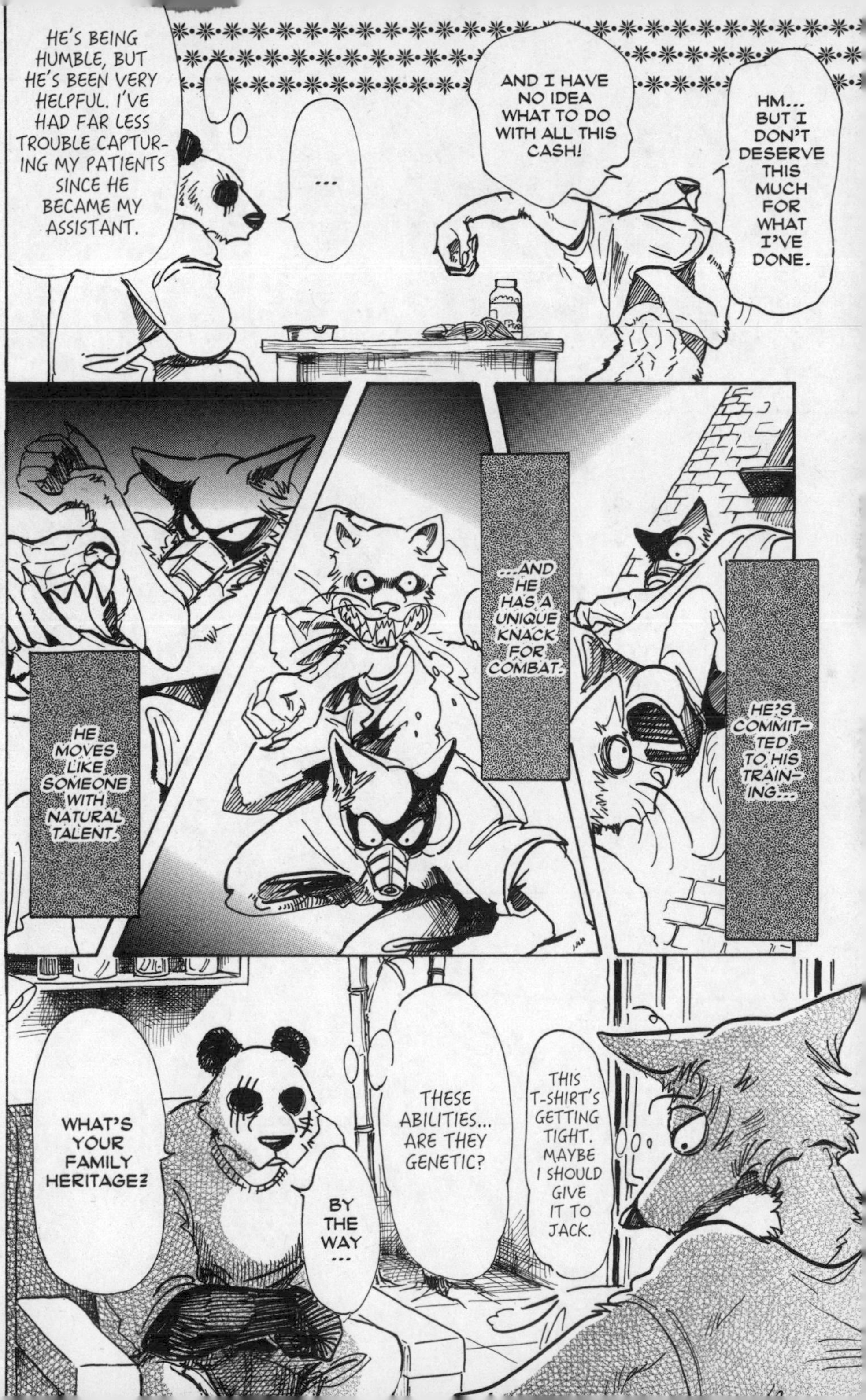
HM... BUT I DON'T DESERVE THIS MUCH FOR WHAT I'VE DONE.
AND I HAVE NO IDEA WHAT TO DO WITH ALL THIS CASH!
...
HE'S BEING HUMBLE, BUT HE'S BEEN VERY HELPFUL. I'VE HAD FAR LESS TROUBLE CAPTURING MY PATIENTS SINCE HE BECAME MY ASSISTANT.
HE'S COMMITTED TO HIS TRAINING...
...AND HE HAS A UNIQUE KNACK FOR COMBAT.
HE MOVES LIKE SOMEONE WITH NATURAL TALENT.
THIS T-SHIRT'S GETTING TIGHT. MAYBE I SHOULD GIVE IT TO JACK.
THESE ABILITIES... ARE THEY GENETIC?
BY THE WAY...
WHAT'S YOUR FAMILY HERITAGE?

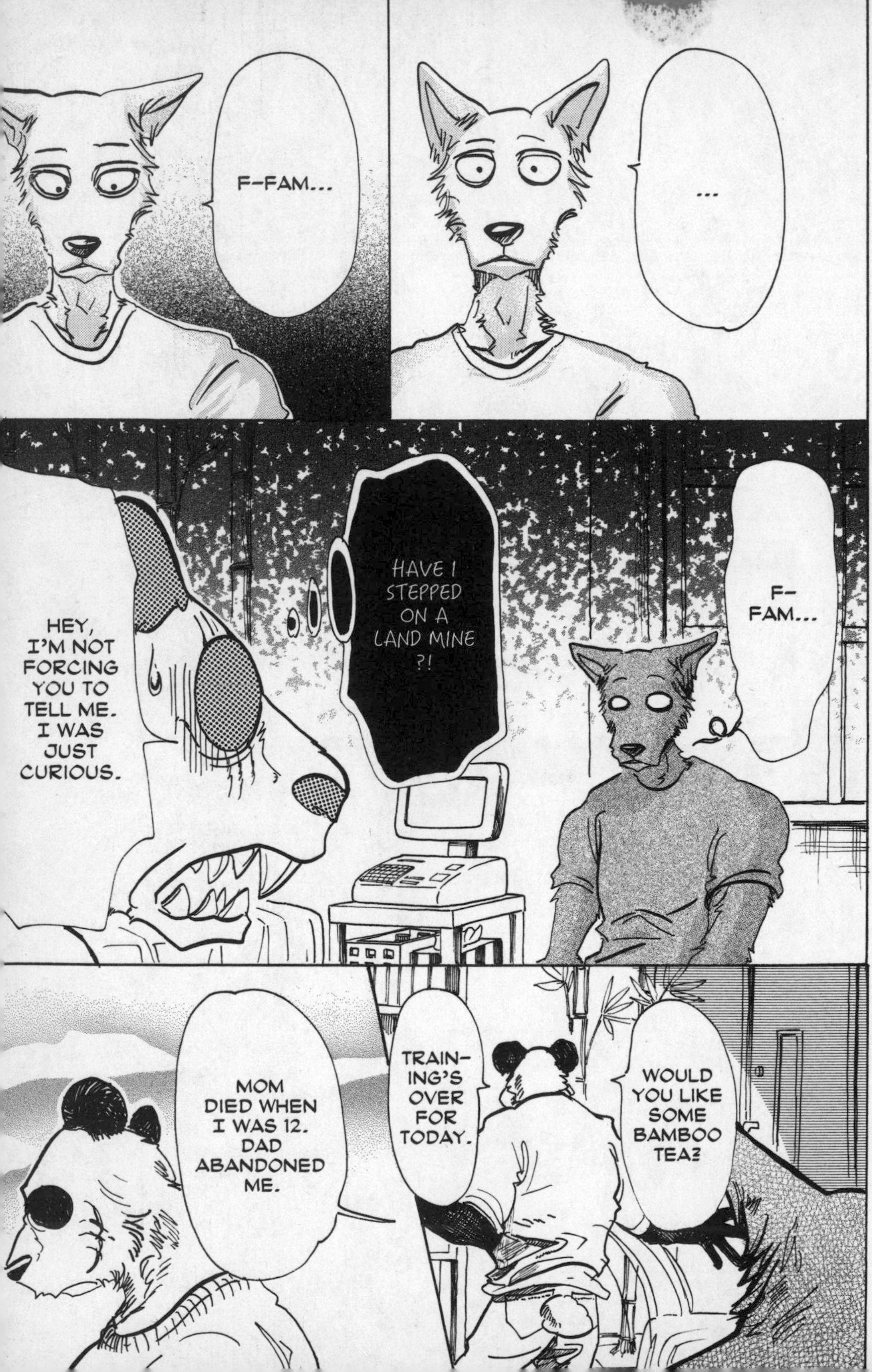
...
F-FAM...
F- FAM...
HAVE I STEPPED ON A LAND MINE ?!
HEY, I'M NOT FORCING YOU TO TELL ME. I WAS JUST CURIOUS.
WOULD YOU LIKE SOME BAMBOO TEA?
TRAINING'S OVER FOR TODAY.
MOM DIED WHEN I WAS 12. DAD ABANDONED ME.

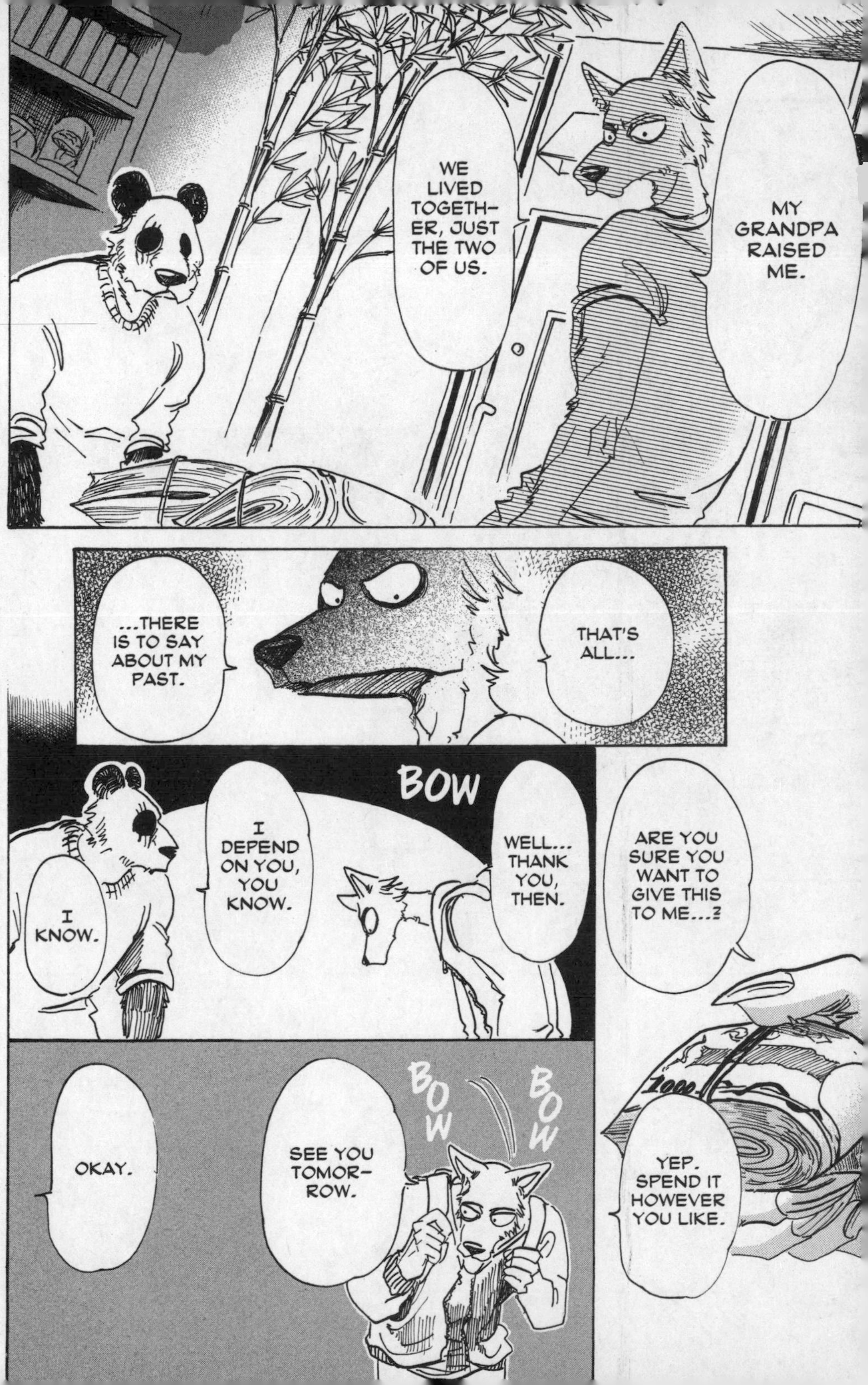
MY GRANDPA RAISED ME.
WE LIVED TOGETH-ER, JUST THE TWO OF US.
THAT'S ALL...
...THERE IS TO SAY ABOUT MY PAST.
ARE YOU SURE YOU WANT TO GIVE THIS TO ME...?
YEP. SPEND IT HOWEVER YOU LIKE.
2000
BOW
WELL... THANK YOU, THEN.
I DEPEND ON YOU, YOU KNOW.
I KNOW.
BOW BOW
SEE YOU TOMOR-ROW.
OKAY.

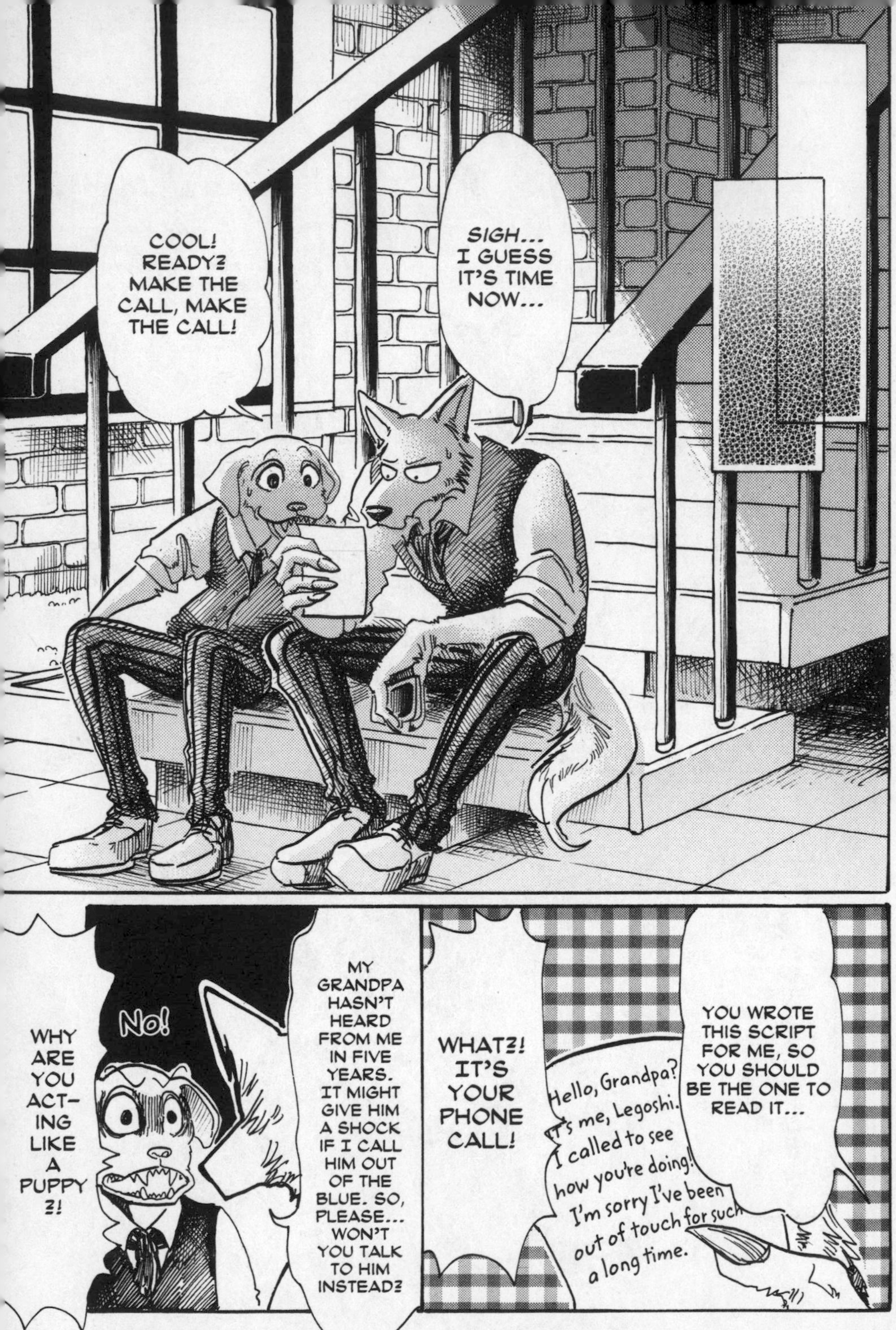
SIGH... I GUESS IT'S TIME NOW...
COOL! READY? MAKE THE CALL, MAKE THE CALL!
YOU WROTE THIS SCRIPT FOR ME, SO YOU SHOULD BE THE ONE TO READ IT...
Hello, Grandpa? It's me, Legoshi. I called to see how you're doing! I'm sorry I've been out of touch for such a long time.
WHAT?! IT'S YOUR PHONE CALL!
MY GRANDPA HASN'T HEARD FROM ME IN FIVE YEARS. IT MIGHT GIVE HIM A SHOCK IF I CALL HIM OUT OF THE BLUE. SO, PLEASE... WON'T YOU TALK TO HIM INSTEAD?
No!
WHY ARE YOU ACT-ING LIKE A PUPPY?!

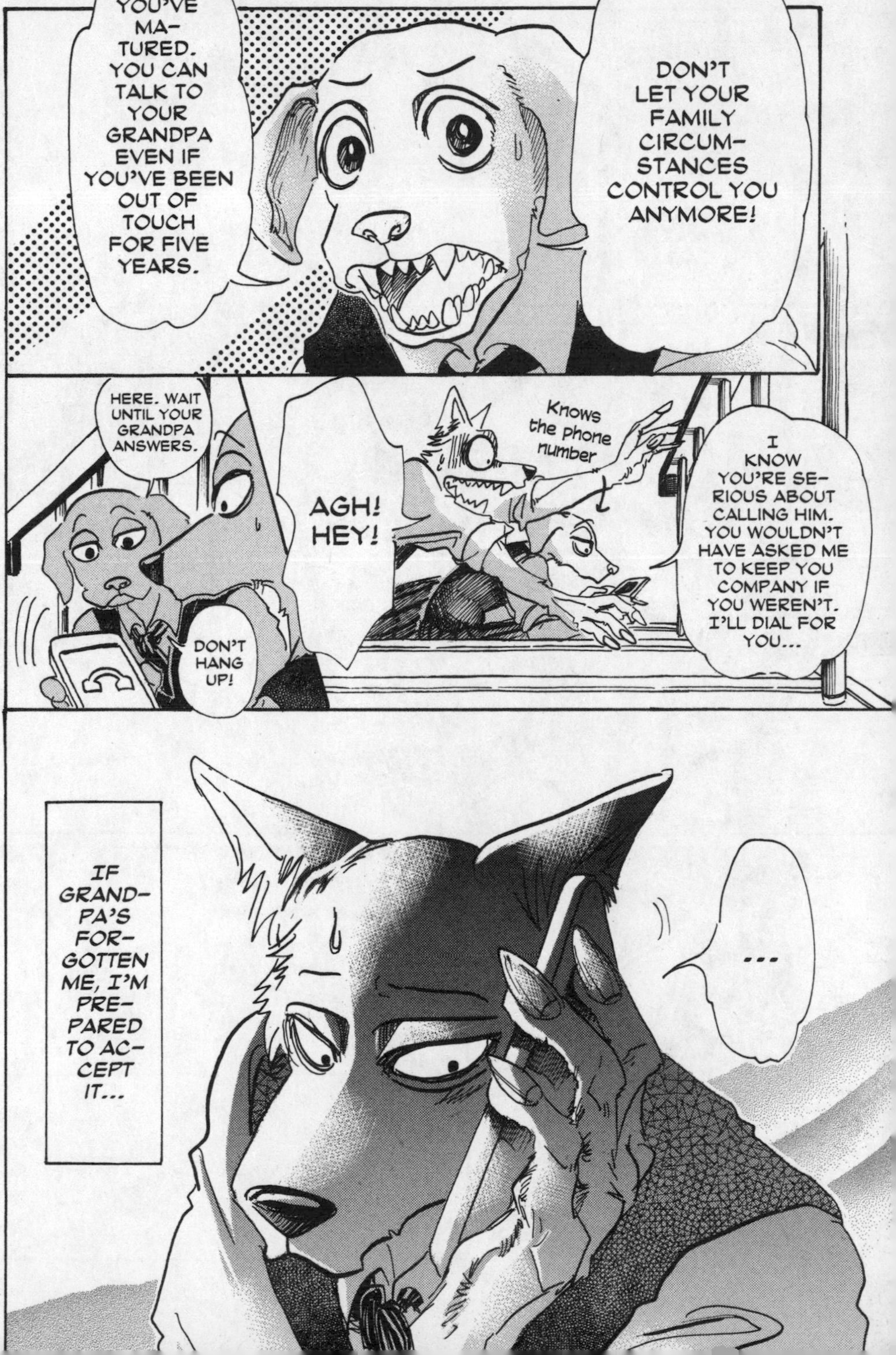
DON'T LET YOUR FAMILY CIRCUMSTANCES CONTROL YOU ANYMORE!
YOU'VE MATURED. YOU CAN TALK TO YOUR GRANDPA EVEN IF YOU'VE BEEN OUT OF TOUCH FOR FIVE YEARS.
I KNOW YOU'RE SERIOUS ABOUT CALLING HIM. YOU WOULDN'T HAVE ASKED ME TO KEEP YOU COMPANY IF YOU WEREN'T. I'LL DIAL FOR YOU...
Knows the phone number
AGH! HEY!
HERE. WAIT UNTIL YOUR GRANDPA ANSWERS.
DON'T HANG UP!
...
IF GRANDPA'S FORGOTTEN ME, I'M PREPARED TO ACCEPT IT...

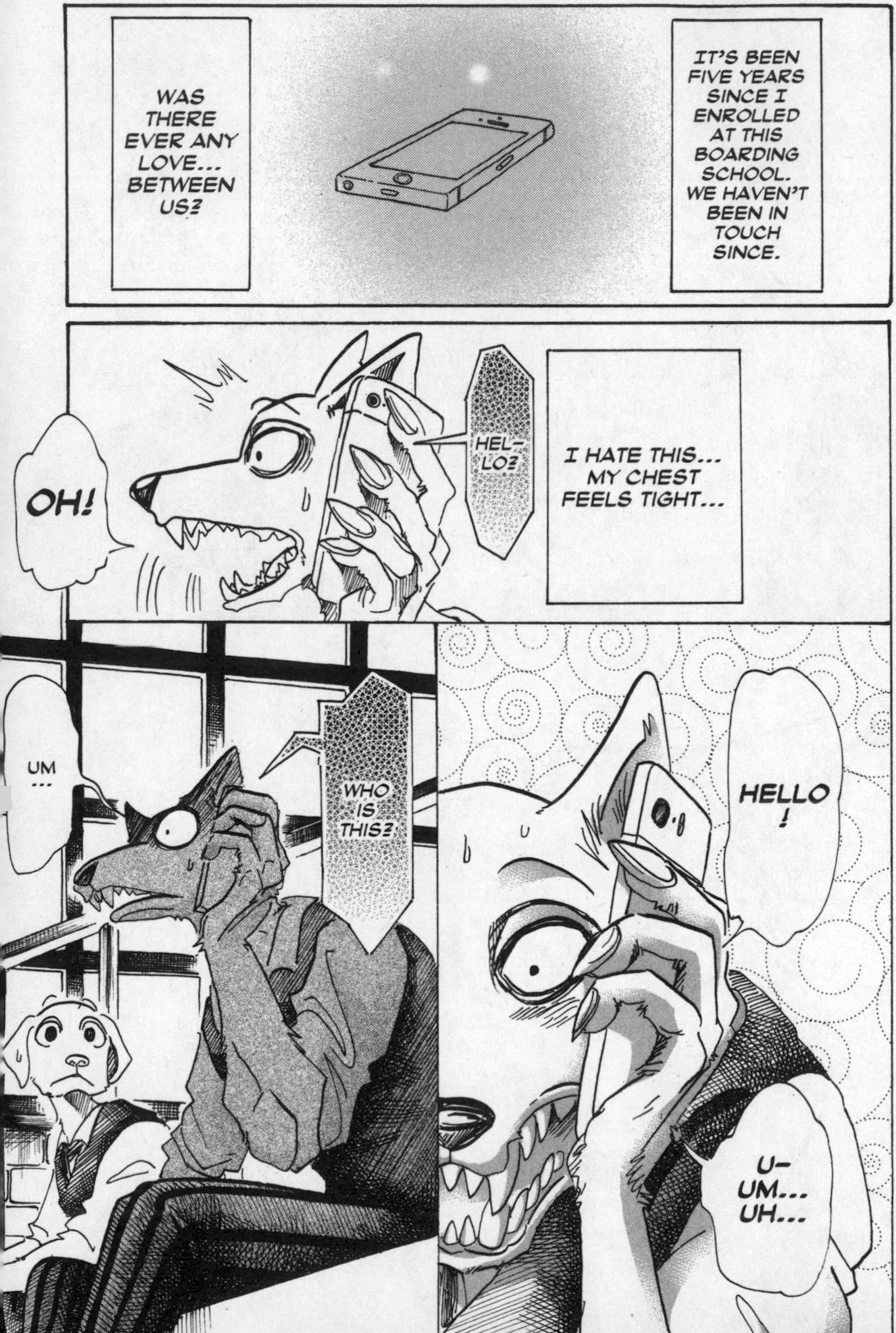
IT'S BEEN FIVE YEARS SINCE I ENROLLED AT THIS BOARDING SCHOOL. WE HAVEN'T BEEN IN TOUCH SINCE.
WAS THERE EVER ANY LOVE... BETWEEN US?
I HATE THIS... MY CHEST FEELS TIGHT...
HEL-LO?
OH!
HELLO!
U-UM... UH...
WHO IS THIS?
UM...

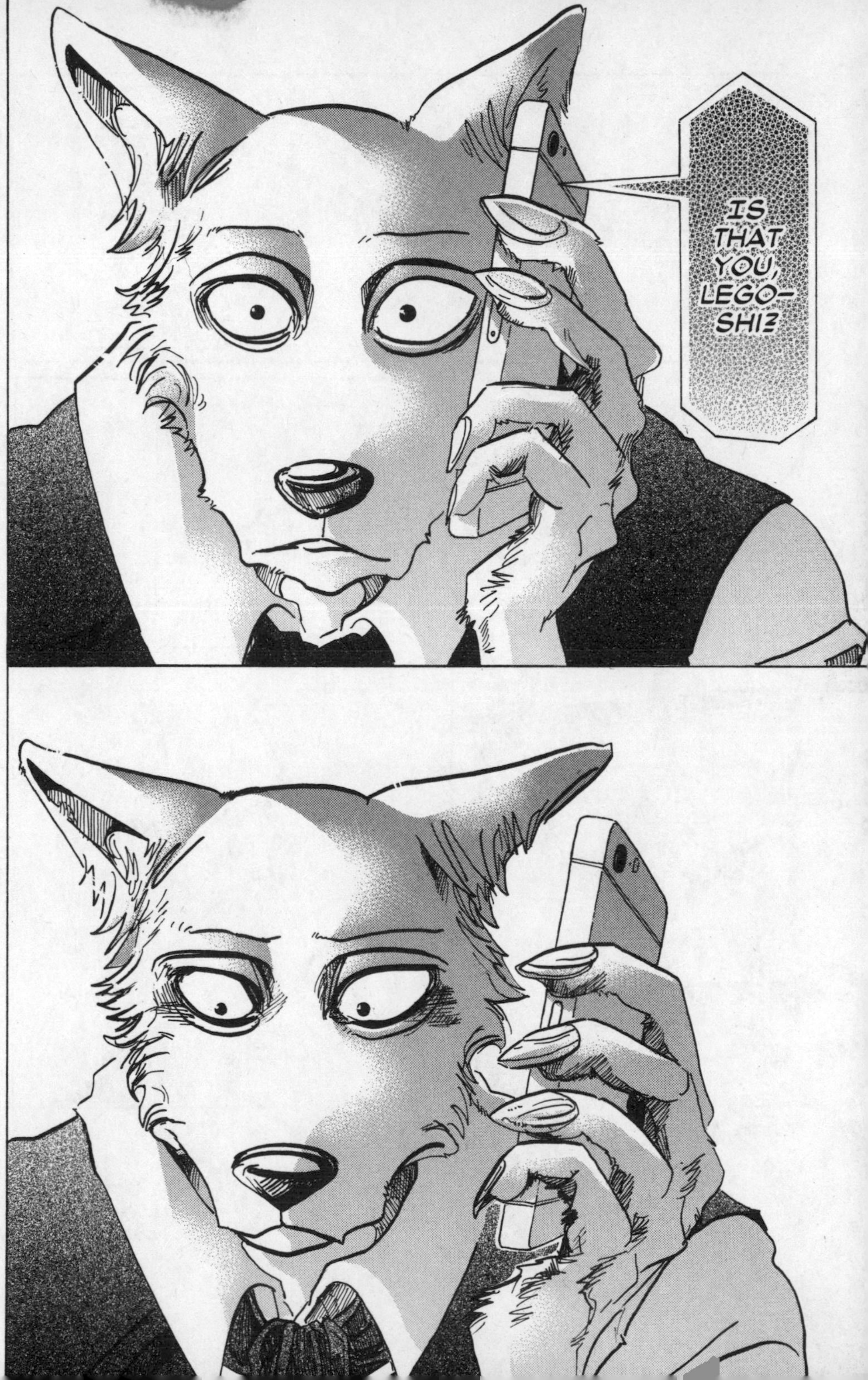
IS THAT YOU, LEGO-SHI?

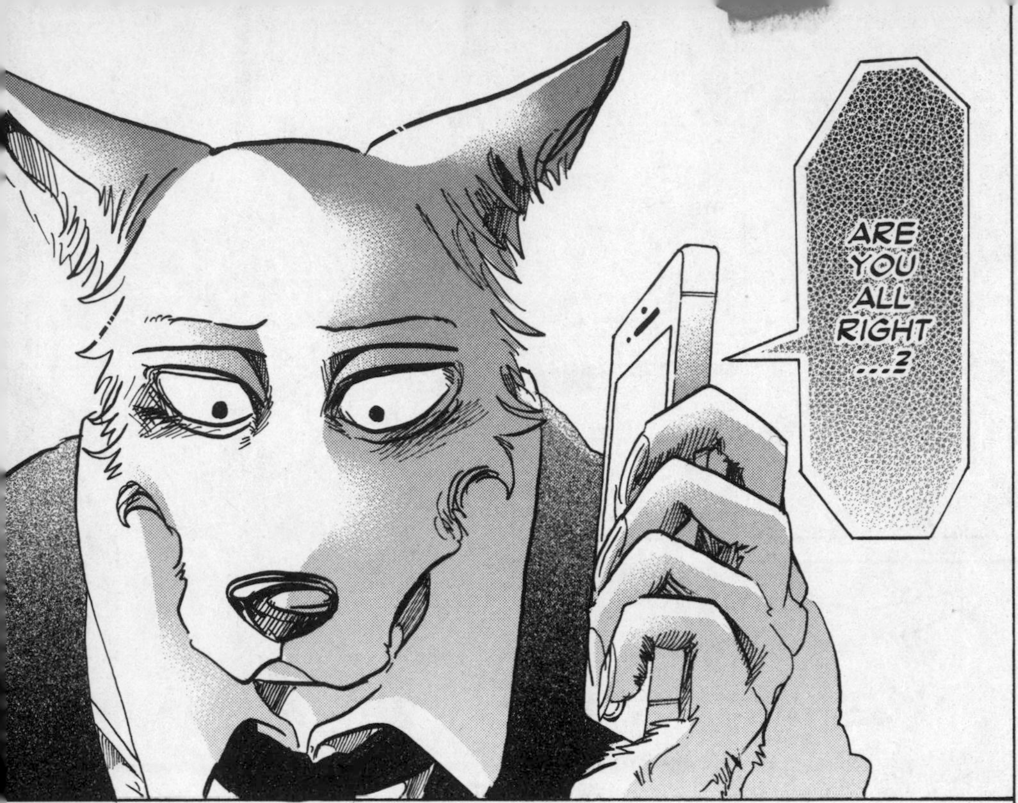
ARE YOU ALL RIGHT ...?
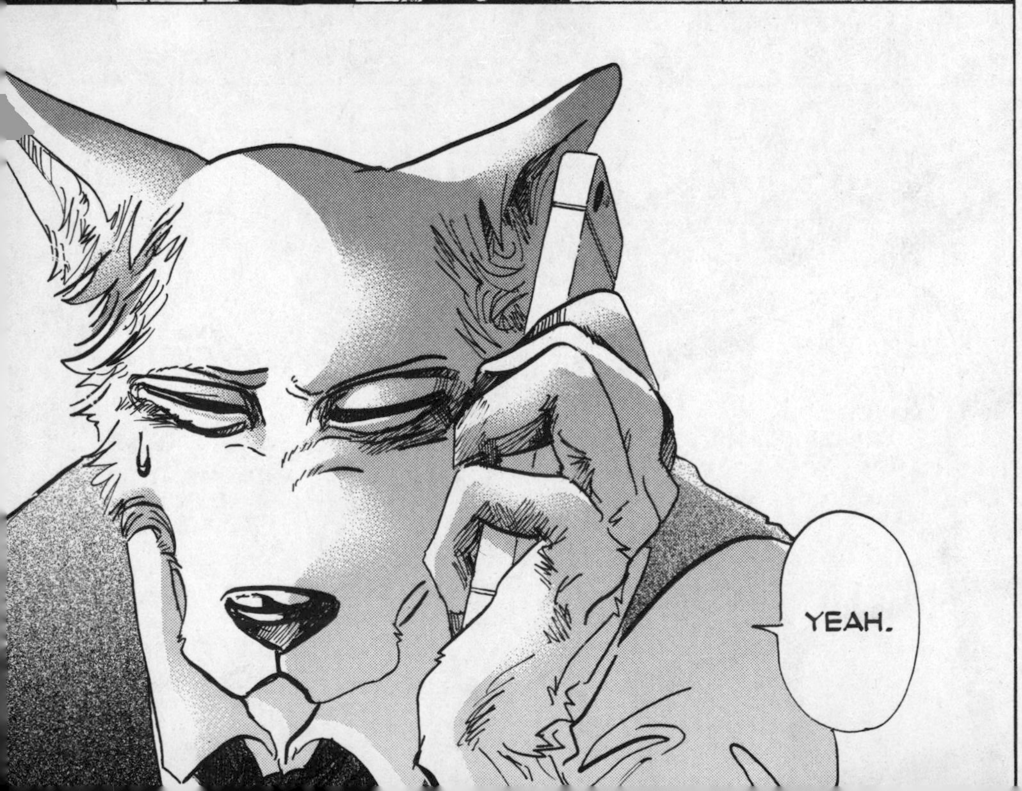
YEAH.

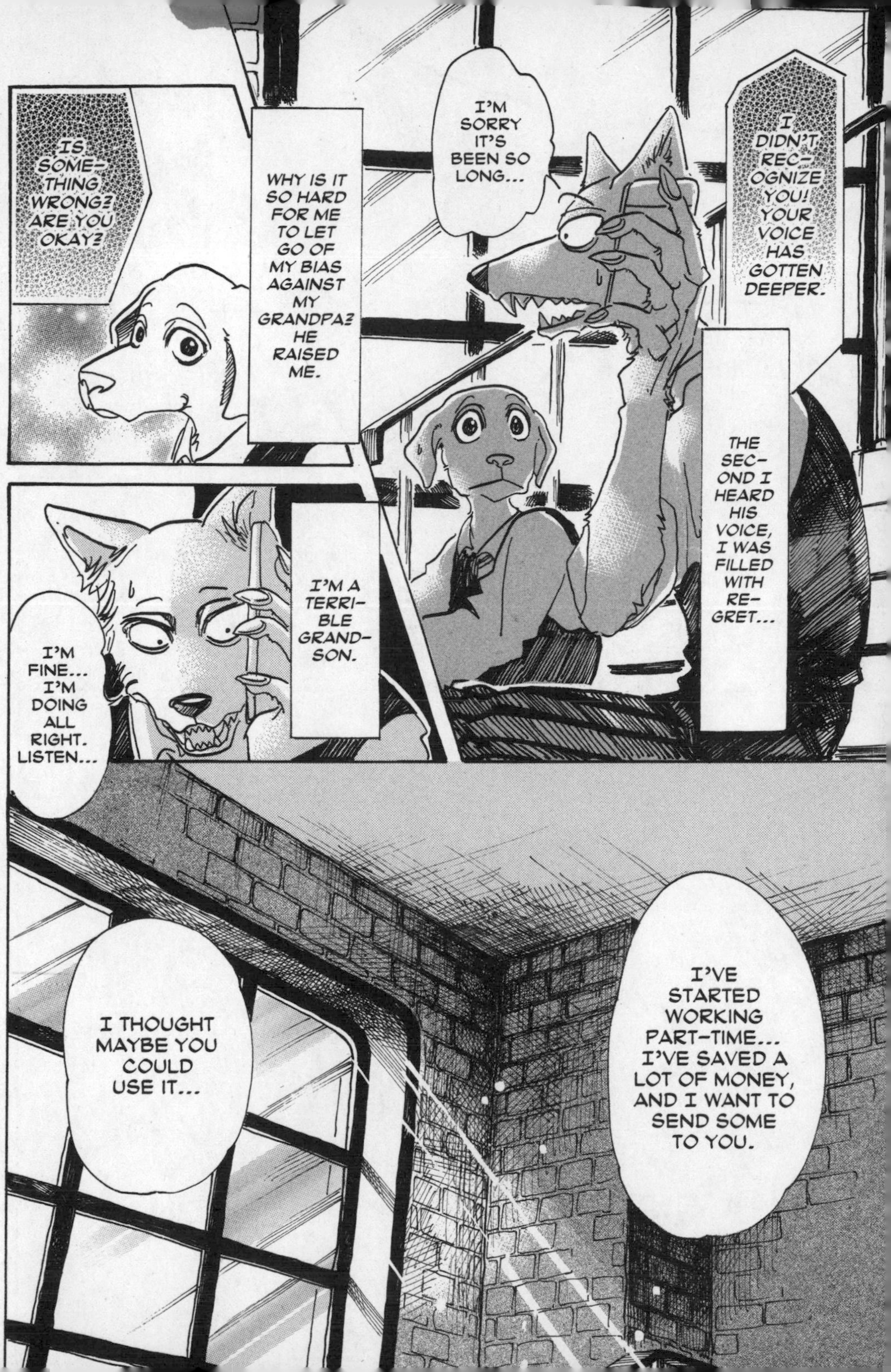
I DIDN'T RECOGNIZE YOU! YOUR VOICE HAS GOTTEN DEEPER.
I'M SORRY IT'S BEEN SO LONG...
THE SECOND I HEARD HIS VOICE, I WAS FILLED WITH REGRET...
WHY IS IT SO HARD FOR ME TO LET GO OF MY BIAS AGAINST MY GRANDPA? HE RAISED ME.
IS SOMETHING WRONG? ARE YOU OKAY?
I'M A TERRIBLE GRANDSON.
I'M FINE... I'M DOING ALL RIGHT. LISTEN...
I'VE STARTED WORKING PART-TIME... I'VE SAVED A LOT OF MONEY, AND I WANT TO SEND SOME TO YOU.
I THOUGHT MAYBE YOU COULD USE IT...

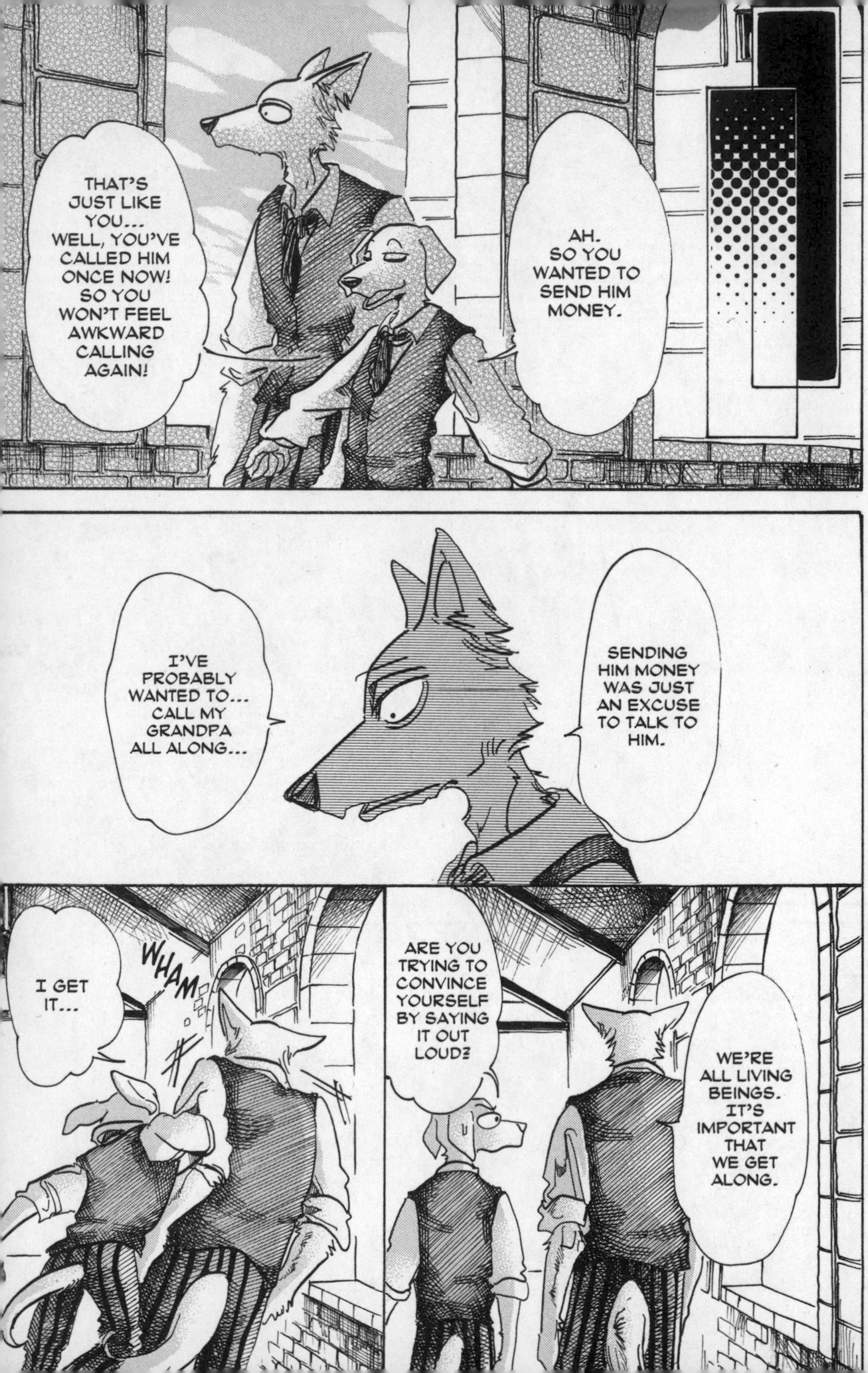
AH. SO YOU WANTED TO SEND HIM MONEY.
THAT'S JUST LIKE YOU... WELL, YOU'VE CALLED HIM ONCE NOW! SO YOU WON'T FEEL AWKWARD CALLING AGAIN!
SENDING HIM MONEY WAS JUST AN EXCUSE TO TALK TO HIM.
I'VE PROBABLY WANTED TO... CALL MY GRANDPA ALL ALONG...
WE'RE ALL LIVING BEINGS. IT'S IMPORTANT THAT WE GET ALONG.
ARE YOU TRYING TO CONVINCE YOURSELF BY SAYING IT OUT LOUD?
WHAM
I GET IT...

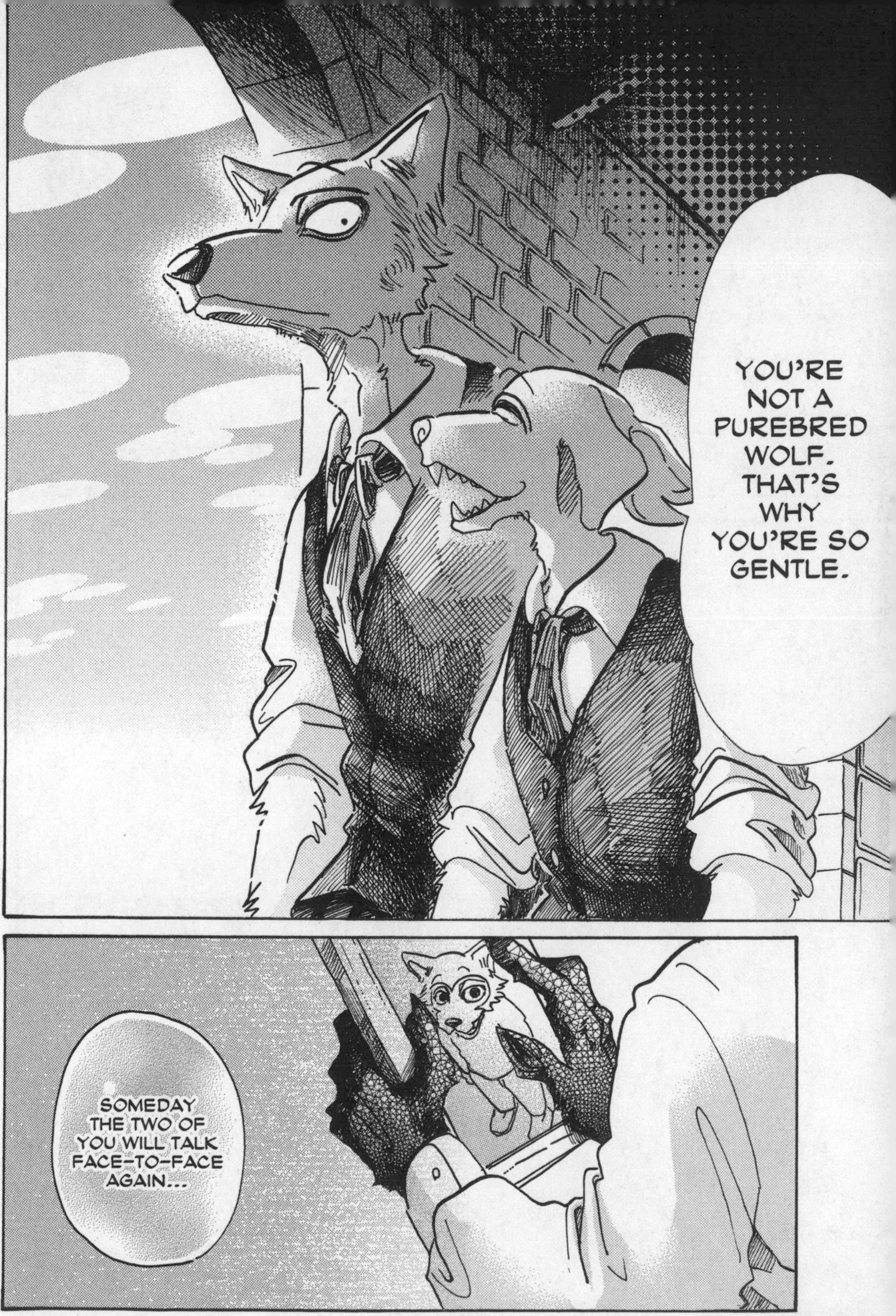
YOU'RE NOT A PUREBRED WOLF. THAT'S WHY YOU'RE SO GENTLE.
SOMEDAY THE TWO OF YOU WILL TALK FACE-TO-FACE AGAIN...

Chapter 74: You're a Solitary Knight

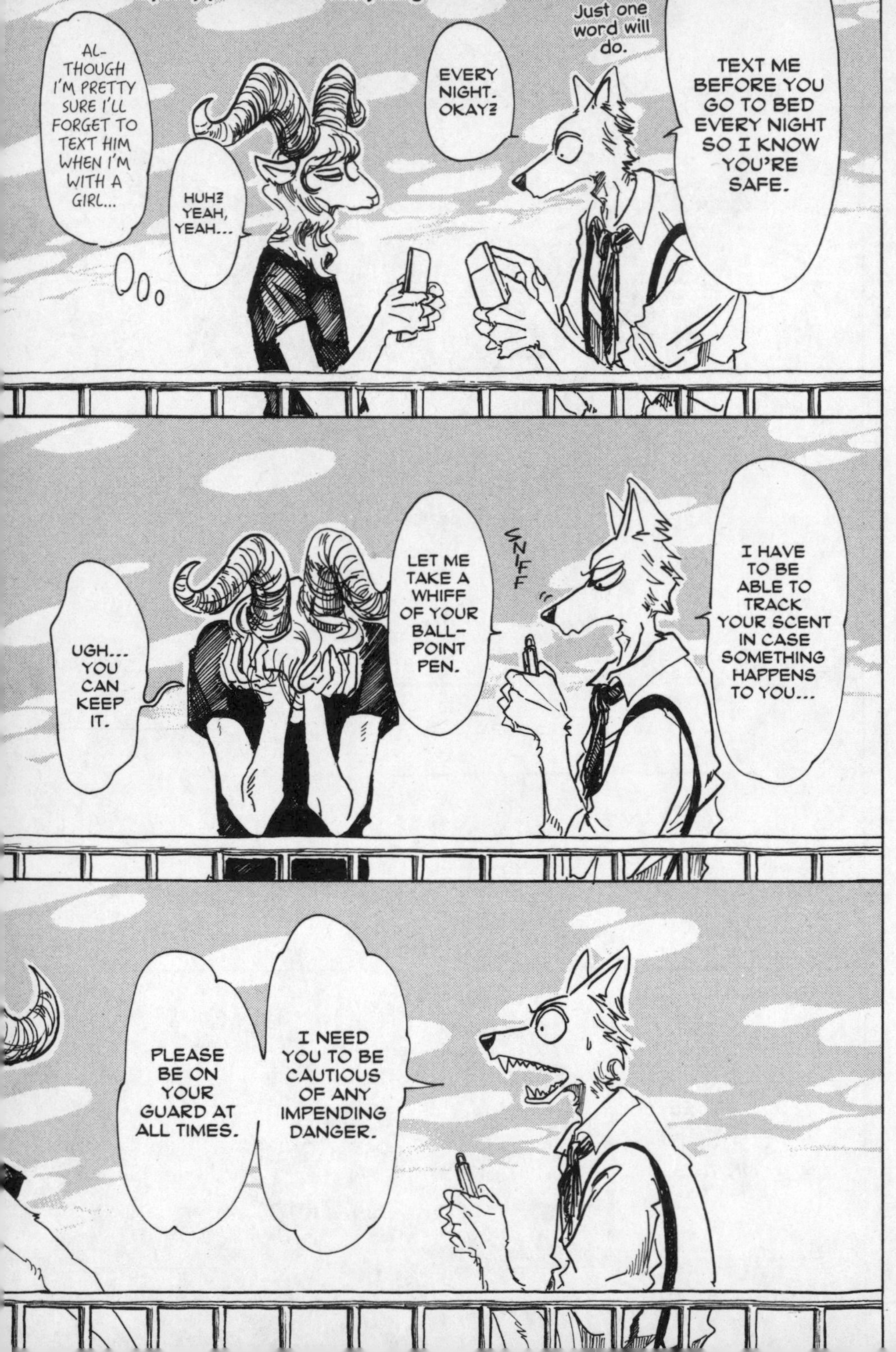
TEXT ME BEFORE YOU GO TO BED EVERY NIGHT SO I KNOW YOU'RE SAFE.
Just one word will do.
EVERY NIGHT. OKAY?
HUH? YEAH, YEAH...
ALTHOUGH I'M PRETTY SURE I'LL FORGET TO TEXT HIM WHEN I'M WITH A GIRL...
I HAVE TO BE ABLE TO TRACK YOUR SCENT IN CASE SOMETHING HAPPENS TO YOU...
SNIFF
LET ME TAKE A WHIFF OF YOUR BALL-POINT PEN.
UGH... YOU CAN KEEP IT.
I NEED YOU TO BE CAUTIOUS OF ANY IMPENDING DANGER.
PLEASE BE ON YOUR GUARD AT ALL TIMES.

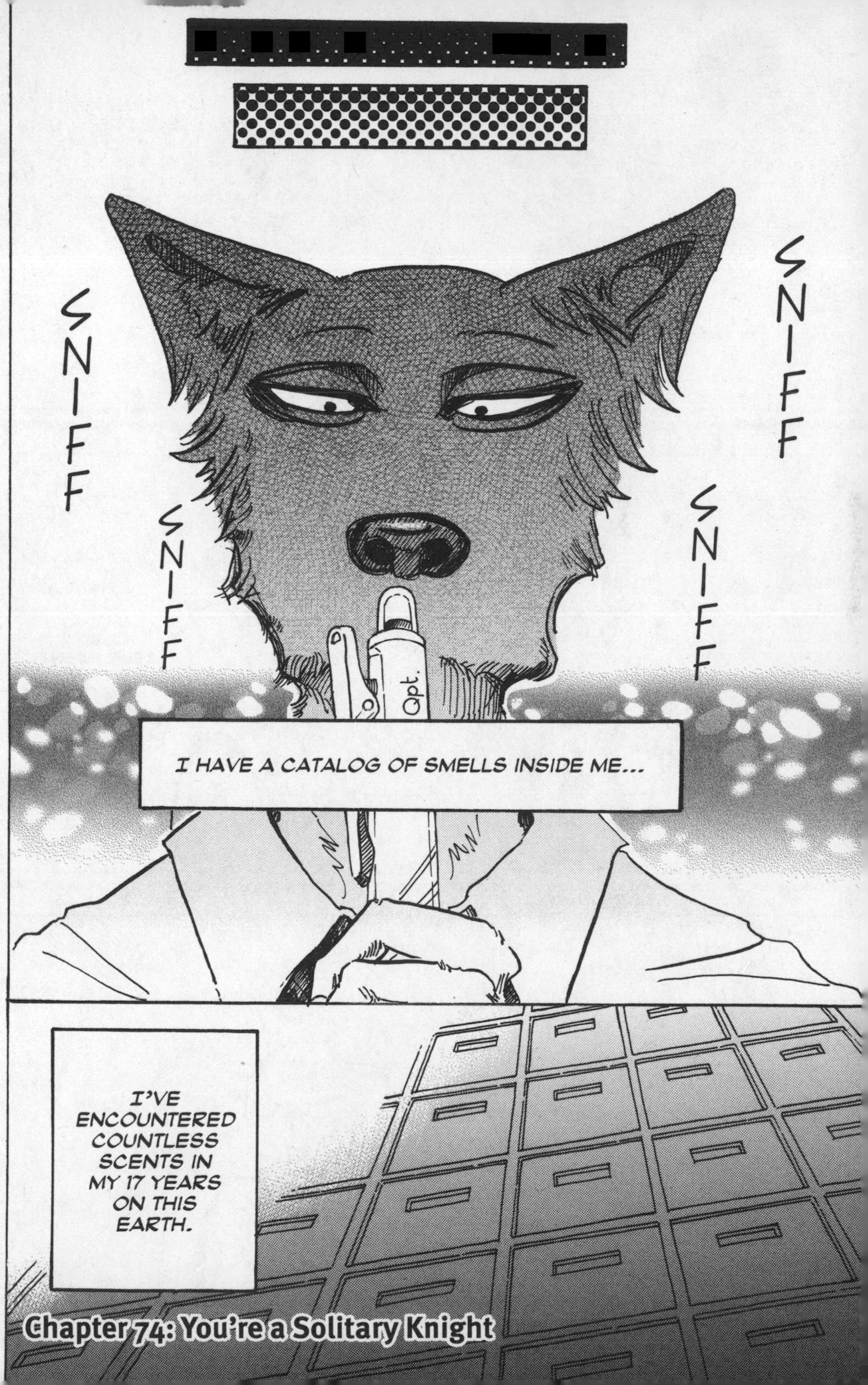
SNIFF
SNIFF
SNIFF
SNIFF
Opt.
I HAVE A CATALOG OF SMELLS INSIDE ME...
I'VE ENCOUNTERED COUNTLESS SCENTS IN MY 17 YEARS ON THIS EARTH.
Chapter 74: You're a Solitary Knight

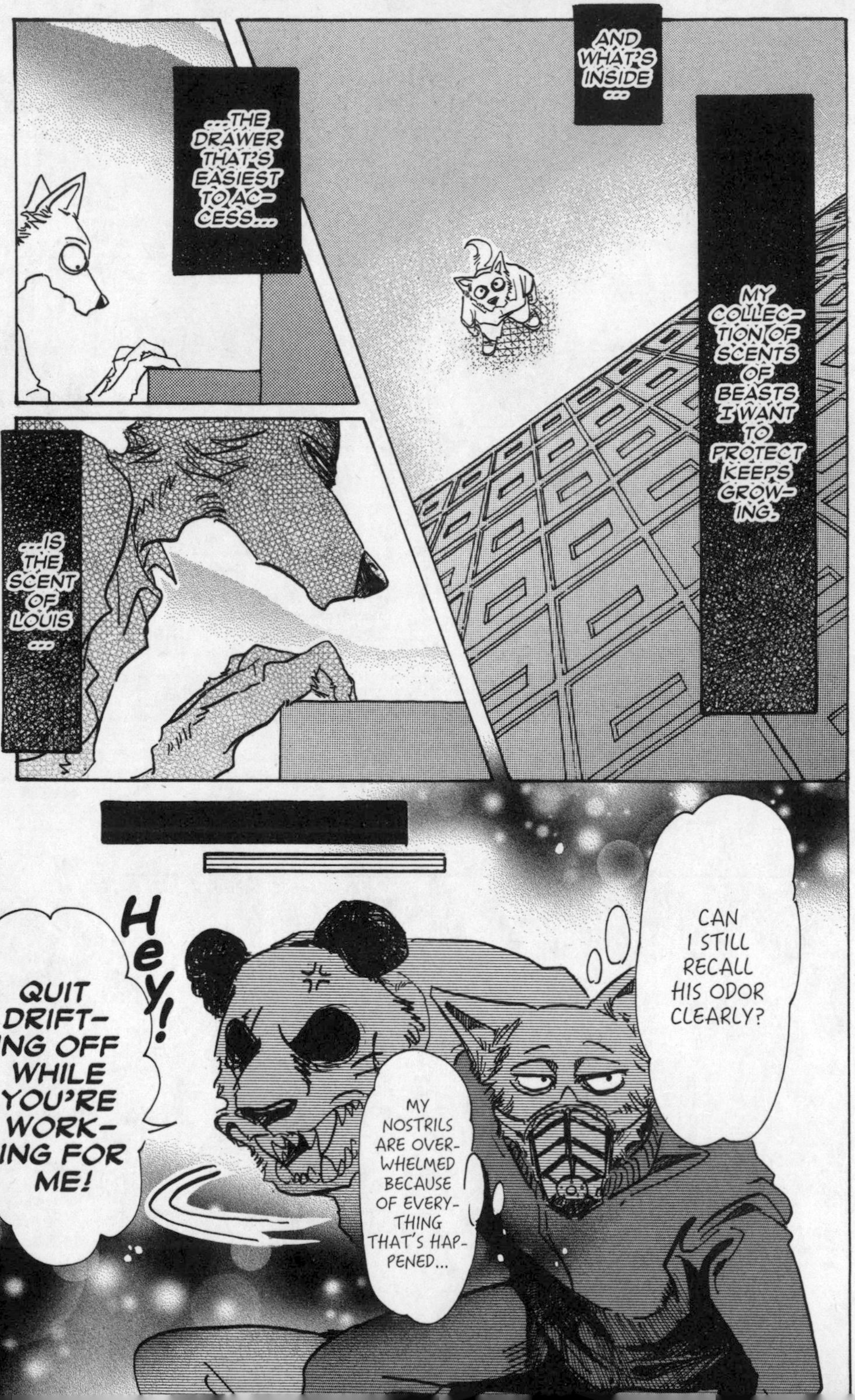
AND WHAT'S INSIDE ...
MY COLLECTION OF SCENTS OF BEASTS I WANT TO PROTECT KEEPS GROWING.
...THE DRAWER THAT'S EASIEST TO AC-CESS...
...IS THE SCENT OF LOUIS ...
CAN I STILL RECALL HIS ODOR CLEARLY?
MY NOSTRILS ARE OVER-WHELMED BECAUSE OF EVERY-THING THAT'S HAP-PENED...
Hey!
QUIT DRIFT-ING OFF WHILE YOU'RE WORK-ING FOR ME!

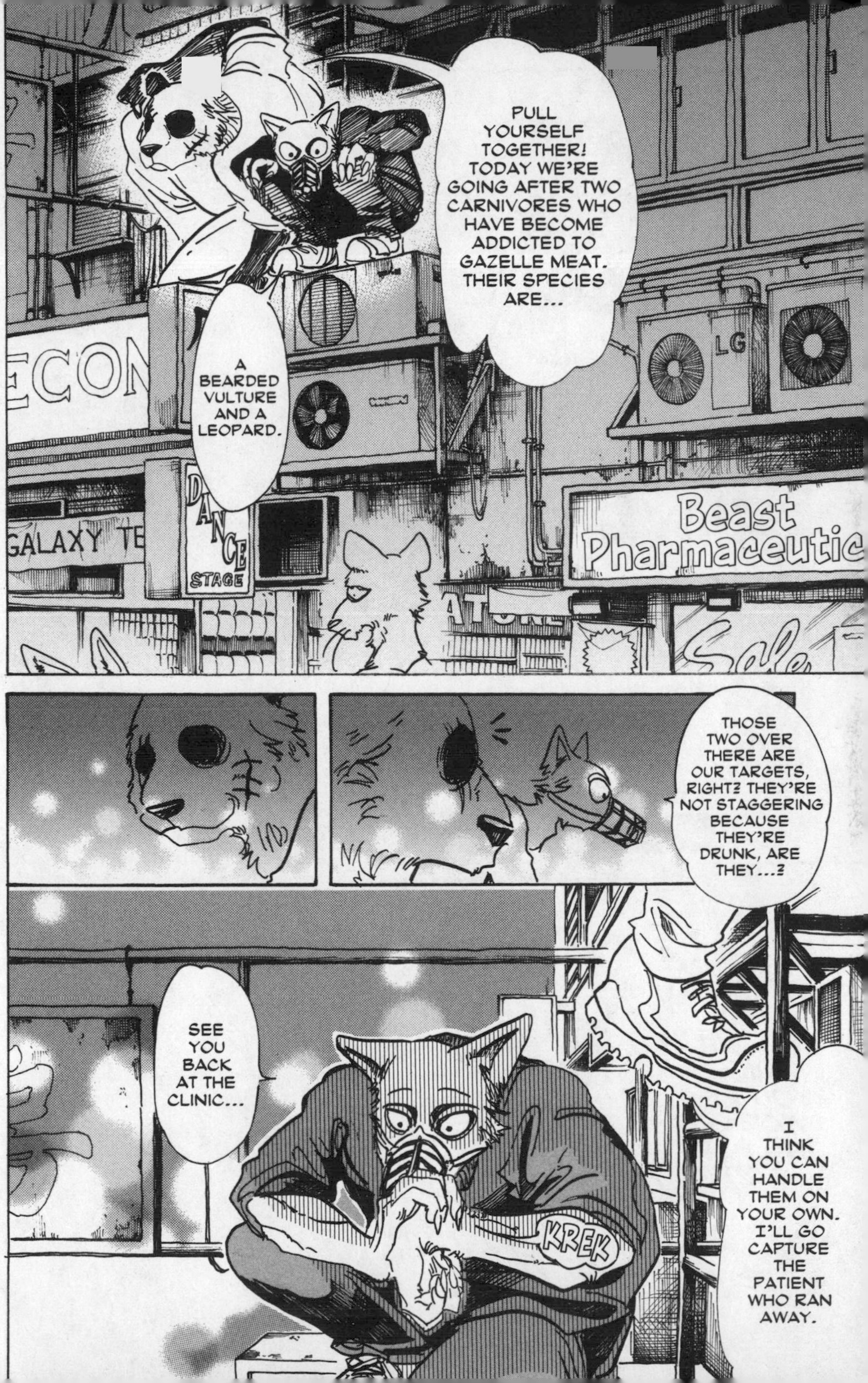
PULL YOURSELF TOGETHER! TODAY WE'RE GOING AFTER TWO CARNIVORES WHO HAVE BECOME ADDICTED TO GAZELLE MEAT. THEIR SPECIES ARE...
A BEARDED VULTURE AND A LEOPARD.
LG
DANCE STAGE
THOSE TWO OVER THERE ARE OUR TARGETS, RIGHT? THEY'RE NOT STAGGERING BECAUSE THEY'RE DRUNK, ARE THEY...?
I THINK YOU CAN HANDLE THEM ON YOUR OWN. I'LL GO CAPTURE THE PATIENT WHO RAN AWAY.
KREK
SEE YOU BACK AT THE CLINIC...

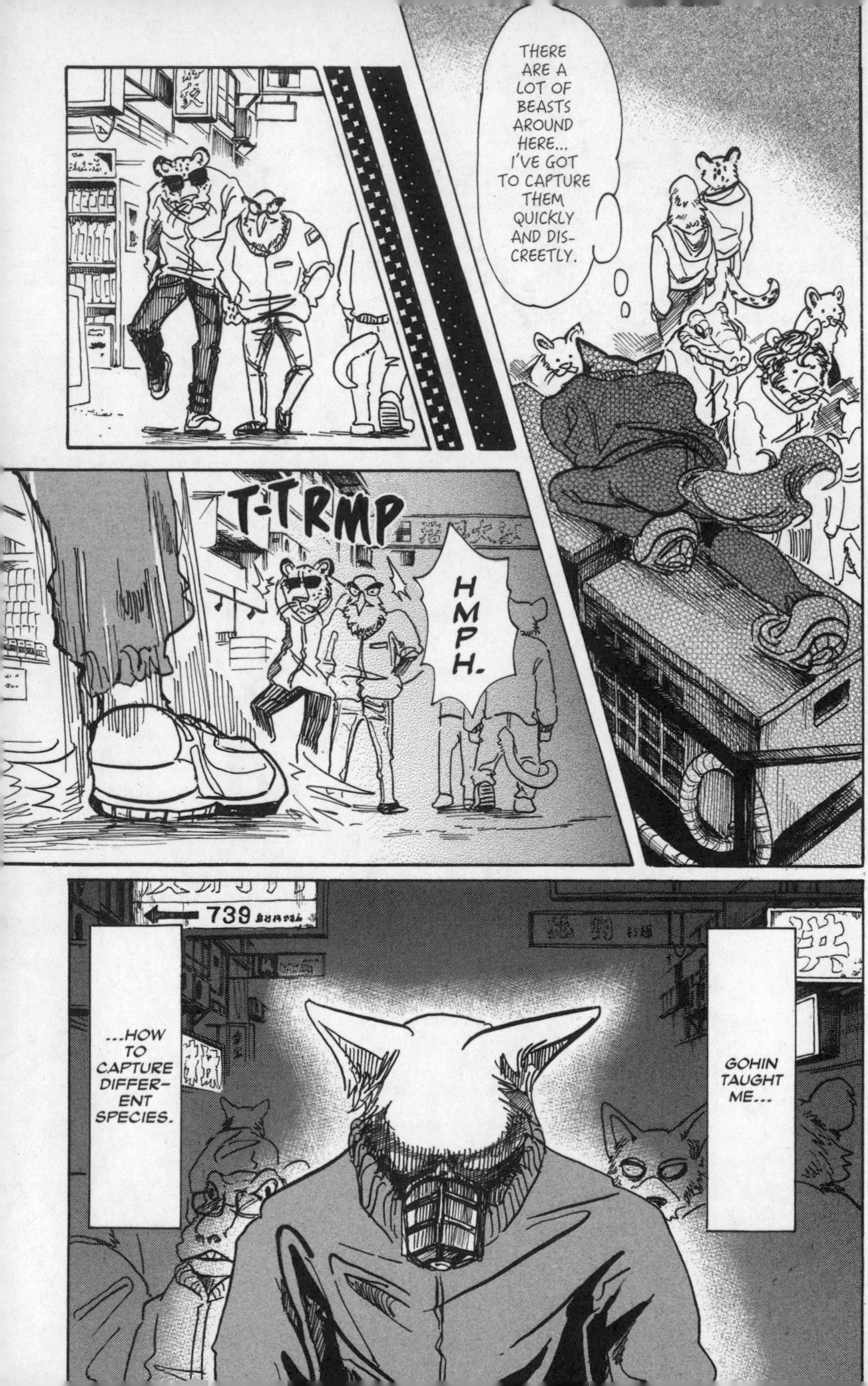
THERE ARE A LOT OF BEASTS AROUND HERE... I'VE GOT TO CAPTURE THEM QUICKLY AND DISCREETLY.
T-TRMP
HMPH.
739
GOHIN TAUGHT ME...
...HOW TO CAPTURE DIFFERENT SPECIES.

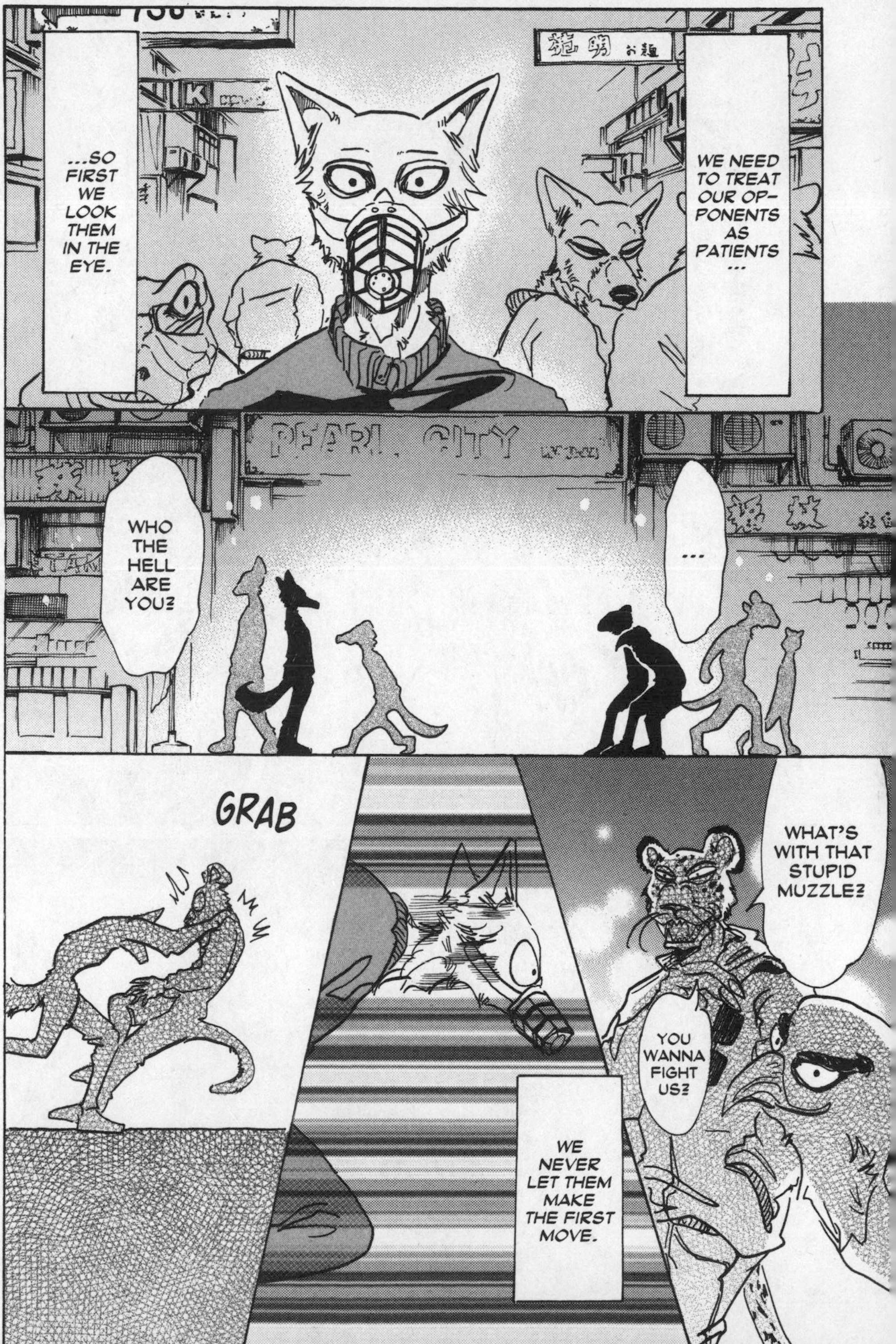
WE NEED TO TREAT OUR OP-PONENTS AS PATIENTS ...
...SO FIRST WE LOOK THEM IN THE EYE.
...
WHO THE HELL ARE YOU?
WHAT'S WITH THAT STUPID MUZZLE?
YOU WANNA FIGHT US?
WE NEVER LET THEM MAKE THE FIRST MOVE.
GRAB

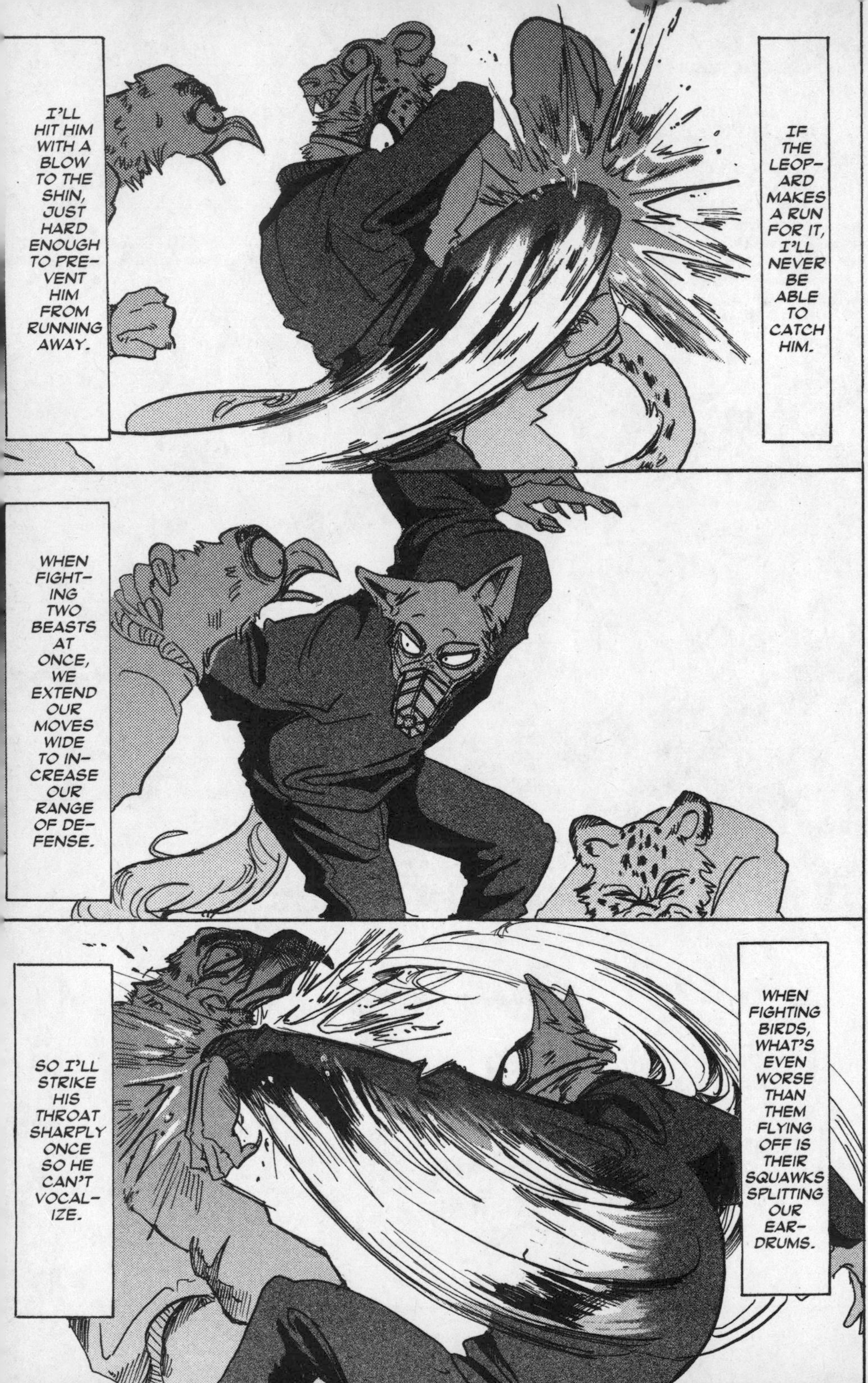
IF THE LEOPARD MAKES A RUN FOR IT, I'LL NEVER BE ABLE TO CATCH HIM.
I'LL HIT HIM WITH A BLOW TO THE SHIN, JUST HARD ENOUGH TO PREVENT HIM FROM RUNNING AWAY.
WHEN FIGHTING TWO BEASTS AT ONCE, WE EXTEND OUR MOVES WIDE TO INCREASE OUR RANGE OF DEFENSE.
WHEN FIGHTING BIRDS, WHAT'S EVEN WORSE THAN THEM FLYING OFF IS THEIR SQUAWKS SPLITTING OUR EARDRUMS.
SO I'LL STRIKE HIS THROAT SHARPLY ONCE SO HE CAN'T VOCALIZE.

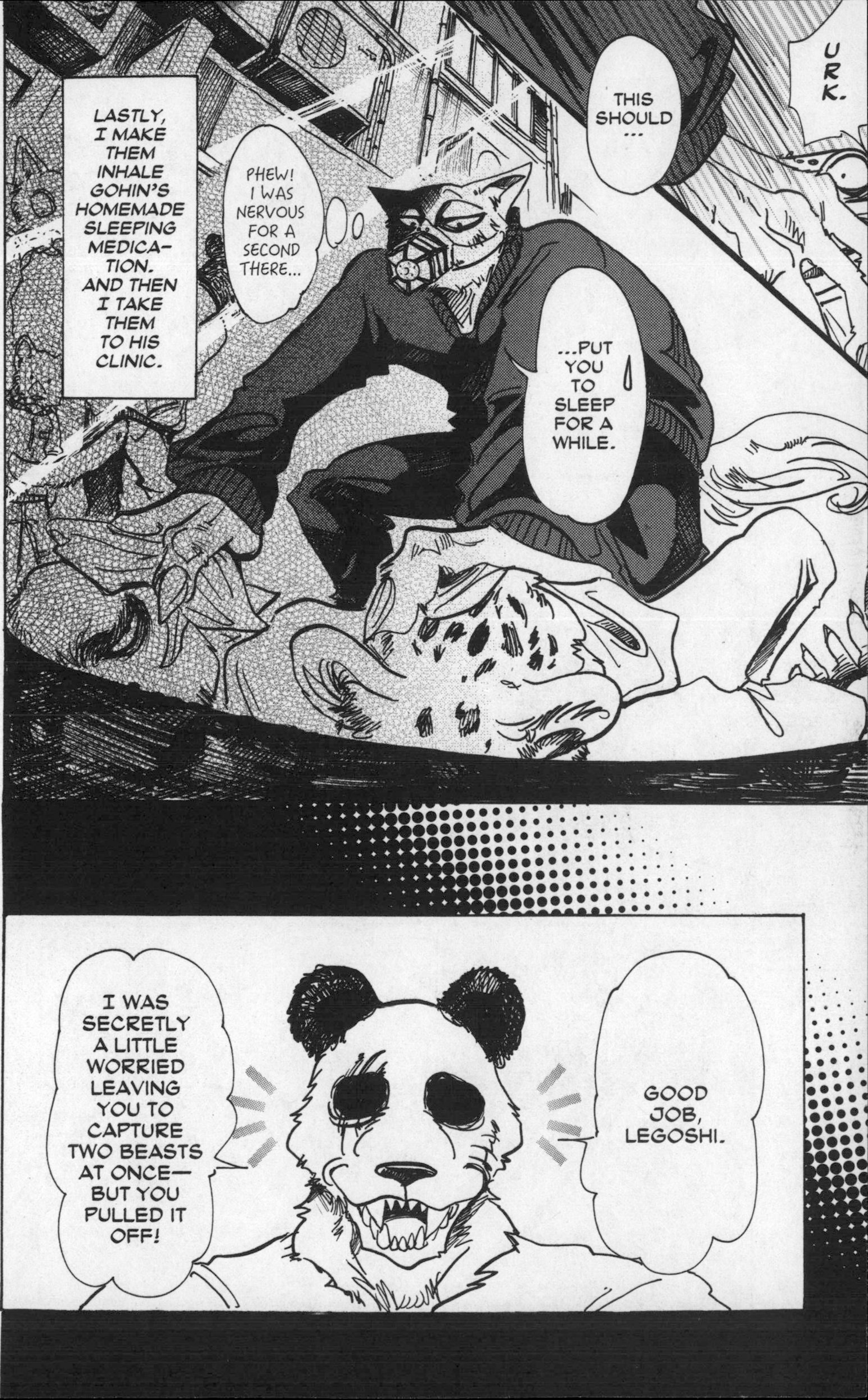
URK.
THIS SHOULD...
...PUT YOU TO SLEEP FOR A WHILE.
PHEW! I WAS NERVOUS FOR A SECOND THERE...
LASTLY, I MAKE THEM INHALE GOHIN'S HOMEMADE SLEEPING MEDICATION. AND THEN I TAKE THEM TO HIS CLINIC.
GOOD JOB, LEGOSHI.
I WAS SECRETLY A LITTLE WORRIED LEAVING YOU TO CAPTURE TWO BEASTS AT ONCE—BUT YOU PULLED IT OFF!

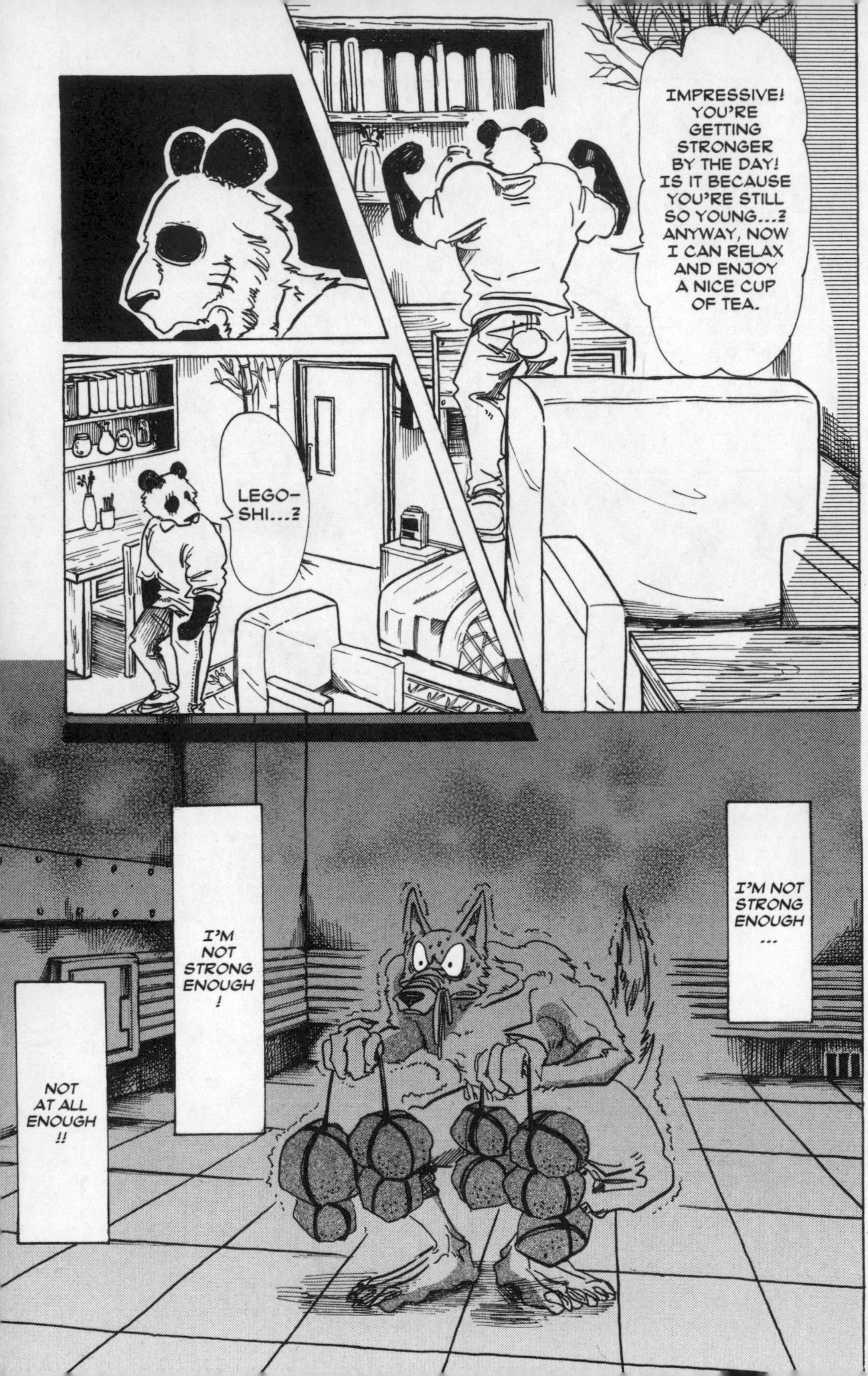
IMPRESSIVE! YOU'RE GETTING STRONGER BY THE DAY! IS IT BECAUSE YOU'RE STILL SO YOUNG...? ANYWAY, NOW I CAN RELAX AND ENJOY A NICE CUP OF TEA.
LEGO-SHI...?
I'M NOT STRONG ENOUGH ...
I'M NOT STRONG ENOUGH !
NOT AT ALL ENOUGH !!

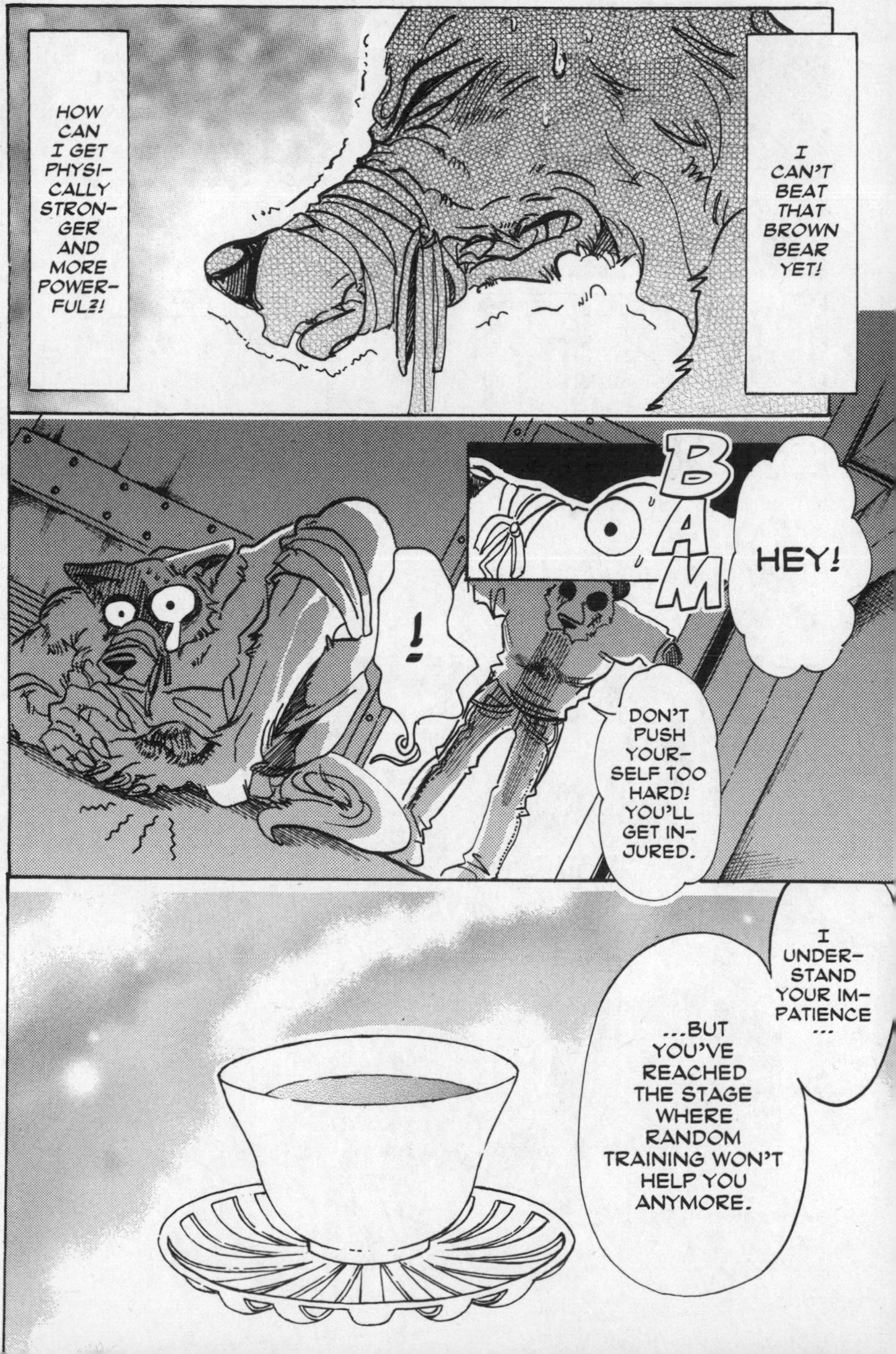
I CAN'T BEAT THAT BROWN BEAR YET!
HOW CAN I GET PHYSICALLY STRONGER AND MORE POWERFUL?!
HEY!
BAM
DON'T PUSH YOURSELF TOO HARD! YOU'LL GET INJURED.
!
I UNDERSTAND YOUR IMPATIENCE...
...BUT YOU'VE REACHED THE STAGE WHERE RANDOM TRAINING WON'T HELP YOU ANYMORE.

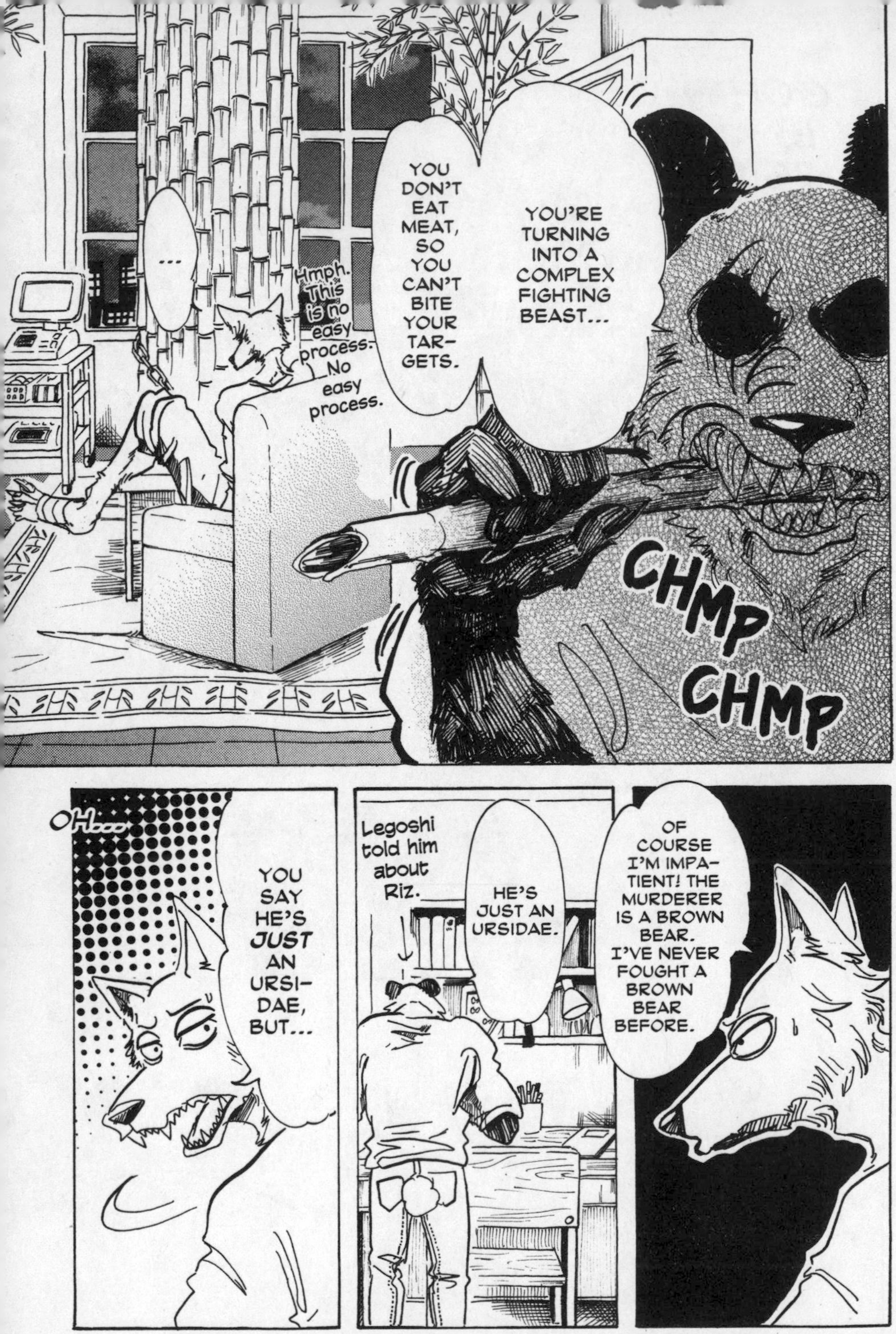
YOU'RE TURNING INTO A COMPLEX FIGHTING BEAST...
YOU DON'T EAT MEAT, SO YOU CAN'T BITE YOUR TAR-GETS.
CHMP CHMP
Hmph. This is no easy process. No easy process.
...
OF COURSE I'M IMPA-TIENT! THE MURDERER IS A BROWN BEAR. I'VE NEVER FOUGHT A BROWN BEAR BEFORE.
HE'S JUST AN URSIDAE.
Legoshi told him about Riz.
YOU SAY HE'S *JUST* AN URSI-DAE, BUT...
OHooo

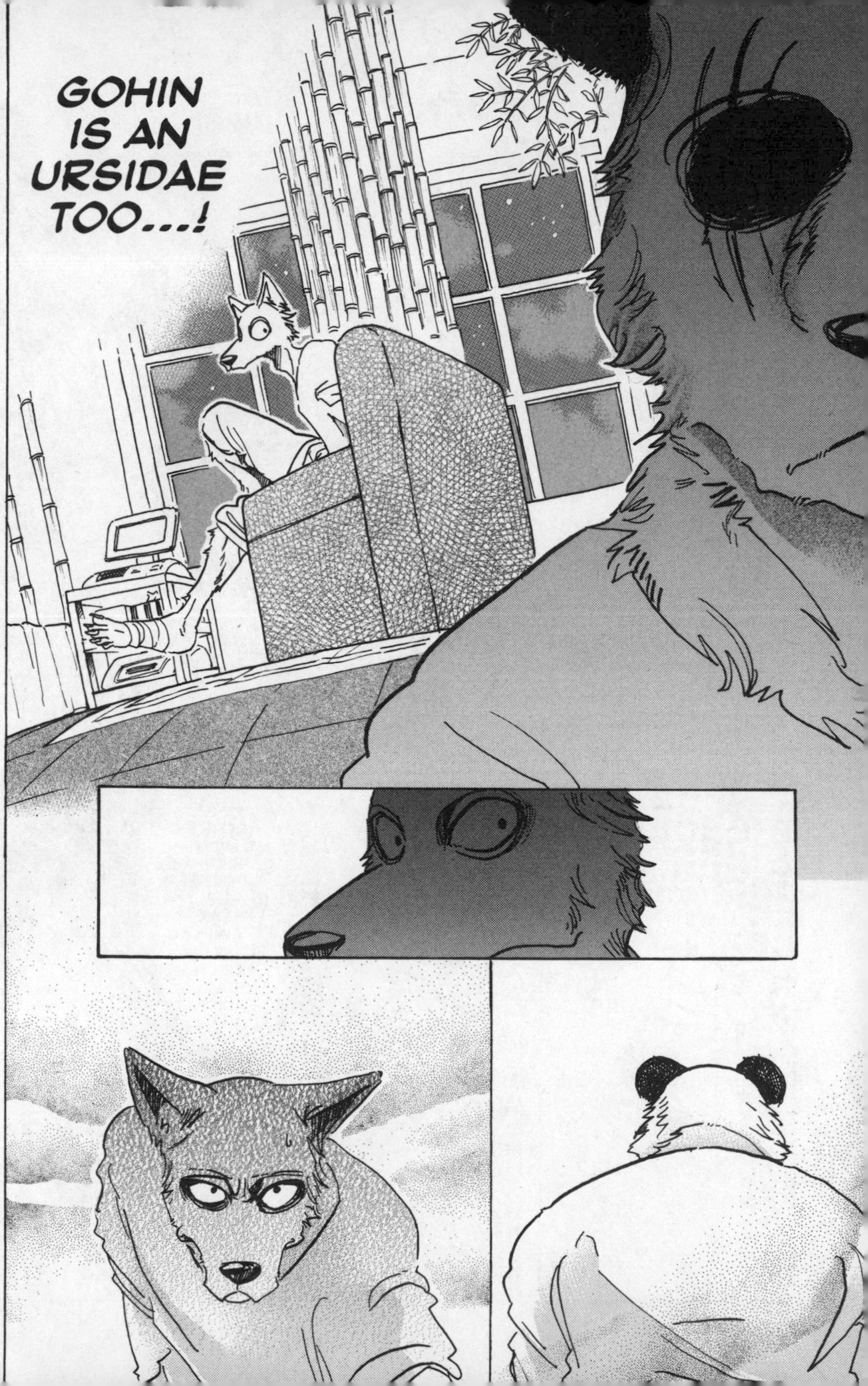
GOHIN IS AN URSIDAE TOO...!

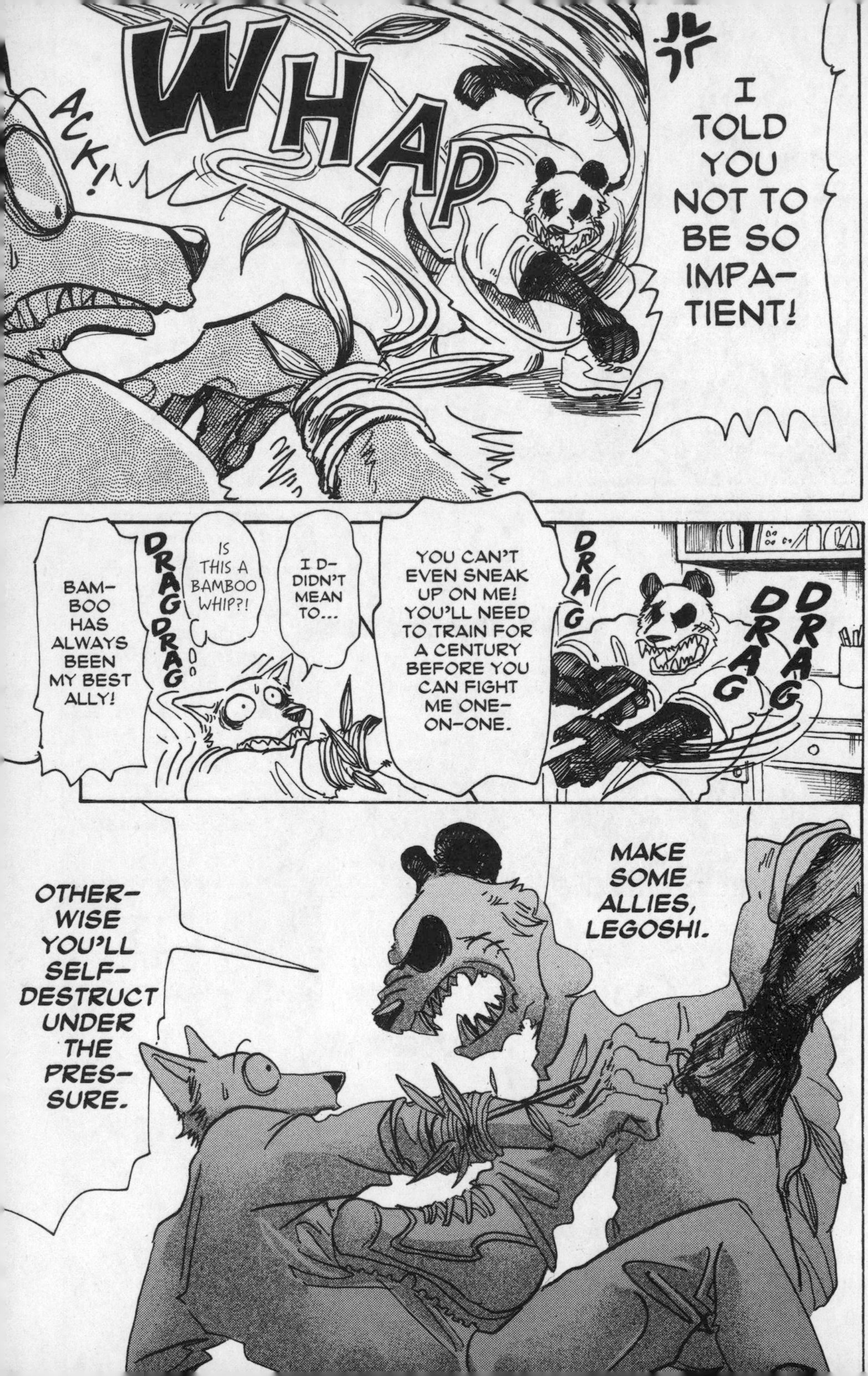
I TOLD YOU NOT TO BE SO IMPA-TIENT!
WHAP
ACK!
DRAG DRAG DRAG
YOU CAN'T EVEN SNEAK UP ON ME! YOU'LL NEED TO TRAIN FOR A CENTURY BEFORE YOU CAN FIGHT ME ONE-ON-ONE.
I D-DIDN'T MEAN TO...
IS THIS A BAMBOO WHIP?!
DRAG DRAG
BAM-BOO HAS ALWAYS BEEN MY BEST ALLY!
MAKE SOME ALLIES, LEGOSHI.
OTHER-WISE YOU'LL SELF-DESTRUCT UNDER THE PRES-SURE.

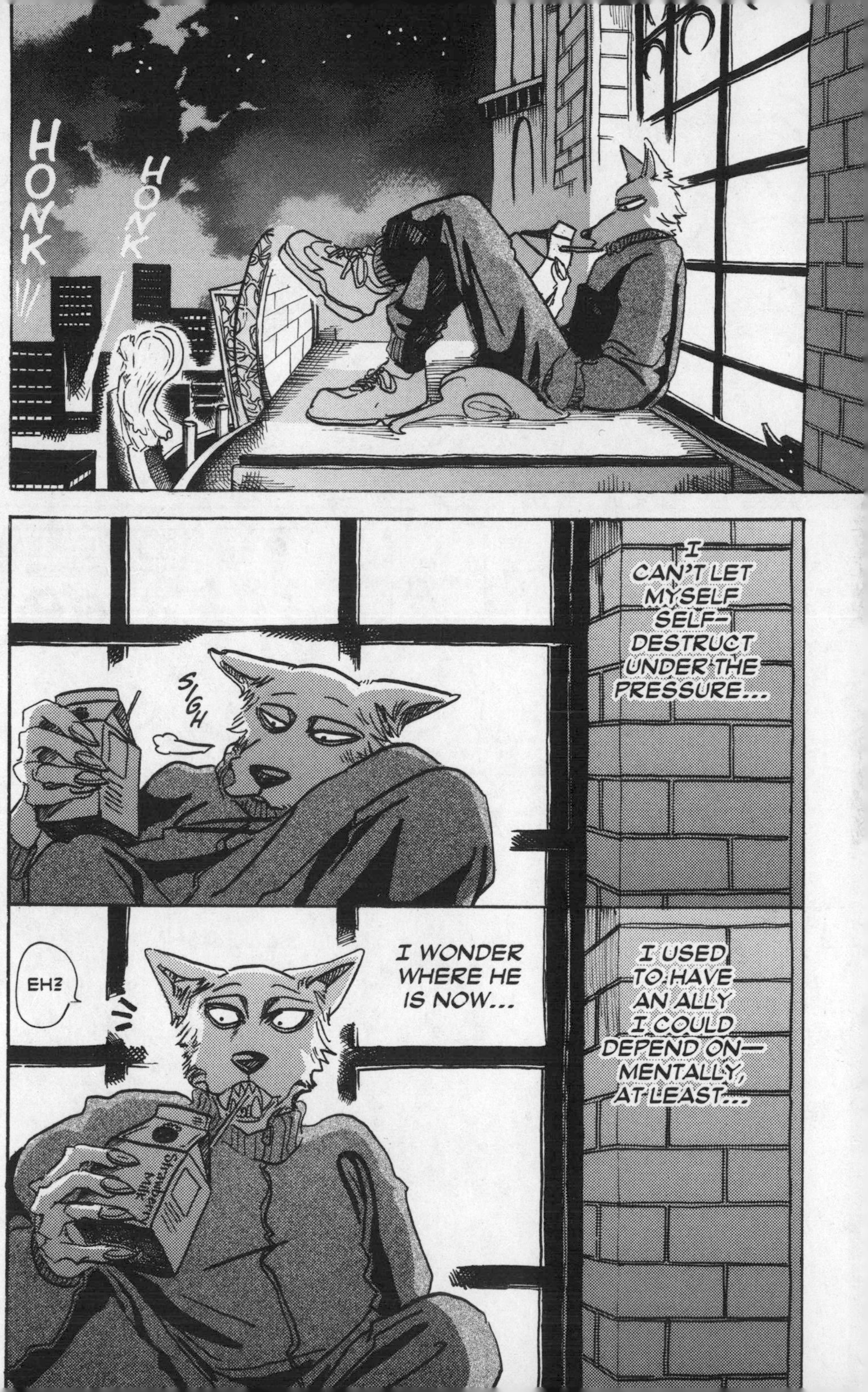
HONK HONK
HONK
I CAN'T LET MYSELF SELF-DESTRUCT UNDER THE PRESSURE...
SIGH
I USED TO HAVE AN ALLY I COULD DEPEND ON—MENTALLY, AT LEAST...
I WONDER WHERE HE IS NOW...
EH?

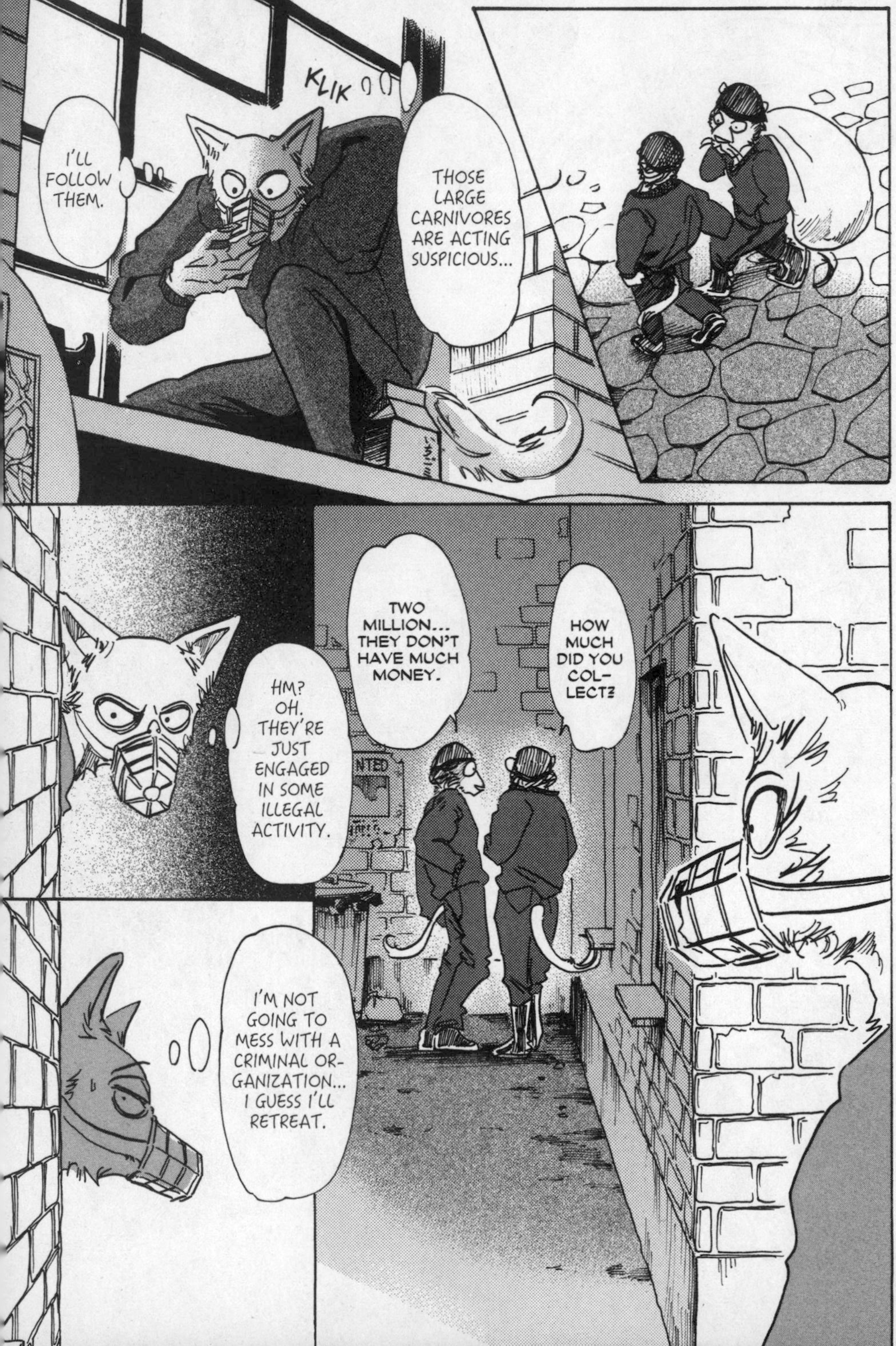
KLIK
THOSE LARGE CARNIVORES ARE ACTING SUSPICIOUS...
I'LL FOLLOW THEM.
HOW MUCH DID YOU COL-LECT?
TWO MILLION... THEY DON'T HAVE MUCH MONEY.
HM? OH. THEY'RE JUST ENGAGED IN SOME ILLEGAL ACTIVITY.
I'M NOT GOING TO MESS WITH A CRIMINAL OR-GANIZATION... I GUESS I'LL RETREAT.

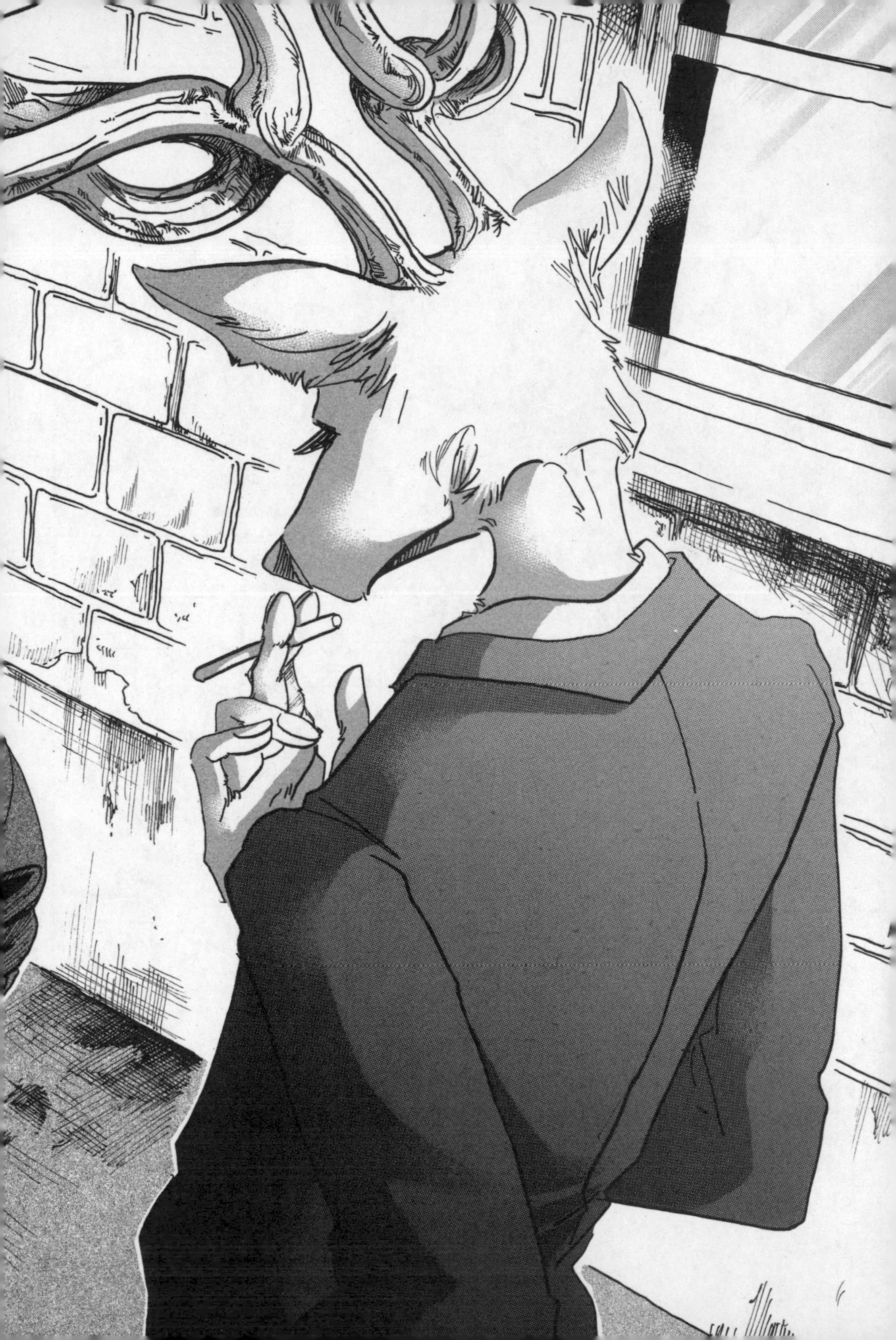

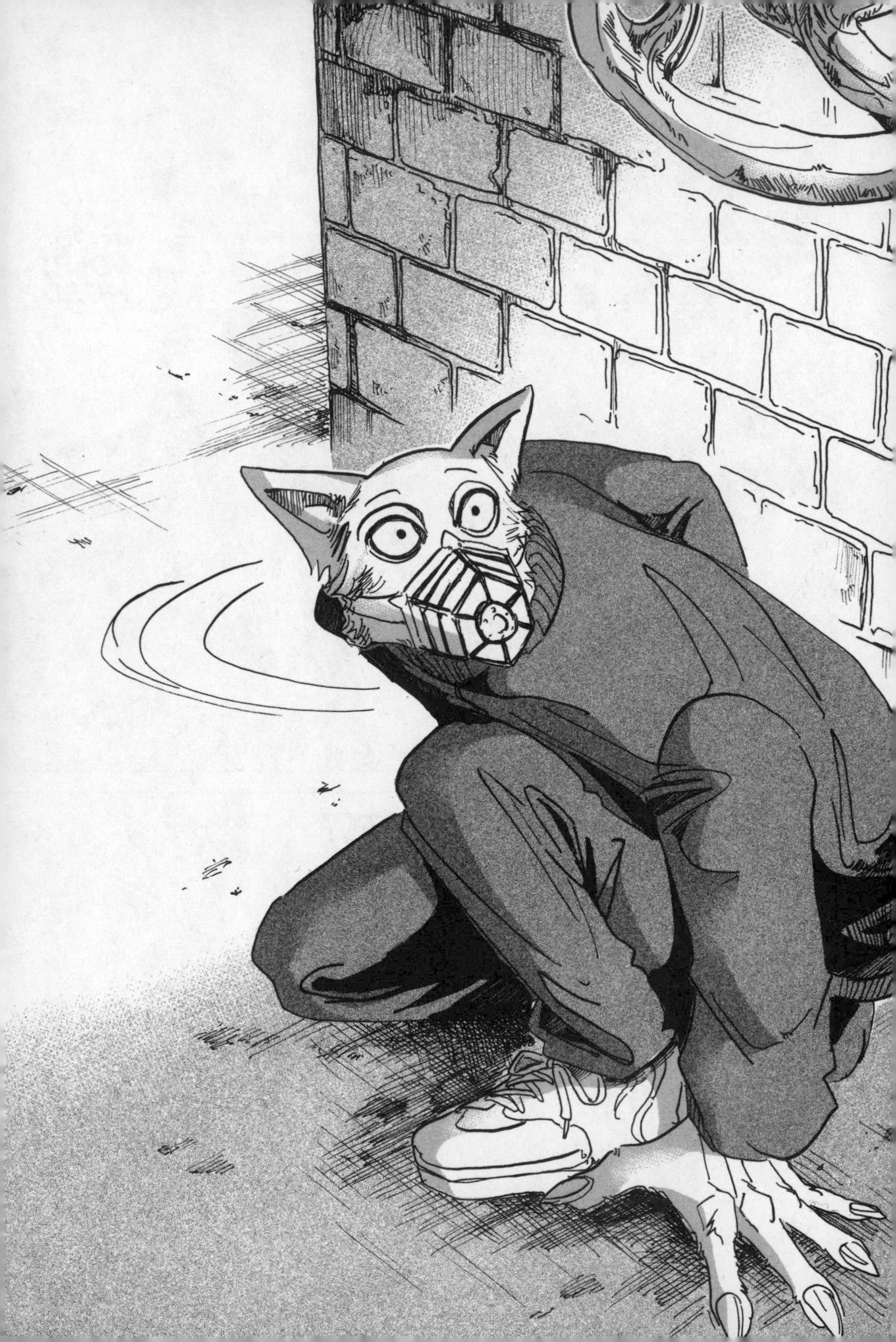

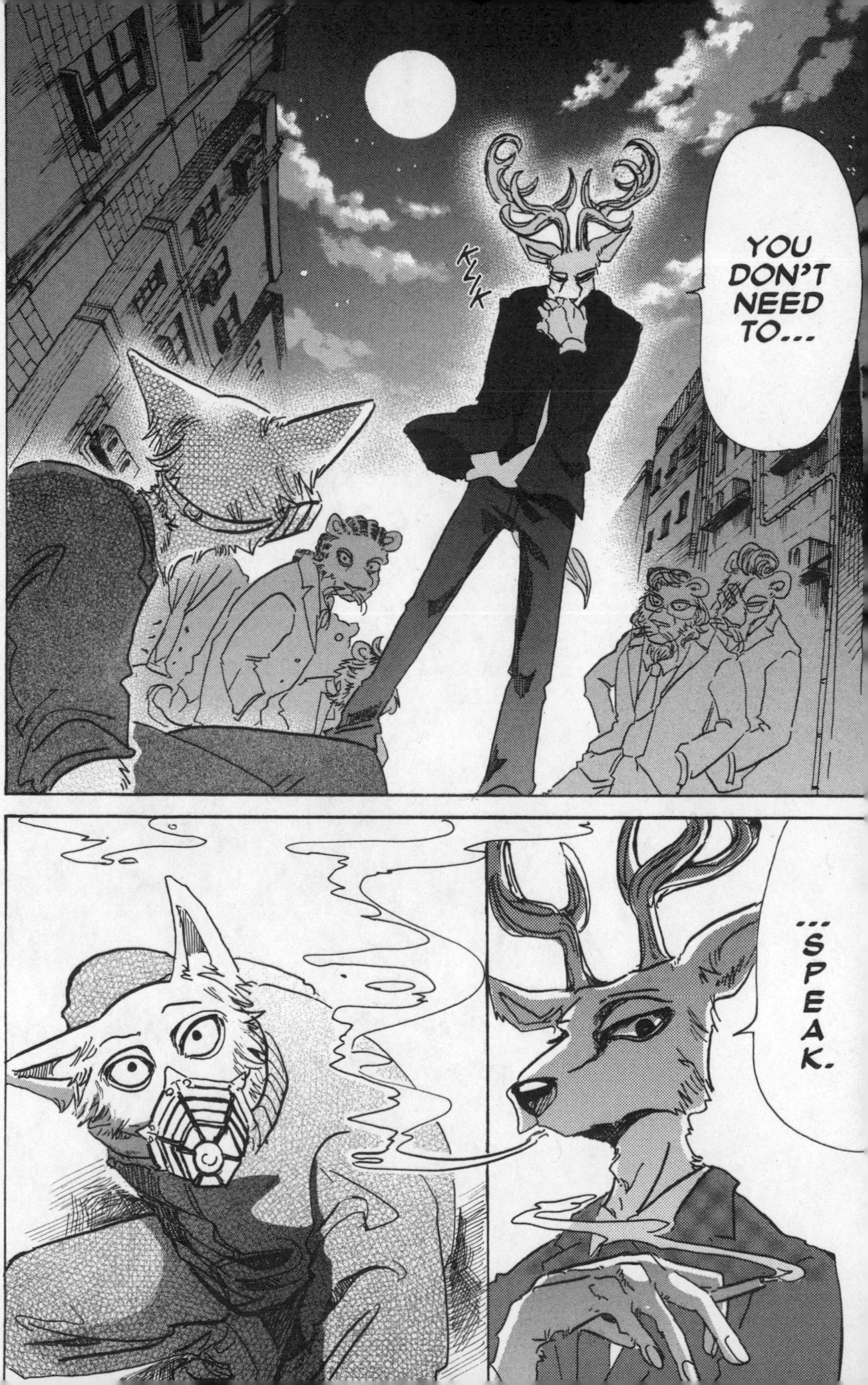
KLIK
YOU DON'T NEED TO...
...SPEAK.

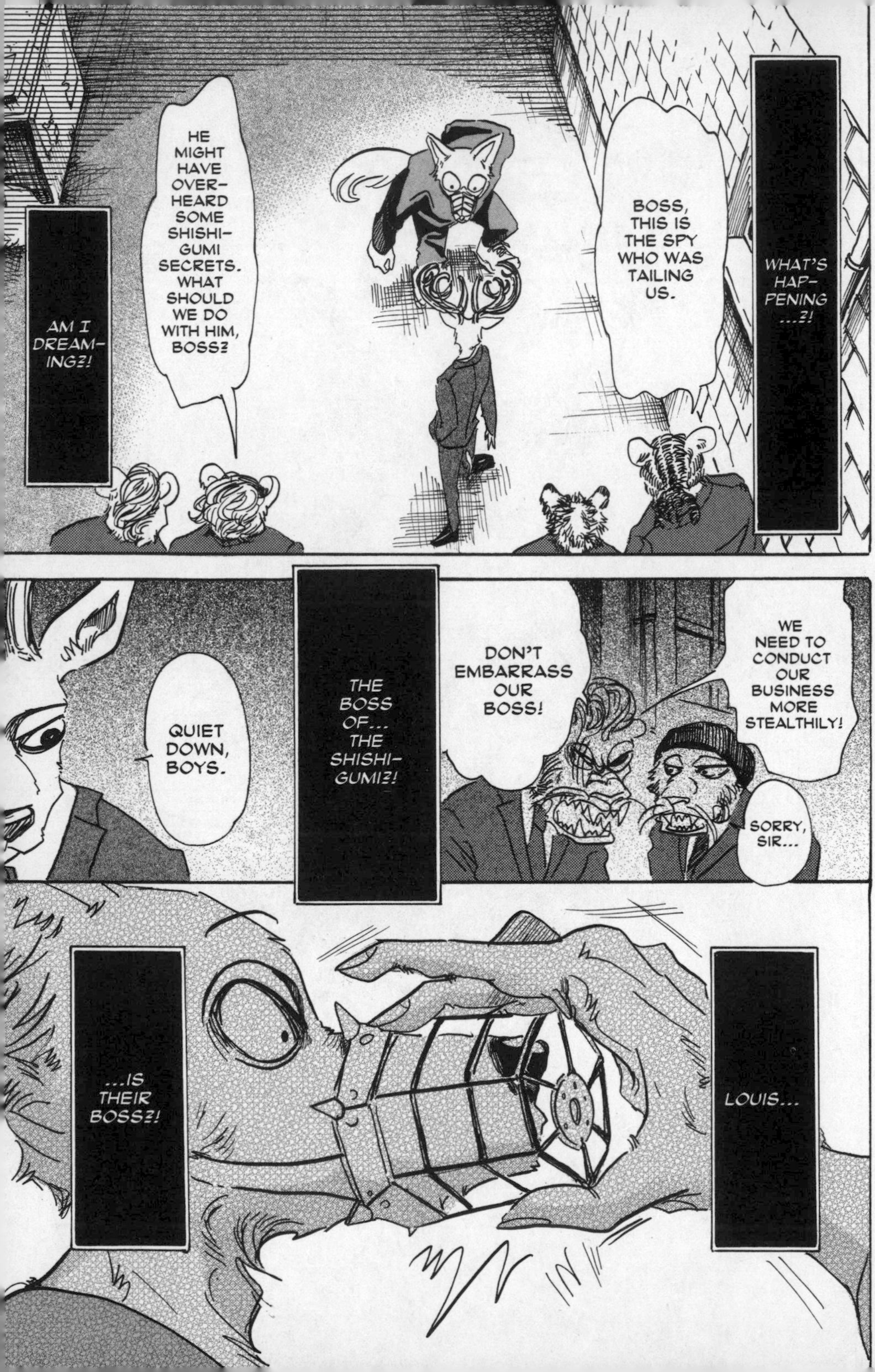
WHAT'S HAP-PENING...?!
BOSS, THIS IS THE SPY WHO WAS TAILING US.
HE MIGHT HAVE OVER-HEARD SOME SHISHI-GUMI SECRETS. WHAT SHOULD WE DO WITH HIM, BOSS?
AM I DREAMING?!
WE NEED TO CONDUCT OUR BUSINESS MORE STEALTHILY!
DON'T EMBARRASS OUR BOSS!
SORRY, SIR...
THE BOSS OF... THE SHISHI-GUMI?!
QUIET DOWN, BOYS.
LOUIS...
...IS THEIR BOSS?!

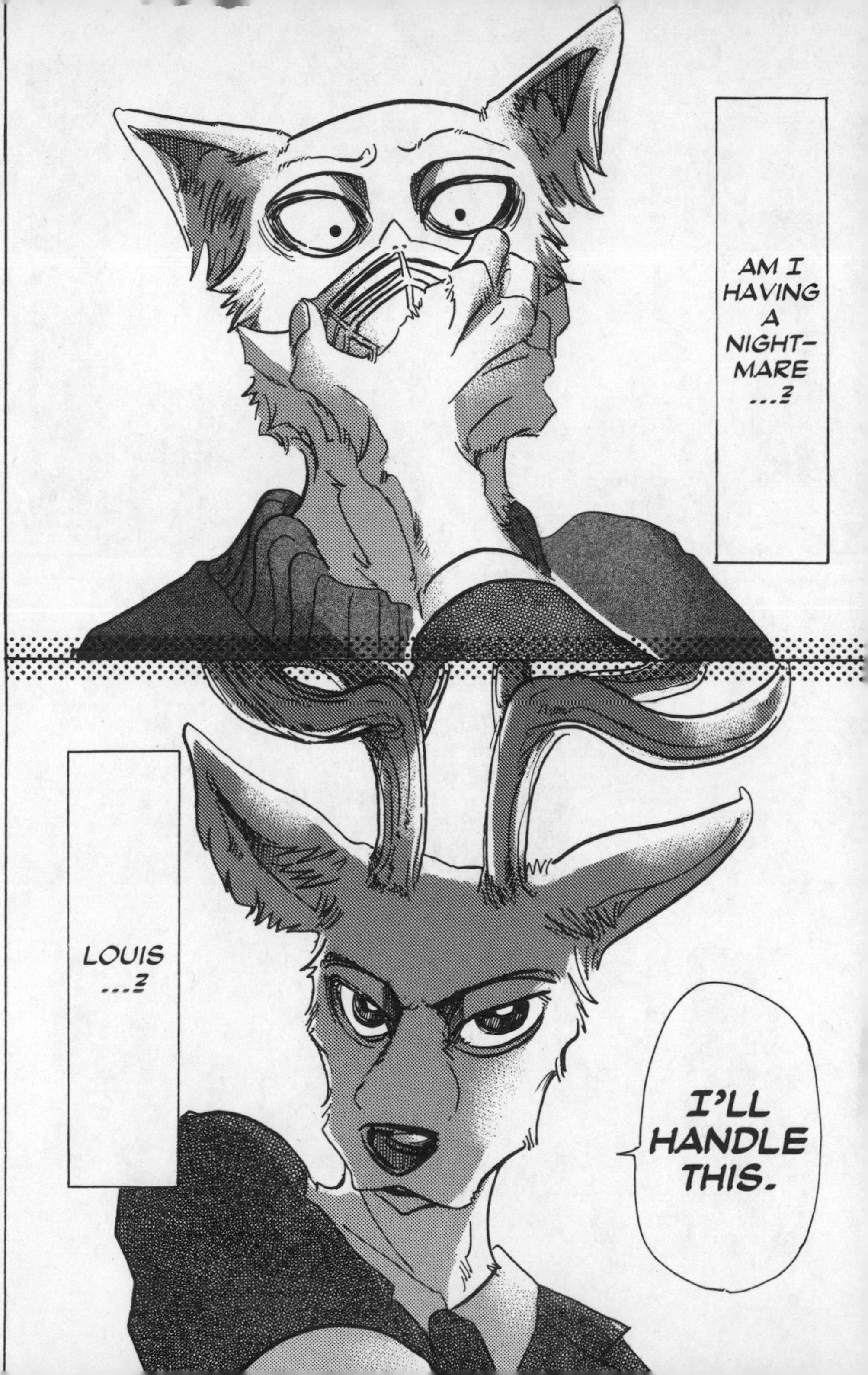
AM I HAVING A NIGHT-MARE ...?
I'LL HANDLE THIS.
LOUIS ...?

Three minutes ago...
BOSS! HE'S A SPY FOR SURE. LET'S KILL 'IM.
I CAN'T BE-LIEVE IT...
OF ALL THE BEASTS...

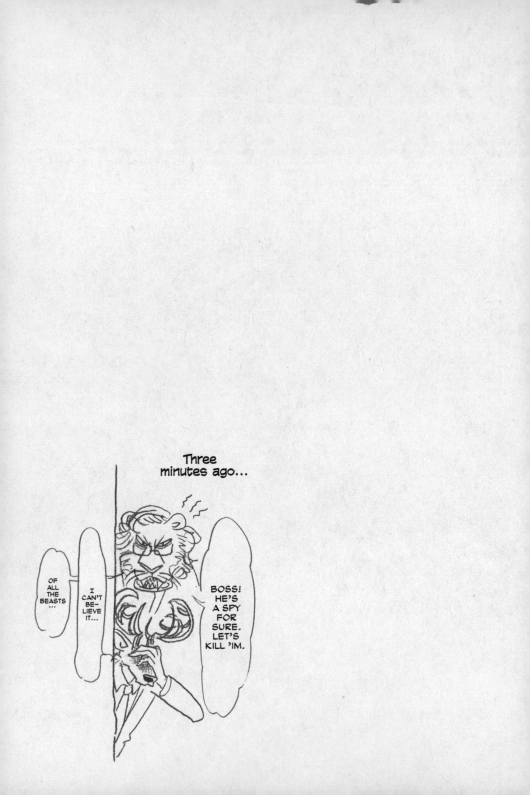

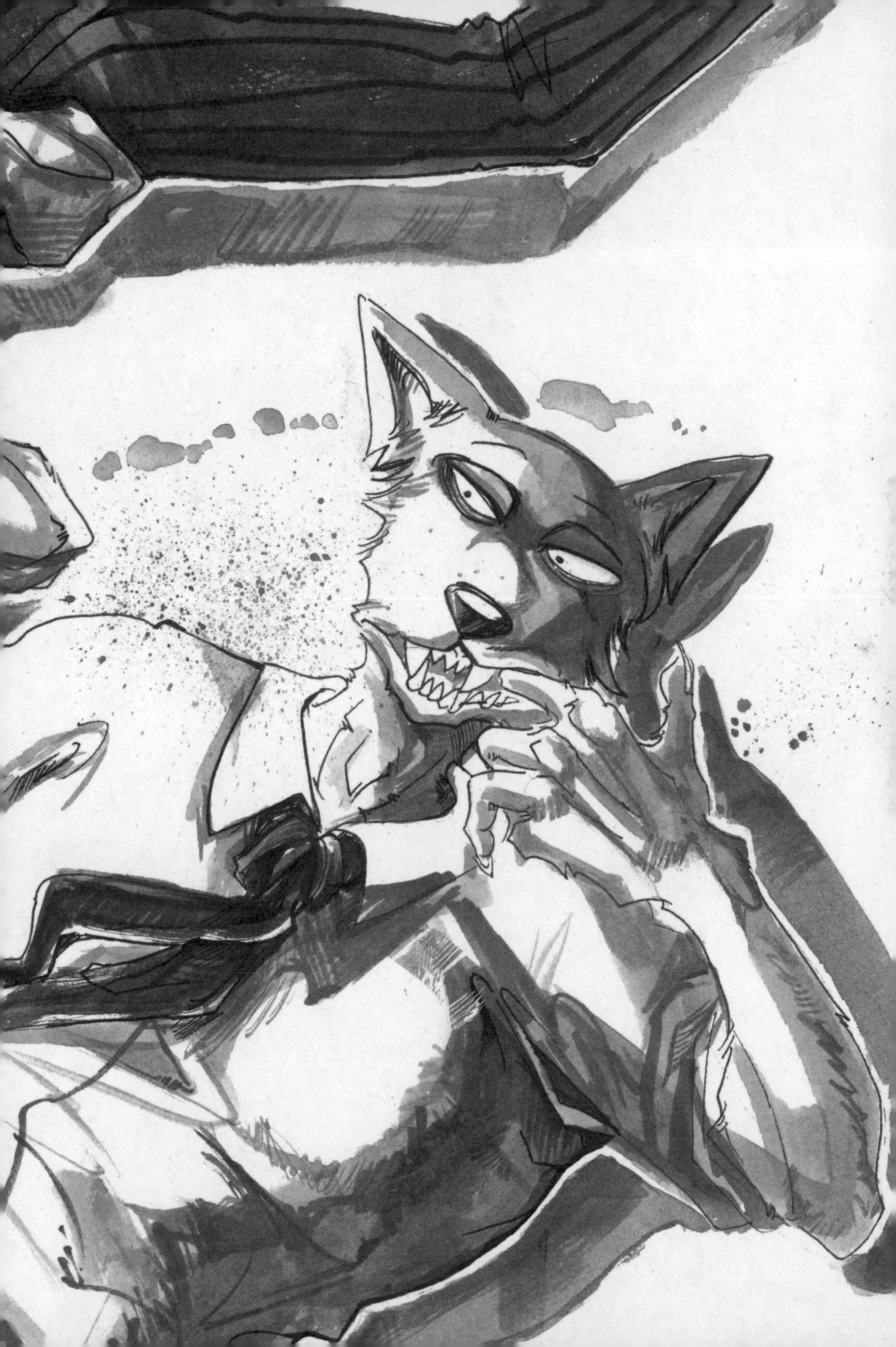

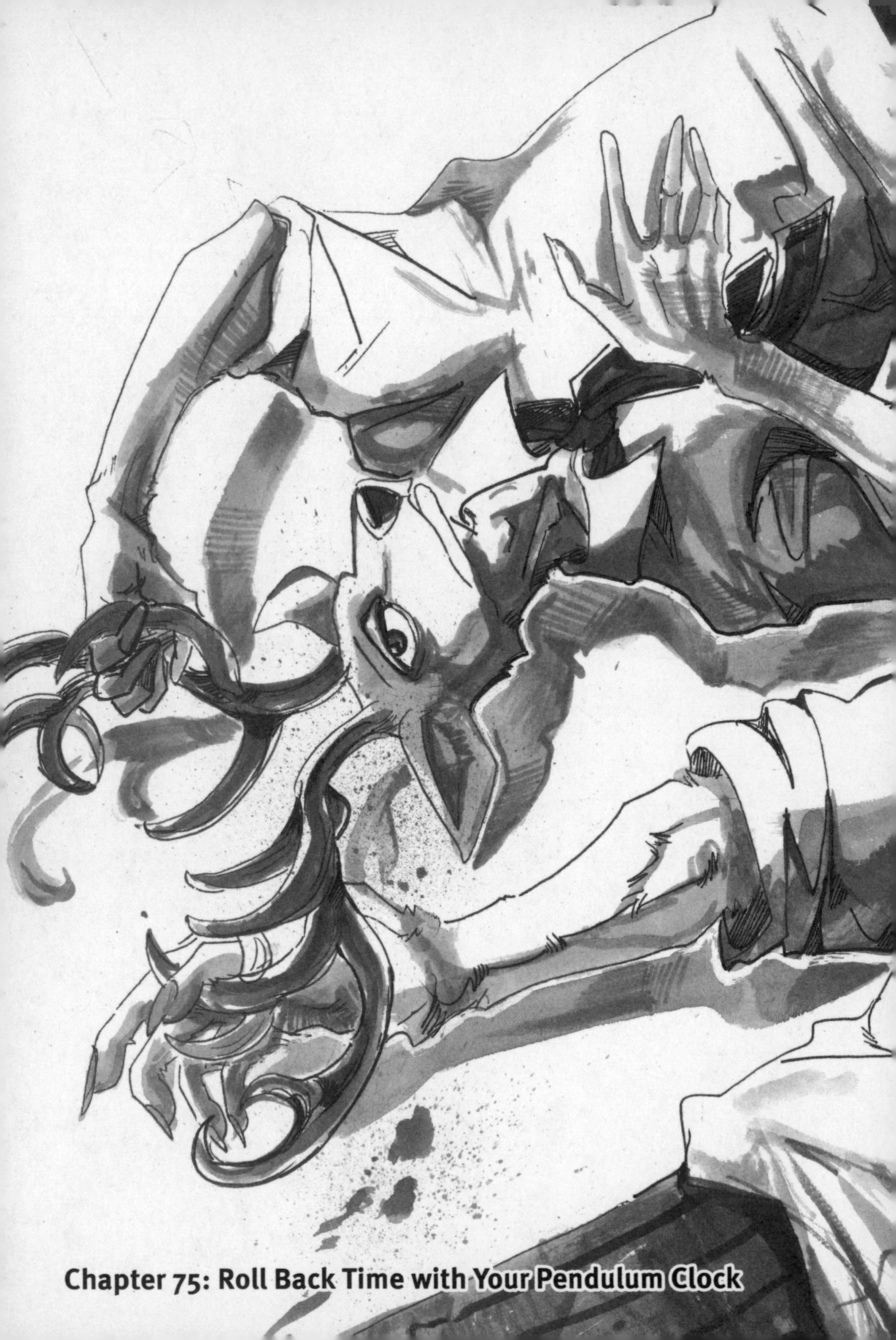

Chapter 75: Roll Back Time with Your Pendulum Clock

BEASTARS
Vol. 9

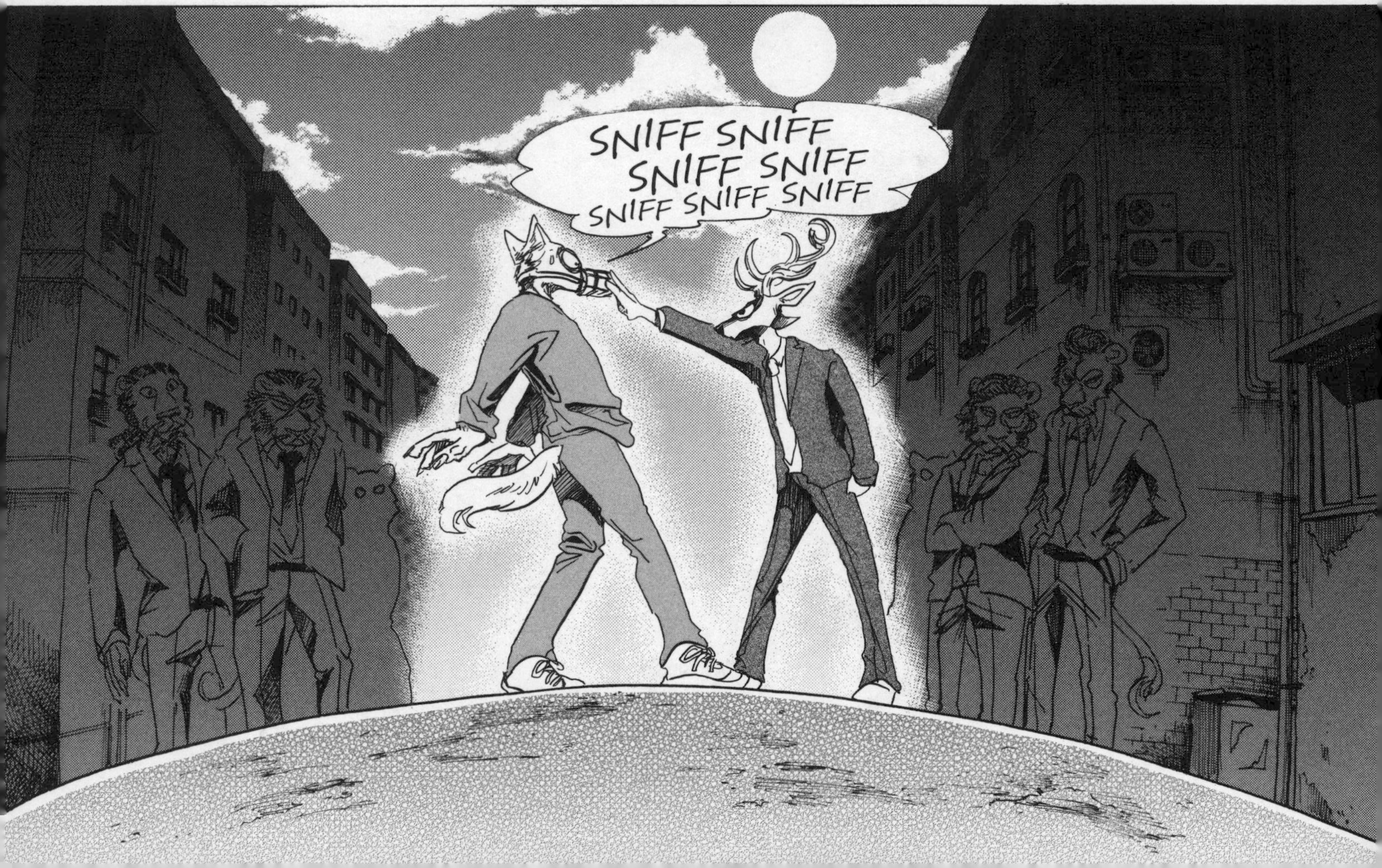
SNIFF SNIFF SNIFF SNIFF SNIFF SNIFF SNIFF

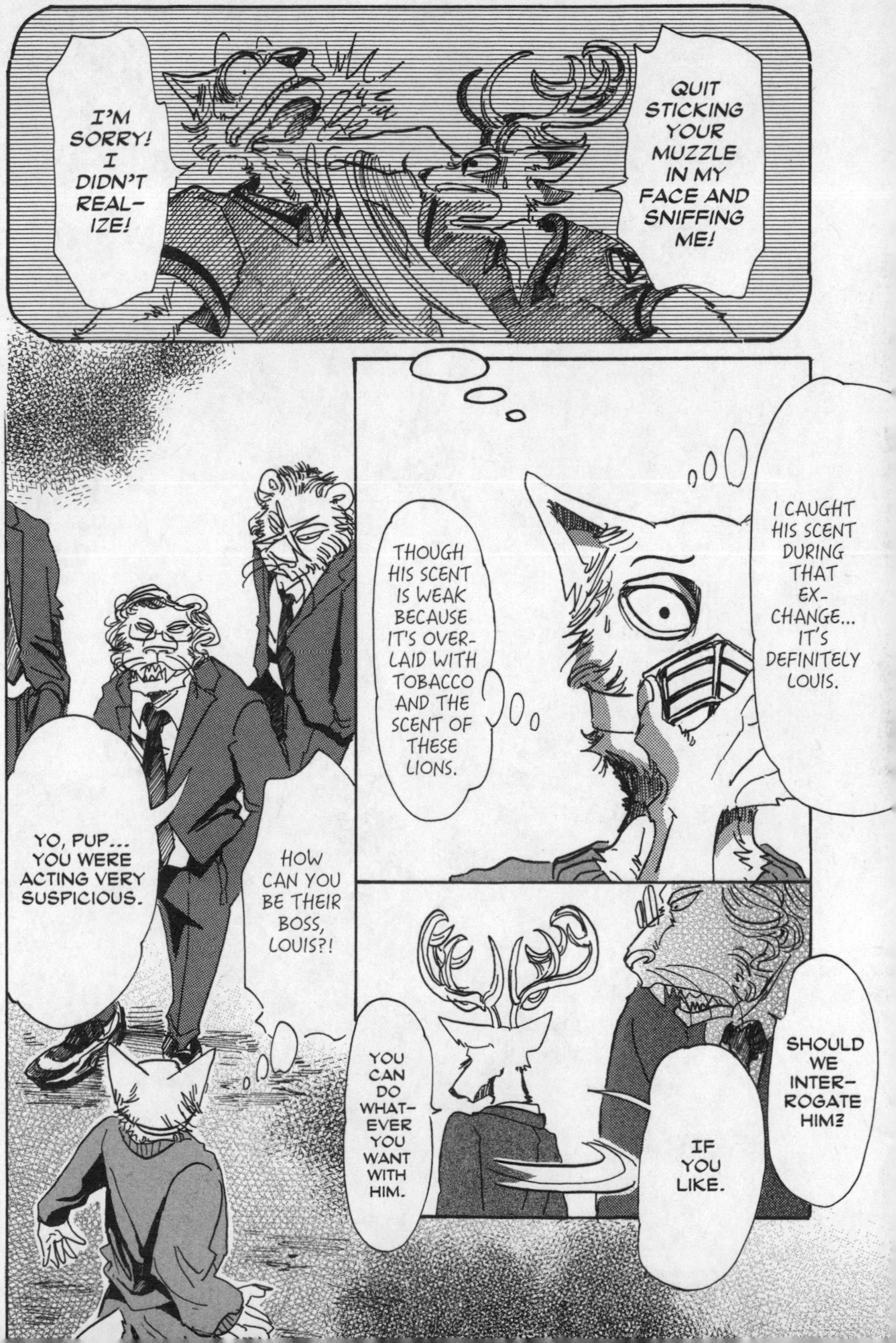
QUIT STICKING YOUR MUZZLE IN MY FACE AND SNIFFING ME!
I'M SORRY! I DIDN'T REAL-IZE!
I CAUGHT HIS SCENT DURING THAT EX-CHANGE... IT'S DEFINITELY LOUIS.
THOUGH HIS SCENT IS WEAK BECAUSE IT'S OVER-LAID WITH TOBACCO AND THE SCENT OF THESE LIONS.
SHOULD WE INTER-ROGATE HIM?
IF YOU LIKE.
YOU CAN DO WHAT-EVER YOU WANT WITH HIM.
HOW CAN YOU BE THEIR BOSS, LOUIS?!
YO, PUP... YOU WERE ACTING VERY SUSPICIOUS.

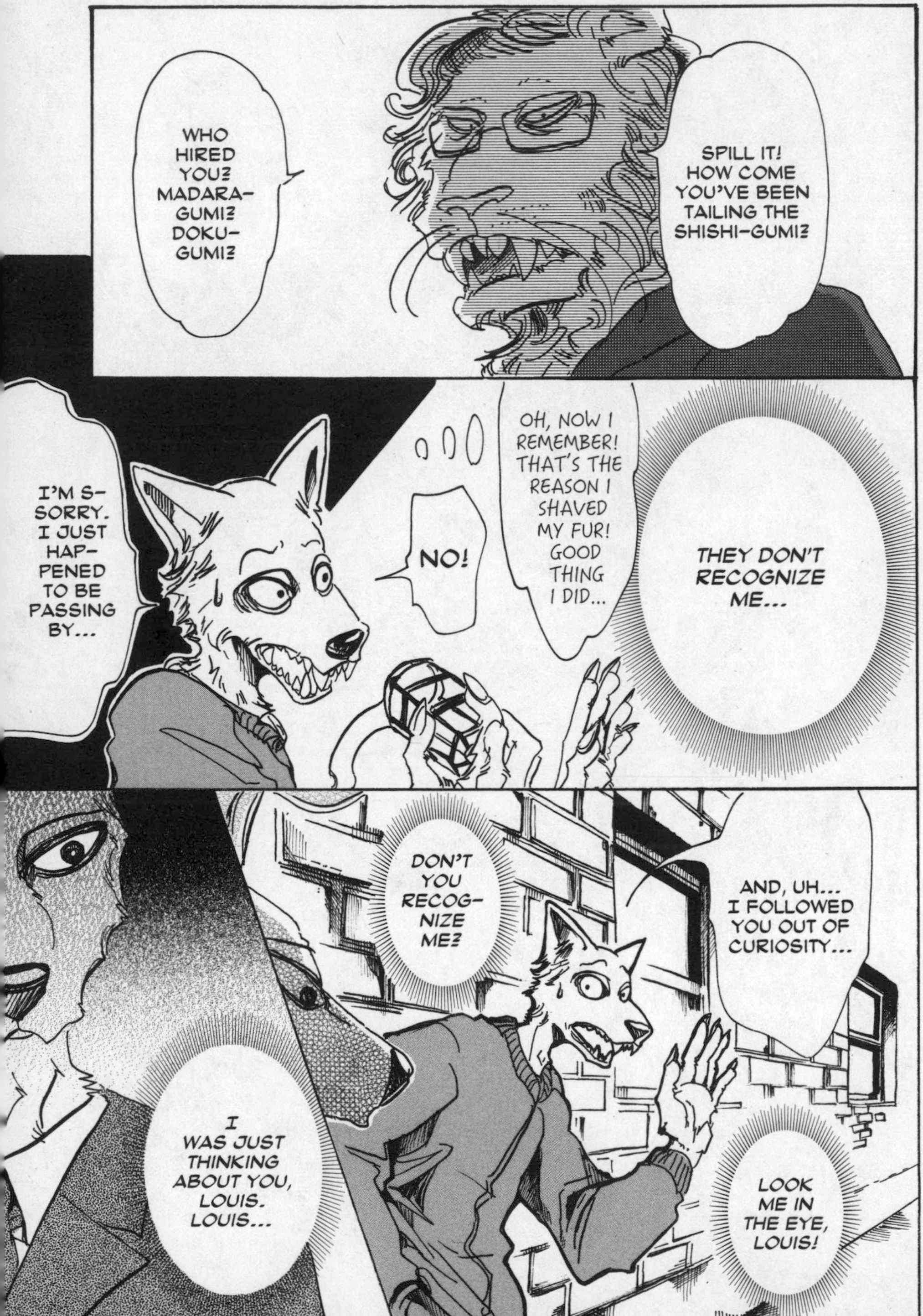
SPILL IT! HOW COME YOU'VE BEEN TAILING THE SHISHI-GUMI?
WHO HIRED YOU? MADARA-GUMI? DOKU-GUMI?
THEY DON'T RECOGNIZE ME...
OH, NOW I REMEMBER! THAT'S THE REASON I SHAVED MY FUR! GOOD THING I DID...
NO!
I'M S-SORRY. I JUST HAP-PENED TO BE PASSING BY...
AND, UH... I FOLLOWED YOU OUT OF CURIOSITY...
LOOK ME IN THE EYE, LOUIS!
DON'T YOU RECOG-NIZE ME?
I WAS JUST THINKING ABOUT YOU, LOUIS. LOUIS...

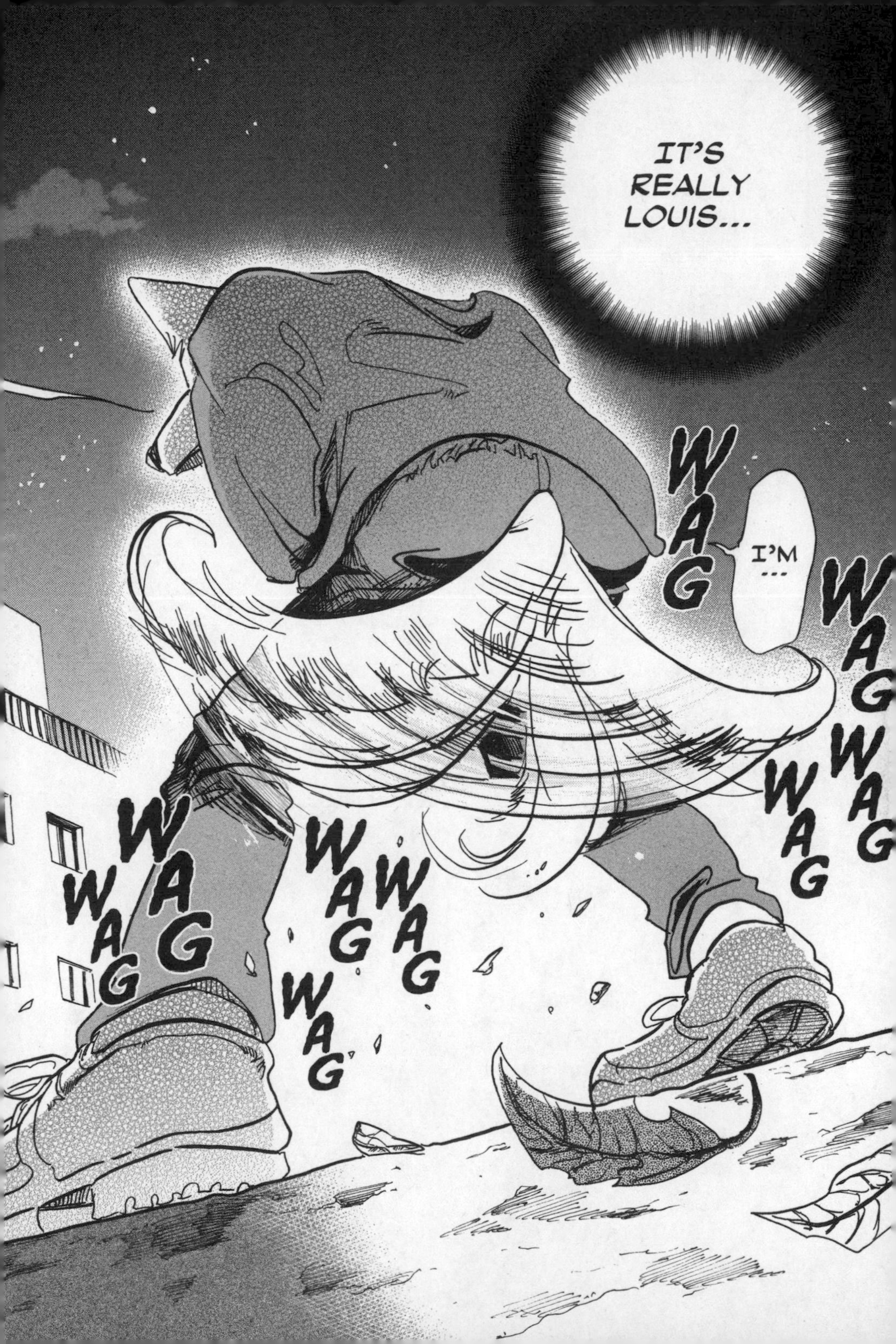
IT'S REALLY LOUIS...
WAG
I'M ...
WAG
WAG
WAG
WAG
WAG
WAG
WAG
WAG
WAG

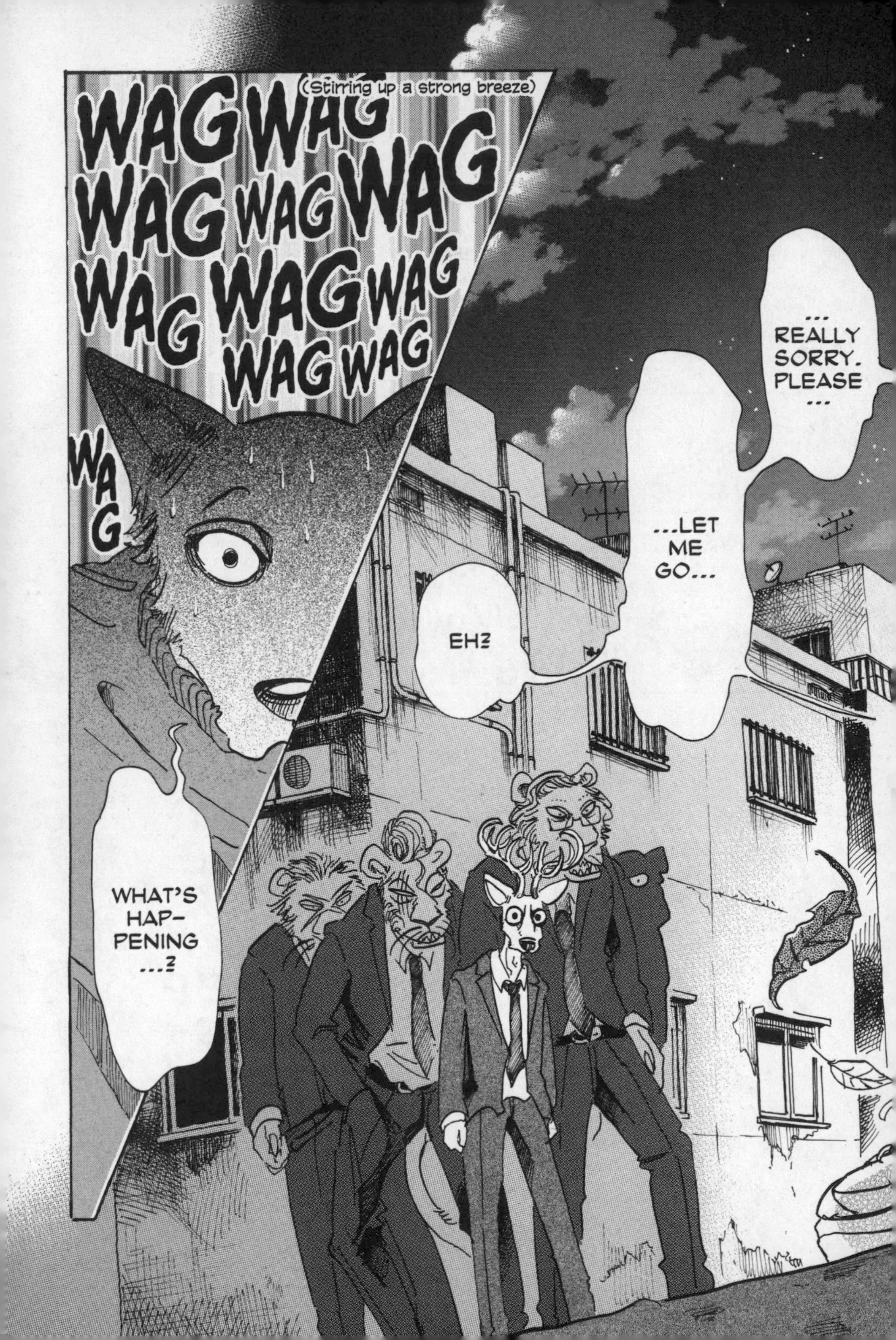
...REALLY SORRY. PLEASE...
...LET ME GO...
EH?
(Stirring up a strong breeze)
WAG WAG WAG WAG WAG WAG WAG WAG WAG WAG WAG
WAG WAG
WHAT'S HAP-PENING...?

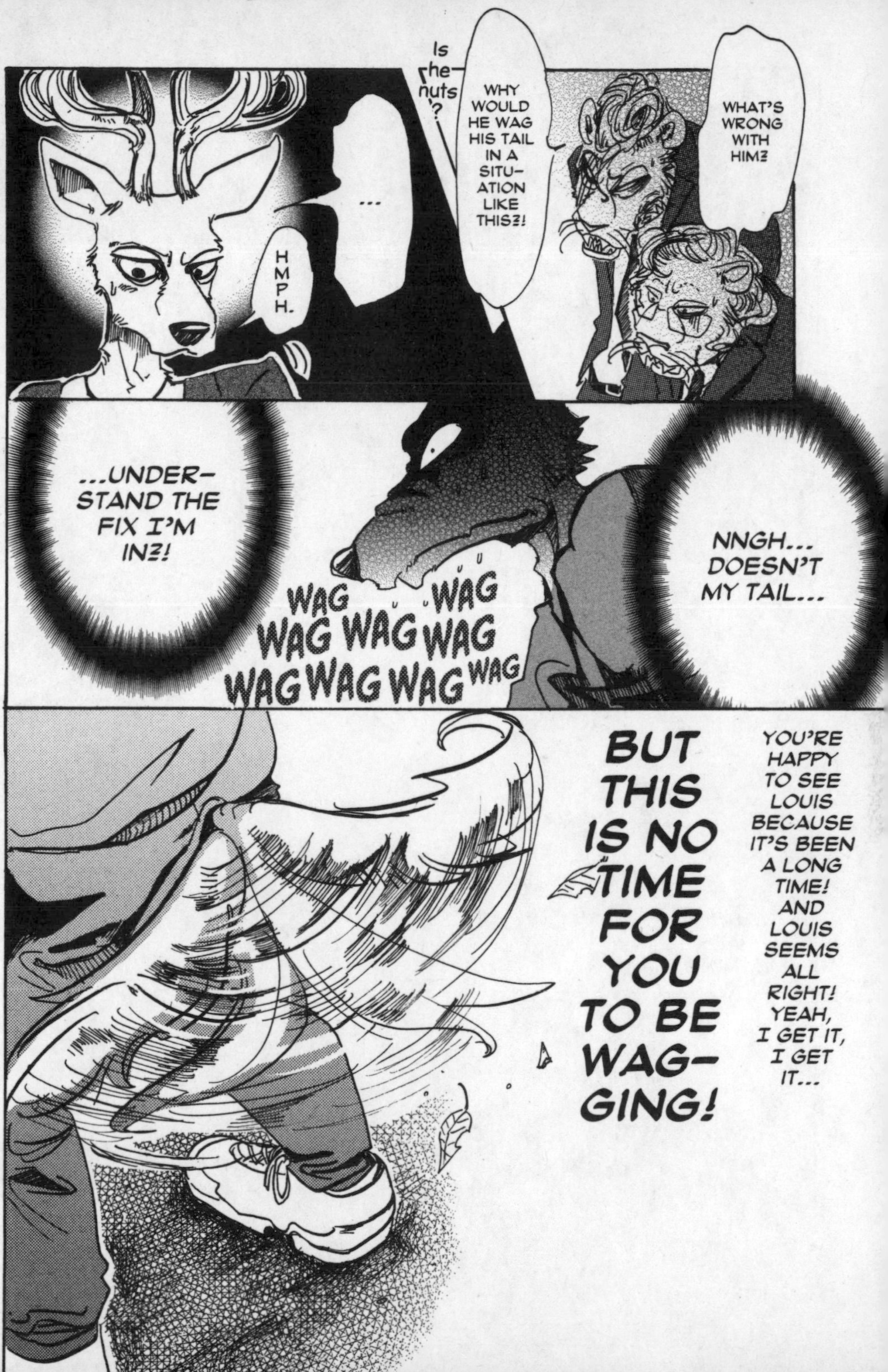
WHAT'S WRONG WITH HIM?
WHY WOULD HE WAG HIS TAIL IN A SITUATION LIKE THIS?!
Is he nuts?
...
HMPH.
NNGH... DOESN'T MY TAIL...
...UNDERSTAND THE FIX I'M IN?!
WAG WAG WAG WAG WAG WAG WAG WAG WAG
YOU'RE HAPPY TO SEE LOUIS BECAUSE IT'S BEEN A LONG TIME! AND LOUIS SEEMS ALL RIGHT! YEAH, I GET IT, I GET IT...
BUT THIS IS NO TIME FOR YOU TO BE WAGGING!

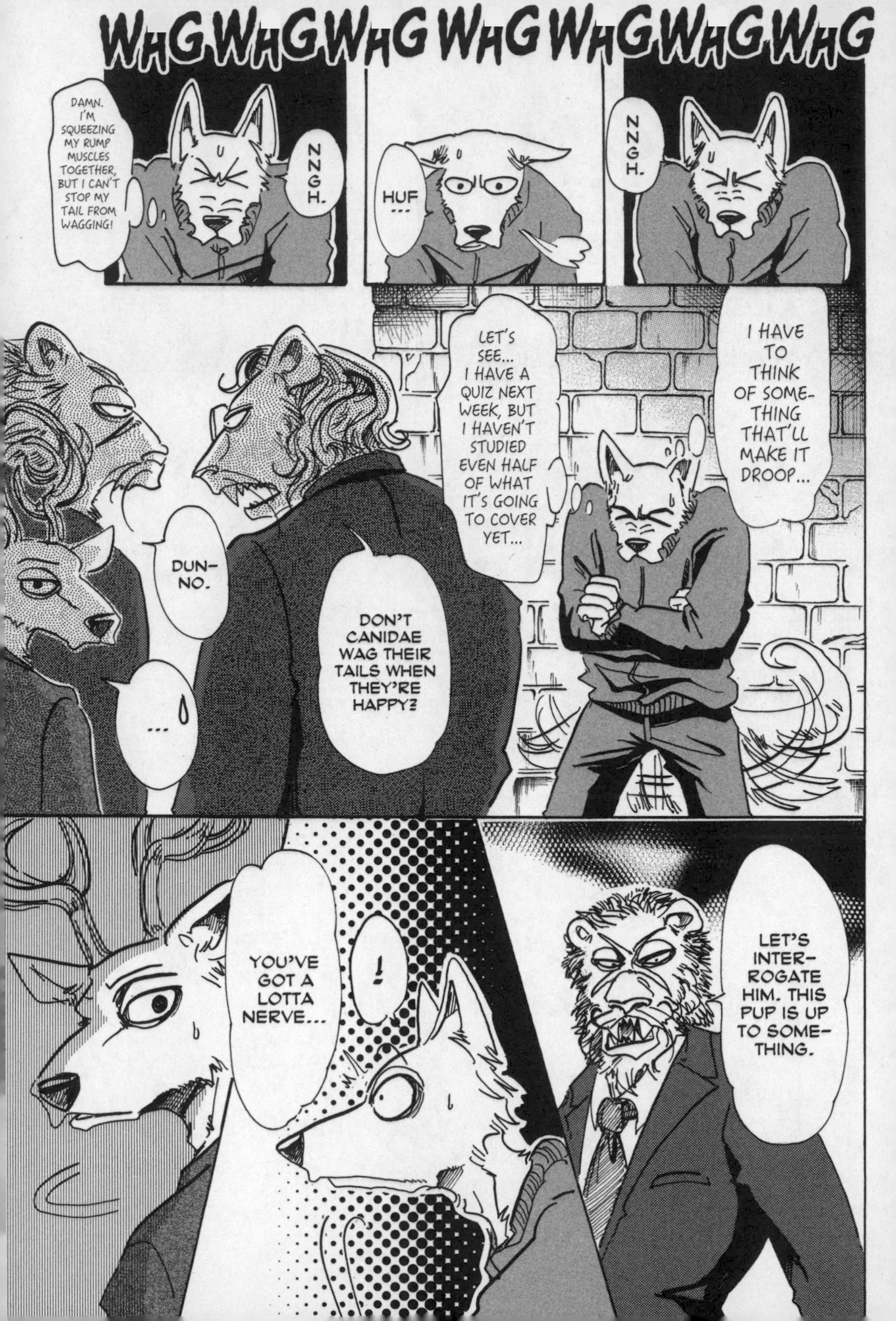
WAG WAG WAG WAG WAG WAG WAG
NNGH.
HUF...
NNGH.
DAMN. I'M SQUEEZING MY RUMP MUSCLES TOGETHER, BUT I CAN'T STOP MY TAIL FROM WAGGING!
I HAVE TO THINK OF SOMETHING THAT'LL MAKE IT DROOP...
LET'S SEE... I HAVE A QUIZ NEXT WEEK, BUT I HAVEN'T STUDIED EVEN HALF OF WHAT IT'S GOING TO COVER YET...
DON'T CANIDAE WAG THEIR TAILS WHEN THEY'RE HAPPY?
DUN-NO.
...
LET'S INTERROGATE HIM. THIS PUP IS UP TO SOMETHING.
!
YOU'VE GOT A LOTTA NERVE...

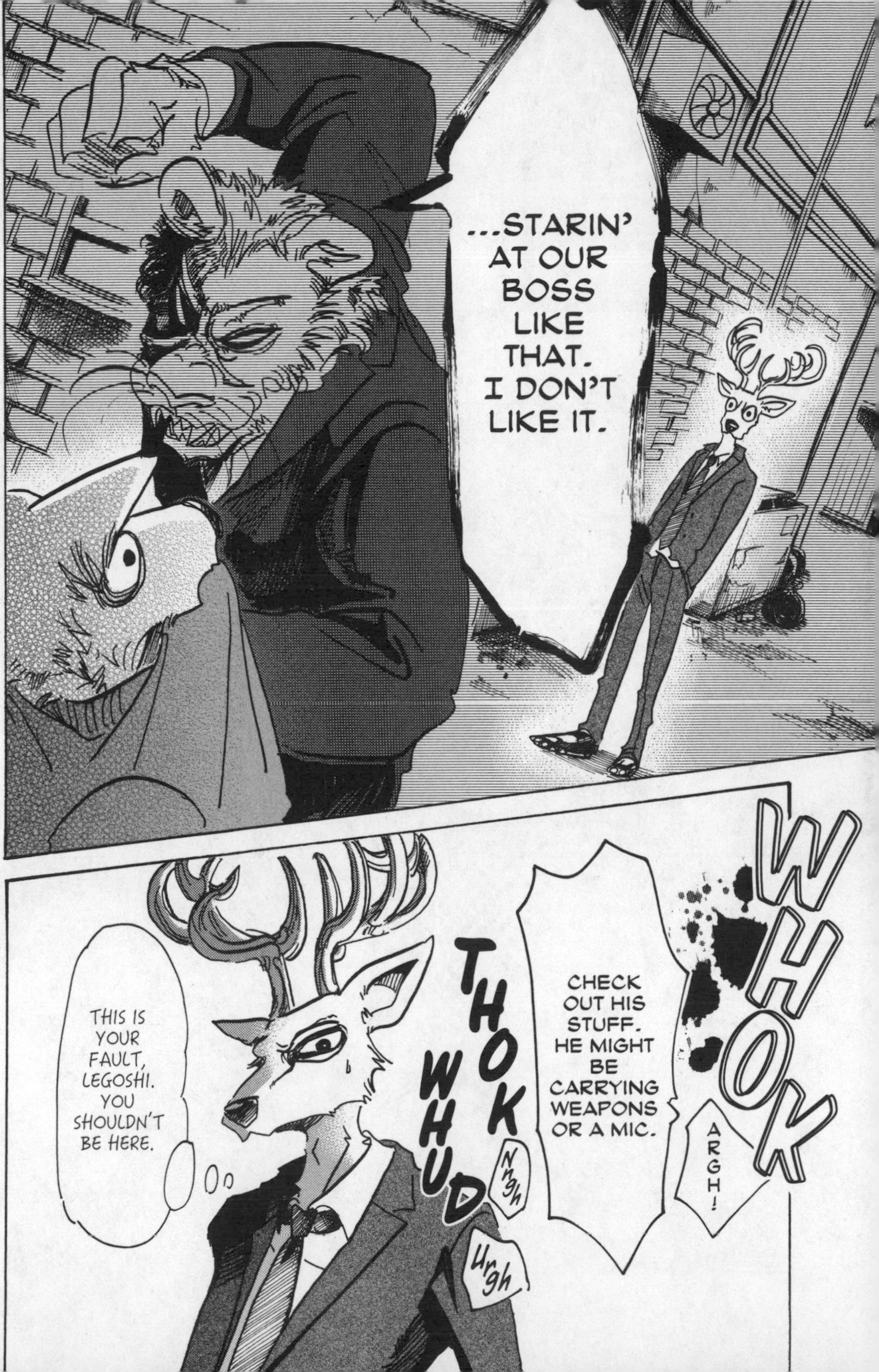
...STARIN' AT OUR BOSS LIKE THAT. I DON'T LIKE IT.
WHOK
ARGH!
CHECK OUT HIS STUFF. HE MIGHT BE CARRYING WEAPONS OR A MIC.
THOK
Nngh
WHUD
Urgh
THIS IS YOUR FAULT, LEGOSHI. YOU SHOULDN'T BE HERE.

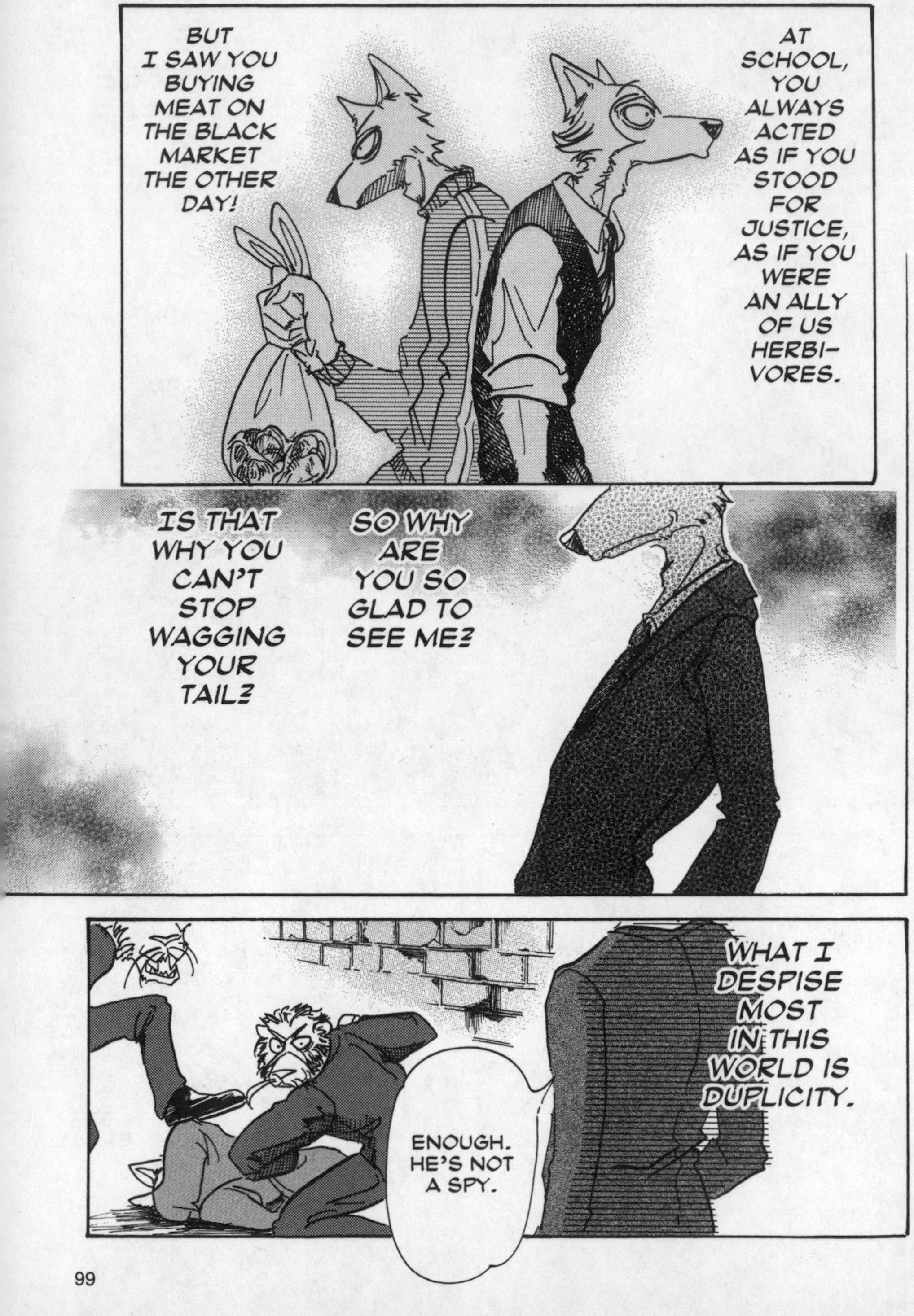
AT SCHOOL, YOU ALWAYS ACTED AS IF YOU STOOD FOR JUSTICE, AS IF YOU WERE AN ALLY OF US HERBI-VORES.
BUT I SAW YOU BUYING MEAT ON THE BLACK MARKET THE OTHER DAY!
SO WHY ARE YOU SO GLAD TO SEE ME?
IS THAT WHY YOU CAN'T STOP WAGGING YOUR TAIL?
WHAT I DESPISE MOST IN THIS WORLD IS DUPLICITY.
ENOUGH. HE'S NOT A SPY.

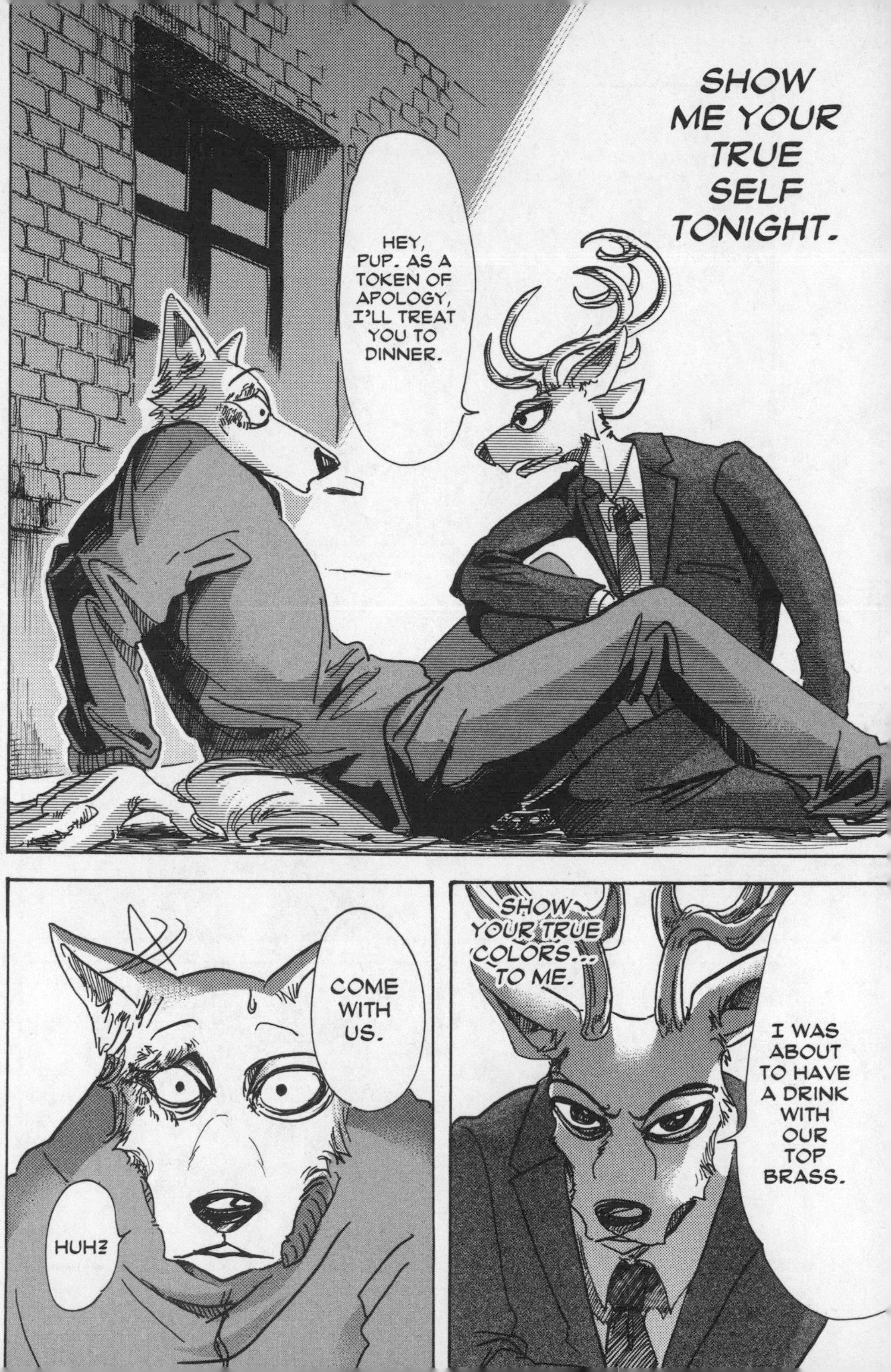
SHOW ME YOUR TRUE SELF TONIGHT.
HEY, PUP. AS A TOKEN OF APOLOGY, I'LL TREAT YOU TO DINNER.
SHOW YOUR TRUE COLORS... TO ME.
I WAS ABOUT TO HAVE A DRINK WITH OUR TOP BRASS.
COME WITH US.
HUH?

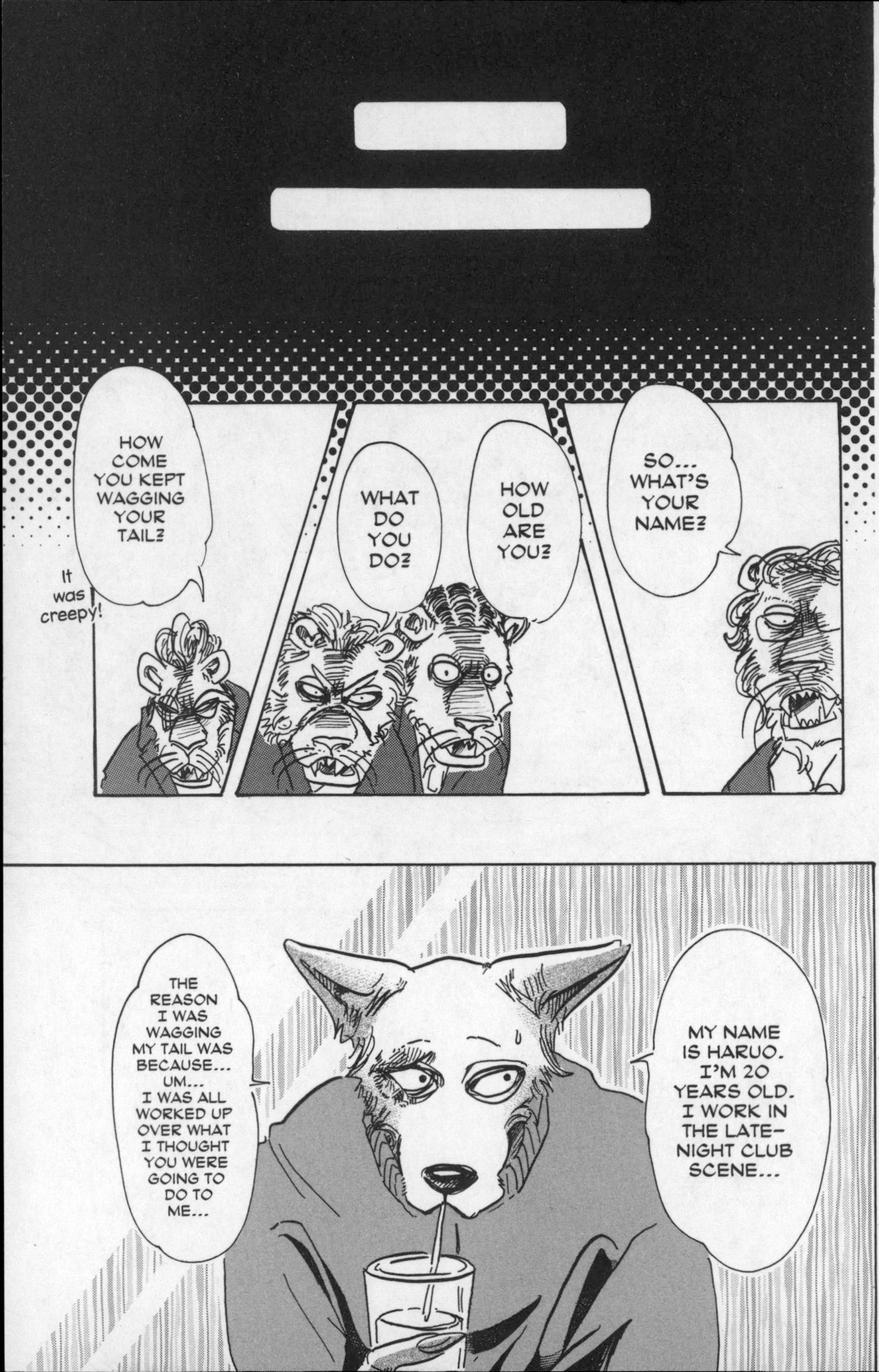
SO... WHAT'S YOUR NAME?
HOW OLD ARE YOU?
WHAT DO YOU DO?
HOW COME YOU KEPT WAGGING YOUR TAIL?
It was creepy!
MY NAME IS HARUO. I'M 20 YEARS OLD. I WORK IN THE LATE-NIGHT CLUB SCENE...
THE REASON I WAS WAGGING MY TAIL WAS BECAUSE... UM... I WAS ALL WORKED UP OVER WHAT I THOUGHT YOU WERE GOING TO DO TO ME...

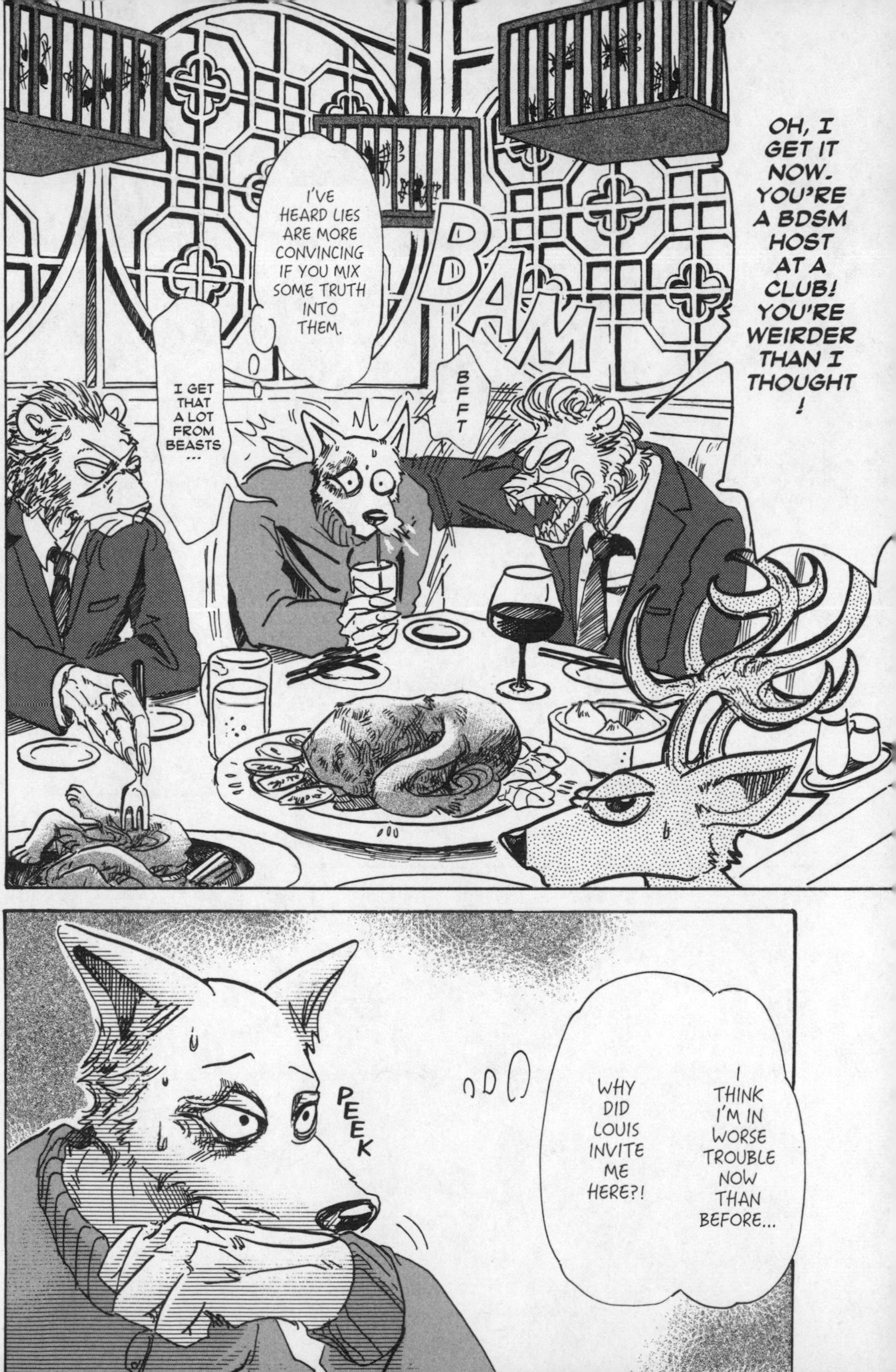
OH, I GET IT NOW. YOU'RE A BDSM HOST AT A CLUB! YOU'RE WEIRDER THAN I THOUGHT!
BAM
BFFT
I'VE HEARD LIES ARE MORE CONVINCING IF YOU MIX SOME TRUTH INTO THEM.
I GET THAT A LOT FROM BEASTS...
I THINK I'M IN WORSE TROUBLE NOW THAN BEFORE...
WHY DID LOUIS INVITE ME HERE?!
PEEK

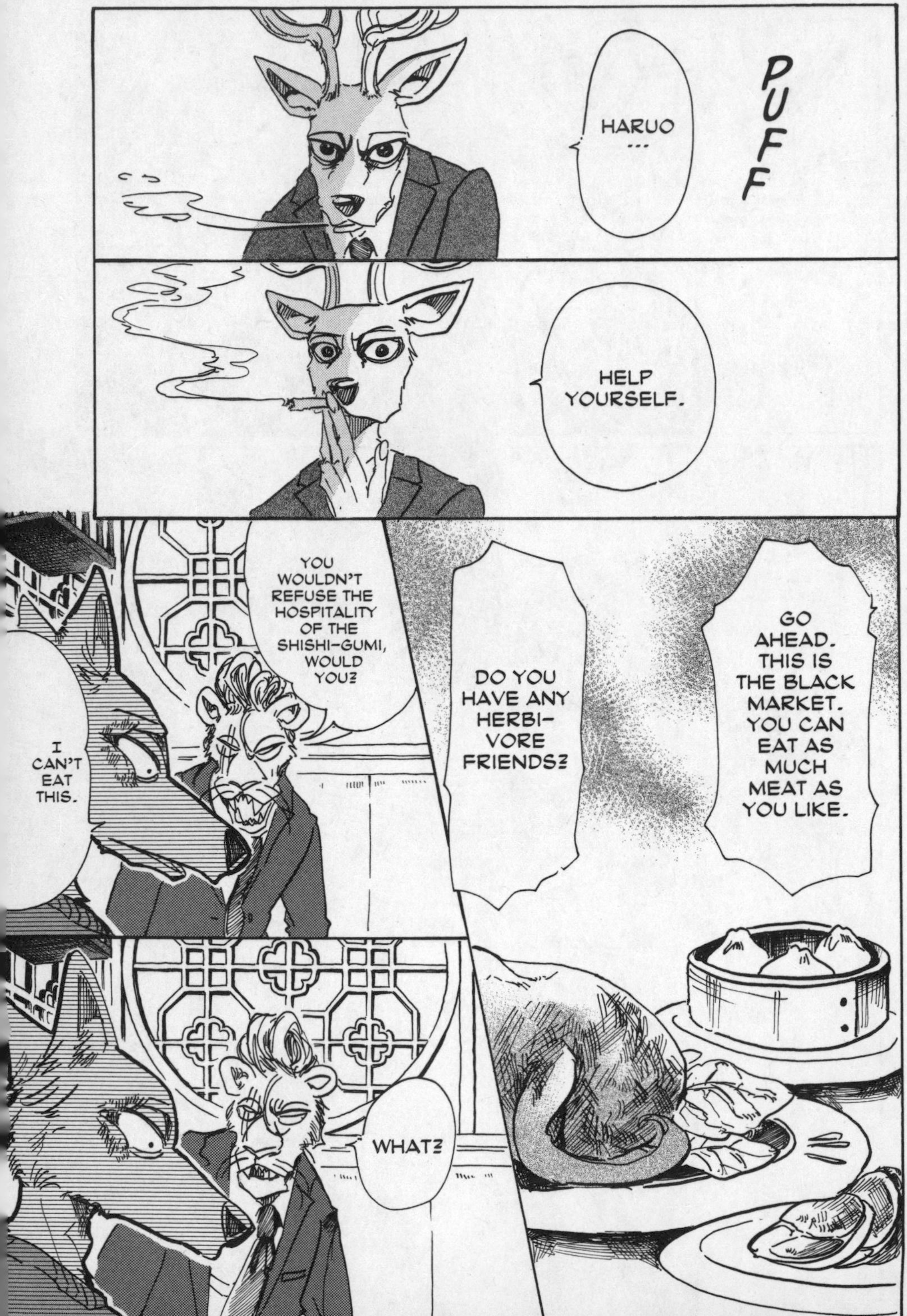
PUFF
HARUO...
HELP YOURSELF.
GO AHEAD. THIS IS THE BLACK MARKET. YOU CAN EAT AS MUCH MEAT AS YOU LIKE.
DO YOU HAVE ANY HERBI-VORE FRIENDS?
YOU WOULDN'T REFUSE THE HOSPITALITY OF THE SHISHI-GUMI, WOULD YOU?
I CAN'T EAT THIS.
WHAT?

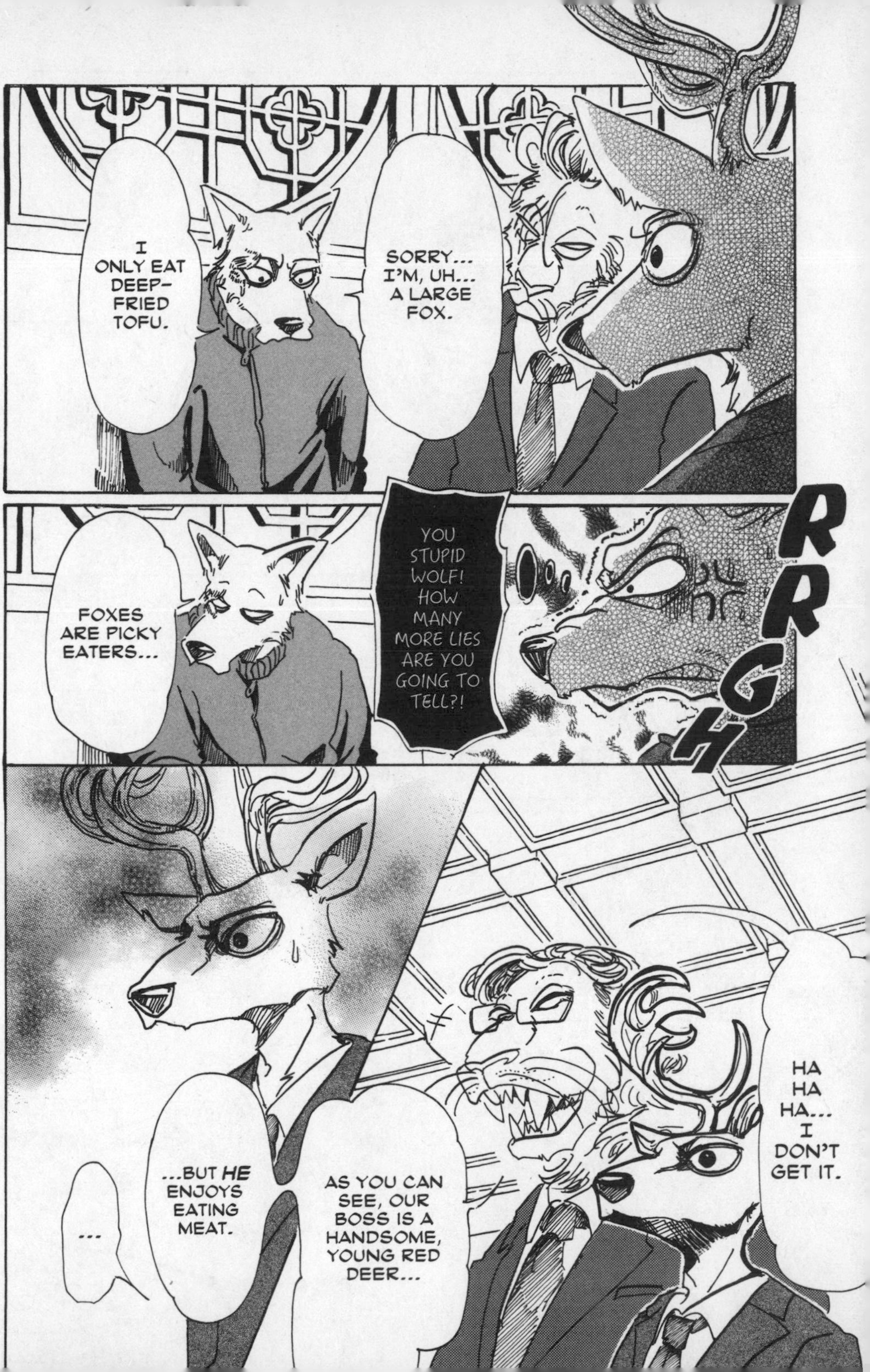
SORRY... I'M, UH... A LARGE FOX.
I ONLY EAT DEEP-FRIED TOFU.
RRRGH
YOU STUPID WOLF! HOW MANY MORE LIES ARE YOU GOING TO TELL?!
FOXES ARE PICKY EATERS...
HA HA HA... I DON'T GET IT.
AS YOU CAN SEE, OUR BOSS IS A HANDSOME, YOUNG RED DEER...
...BUT HE ENJOYS EATING MEAT.
...

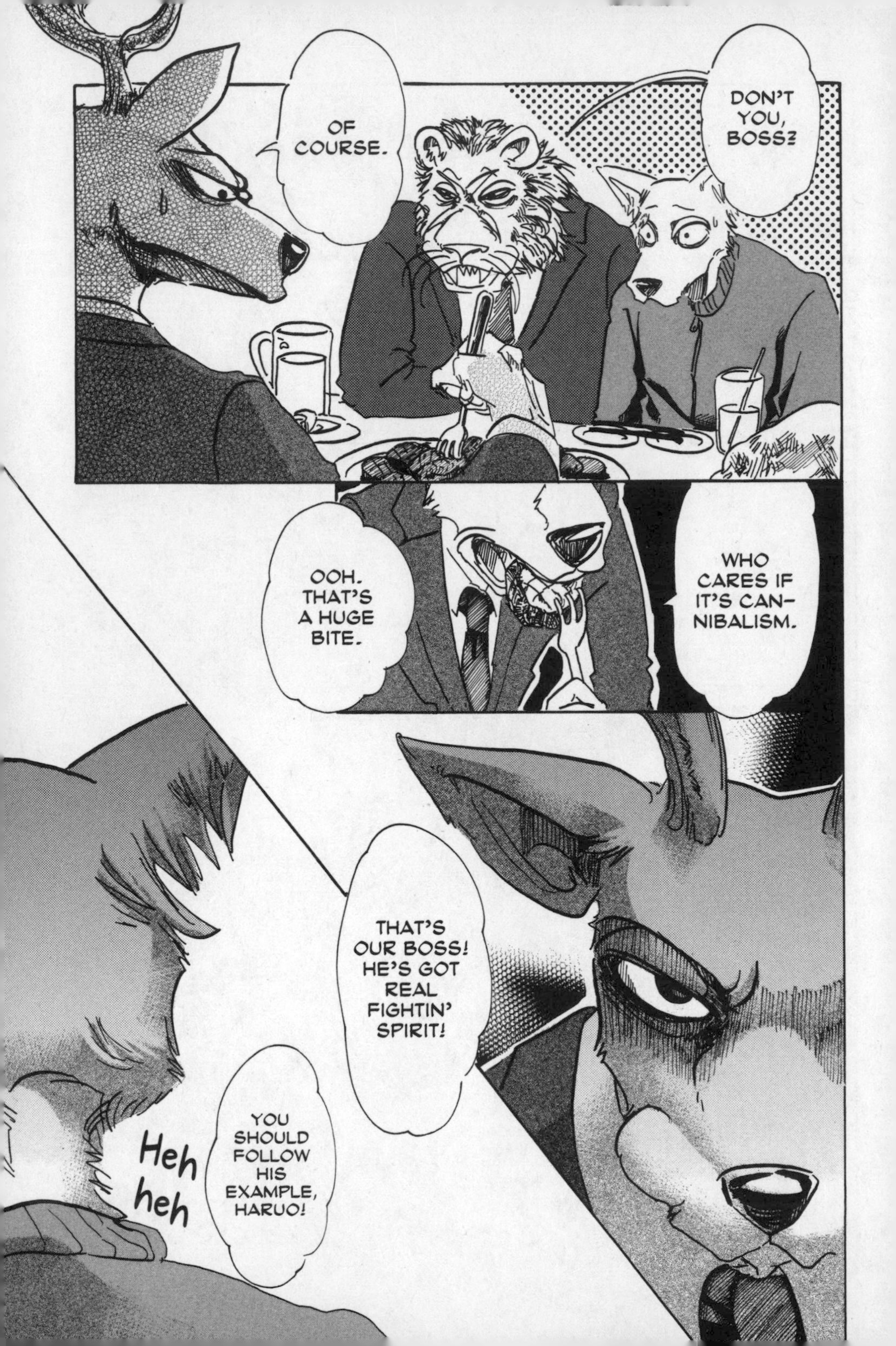
DON'T YOU, BOSS?
OF COURSE.
WHO CARES IF IT'S CAN-NIBALISM.
OOH. THAT'S A HUGE BITE.
THAT'S OUR BOSS! HE'S GOT REAL FIGHTIN' SPIRIT!
YOU SHOULD FOLLOW HIS EXAMPLE, HARUO!
Heh heh

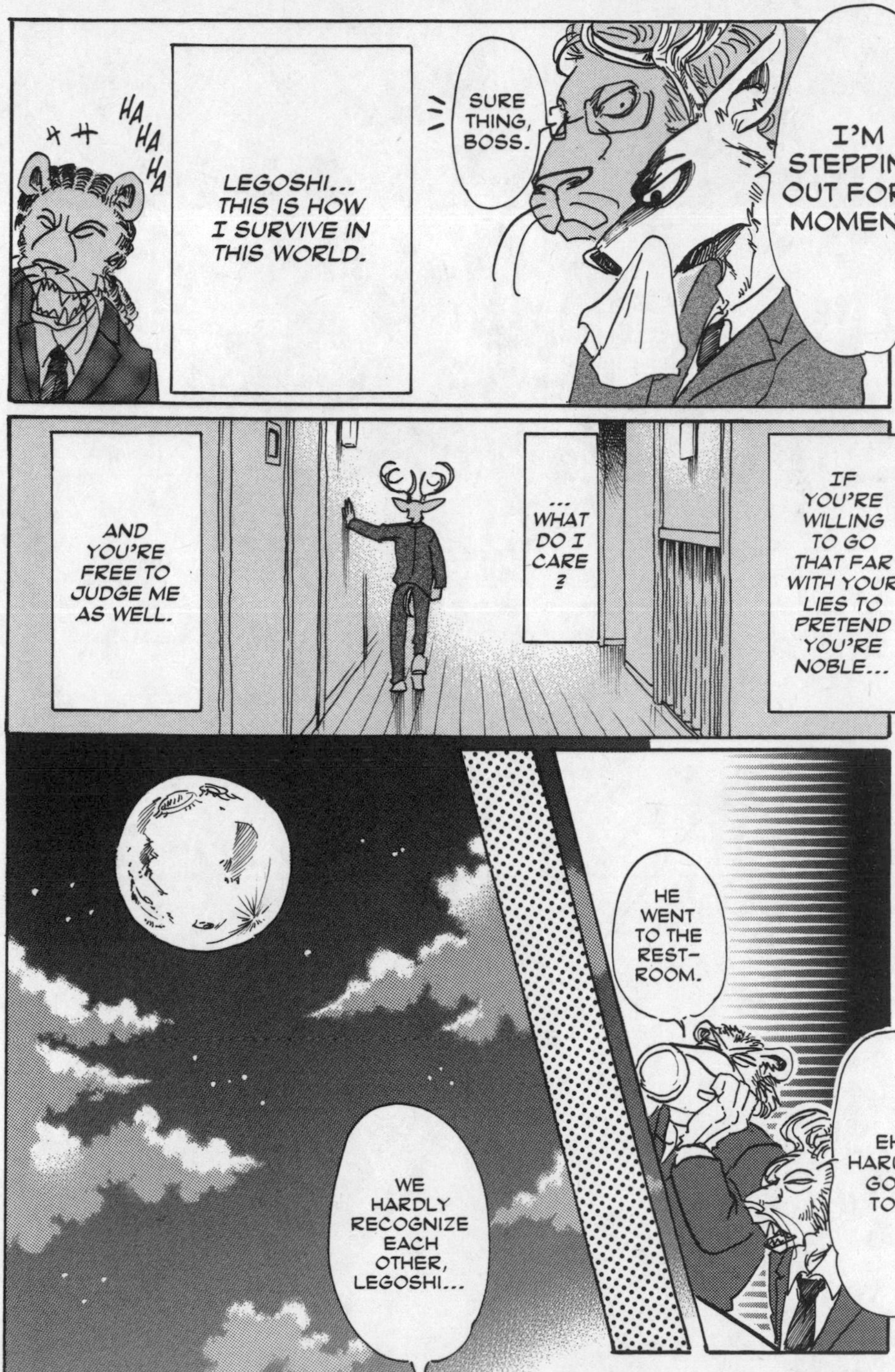
I'M STEPPING OUT FOR A MOMENT.
SURE THING, BOSS.
LEGOSHI... THIS IS HOW I SURVIVE IN THIS WORLD.
HAHAHAHA
IF YOU'RE WILLING TO GO THAT FAR WITH YOUR LIES TO PRETEND YOU'RE NOBLE...
...WHAT DO I CARE?
AND YOU'RE FREE TO JUDGE ME AS WELL.
EH? HARUO'S GONE TOO.
HE WENT TO THE REST-ROOM.
WE HARDLY RECOGNIZE EACH OTHER, LEGOSHI...

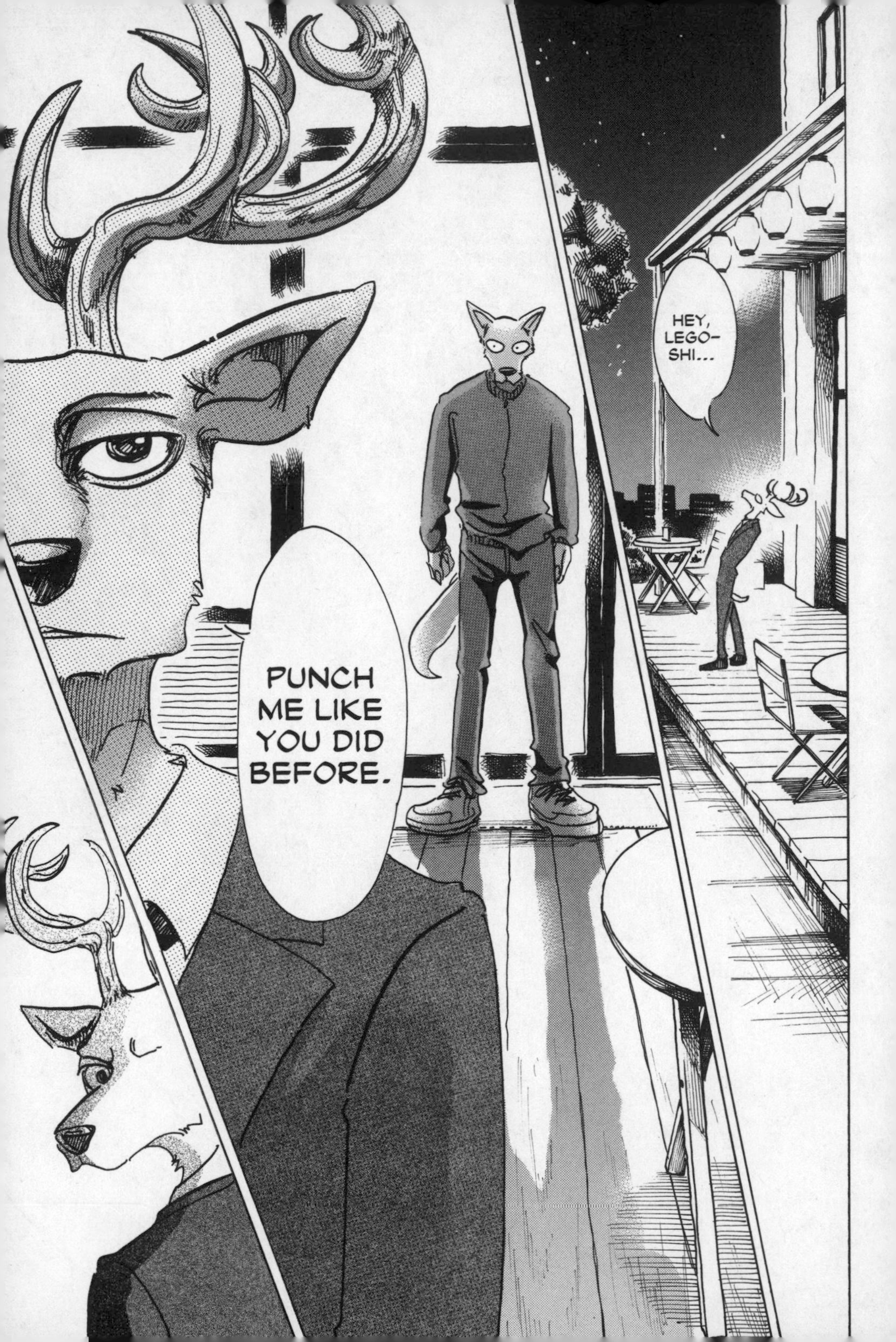
HEY, LEGO-SHI...
PUNCH ME LIKE YOU DID BEFORE.

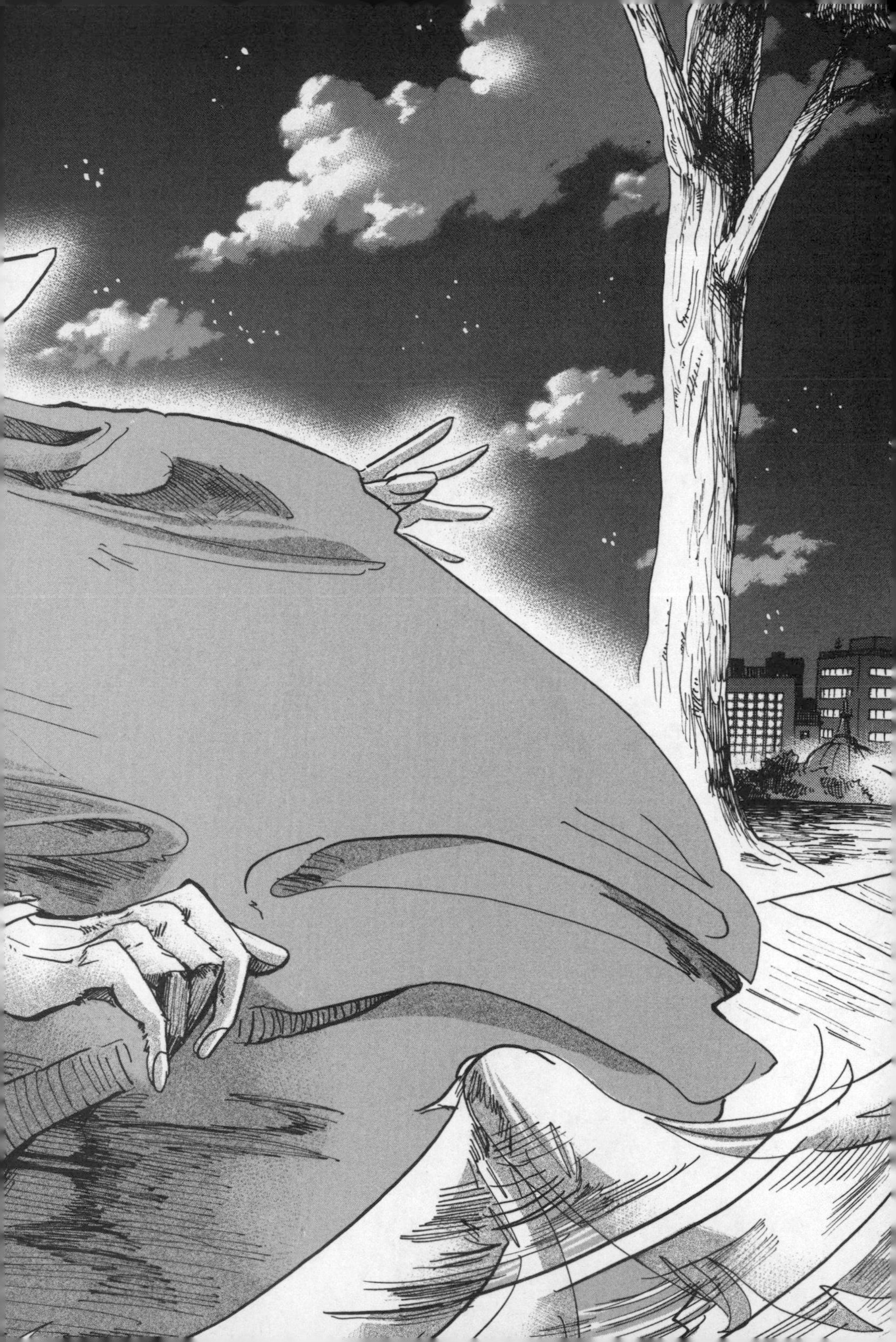

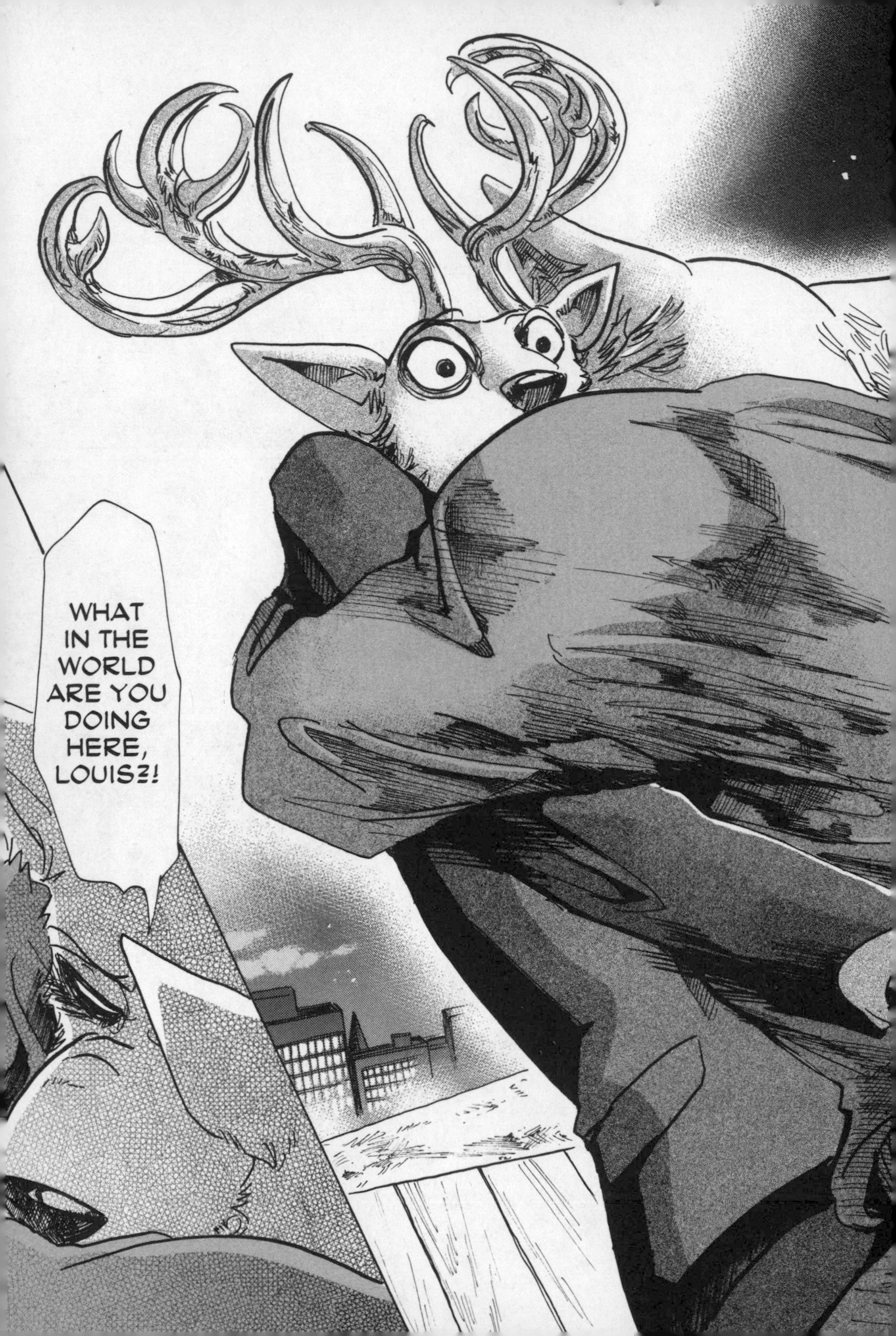
WHAT IN THE WORLD ARE YOU DOING HERE, LOUIS?!

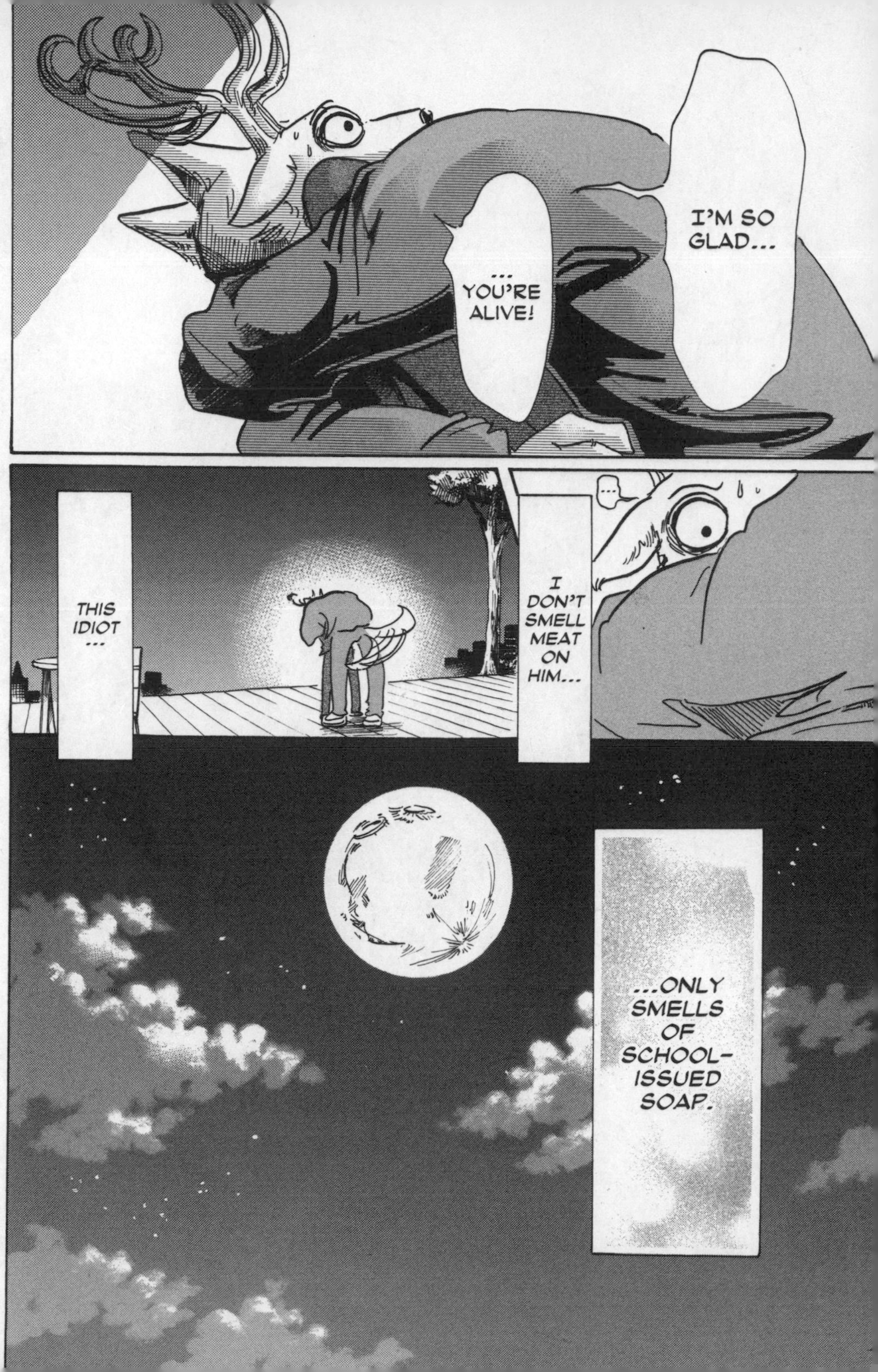
I'M SO GLAD...
...YOU'RE ALIVE!
...
I DON'T SMELL MEAT ON HIM...
THIS IDIOT ...
...ONLY SMELLS OF SCHOOL-ISSUED SOAP.

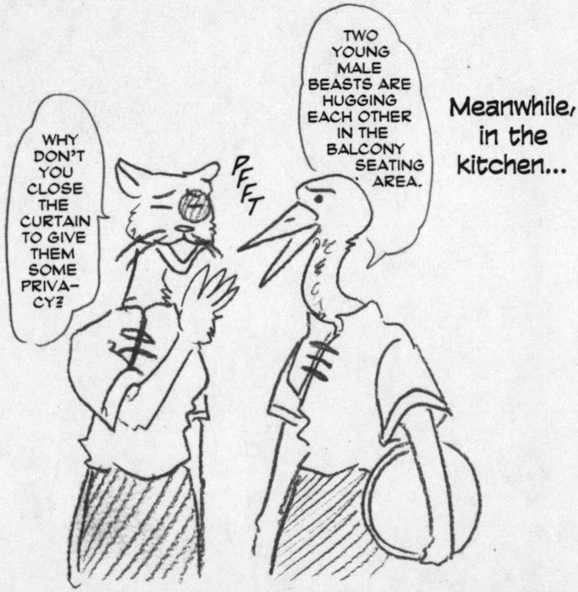
Meanwhile, in the kitchen...
TWO YOUNG MALE BEASTS ARE HUGGING EACH OTHER IN THE BALCONY SEATING AREA.
PFFT
WHY DON'T YOU CLOSE THE CURTAIN TO GIVE THEM SOME PRIVA-CY?

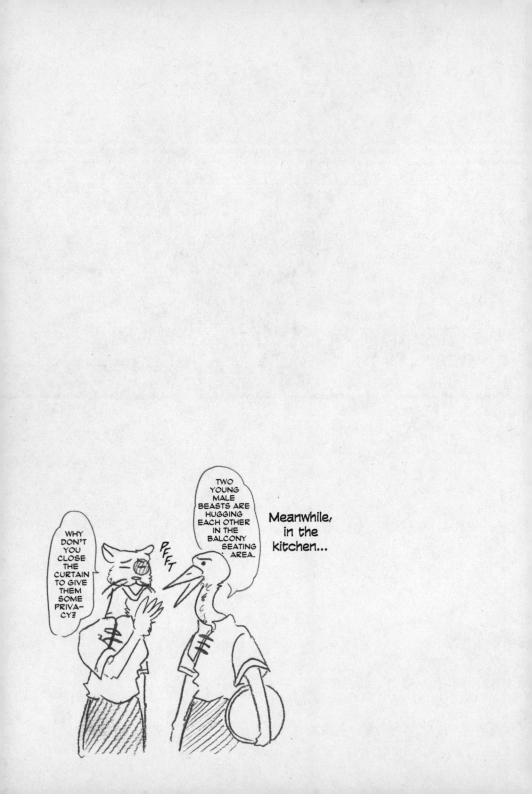

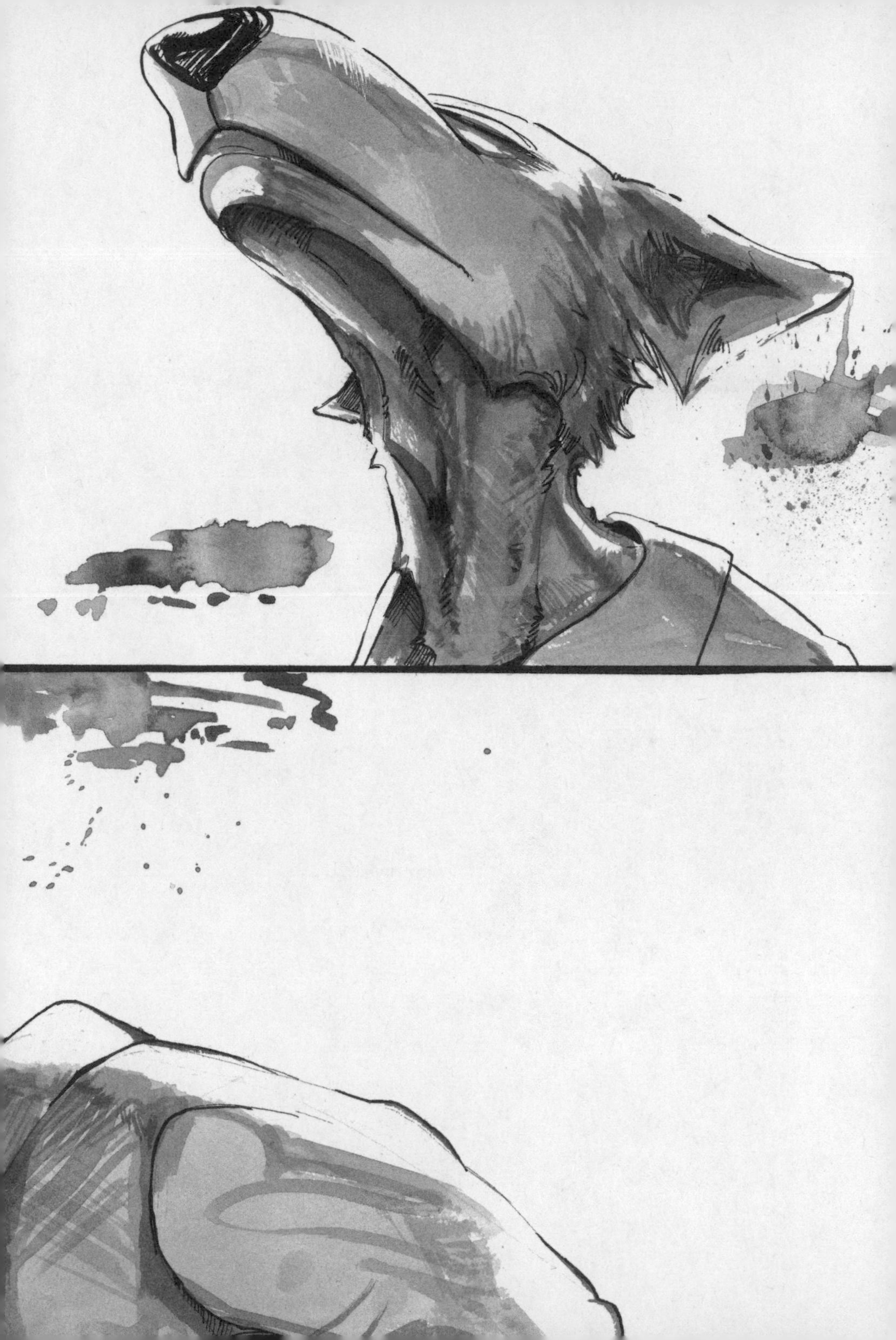

Chapter 76: Rhapsody of Requesting the Impossible

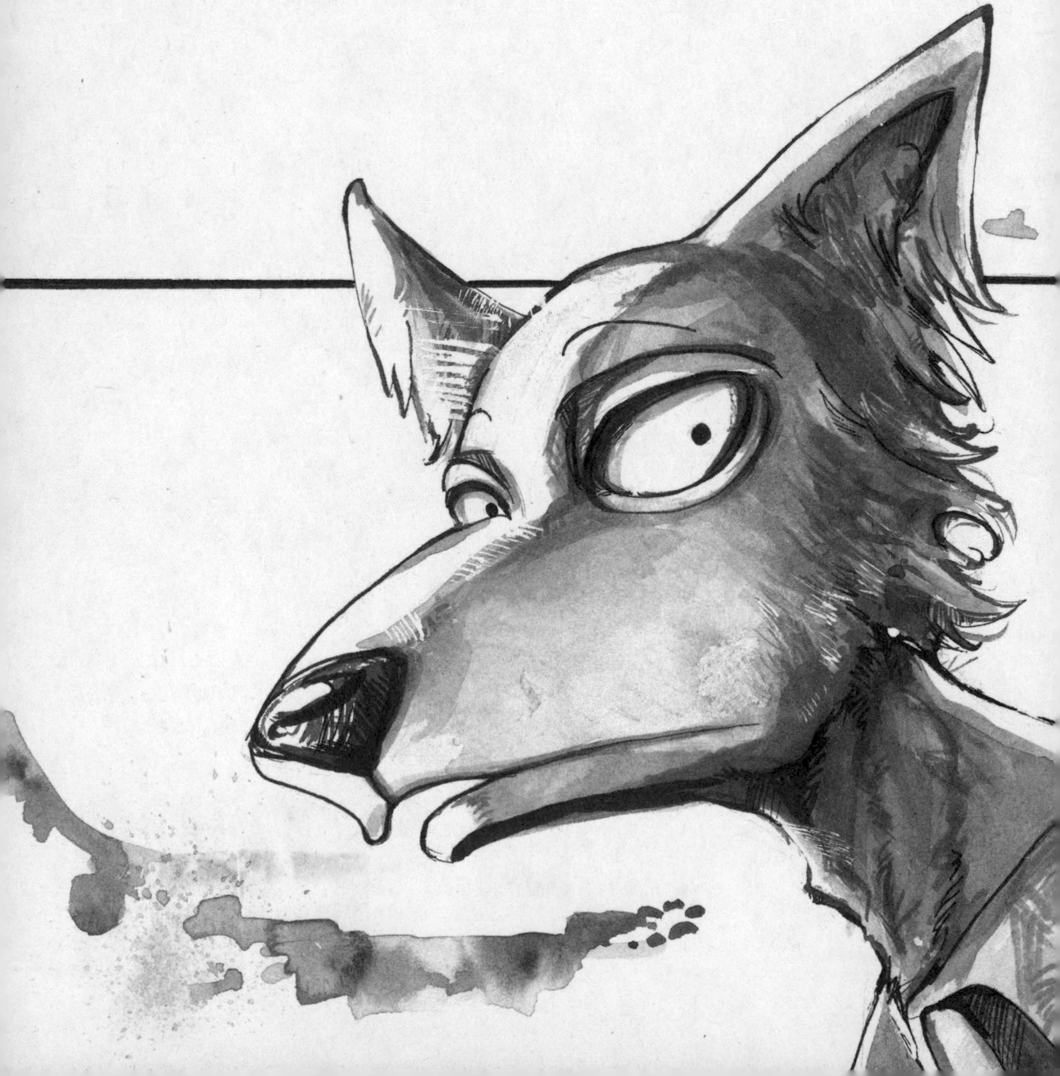

BEASTARS
Vol. 9

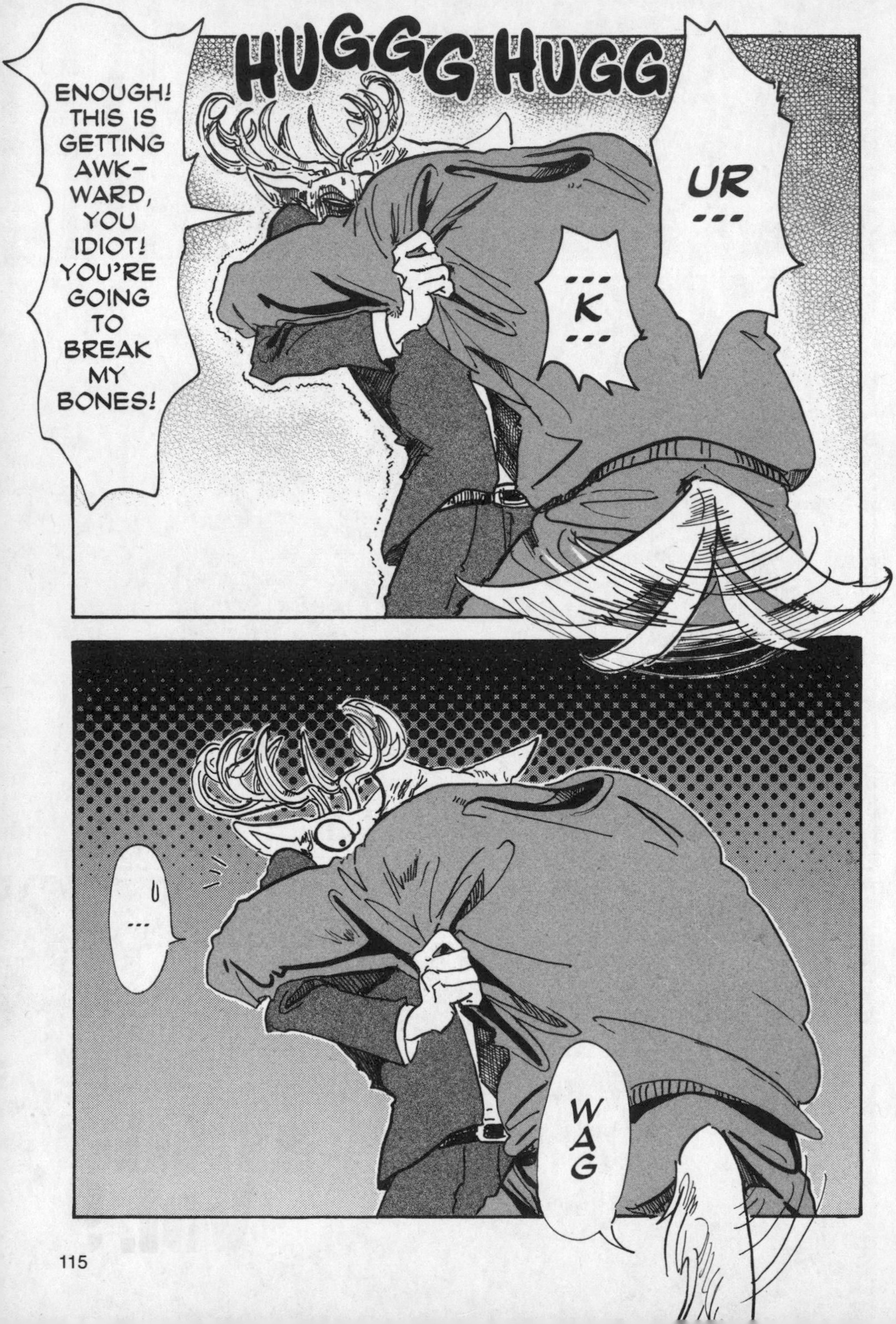
UR ---
HUGGG HUGG
--- K ---
ENOUGH! THIS IS GETTING AWK-WARD, YOU IDIOT! YOU'RE GOING TO BREAK MY BONES!
WAG
U ...

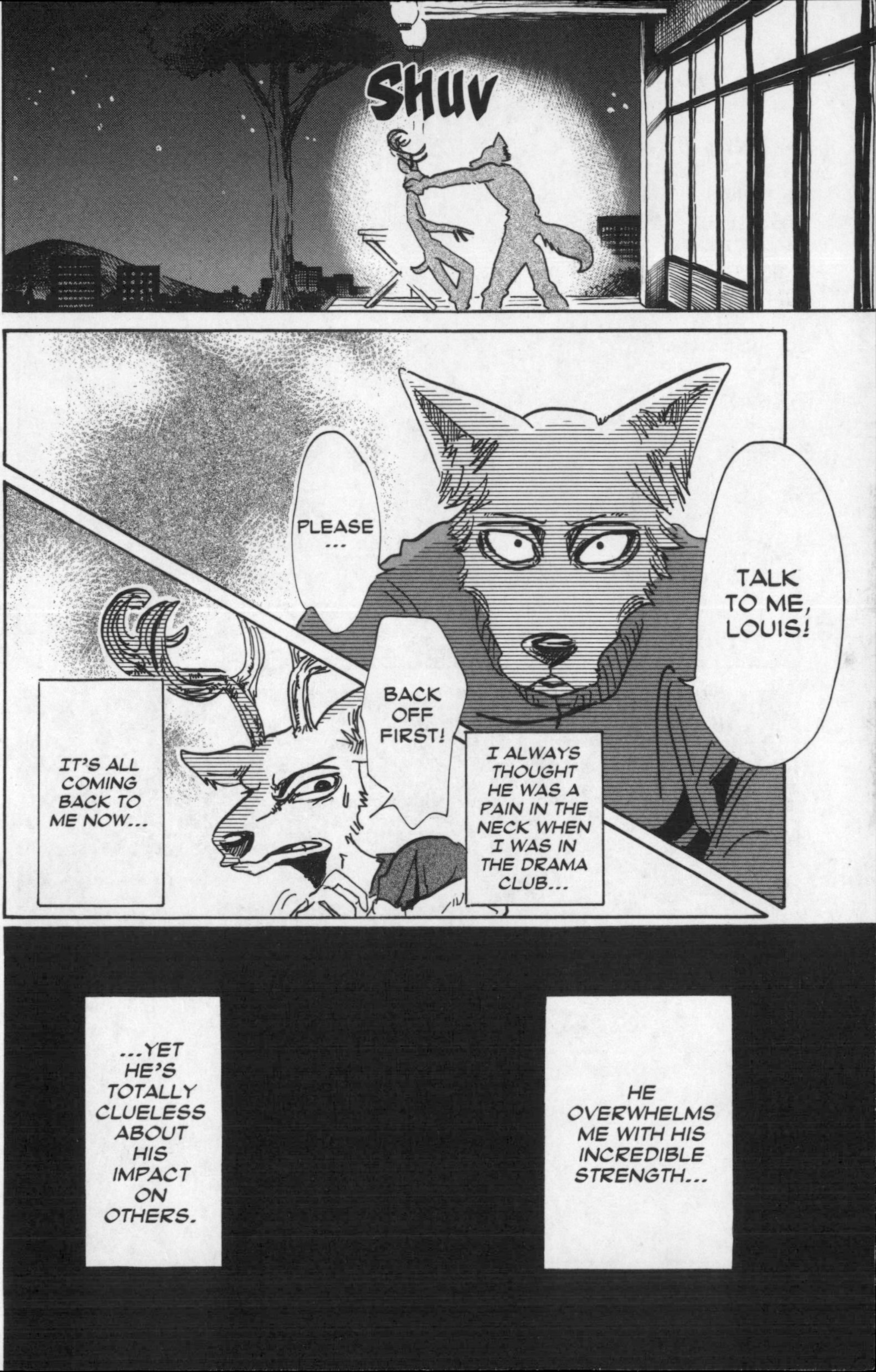
SHUV
TALK TO ME, LOUIS!
PLEASE...
BACK OFF FIRST!
I ALWAYS THOUGHT HE WAS A PAIN IN THE NECK WHEN I WAS IN THE DRAMA CLUB...
IT'S ALL COMING BACK TO ME NOW...
HE OVERWHELMS ME WITH HIS INCREDIBLE STRENGTH...
...YET HE'S TOTALLY CLUELESS ABOUT HIS IMPACT ON OTHERS.

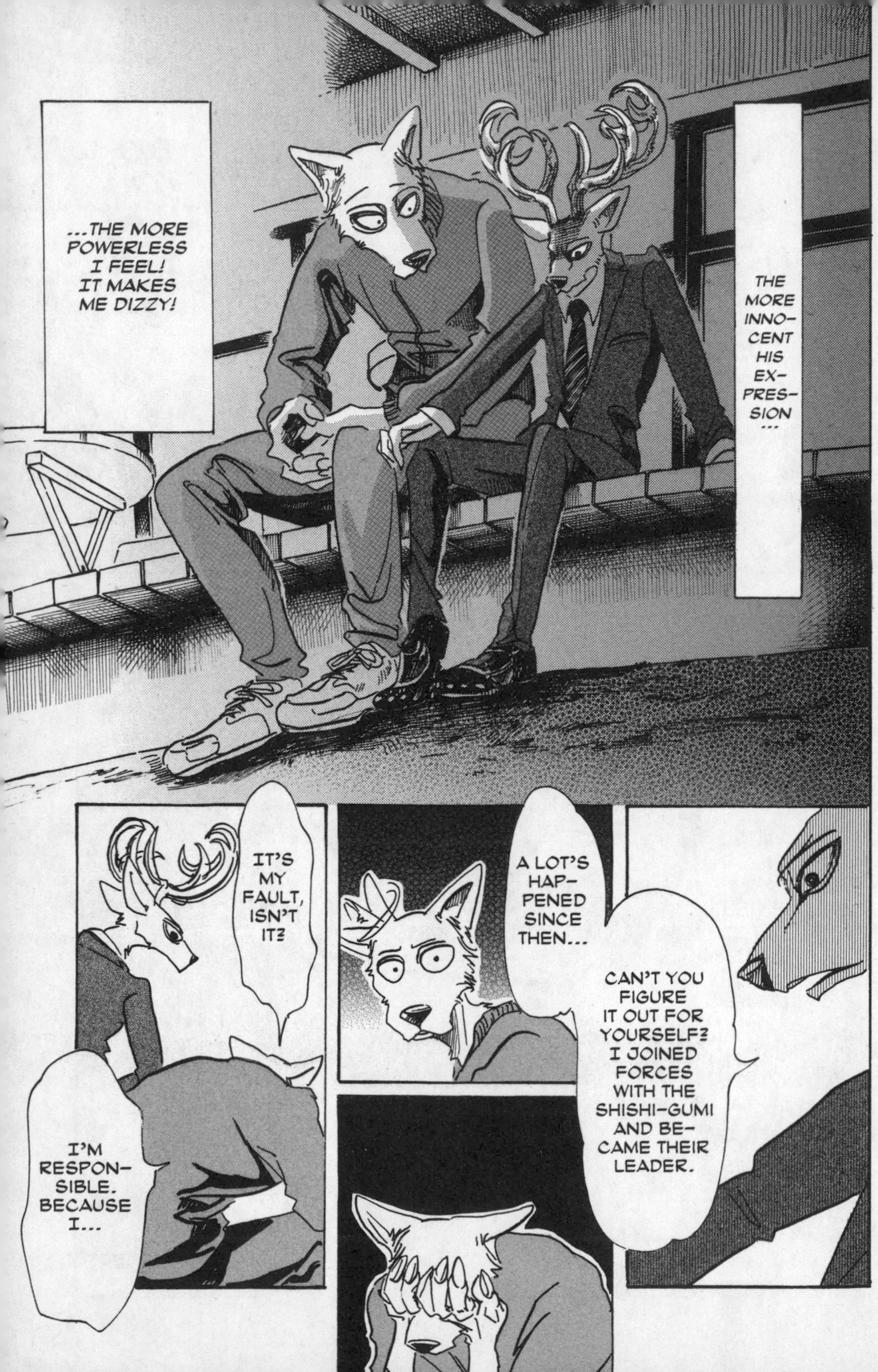

THE MORE INNOCENT HIS EXPRESSION...
...THE MORE POWERLESS I FEEL! IT MAKES ME DIZZY!
A LOT'S HAPPENED SINCE THEN...
CAN'T YOU FIGURE IT OUT FOR YOURSELF? I JOINED FORCES WITH THE SHISHI-GUMI AND BECAME THEIR LEADER.
IT'S MY FAULT, ISN'T IT?
I'M RESPONSIBLE. BECAUSE I...

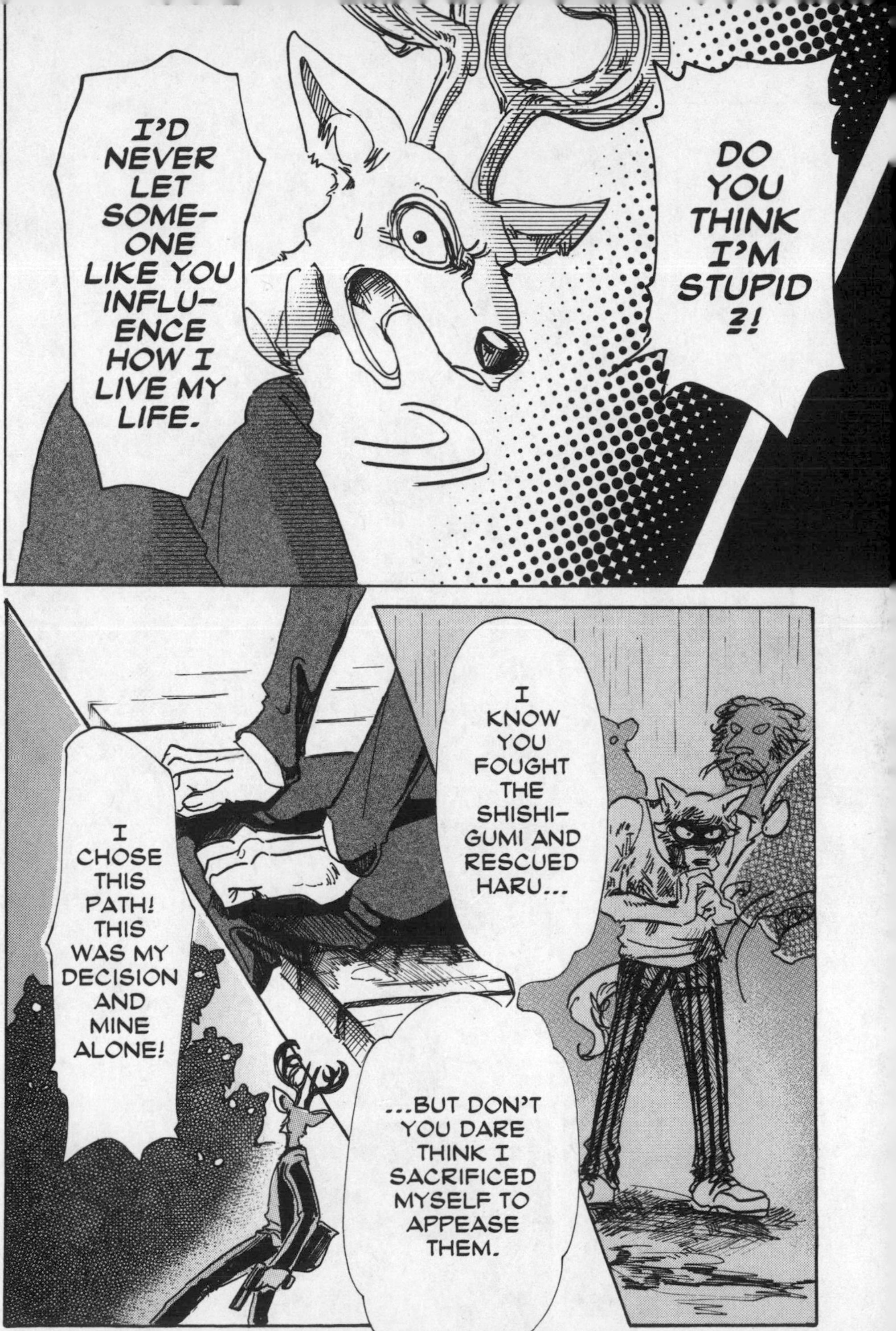
DO YOU THINK I'M STUPID?!
I'D NEVER LET SOME-ONE LIKE YOU INFLU-ENCE HOW I LIVE MY LIFE.
I KNOW YOU FOUGHT THE SHISHI-GUMI AND RESCUED HARU...
...BUT DON'T YOU DARE THINK I SACRIFICED MYSELF TO APPEASE THEM.
I CHOSE THIS PATH! THIS WAS MY DECISION AND MINE ALONE!

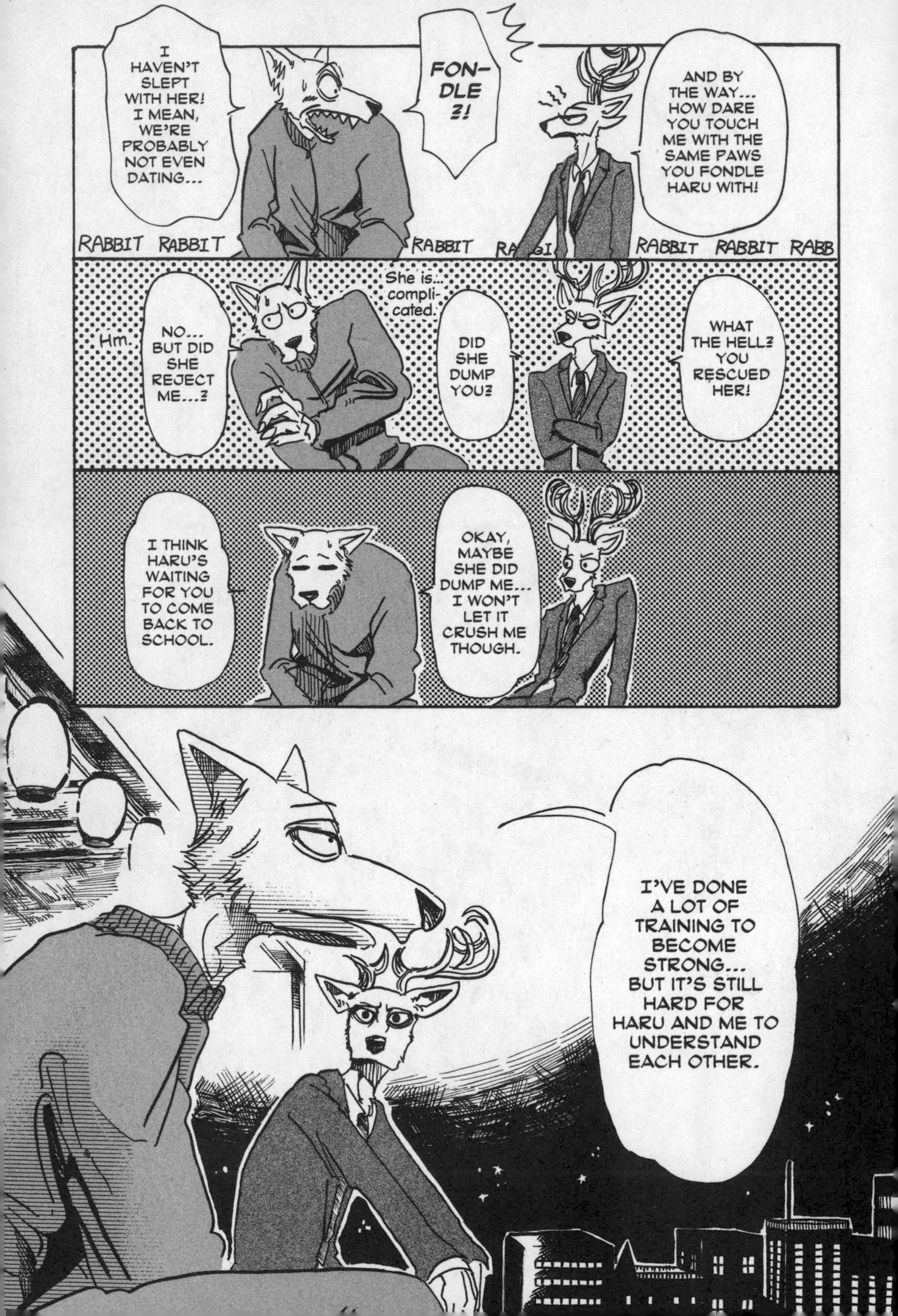
AND BY THE WAY... HOW DARE YOU TOUCH ME WITH THE SAME PAWS YOU FONDLE HARU WITH!
FON-DLE?!
I HAVEN'T SLEPT WITH HER! I MEAN, WE'RE PROBABLY NOT EVEN DATING...
RABBIT RABBIT RABBIT RABGI RABBIT RABBIT RABB
WHAT THE HELL? YOU RESCUED HER!
DID SHE DUMP YOU?
She is... compli-cated.
NO... BUT DID SHE REJECT ME...?
Hm.
OKAY, MAYBE SHE DID DUMP ME... I WON'T LET IT CRUSH ME THOUGH.
I THINK HARU'S WAITING FOR YOU TO COME BACK TO SCHOOL.
I'VE DONE A LOT OF TRAINING TO BECOME STRONG... BUT IT'S STILL HARD FOR HARU AND ME TO UNDERSTAND EACH OTHER.

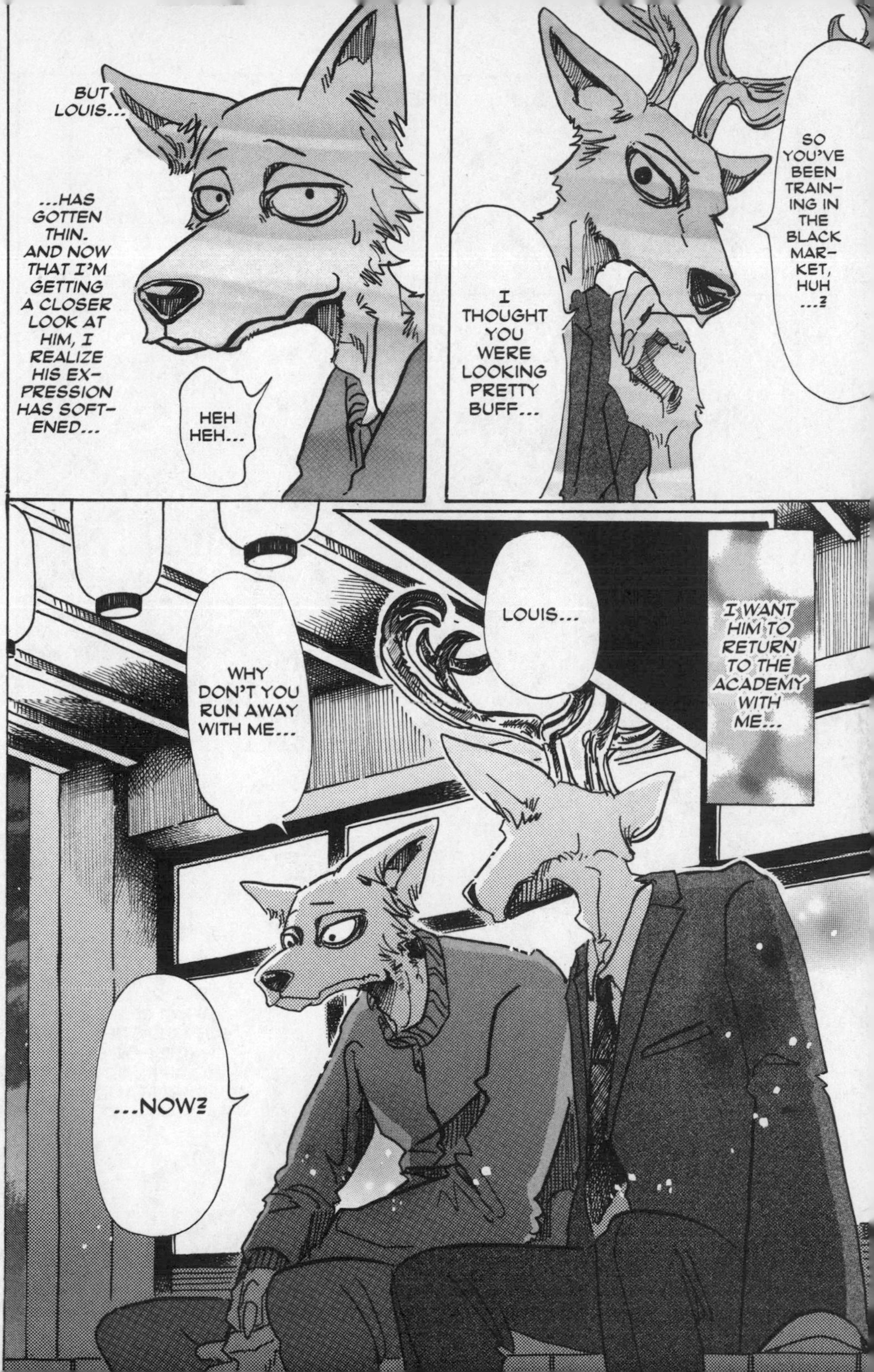
SO YOU'VE BEEN TRAINING IN THE BLACK MARKET, HUH...?
I THOUGHT YOU WERE LOOKING PRETTY BUFF...
BUT LOUIS...
...HAS GOTTEN THIN. AND NOW THAT I'M GETTING A CLOSER LOOK AT HIM, I REALIZE HIS EXPRESSION HAS SOFTENED...
HEH HEH...
I WANT HIM TO RETURN TO THE ACADEMY WITH ME...
LOUIS...
WHY DON'T YOU RUN AWAY WITH ME...
...NOW?

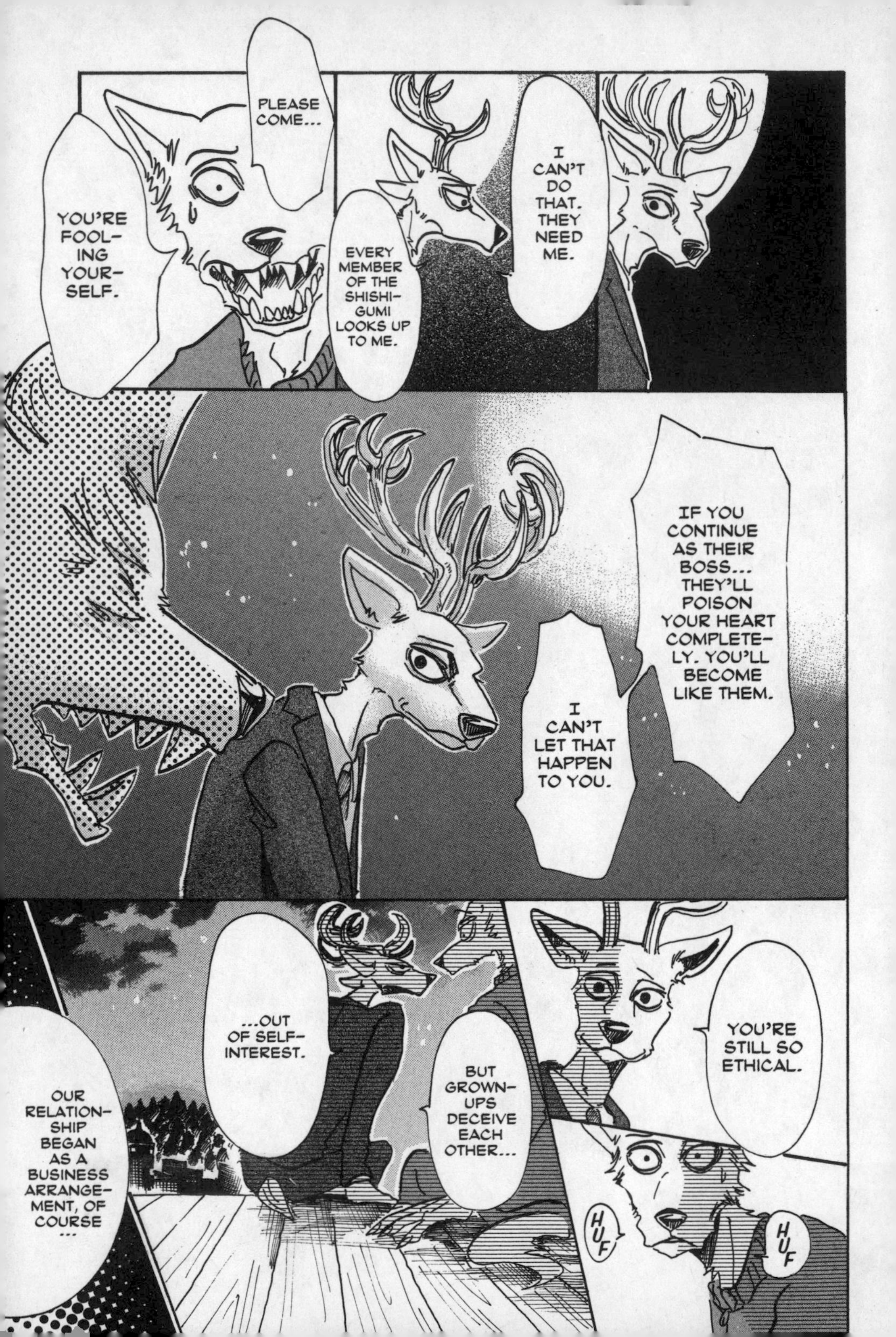
I CAN'T DO THAT. THEY NEED ME.
EVERY MEMBER OF THE SHISHI-GUMI LOOKS UP TO ME.
PLEASE COME...
YOU'RE FOOL-ING YOUR-SELF.
IF YOU CONTINUE AS THEIR BOSS... THEY'LL POISON YOUR HEART COMPLETE-LY. YOU'LL BECOME LIKE THEM.
I CAN'T LET THAT HAPPEN TO YOU.
YOU'RE STILL SO ETHICAL.
HUF
HUF
BUT GROWN-UPS DECEIVE EACH OTHER...
...OUT OF SELF-INTEREST.
OUR RELATION-SHIP BEGAN AS A BUSINESS ARRANGE-MENT, OF COURSE...

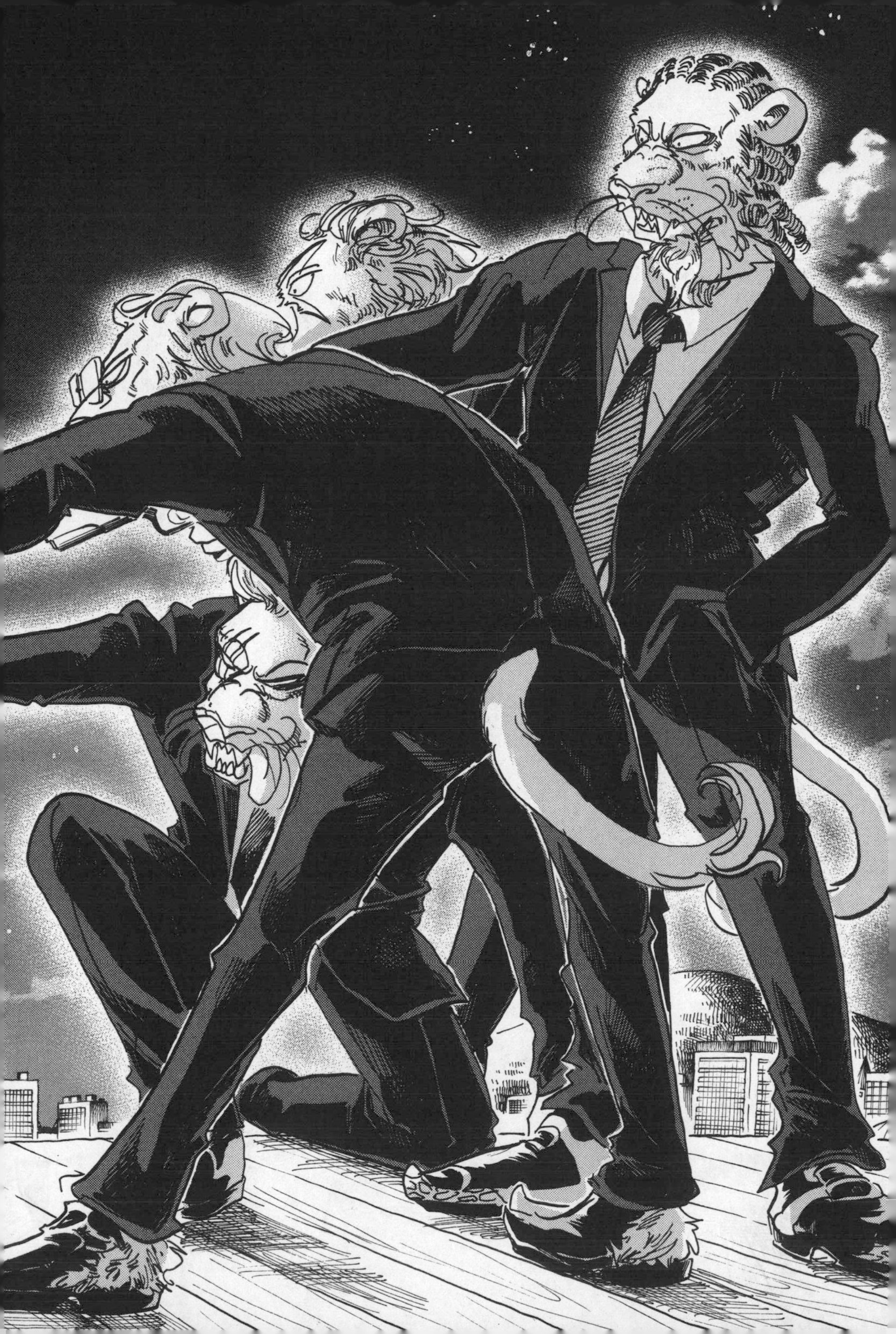

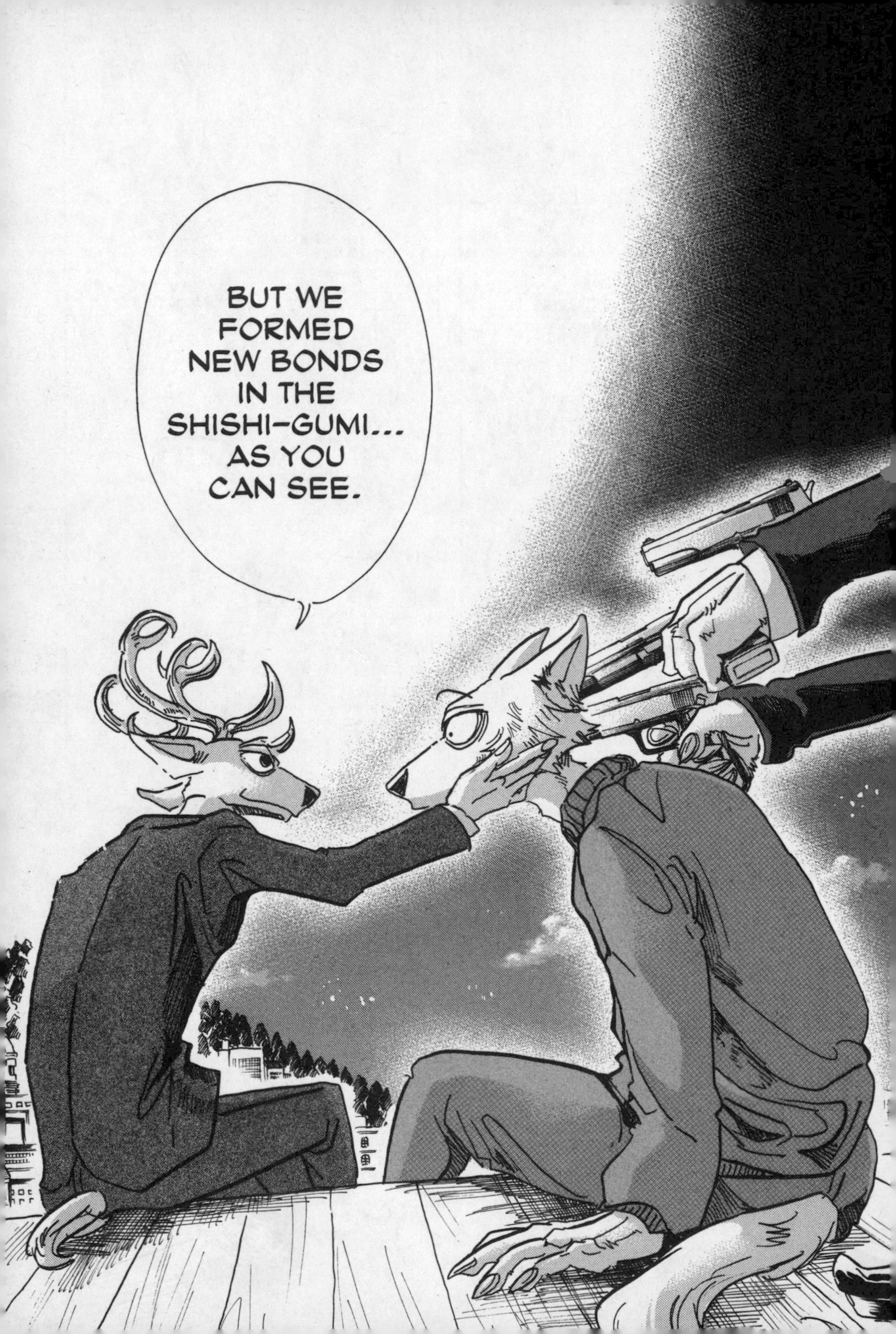
BUT WE FORMED NEW BONDS IN THE SHISHI-GUMI... AS YOU CAN SEE.

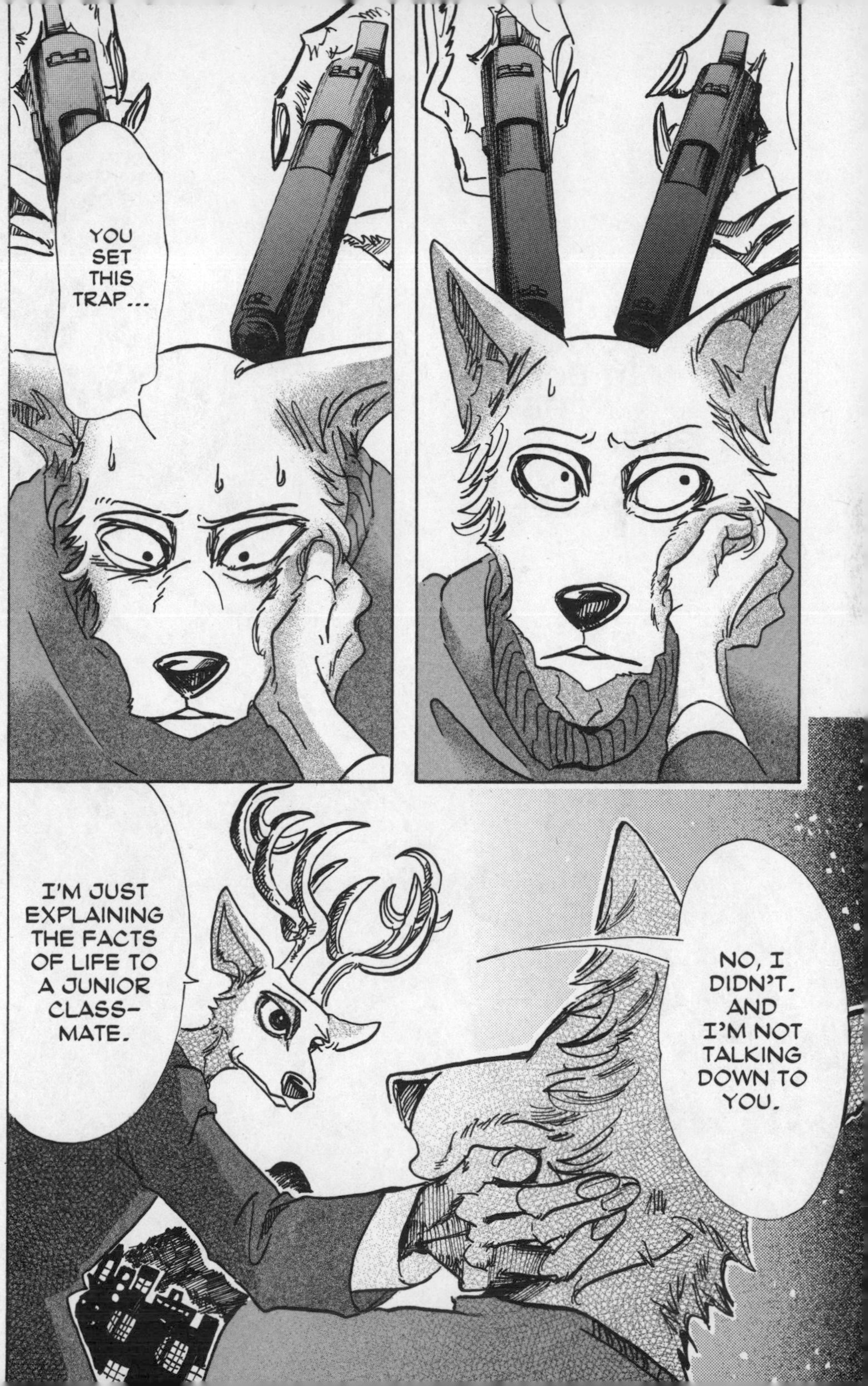
YOU SET THIS TRAP...
NO, I DIDN'T. AND I'M NOT TALKING DOWN TO YOU.
I'M JUST EXPLAINING THE FACTS OF LIFE TO A JUNIOR CLASS-MATE.

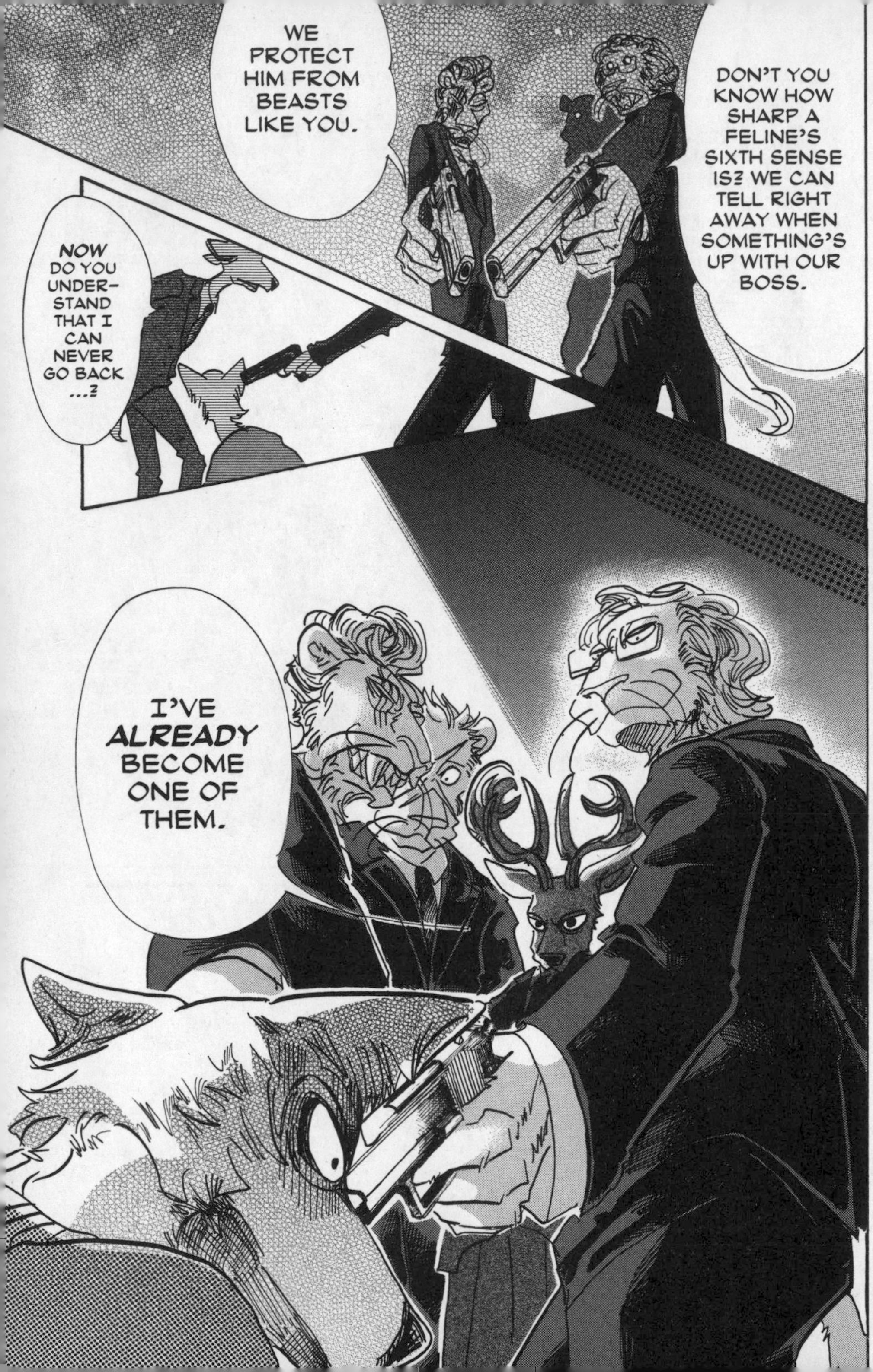
DON'T YOU KNOW HOW SHARP A FELINE'S SIXTH SENSE IS? WE CAN TELL RIGHT AWAY WHEN SOMETHING'S UP WITH OUR BOSS.
WE PROTECT HIM FROM BEASTS LIKE YOU.
NOW DO YOU UNDERSTAND THAT I CAN NEVER GO BACK ...?
I'VE *ALREADY* BECOME ONE OF THEM.

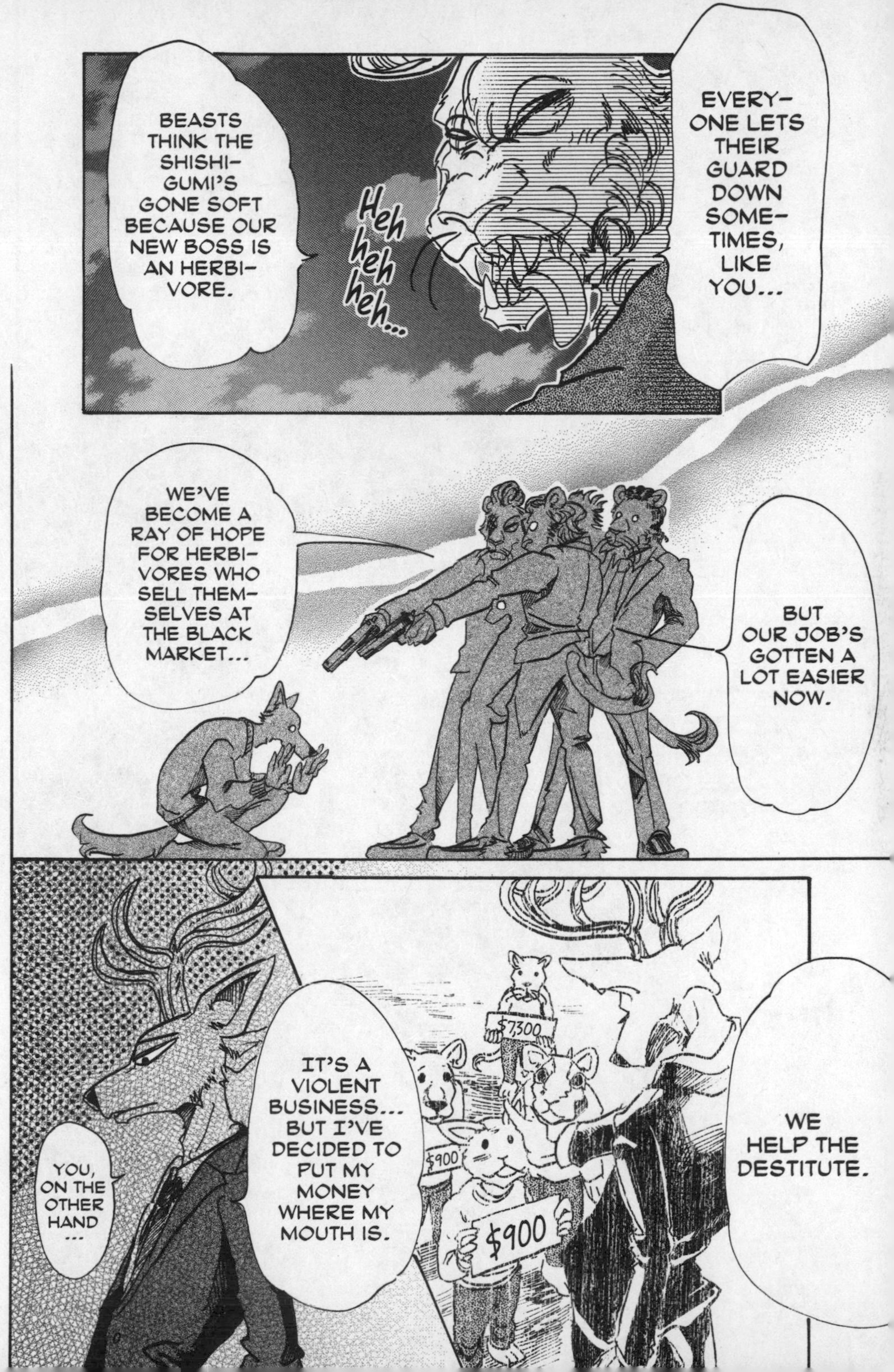
EVERYONE LETS THEIR GUARD DOWN SOMETIMES, LIKE YOU...
Heh heh heh...
BEASTS THINK THE SHISHIGUMI'S GONE SOFT BECAUSE OUR NEW BOSS IS AN HERBIVORE.
BUT OUR JOB'S GOTTEN A LOT EASIER NOW.
WE'VE BECOME A RAY OF HOPE FOR HERBIVORES WHO SELL THEMSELVES AT THE BLACK MARKET...
WE HELP THE DESTITUTE.
$7,300
$900
$900
IT'S A VIOLENT BUSINESS... BUT I'VE DECIDED TO PUT MY MONEY WHERE MY MOUTH IS.
YOU, ON THE OTHER HAND...

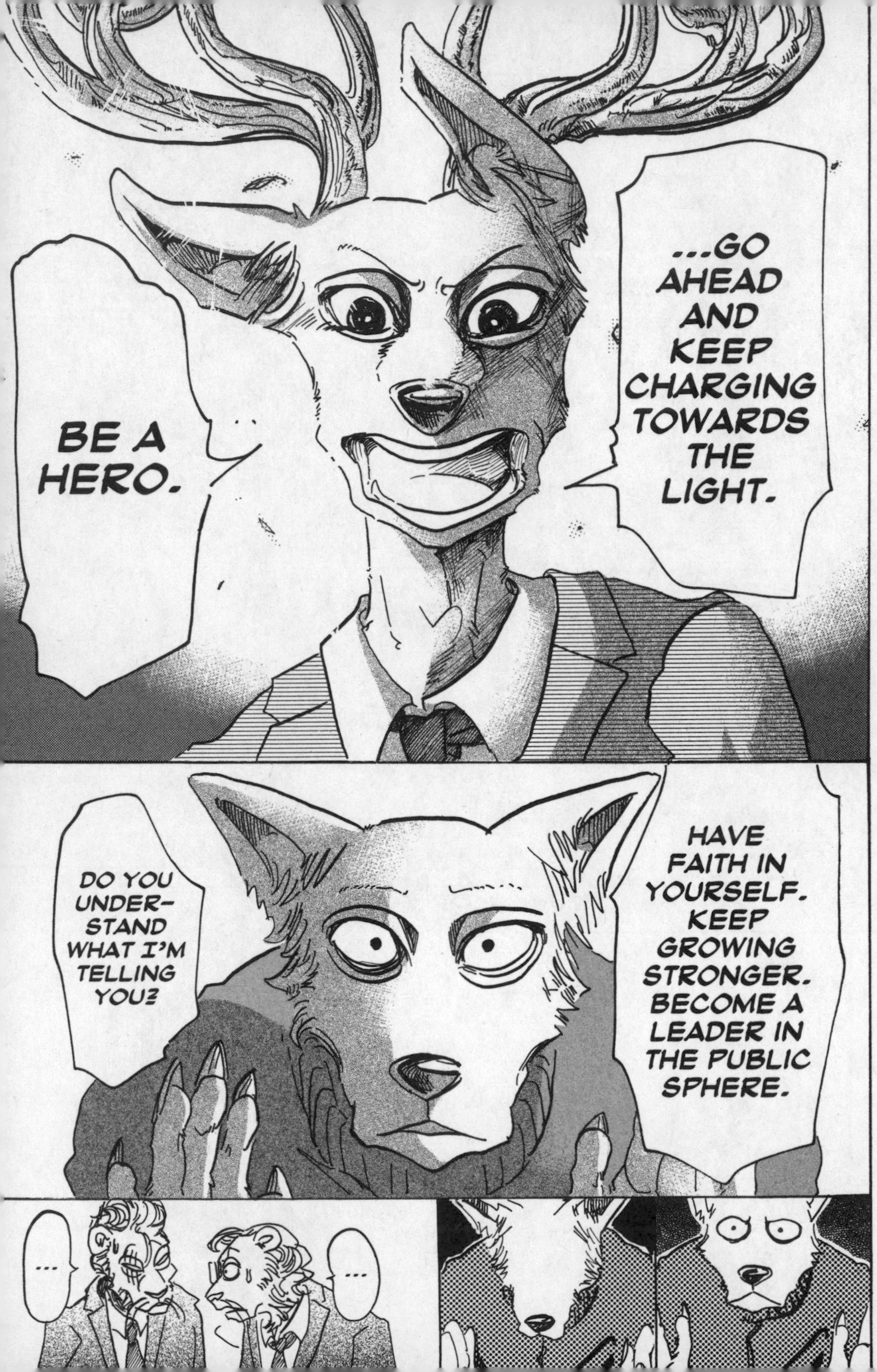
...GO AHEAD AND KEEP CHARGING TOWARDS THE LIGHT.
BE A HERO.
HAVE FAITH IN YOURSELF. KEEP GROWING STRONGER. BECOME A LEADER IN THE PUBLIC SPHERE.
DO YOU UNDER-STAND WHAT I'M TELLING YOU?
...
...

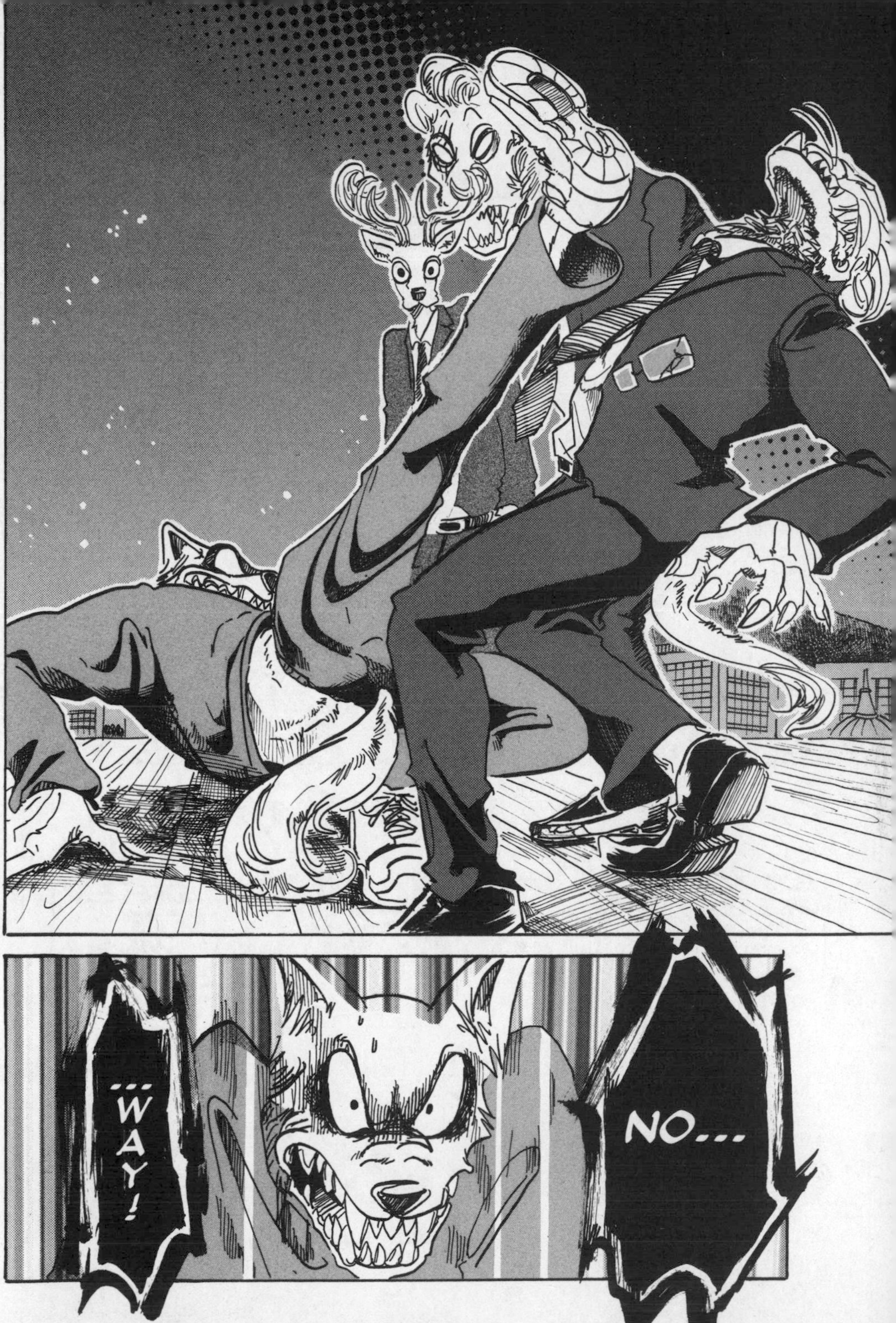
NO...
...WAY!

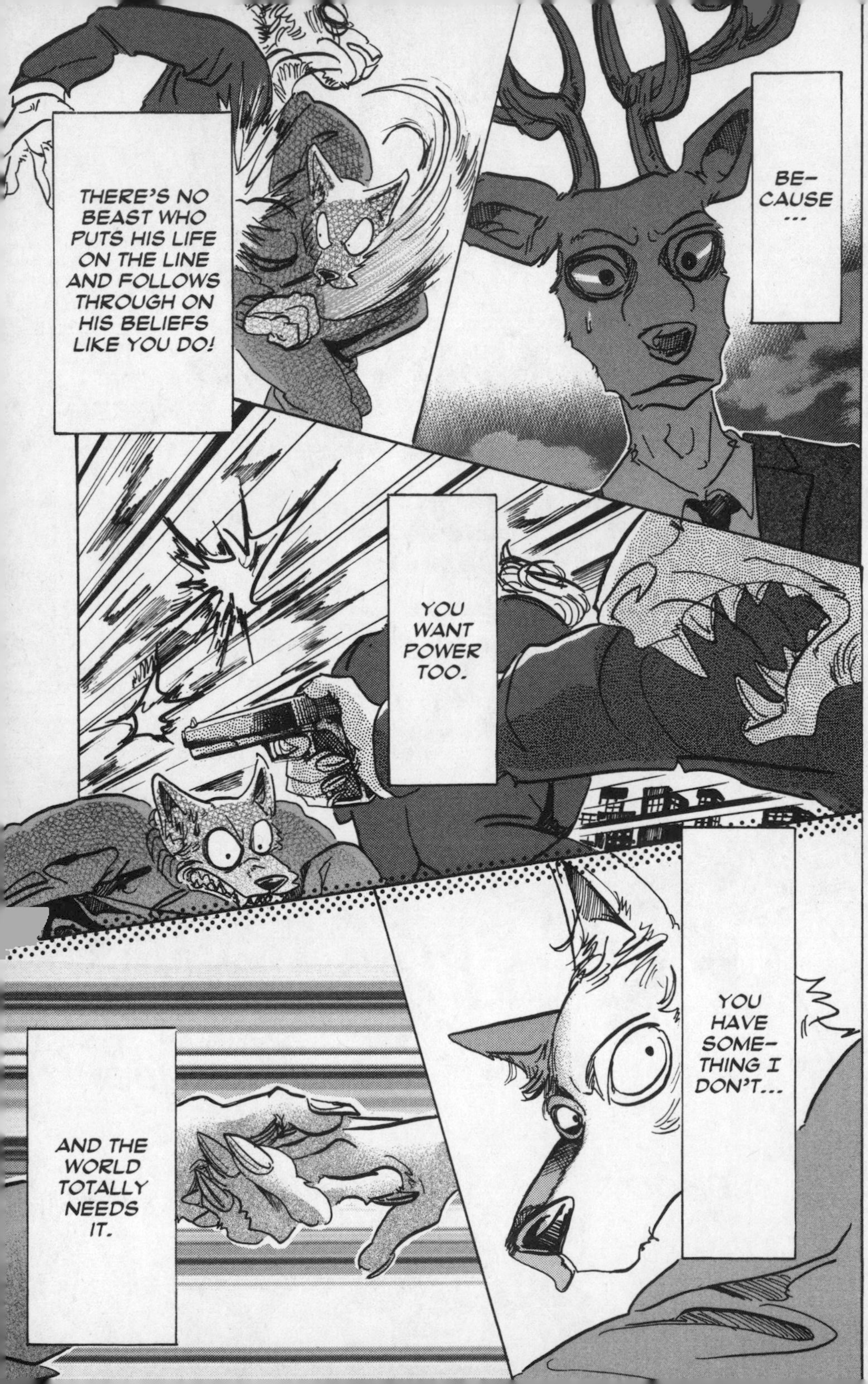

BE-CAUSE...
THERE'S NO BEAST WHO PUTS HIS LIFE ON THE LINE AND FOLLOWS THROUGH ON HIS BELIEFS LIKE YOU DO!
YOU WANT POWER TOO.
YOU HAVE SOME-THING I DON'T...
AND THE WORLD TOTALLY NEEDS IT.

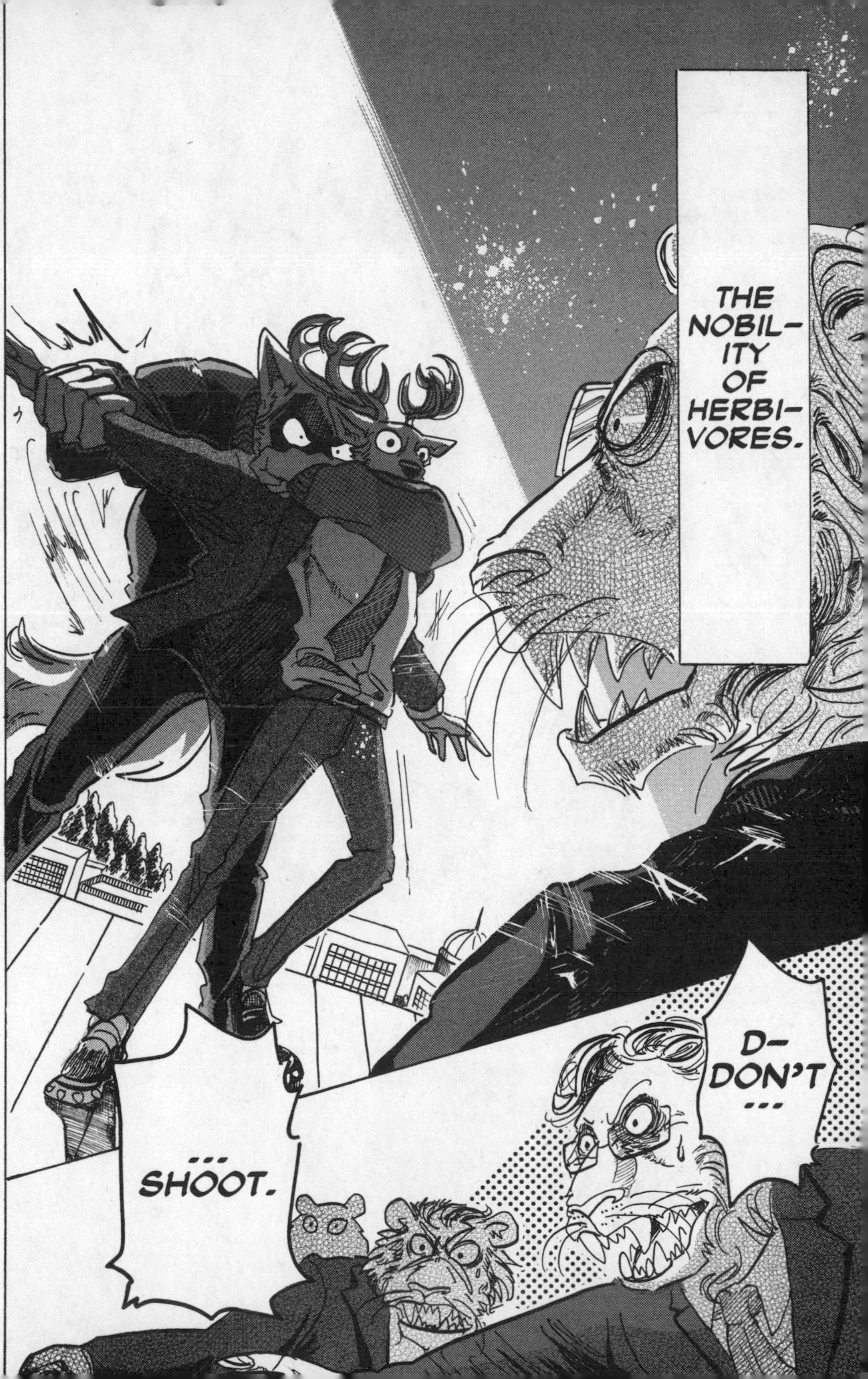
THE NOBIL-ITY OF HERBI-VORES.
D-DON'T ...
... SHOOT.

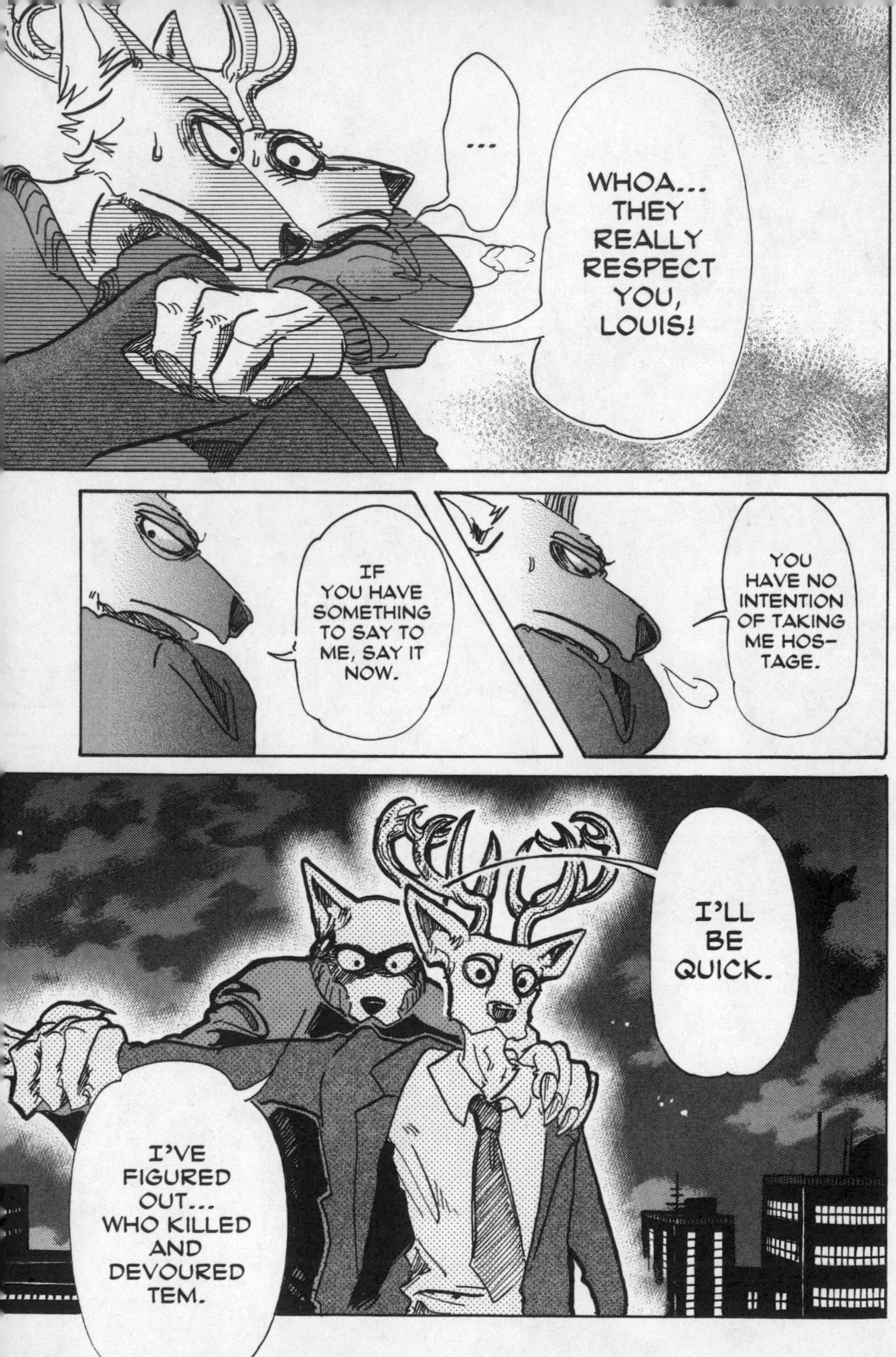
WHOA... THEY REALLY RESPECT YOU, LOUIS!
...
YOU HAVE NO INTENTION OF TAKING ME HOS-TAGE.
IF YOU HAVE SOMETHING TO SAY TO ME, SAY IT NOW.
I'LL BE QUICK.
I'VE FIGURED OUT... WHO KILLED AND DEVOURED TEM.

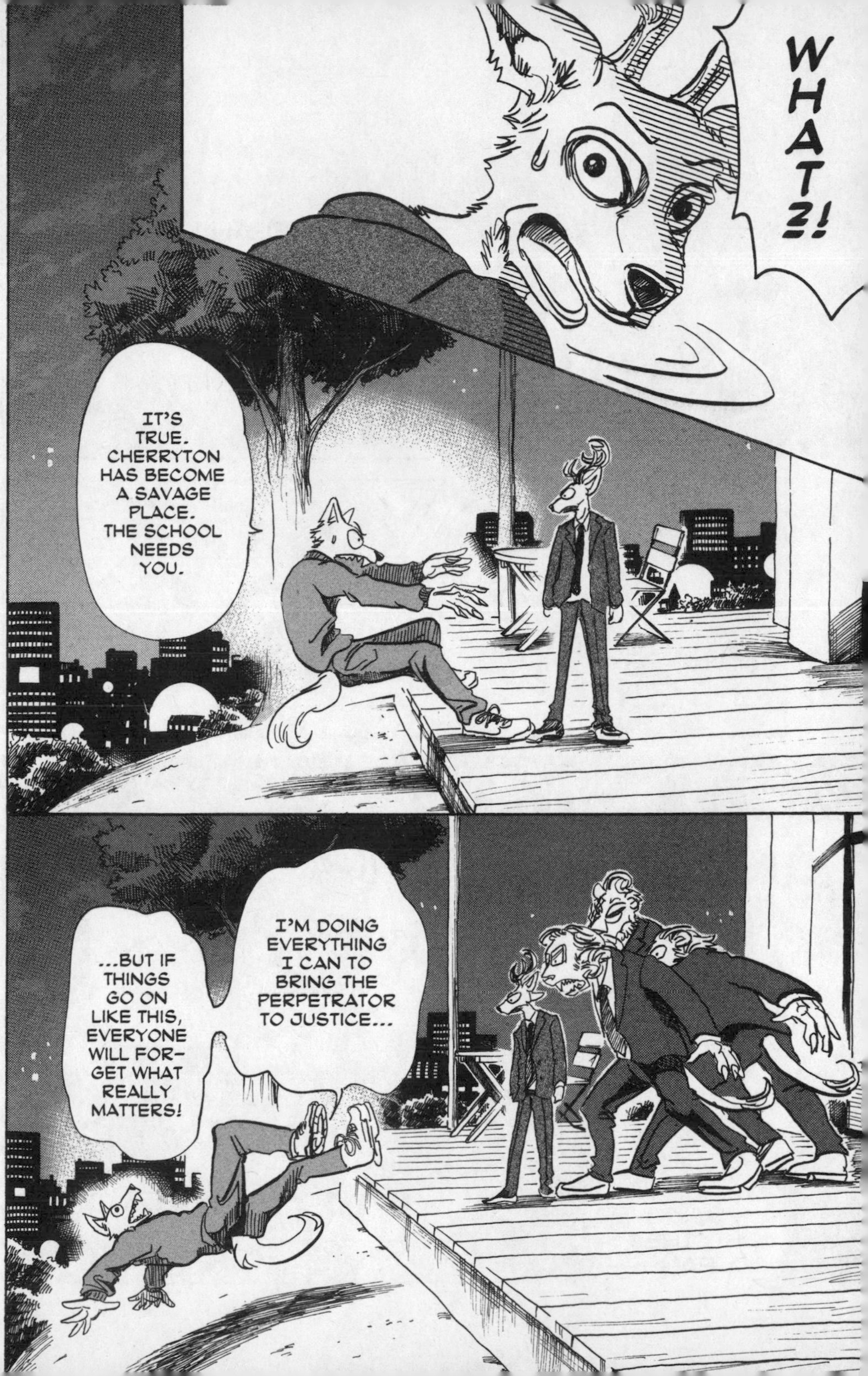
WHAT?!
IT'S TRUE. CHERRYTON HAS BECOME A SAVAGE PLACE. THE SCHOOL NEEDS YOU.
I'M DOING EVERYTHING I CAN TO BRING THE PERPETRATOR TO JUSTICE...
...BUT IF THINGS GO ON LIKE THIS, EVERYONE WILL FOR-GET WHAT REALLY MATTERS!

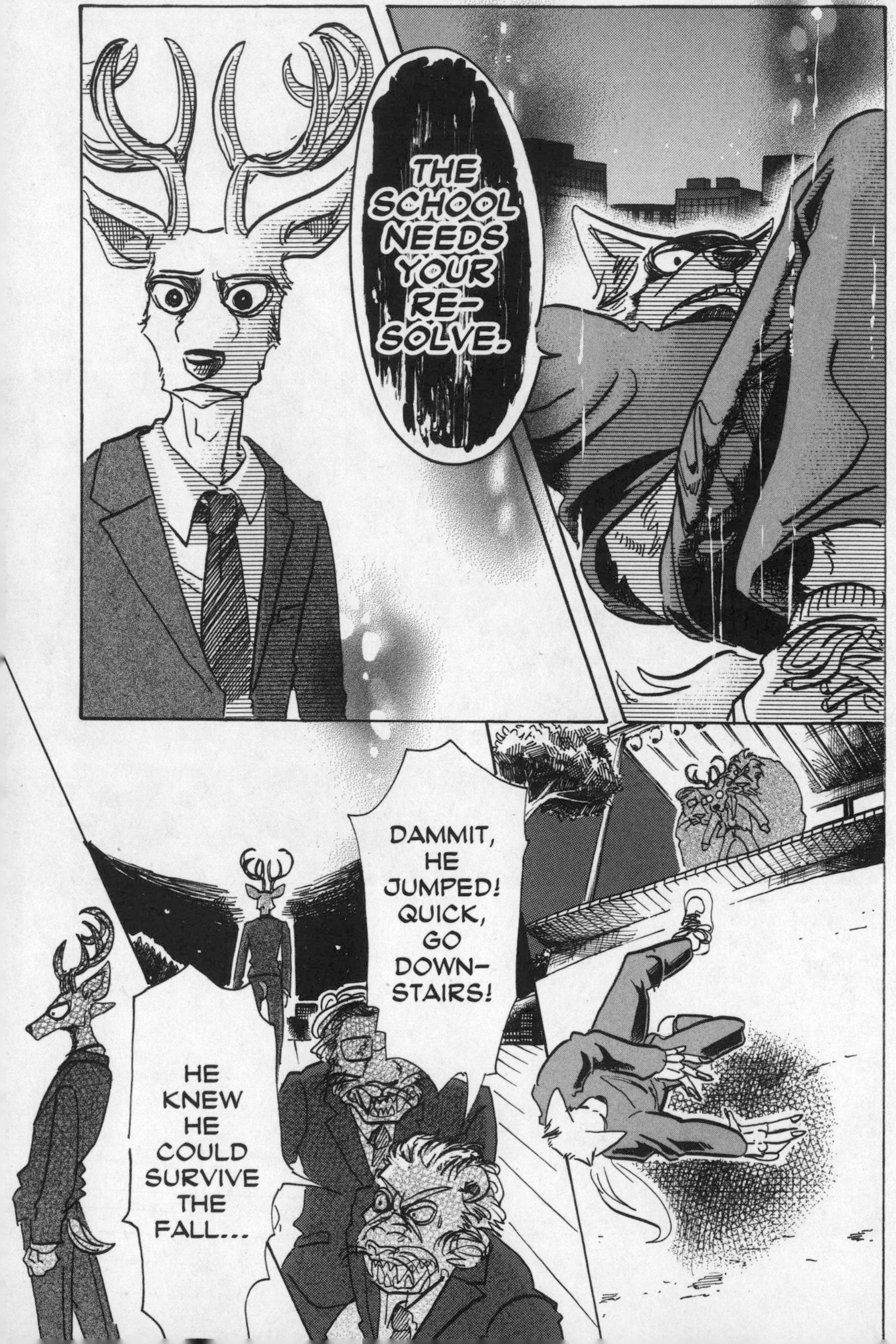
THE SCHOOL NEEDS YOUR RE-SOLVE.
DAMMIT, HE JUMPED! QUICK, GO DOWN-STAIRS!
HE KNEW HE COULD SURVIVE THE FALL...

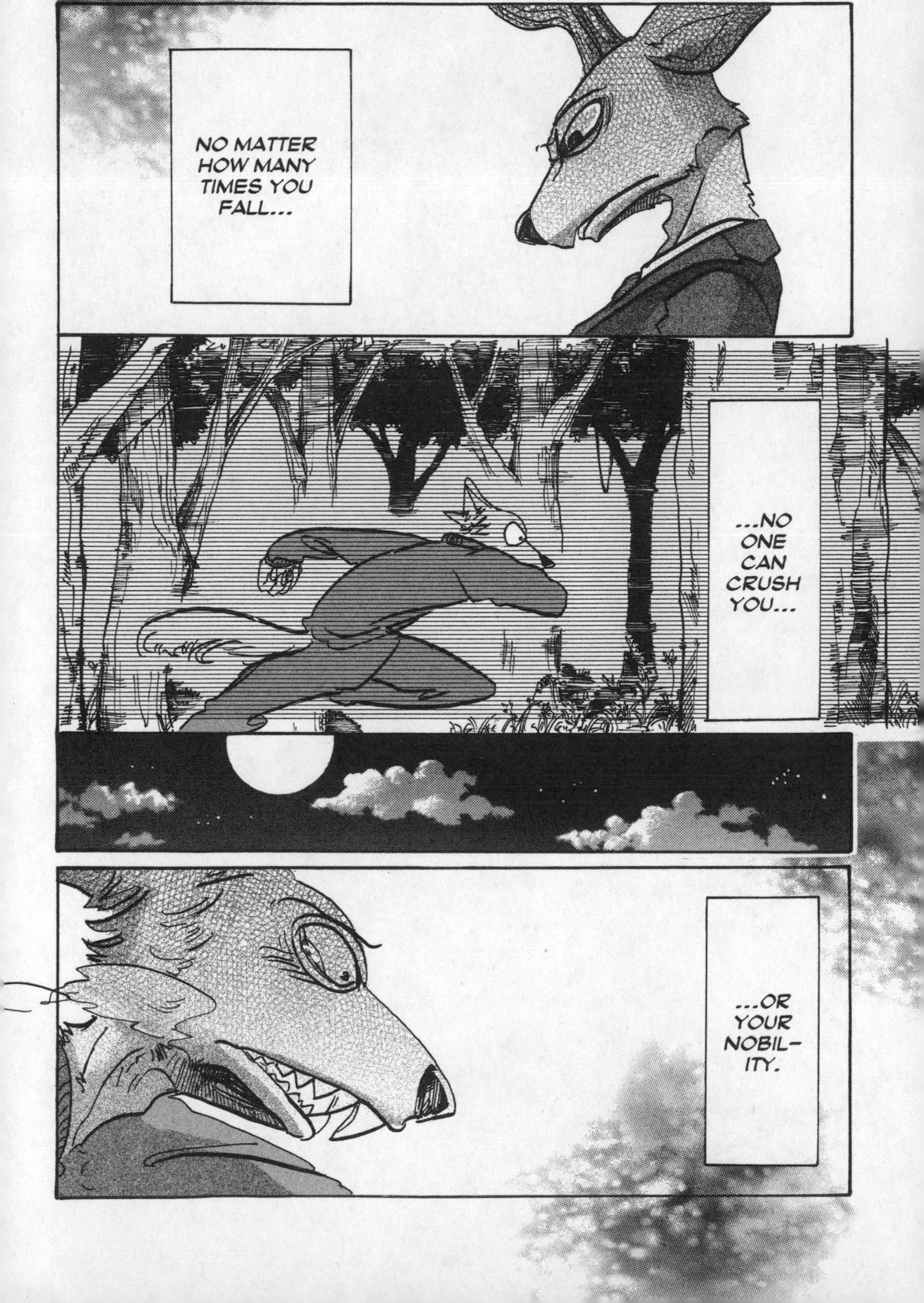
NO MATTER HOW MANY TIMES YOU FALL...
...NO ONE CAN CRUSH YOU...
...OR YOUR NOBIL-ITY.

Chapter 77: Honey Hunt's Pure Heart

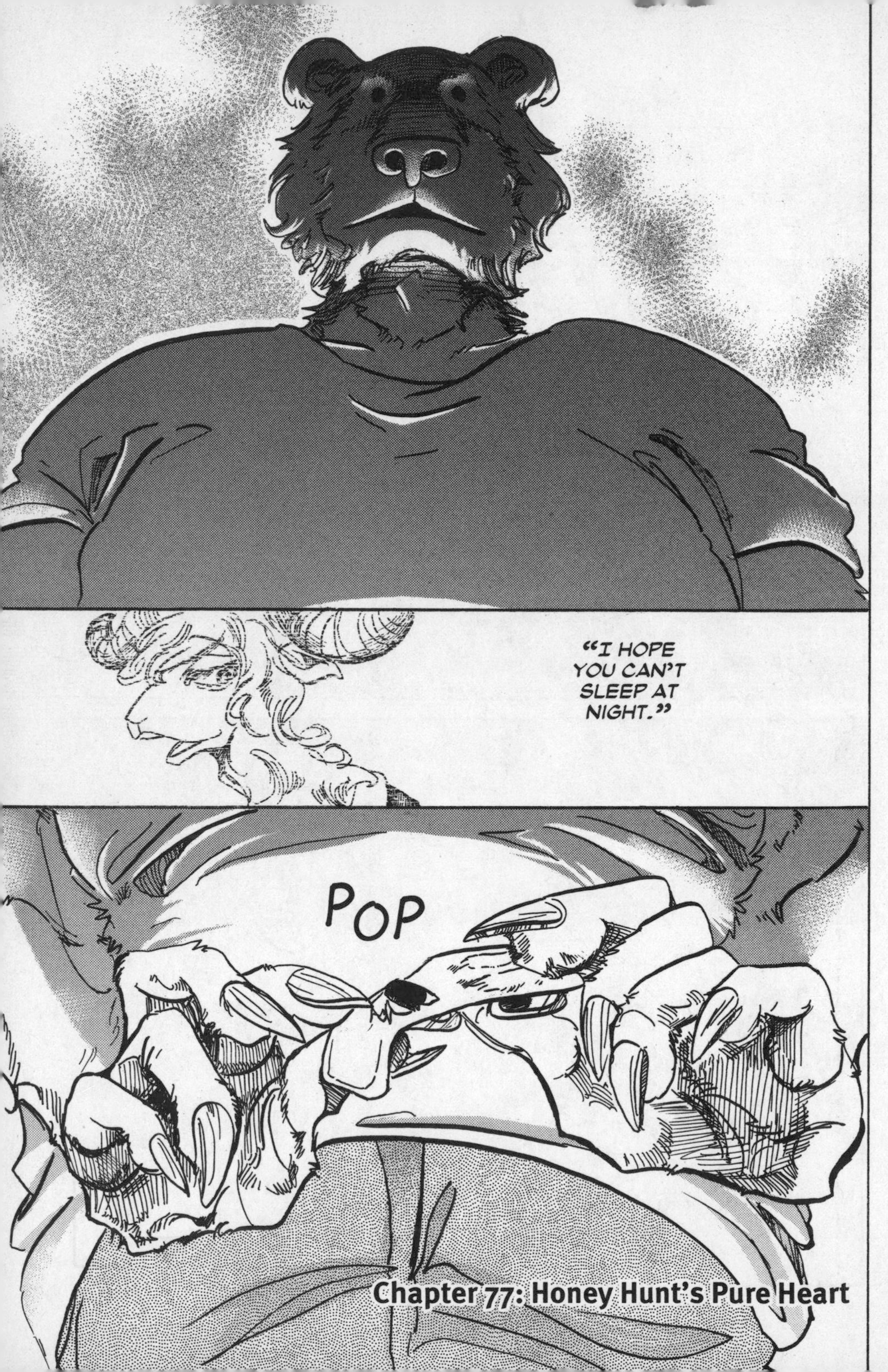
"I HOPE YOU CAN'T SLEEP AT NIGHT."
POP

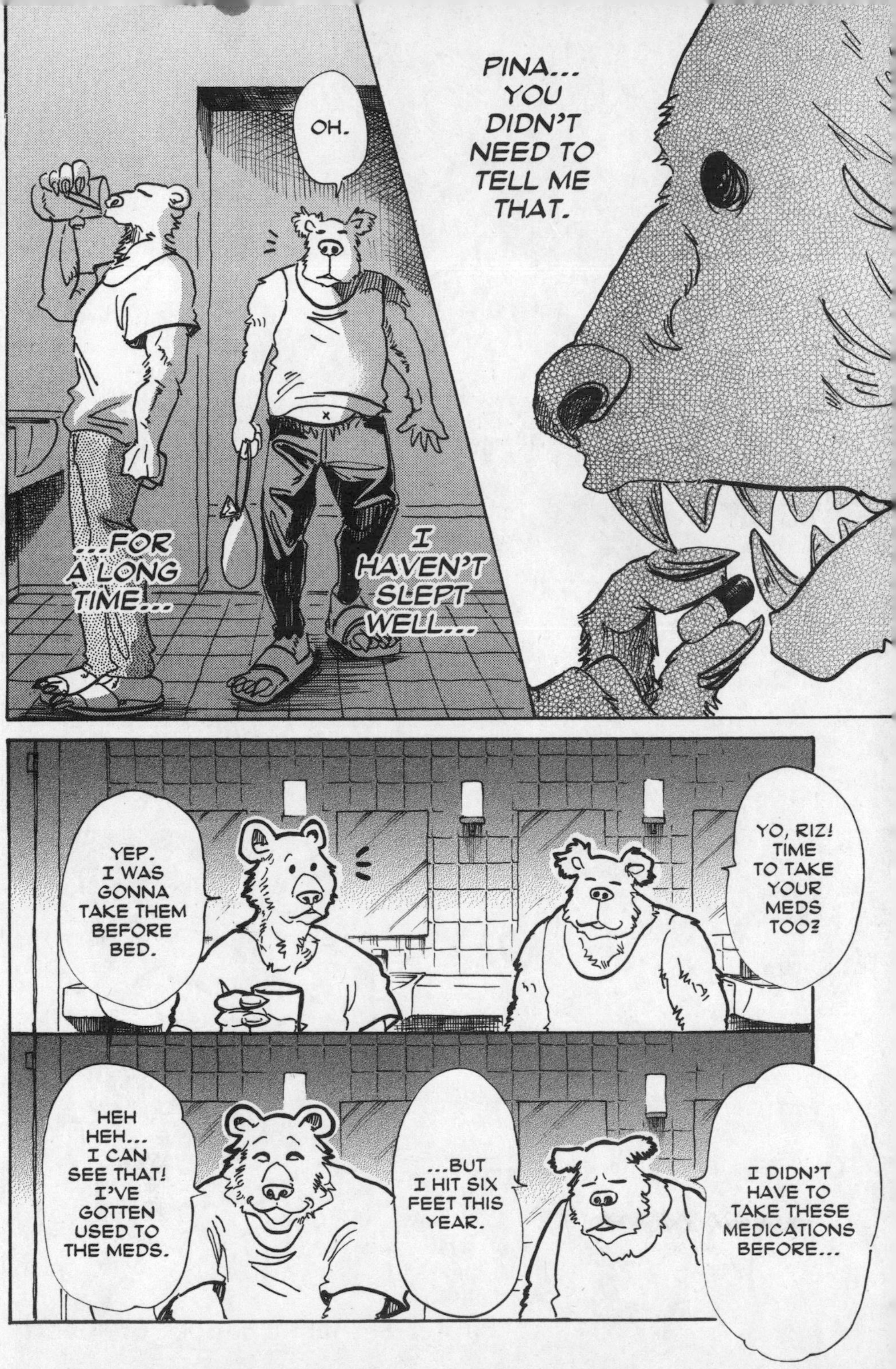
PINA... YOU DIDN'T NEED TO TELL ME THAT.
OH.
I HAVEN'T SLEPT WELL...
...FOR A LONG TIME...
YO, RIZ! TIME TO TAKE YOUR MEDS TOO?
YEP. I WAS GONNA TAKE THEM BEFORE BED.
I DIDN'T HAVE TO TAKE THESE MEDICATIONS BEFORE...
...BUT I HIT SIX FEET THIS YEAR.
HEH HEH... I CAN SEE THAT! I'VE GOTTEN USED TO THE MEDS.

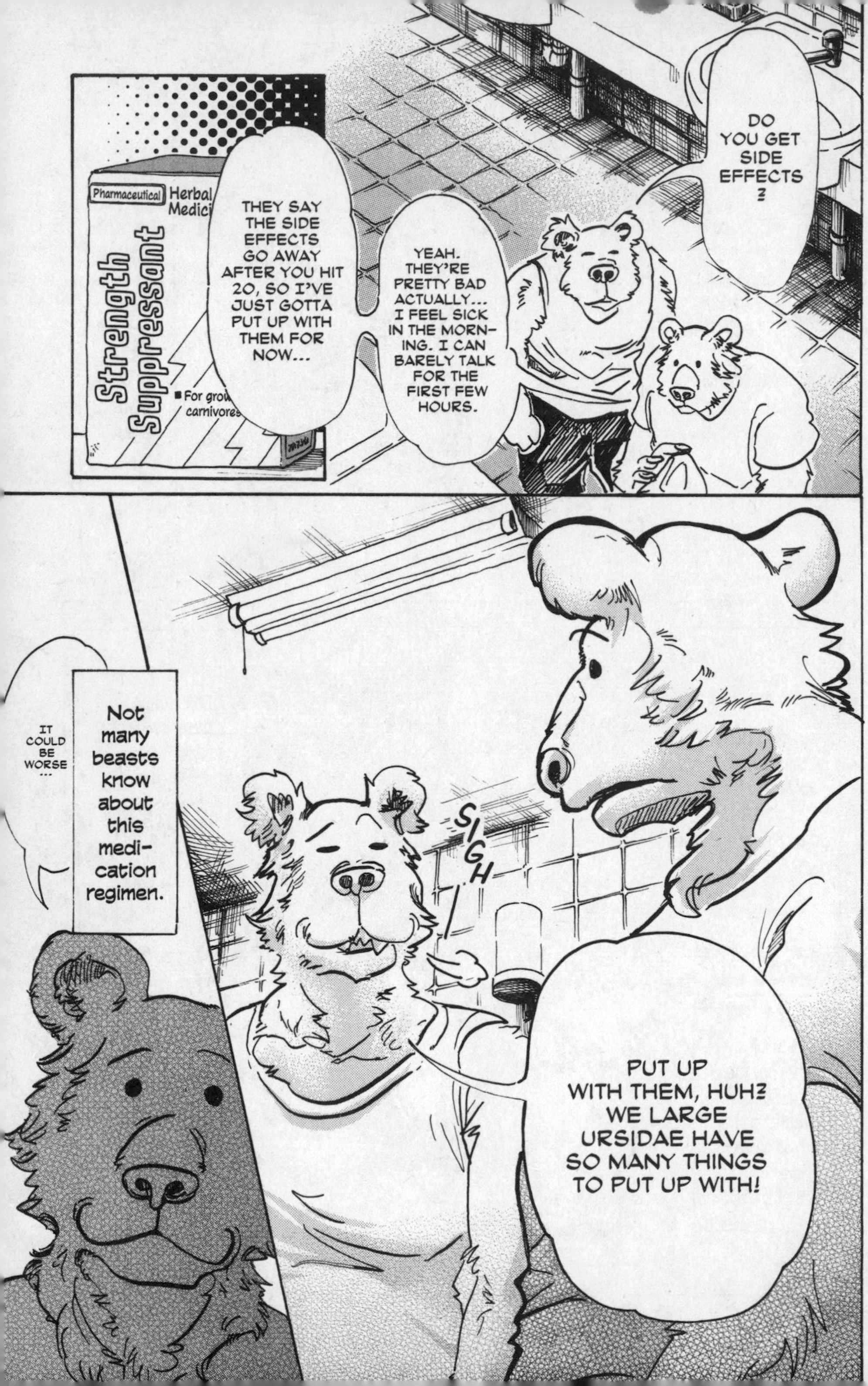
DO YOU GET SIDE EFFECTS?
YEAH. THEY'RE PRETTY BAD ACTUALLY... I FEEL SICK IN THE MORNING. I CAN BARELY TALK FOR THE FIRST FEW HOURS.
THEY SAY THE SIDE EFFECTS GO AWAY AFTER YOU HIT 20, SO I'VE JUST GOTTA PUT UP WITH THEM FOR NOW...
Pharmaceutical
Herbal
Strength Suppressant
PUT UP WITH THEM, HUH? WE LARGE URSIDAE HAVE SO MANY THINGS TO PUT UP WITH!
SIGH
Not many beasts know about this medication regimen.
IT COULD BE WORSE...

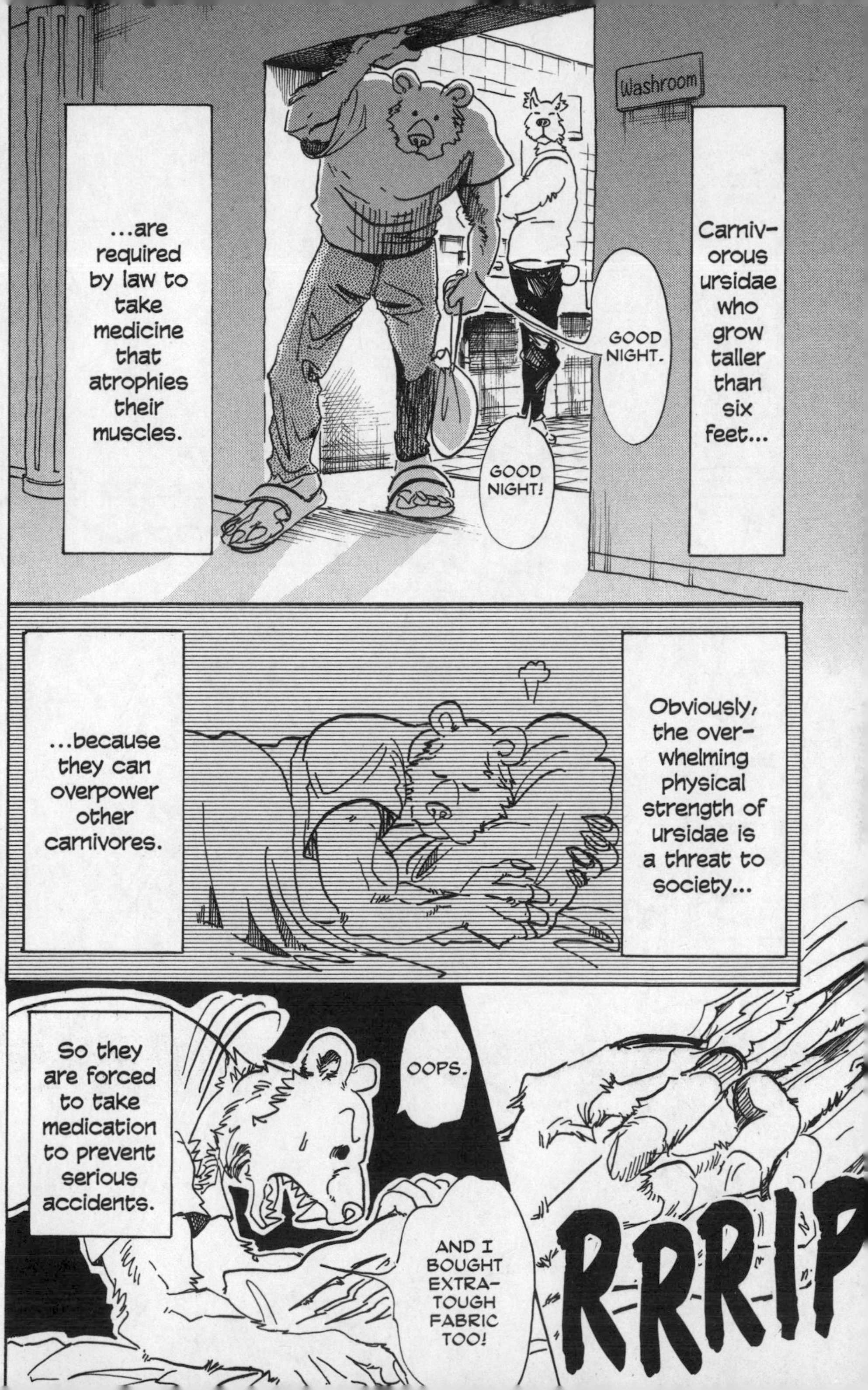
Washroom
Carnivorous ursidae who grow taller than six feet...
GOOD NIGHT.
GOOD NIGHT!
...are required by law to take medicine that atrophies their muscles.
Obviously, the over-whelming physical strength of ursidae is a threat to society...
...because they can overpower other carnivores.
So they are forced to take medication to prevent serious accidents.
RRRIP
OOPS.
AND I BOUGHT EXTRA-TOUGH FABRIC TOO!

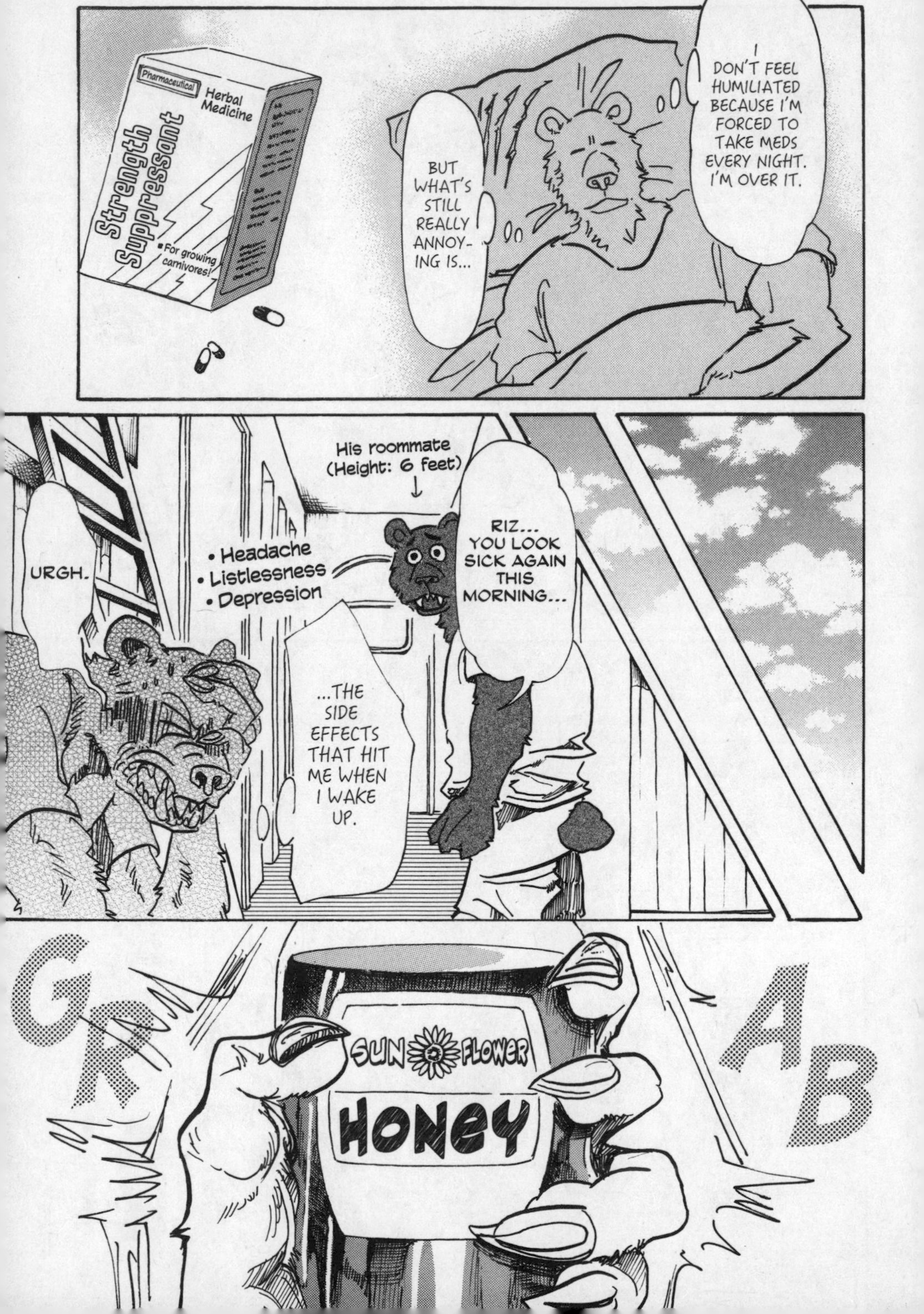
I DON'T FEEL HUMILIATED BECAUSE I'M FORCED TO TAKE MEDS EVERY NIGHT. I'M OVER IT.
BUT WHAT'S STILL REALLY ANNOY-ING IS...
Pharmaceutical
Herbal Medicine
Strength Suppressant
■For growing carnivores!
His roommate (Height: 6 feet)
RIZ... YOU LOOK SICK AGAIN THIS MORNING...
...THE SIDE EFFECTS THAT HIT ME WHEN I WAKE UP.
• Headache
• Listlessness
• Depression
URGH.
GRAB
SUN FLOWER
HONEY

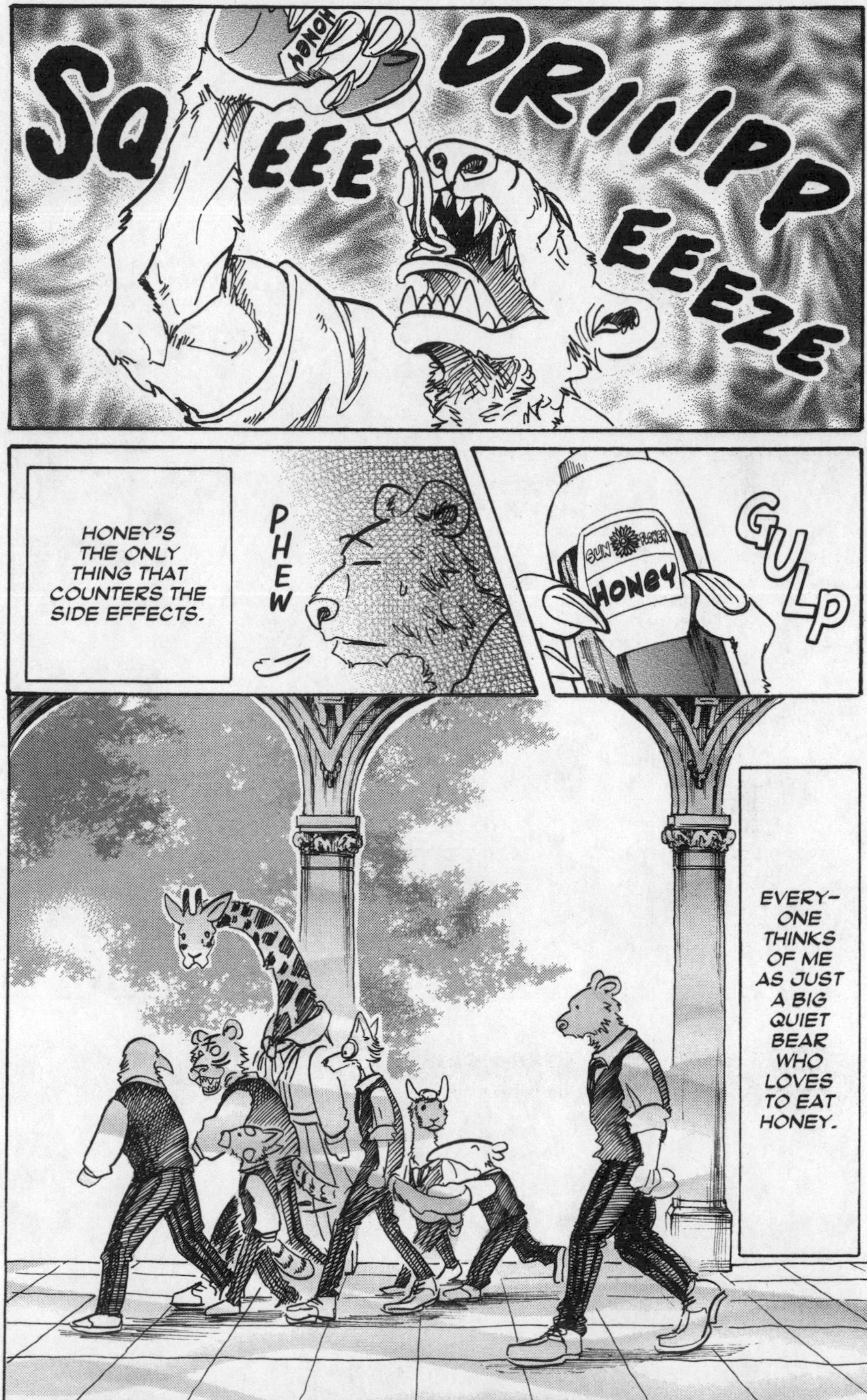

DRIIIPP
SQEEE EEEEZE
HONEY
SUN FLOWER
HONEY
GULP
PHEW
HONEY'S THE ONLY THING THAT COUNTERS THE SIDE EFFECTS.
EVERY-ONE THINKS OF ME AS JUST A BIG QUIET BEAR WHO LOVES TO EAT HONEY.

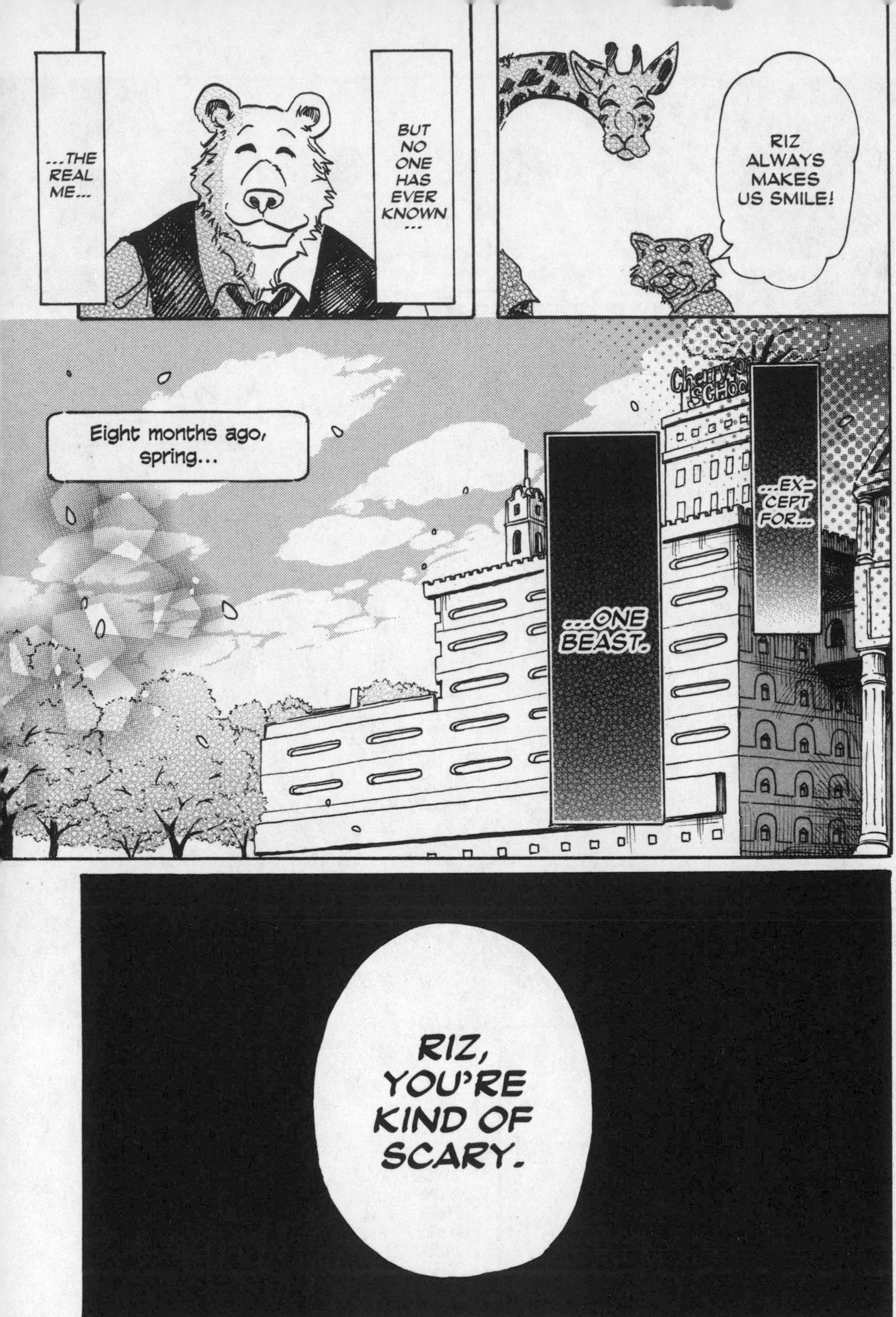
RIZ ALWAYS MAKES US SMILE!
BUT NO ONE HAS EVER KNOWN...
...THE REAL ME...
...EX-CEPT FOR...
...ONE BEAST.
Eight months ago, spring...
RIZ, YOU'RE KIND OF SCARY.

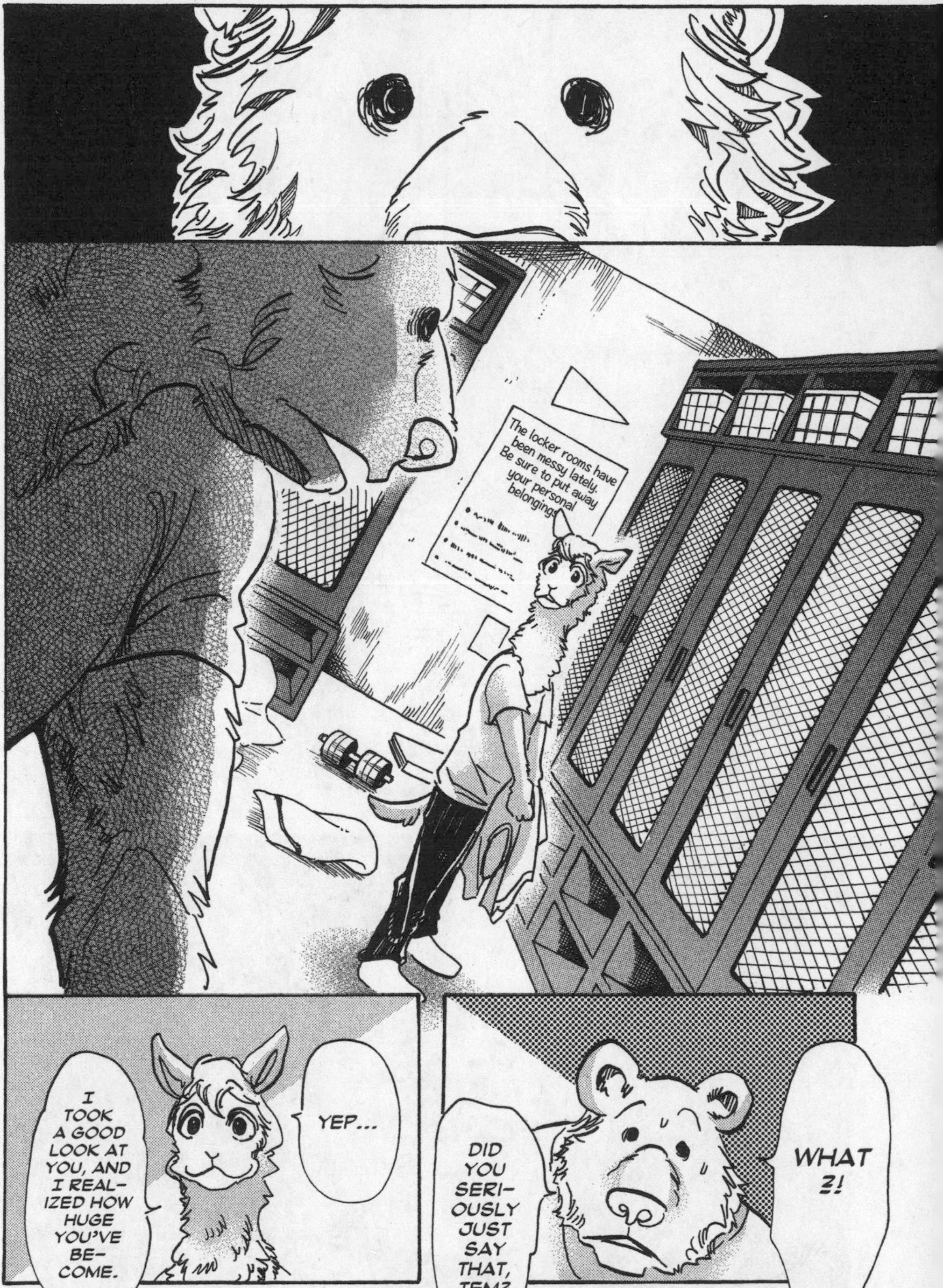
The locker rooms have been messy lately. Be sure to put away your personal belongings.
WHAT?!
DID YOU SERIOUSLY JUST SAY THAT, TEM?
YEP...
I TOOK A GOOD LOOK AT YOU, AND I REALIZED HOW HUGE YOU'VE BECOME.

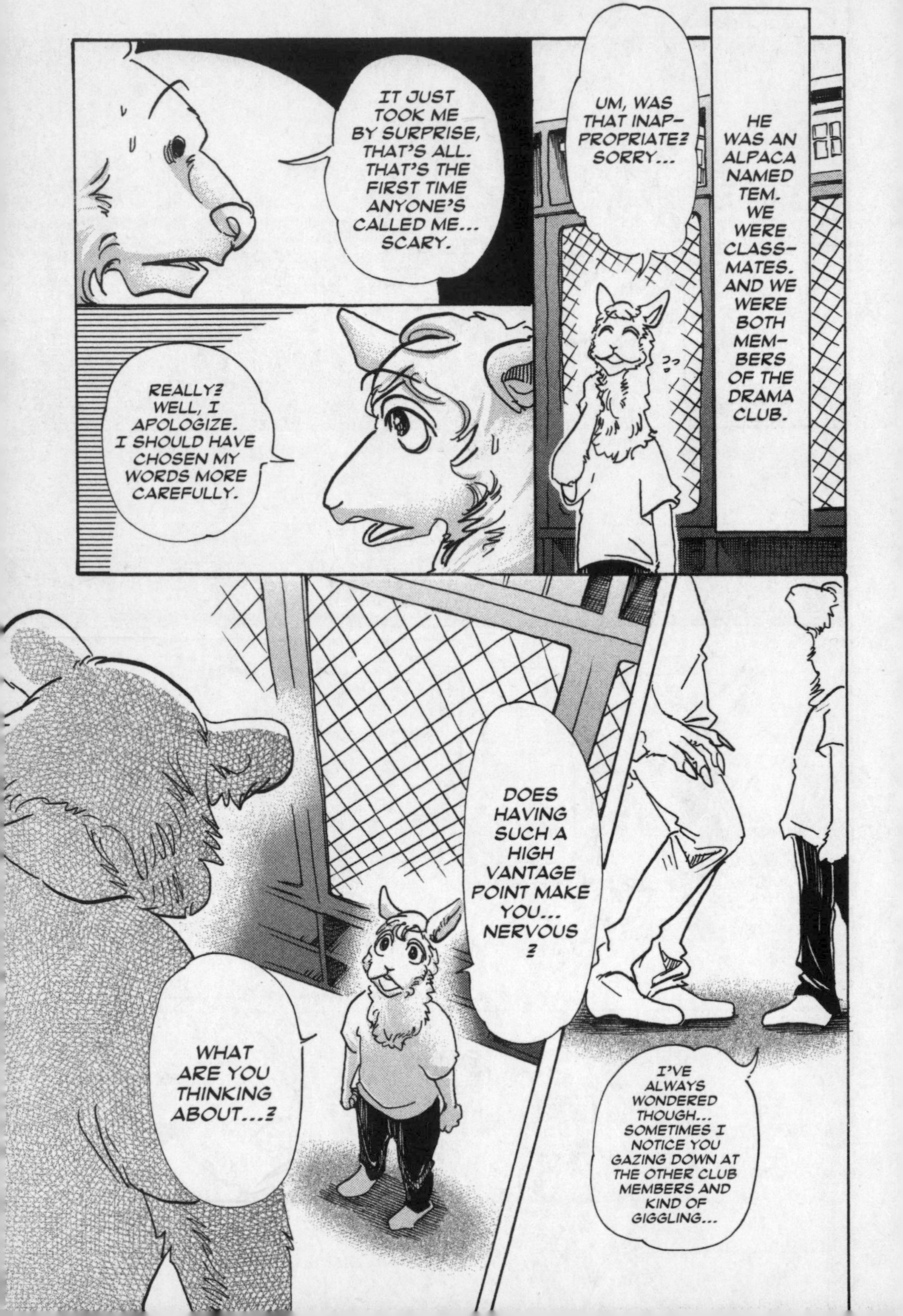
HE WAS AN ALPACA NAMED TEM. WE WERE CLASSMATES. AND WE WERE BOTH MEMBERS OF THE DRAMA CLUB.
UM, WAS THAT INAPPROPRIATE? SORRY...
IT JUST TOOK ME BY SURPRISE, THAT'S ALL. THAT'S THE FIRST TIME ANYONE'S CALLED ME... SCARY.
REALLY? WELL, I APOLOGIZE. I SHOULD HAVE CHOSEN MY WORDS MORE CAREFULLY.
I'VE ALWAYS WONDERED THOUGH... SOMETIMES I NOTICE YOU GAZING DOWN AT THE OTHER CLUB MEMBERS AND KIND OF GIGGLING...
DOES HAVING SUCH A HIGH VANTAGE POINT MAKE YOU... NERVOUS?
WHAT ARE YOU THINKING ABOUT...?

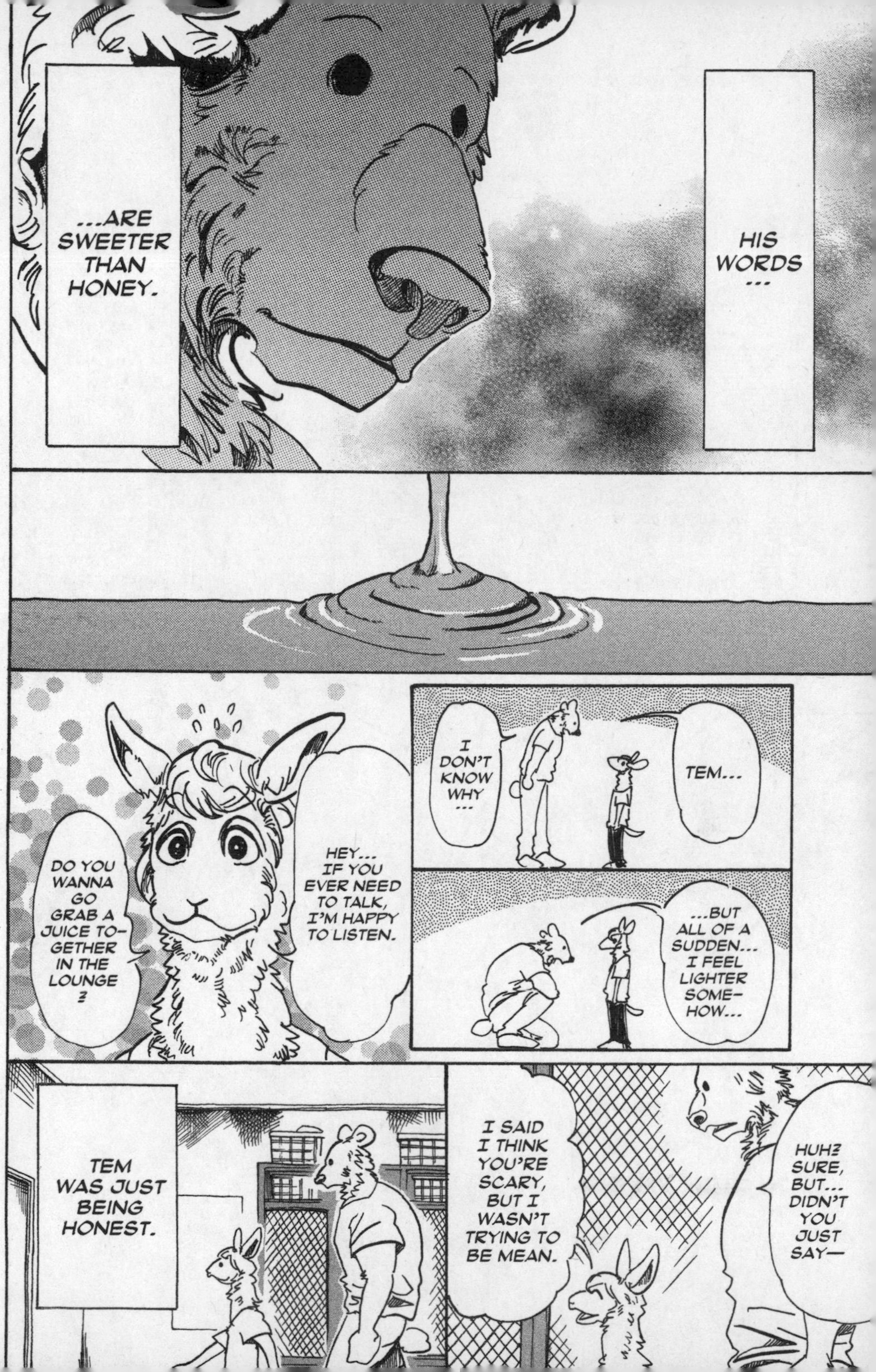
HIS WORDS ...
...ARE SWEETER THAN HONEY.
TEM...
I DON'T KNOW WHY ...
...BUT ALL OF A SUDDEN... I FEEL LIGHTER SOME-HOW...
HEY... IF YOU EVER NEED TO TALK, I'M HAPPY TO LISTEN.
DO YOU WANNA GO GRAB A JUICE TO-GETHER IN THE LOUNGE?
HUH? SURE, BUT... DIDN'T YOU JUST SAY—
I SAID I THINK YOU'RE SCARY, BUT I WASN'T TRYING TO BE MEAN.
TEM WAS JUST BEING HONEST.

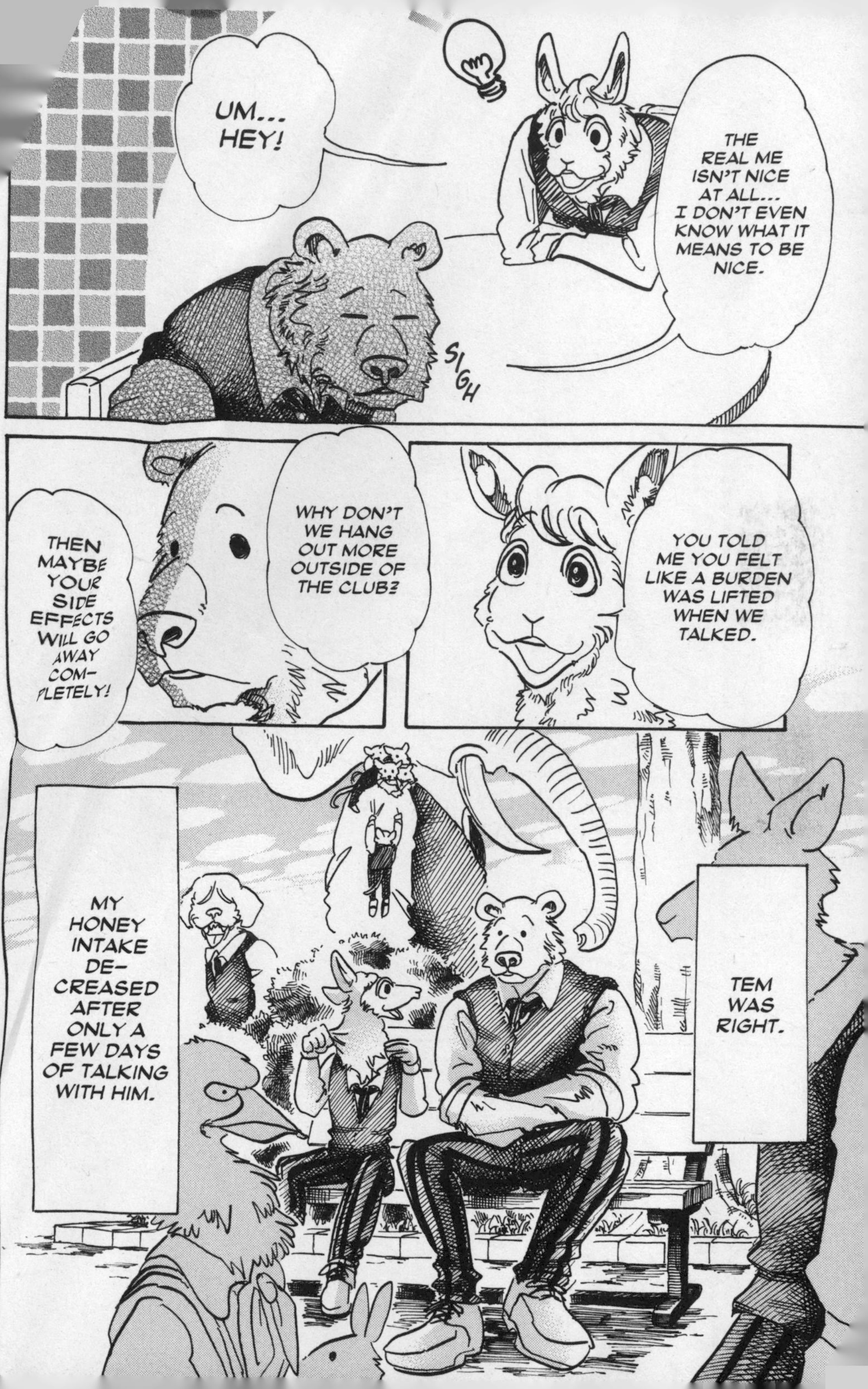
THE REAL ME ISN'T NICE AT ALL... I DON'T EVEN KNOW WHAT IT MEANS TO BE NICE.
UM... HEY!
SIGH
YOU TOLD ME YOU FELT LIKE A BURDEN WAS LIFTED WHEN WE TALKED.
WHY DON'T WE HANG OUT MORE OUTSIDE OF THE CLUB?
THEN MAYBE YOUR SIDE EFFECTS WILL GO AWAY COM-PLETELY!
TEM WAS RIGHT.
MY HONEY INTAKE DE-CREASED AFTER ONLY A FEW DAYS OF TALKING WITH HIM.

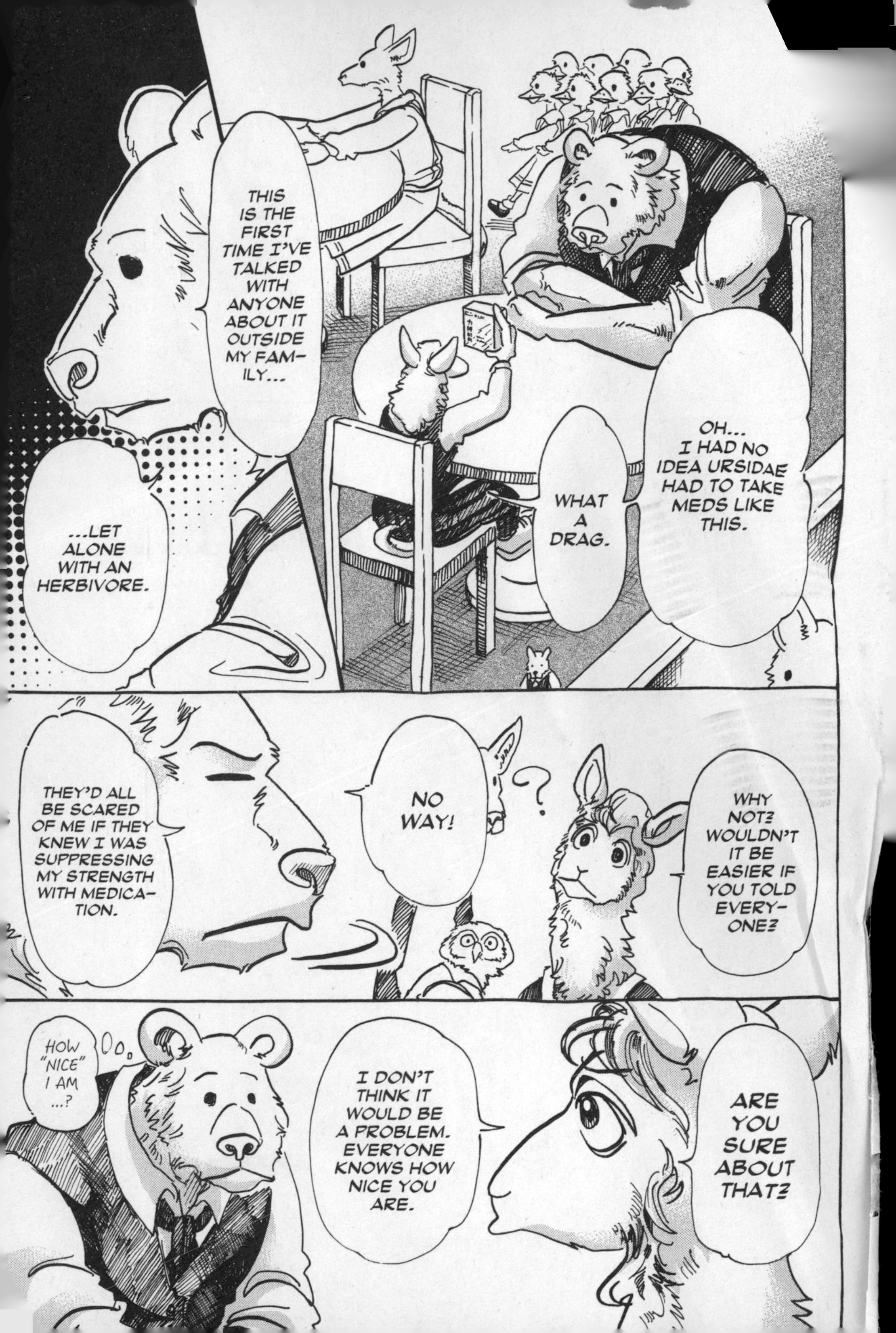
OH... I HAD NO IDEA URSIDAE HAD TO TAKE MEDS LIKE THIS.
WHAT A DRAG.
THIS IS THE FIRST TIME I'VE TALKED WITH ANYONE ABOUT IT OUTSIDE MY FAM-ILY...
...LET ALONE WITH AN HERBIVORE.
WHY NOT? WOULDN'T IT BE EASIER IF YOU TOLD EVERY-ONE?
NO WAY!
THEY'D ALL BE SCARED OF ME IF THEY KNEW I WAS SUPPRESSING MY STRENGTH WITH MEDICA-TION.
ARE YOU SURE ABOUT THAT?
I DON'T THINK IT WOULD BE A PROBLEM. EVERYONE KNOWS HOW NICE YOU ARE.
HOW "NICE" I AM ...?

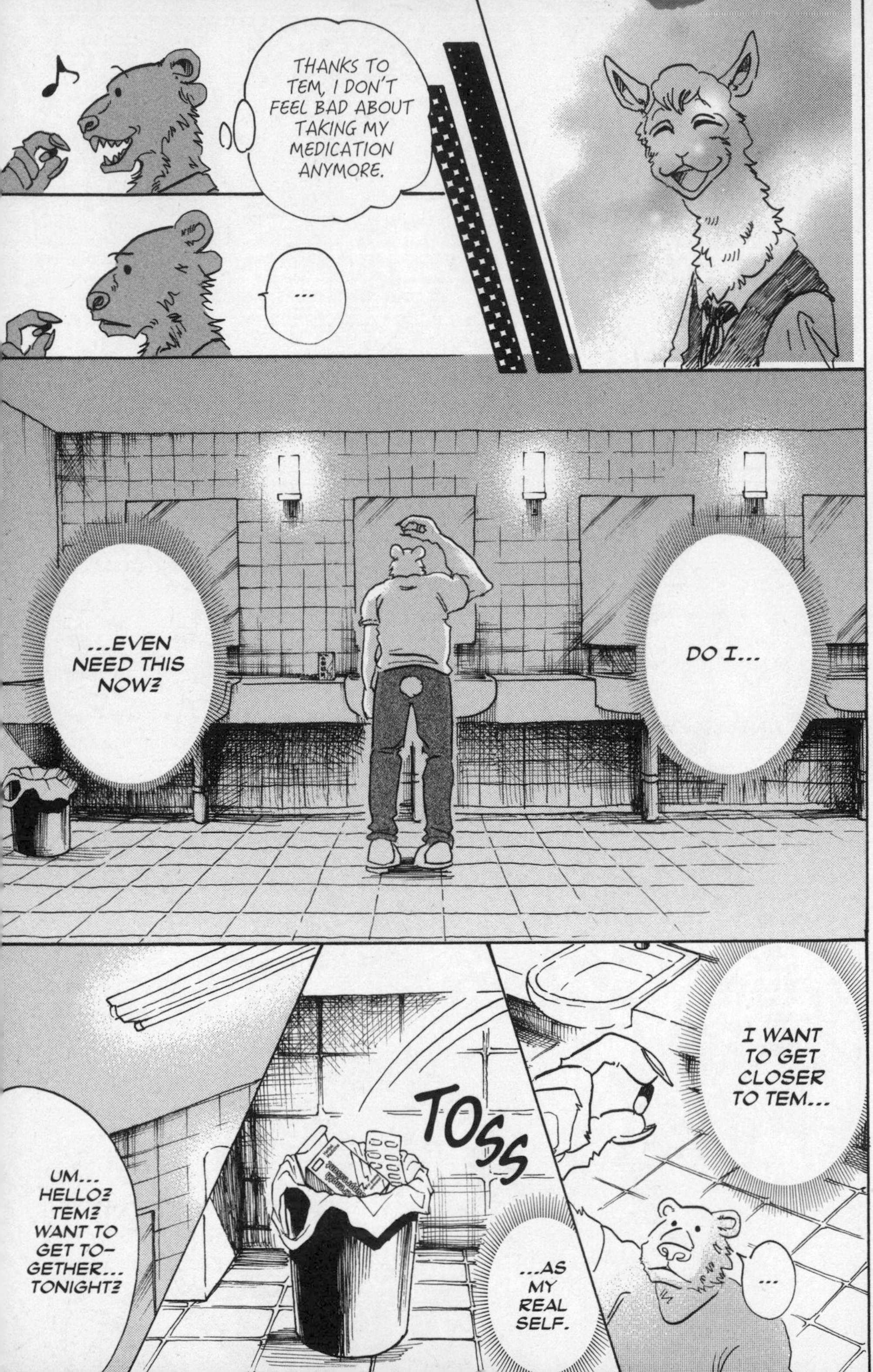
THANKS TO TEM, I DON'T FEEL BAD ABOUT TAKING MY MEDICATION ANYMORE.
...
DO I...
...EVEN NEED THIS NOW?
I WANT TO GET CLOSER TO TEM...
...AS MY REAL SELF.
...
TOSS
UM... HELLO? TEM? WANT TO GET TO-GETHER... TONIGHT?

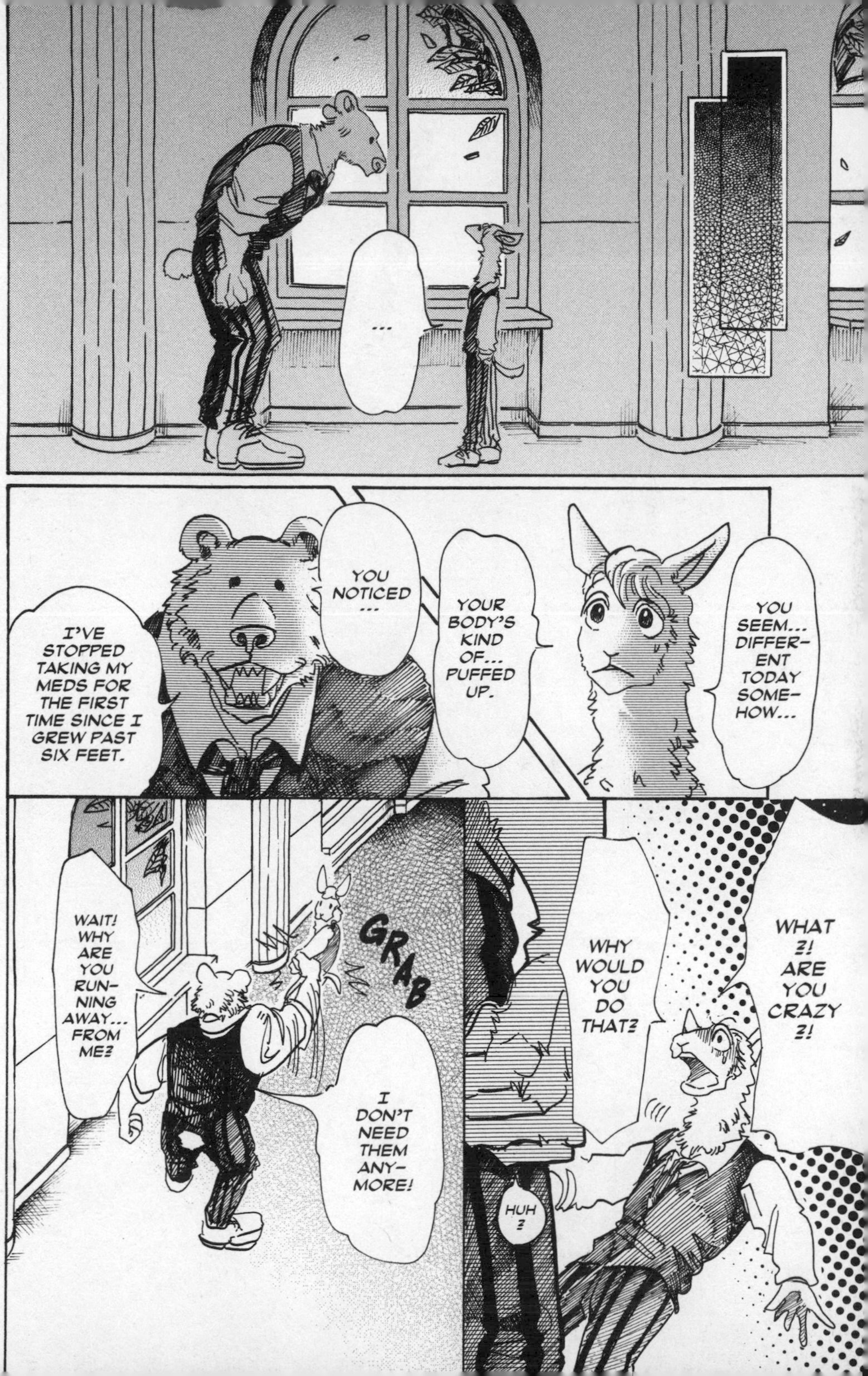
...
YOU SEEM... DIFFERENT TODAY SOMEHOW...
YOUR BODY'S KIND OF... PUFFED UP.
YOU NOTICED ...
I'VE STOPPED TAKING MY MEDS FOR THE FIRST TIME SINCE I GREW PAST SIX FEET.
WHAT?! ARE YOU CRAZY?!
WHY WOULD YOU DO THAT?
HUH?
GRAB
I DON'T NEED THEM ANYMORE!
WAIT! WHY ARE YOU RUNNING AWAY... FROM ME?

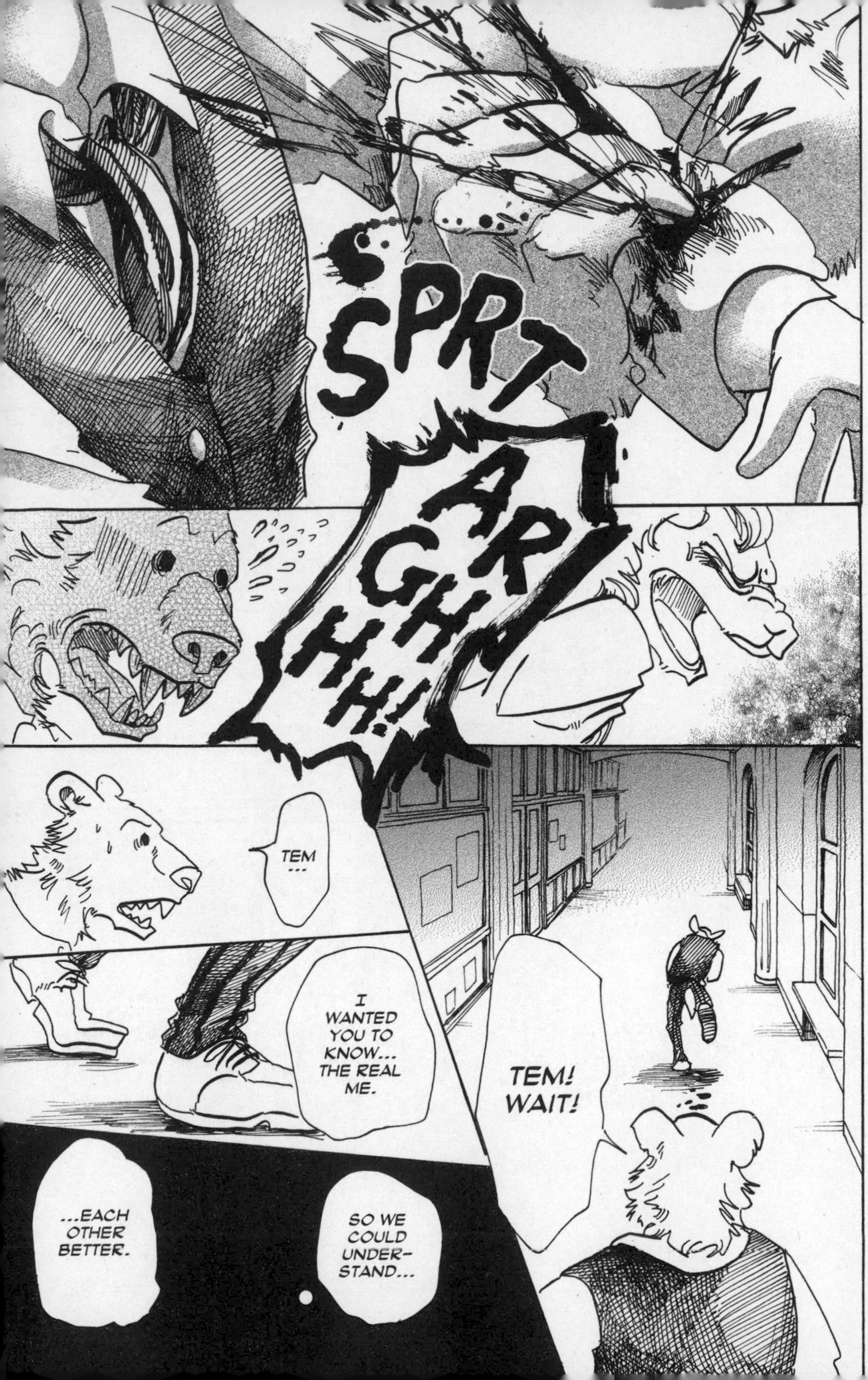
SPRT
ARGHHHH!
TEM! WAIT!
TEM---
I WANTED YOU TO KNOW... THE REAL ME.
SO WE COULD UNDER-STAND...
...EACH OTHER BETTER.

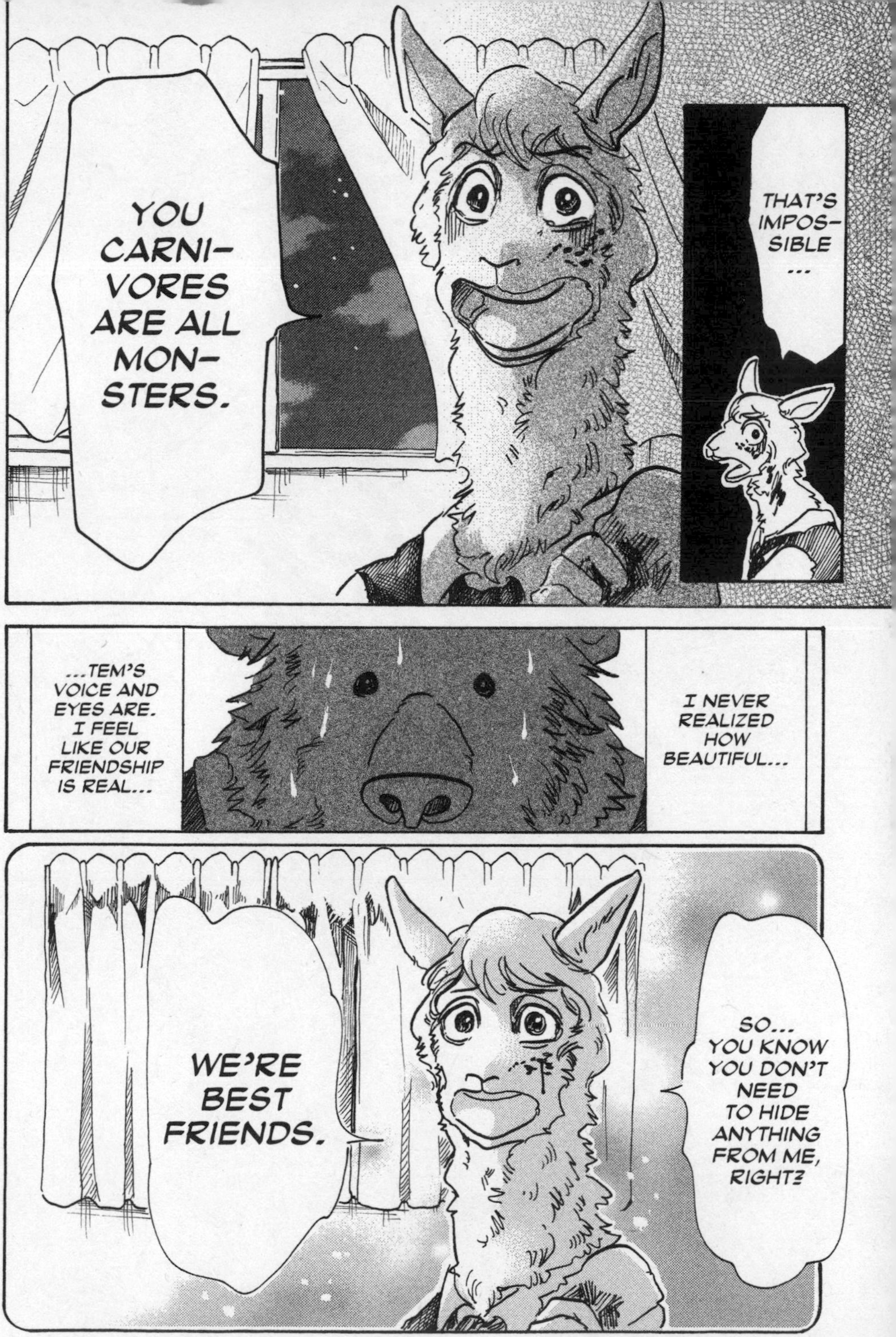
THAT'S IMPOSSIBLE...
YOU CARNIVORES ARE ALL MONSTERS.
I NEVER REALIZED HOW BEAUTIFUL...
...TEM'S VOICE AND EYES ARE. I FEEL LIKE OUR FRIENDSHIP IS REAL...
SO... YOU KNOW YOU DON'T NEED TO HIDE ANYTHING FROM ME, RIGHT?
WE'RE BEST FRIENDS.

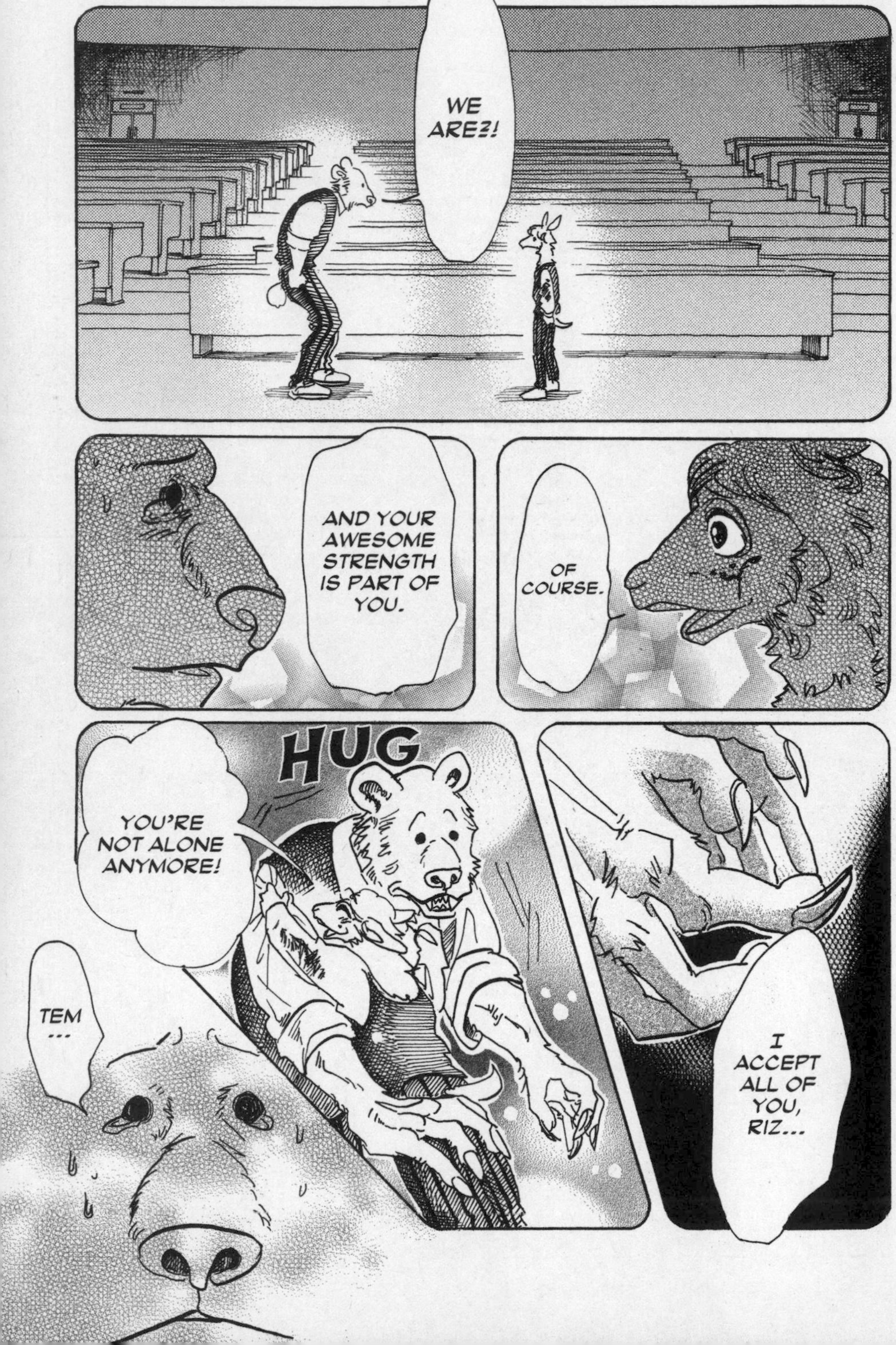
WE ARE?!
OF COURSE.
AND YOUR AWESOME STRENGTH IS PART OF YOU.
I ACCEPT ALL OF YOU, RIZ...
HUG
YOU'RE NOT ALONE ANYMORE!
TEM...

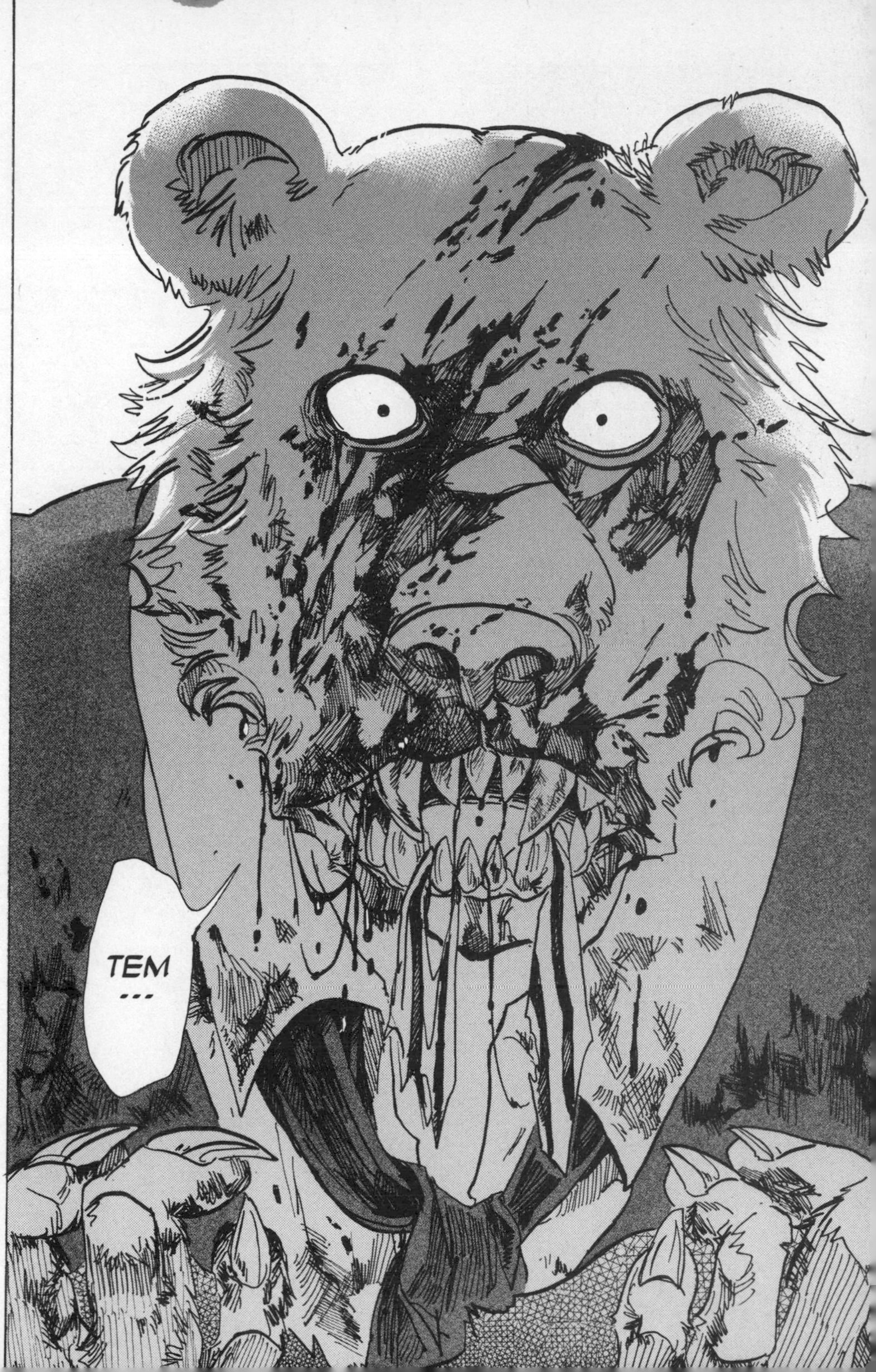
TEM...

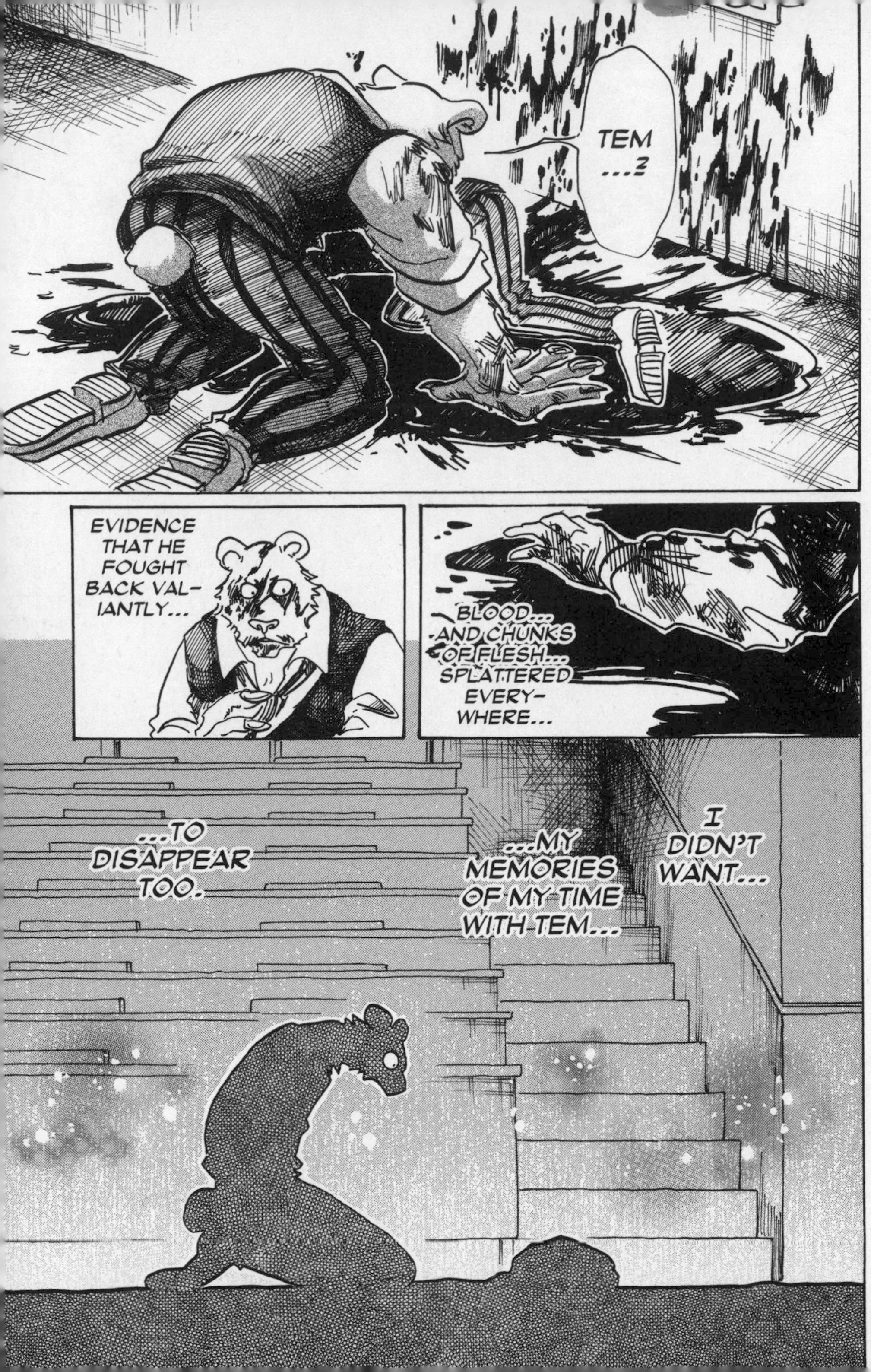
TEM ...?
BLOOD... AND CHUNKS OF FLESH... SPLATTERED EVERY-WHERE...
EVIDENCE THAT HE FOUGHT BACK VAL-IANTLY...
I DIDN'T WANT...
...MY MEMORIES OF MY TIME WITH TEM...
...TO DISAPPEAR TOO.

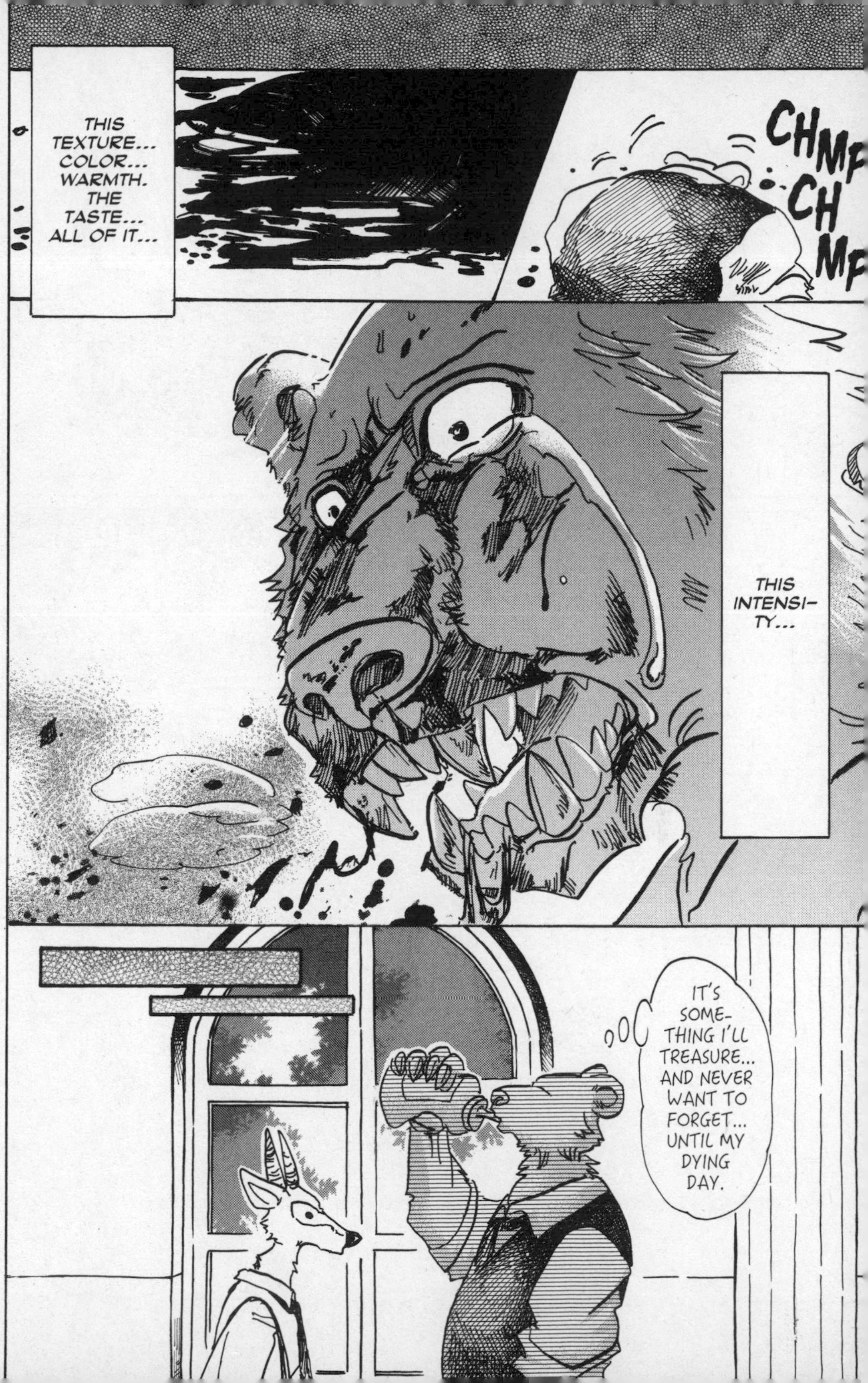
CHMF CH MF
THIS TEXTURE... COLOR... WARMTH. THE TASTE... ALL OF IT...
THIS INTENSI-TY...
IT'S SOME-THING I'LL TREASURE... AND NEVER WANT TO FORGET... UNTIL MY DYING DAY.

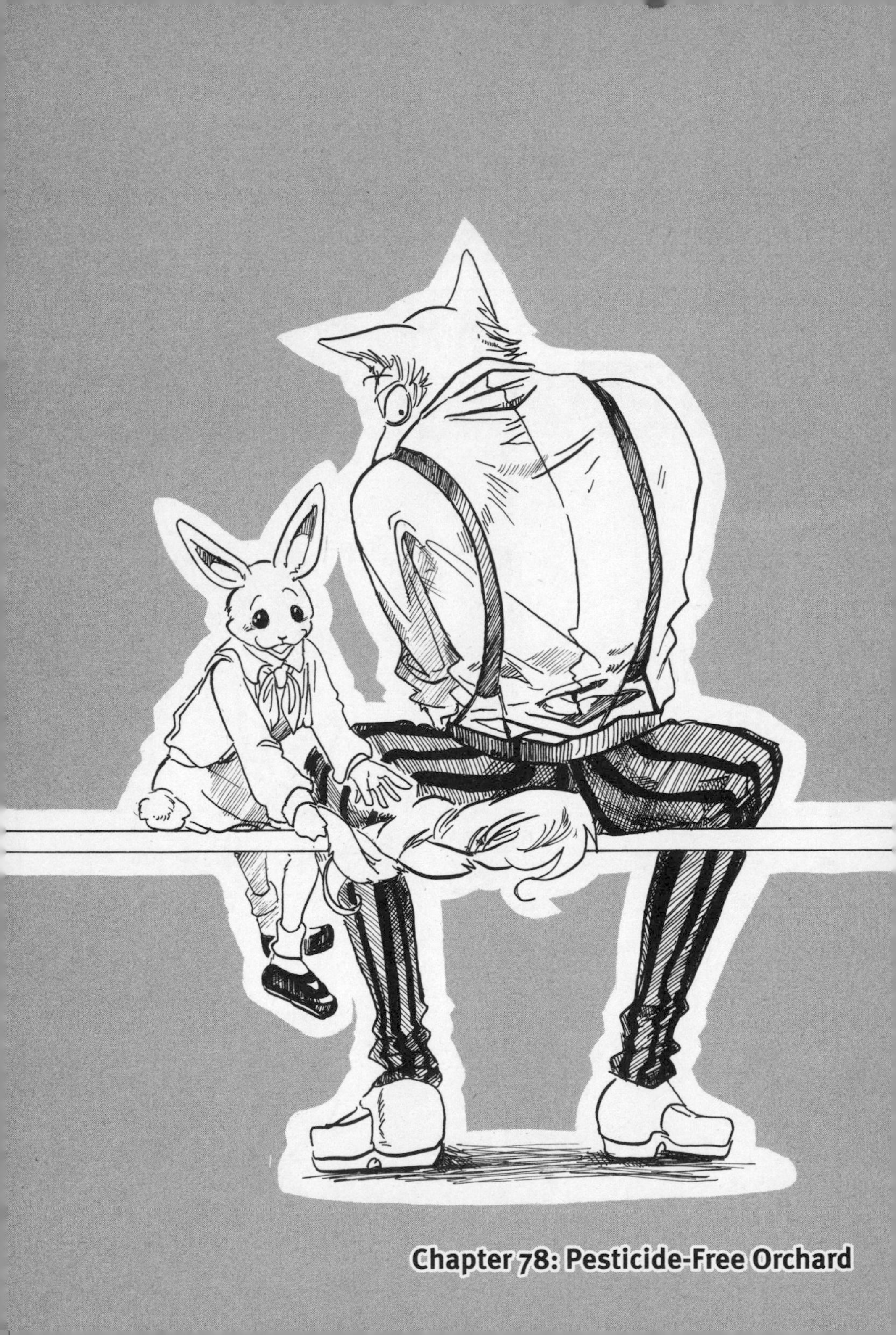

Chapter 78: Pesticide-Free Orchard

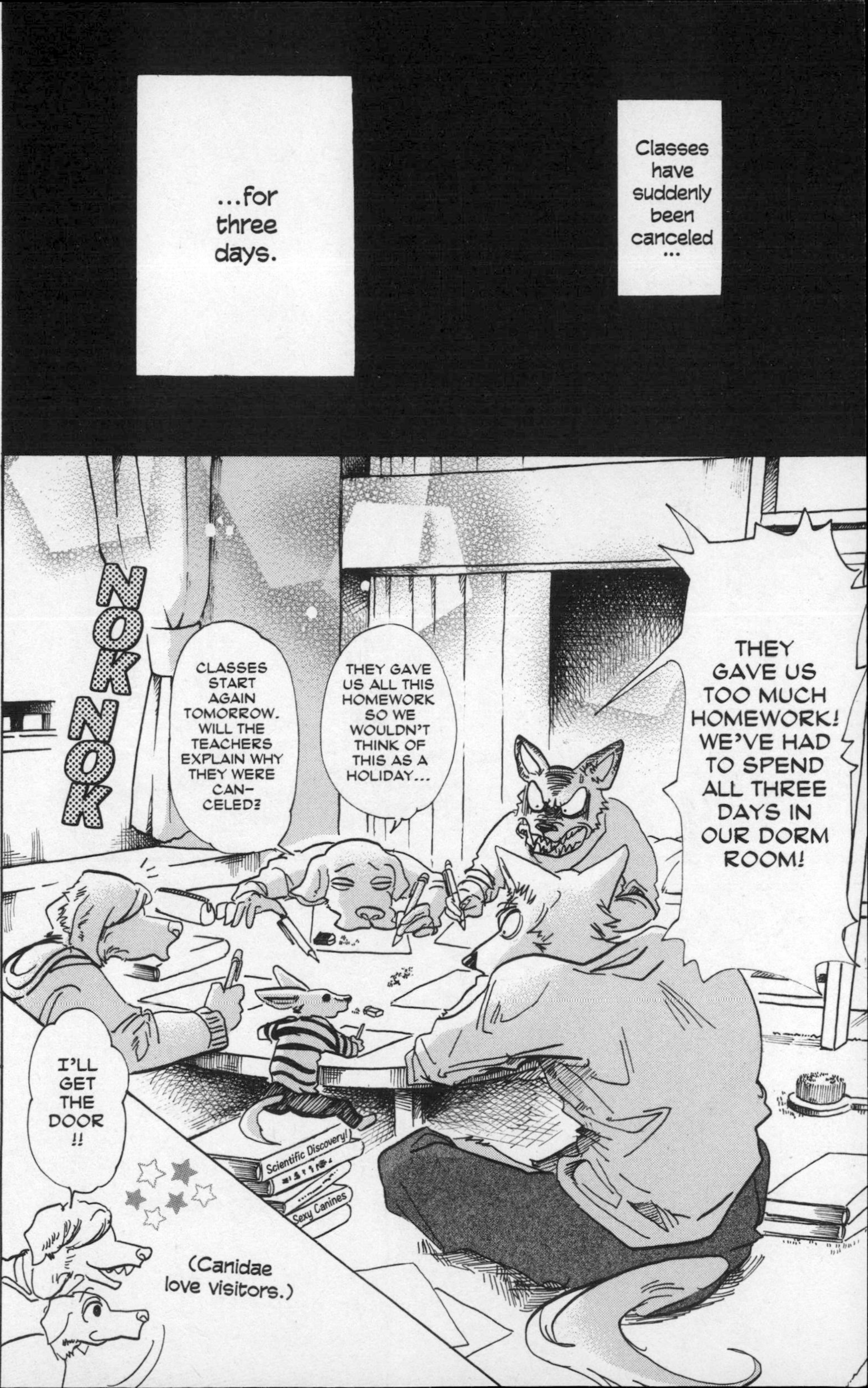
Classes have suddenly been canceled ...
...for three days.
THEY GAVE US TOO MUCH HOMEWORK! WE'VE HAD TO SPEND ALL THREE DAYS IN OUR DORM ROOM!
THEY GAVE US ALL THIS HOMEWORK SO WE WOULDN'T THINK OF THIS AS A HOLIDAY...
CLASSES START AGAIN TOMORROW. WILL THE TEACHERS EXPLAIN WHY THEY WERE CAN-CELED?
NOK NOK
I'LL GET THE DOOR !!
Scientific Discovery!
Sexy Canines
(Canidae love visitors.)

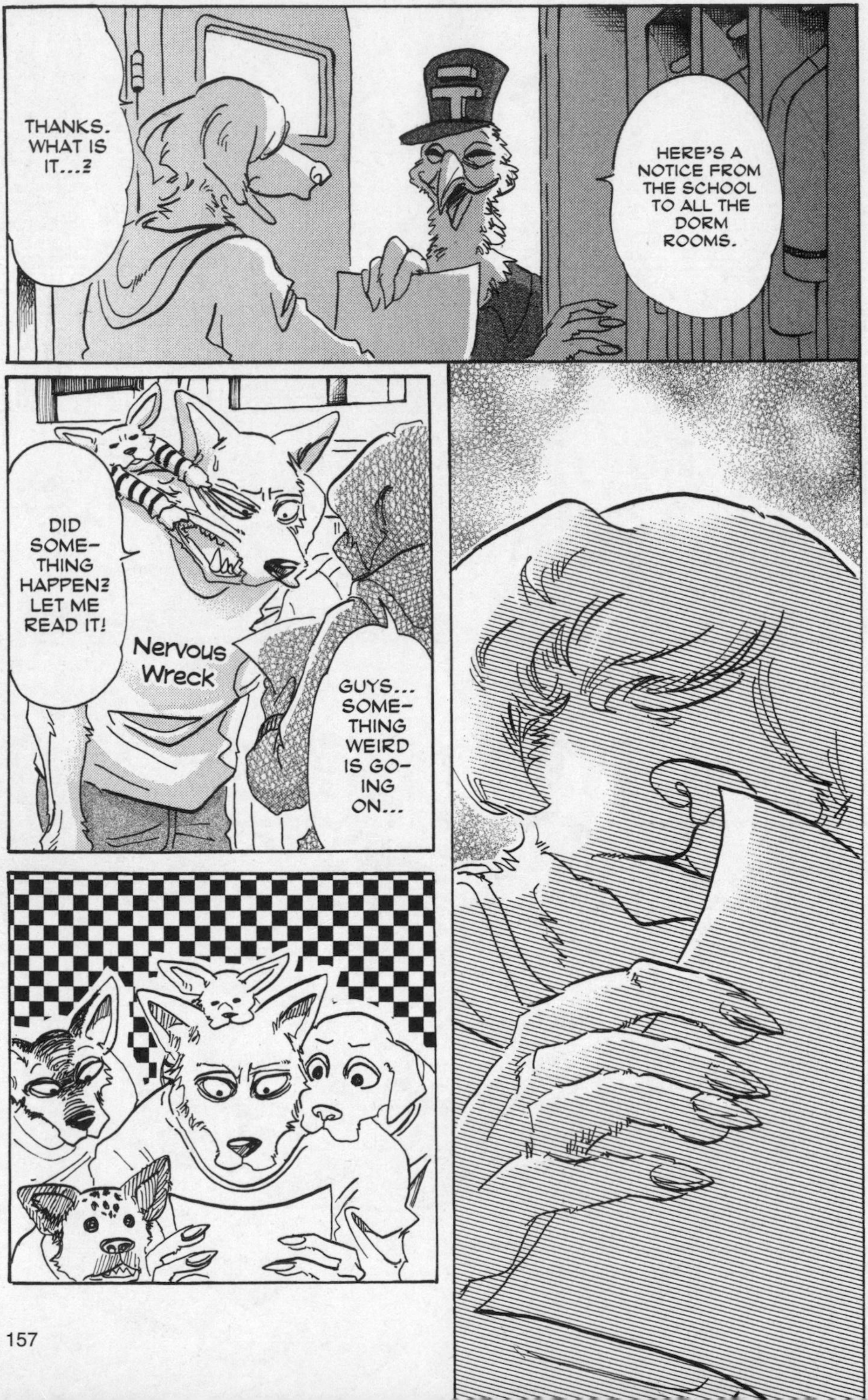
HERE'S A NOTICE FROM THE SCHOOL TO ALL THE DORM ROOMS.
THANKS. WHAT IS IT...?
GUYS... SOME-THING WEIRD IS GO-ING ON...
Nervous Wreck
DID SOME-THING HAPPEN? LET ME READ IT!

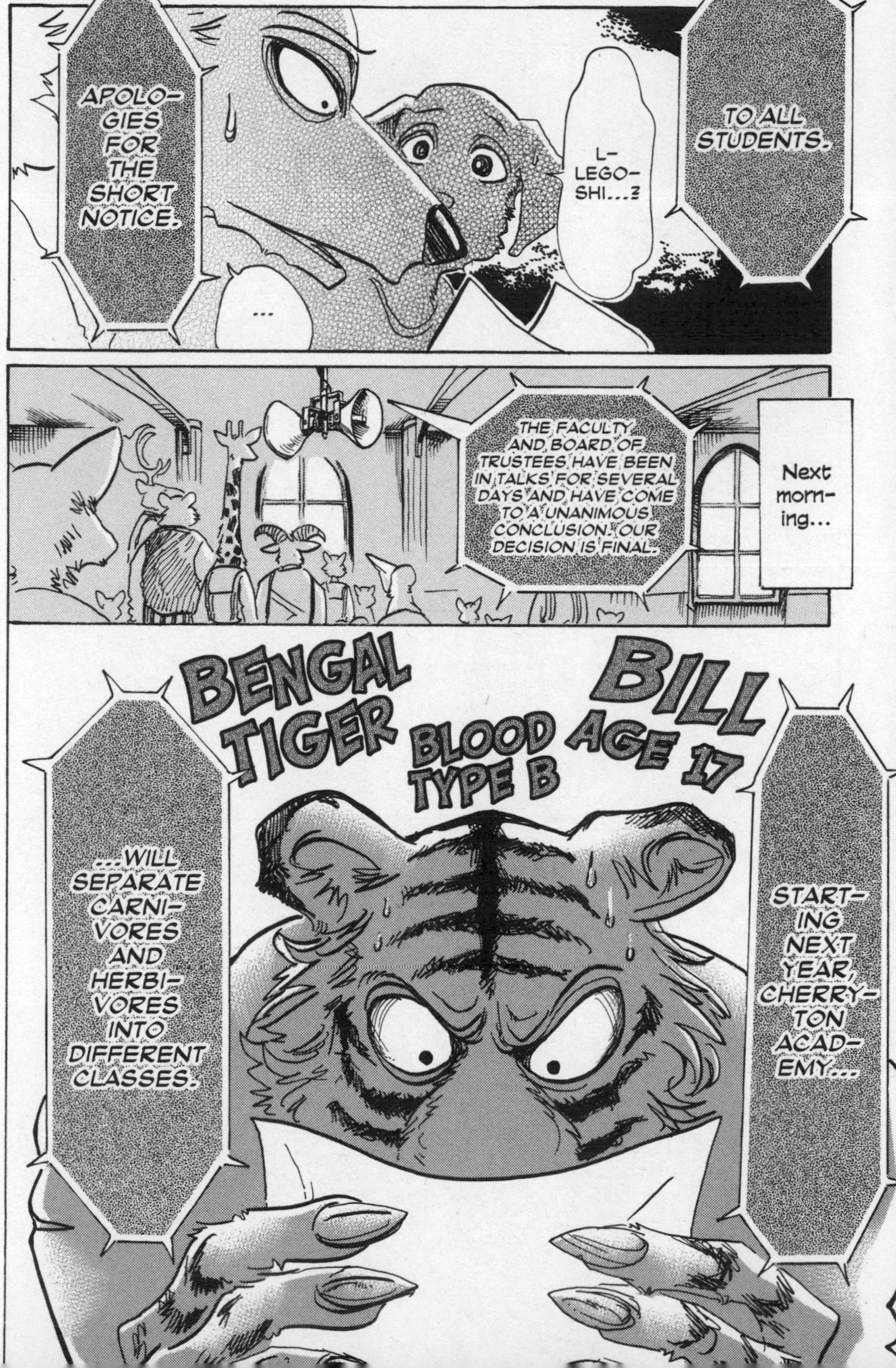
TO ALL STUDENTS.
L-LEGOSHI...?
APOLOGIES FOR THE SHORT NOTICE.
...
Next morning...
THE FACULTY AND BOARD OF TRUSTEES HAVE BEEN IN TALKS FOR SEVERAL DAYS AND HAVE COME TO A UNANIMOUS CONCLUSION. OUR DECISION IS FINAL.
STARTING NEXT YEAR, CHERRYTON ACADEMY...
BENGAL TIGER BILL
AGE 17
BLOOD TYPE B
...WILL SEPARATE CARNIVORES AND HERBIVORES INTO DIFFERENT CLASSES.

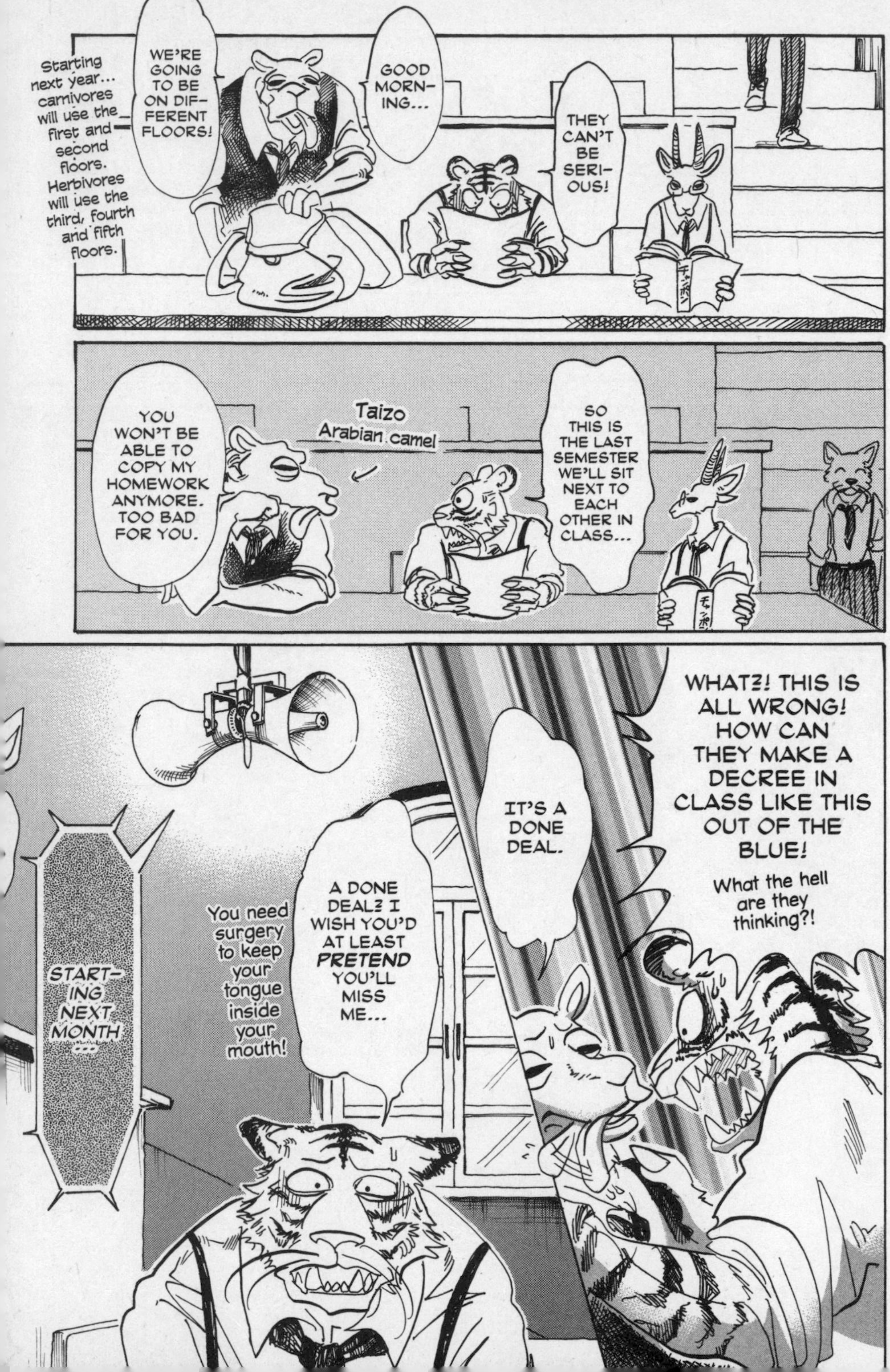
THEY CAN'T BE SERIOUS!
GOOD MORNING...
WE'RE GOING TO BE ON DIFFERENT FLOORS!
Starting next year... carnivores will use the first and second floors. Herbivores will use the third, fourth and fifth floors.
SO THIS IS THE LAST SEMESTER WE'LL SIT NEXT TO EACH OTHER IN CLASS...
Taizo
Arabian camel
YOU WON'T BE ABLE TO COPY MY HOMEWORK ANYMORE. TOO BAD FOR YOU.
WHAT?! THIS IS ALL WRONG! HOW CAN THEY MAKE A DECREE IN CLASS LIKE THIS OUT OF THE BLUE!
What the hell are they thinking?!
IT'S A DONE DEAL.
A DONE DEAL? I WISH YOU'D AT LEAST *PRETEND* YOU'LL MISS ME...
You need surgery to keep your tongue inside your mouth!
STARTING NEXT MONTH...

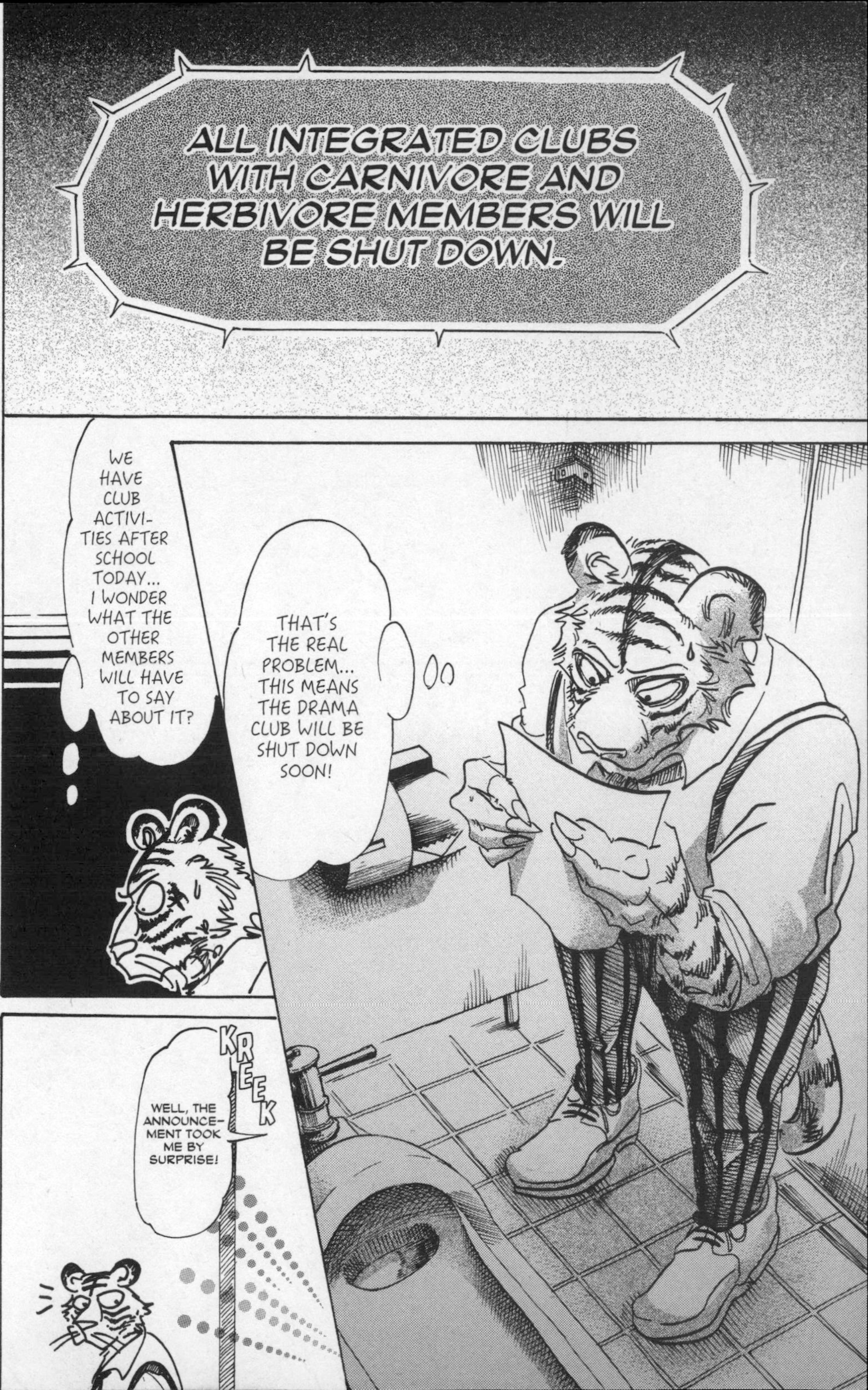
ALL INTEGRATED CLUBS WITH CARNIVORE AND HERBIVORE MEMBERS WILL BE SHUT DOWN.
THAT'S THE REAL PROBLEM... THIS MEANS THE DRAMA CLUB WILL BE SHUT DOWN SOON!
WE HAVE CLUB ACTIVITIES AFTER SCHOOL TODAY... I WONDER WHAT THE OTHER MEMBERS WILL HAVE TO SAY ABOUT IT?
KREEK
WELL, THE ANNOUNCEMENT TOOK ME BY SURPRISE!

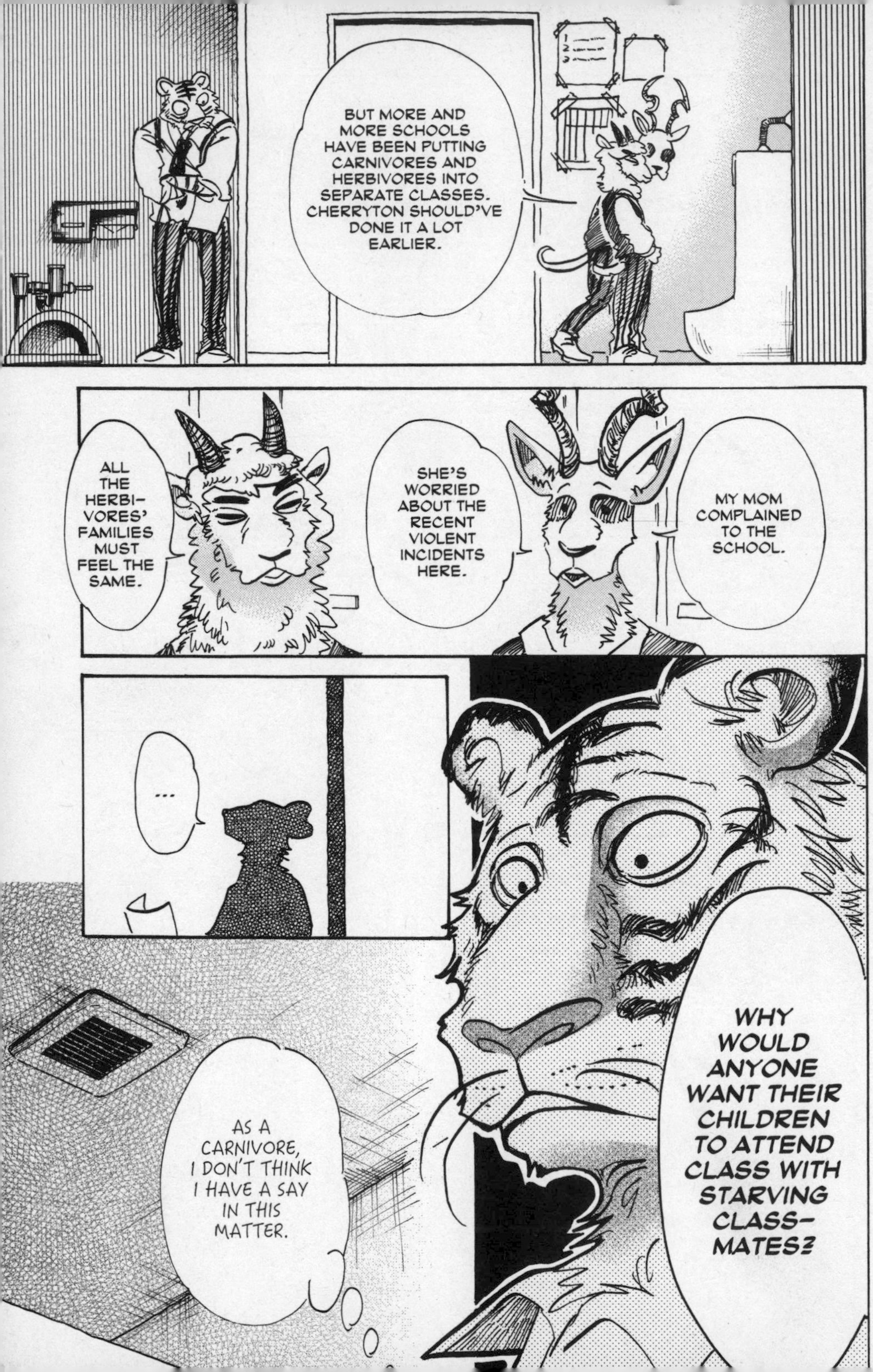
BUT MORE AND MORE SCHOOLS HAVE BEEN PUTTING CARNIVORES AND HERBIVORES INTO SEPARATE CLASSES. CHERRYTON SHOULD'VE DONE IT A LOT EARLIER.
MY MOM COMPLAINED TO THE SCHOOL.
SHE'S WORRIED ABOUT THE RECENT VIOLENT INCIDENTS HERE.
ALL THE HERBI-VORES' FAMILIES MUST FEEL THE SAME.
WHY WOULD ANYONE WANT THEIR CHILDREN TO ATTEND CLASS WITH STARVING CLASS-MATES?
...
AS A CARNIVORE, I DON'T THINK I HAVE A SAY IN THIS MATTER.

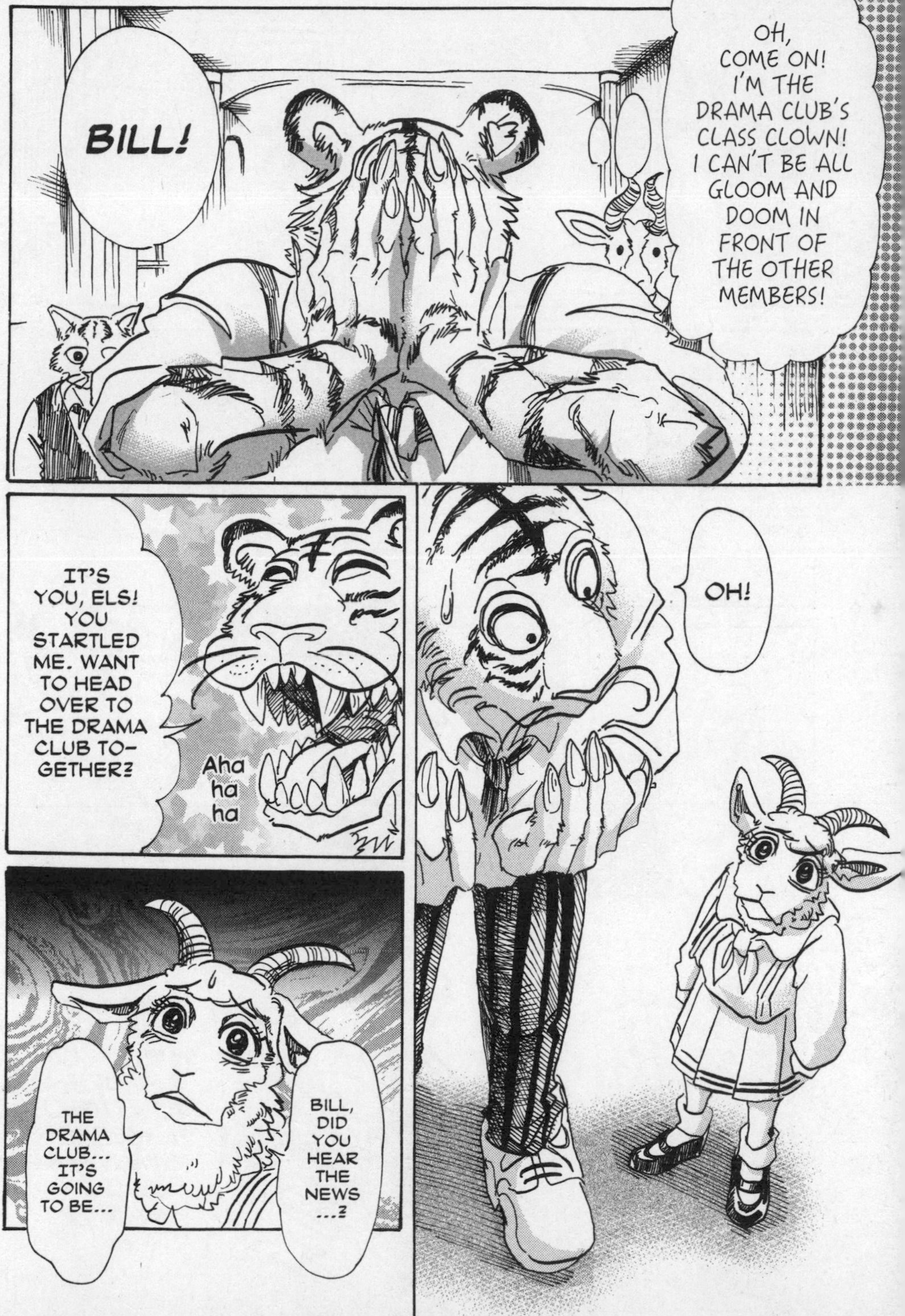

OH, COME ON! I'M THE DRAMA CLUB'S CLASS CLOWN! I CAN'T BE ALL GLOOM AND DOOM IN FRONT OF THE OTHER MEMBERS!
BILL!
OH!
IT'S YOU, ELS! YOU STARTLED ME. WANT TO HEAD OVER TO THE DRAMA CLUB TOGETHER?
Aha ha ha
BILL, DID YOU HEAR THE NEWS...?
THE DRAMA CLUB... IT'S GOING TO BE...

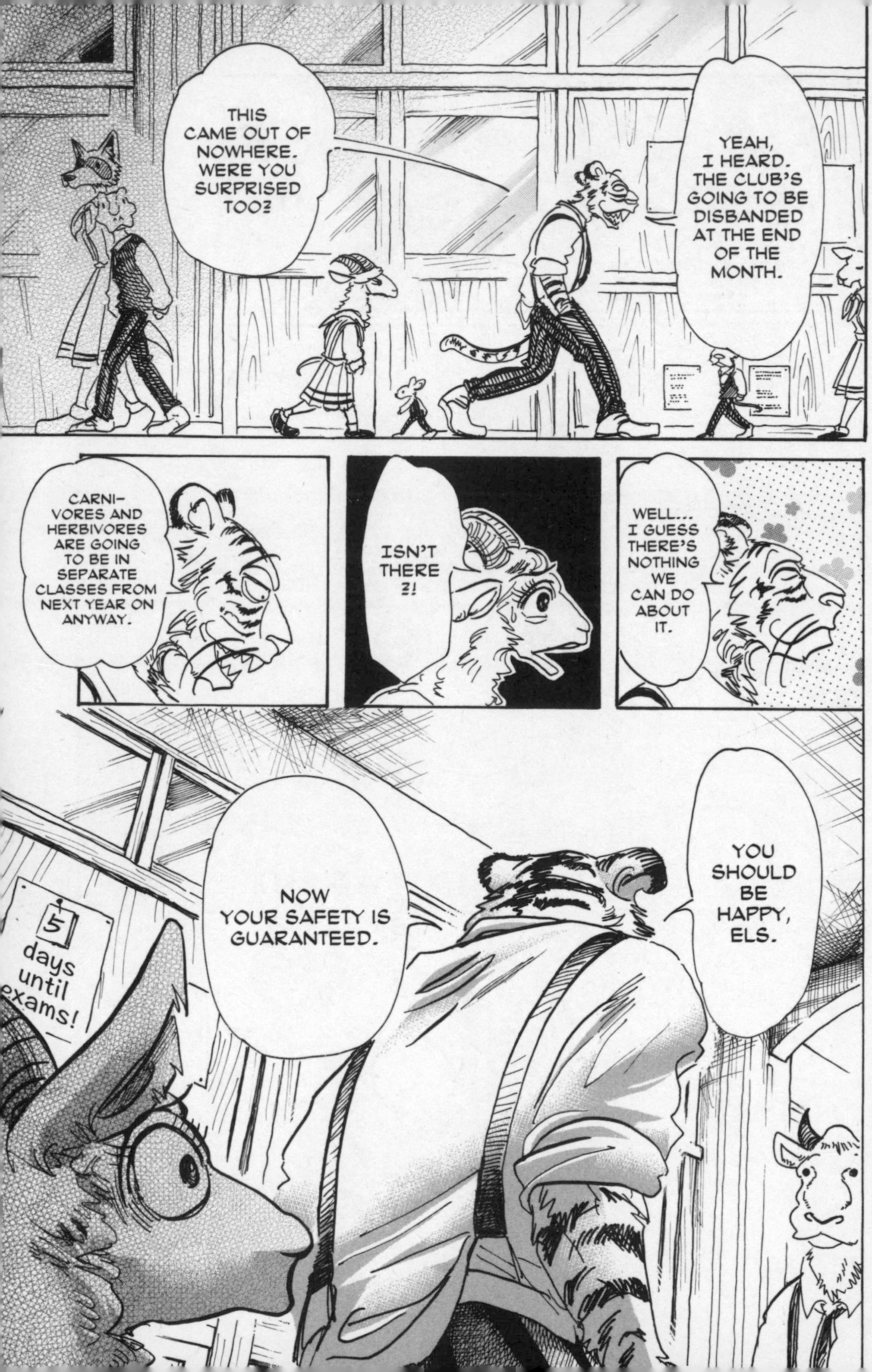
YEAH, I HEARD. THE CLUB'S GOING TO BE DISBANDED AT THE END OF THE MONTH.
THIS CAME OUT OF NOWHERE. WERE YOU SURPRISED TOO?
WELL... I GUESS THERE'S NOTHING WE CAN DO ABOUT IT.
ISN'T THERE ?!
CARNI-VORES AND HERBIVORES ARE GOING TO BE IN SEPARATE CLASSES FROM NEXT YEAR ON ANYWAY.
YOU SHOULD BE HAPPY, ELS.
NOW YOUR SAFETY IS GUARANTEED.
5 days until exams!

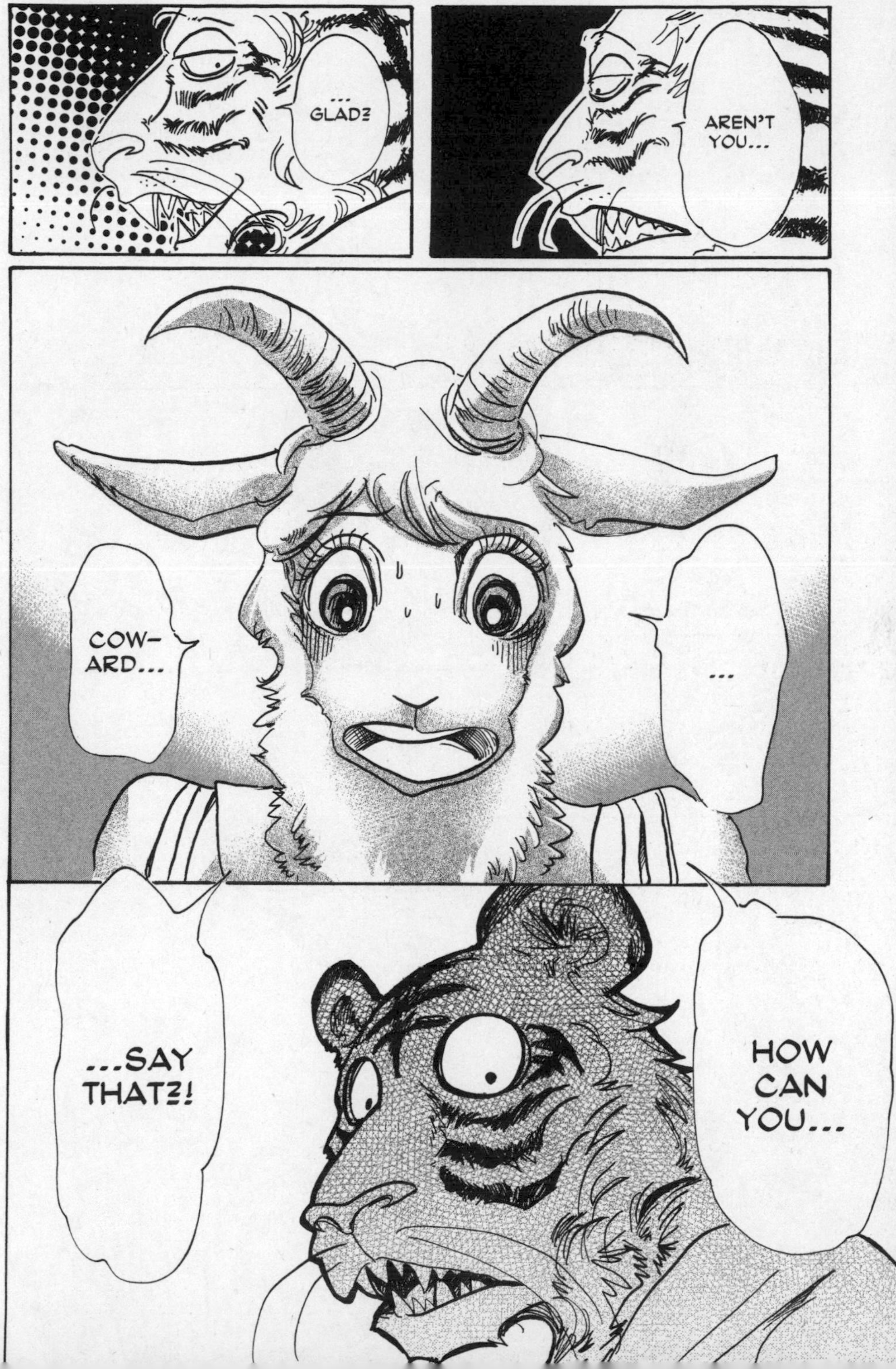
AREN'T YOU...
...GLAD?!
...
COW-ARD...
HOW CAN YOU...
...SAY THAT?!

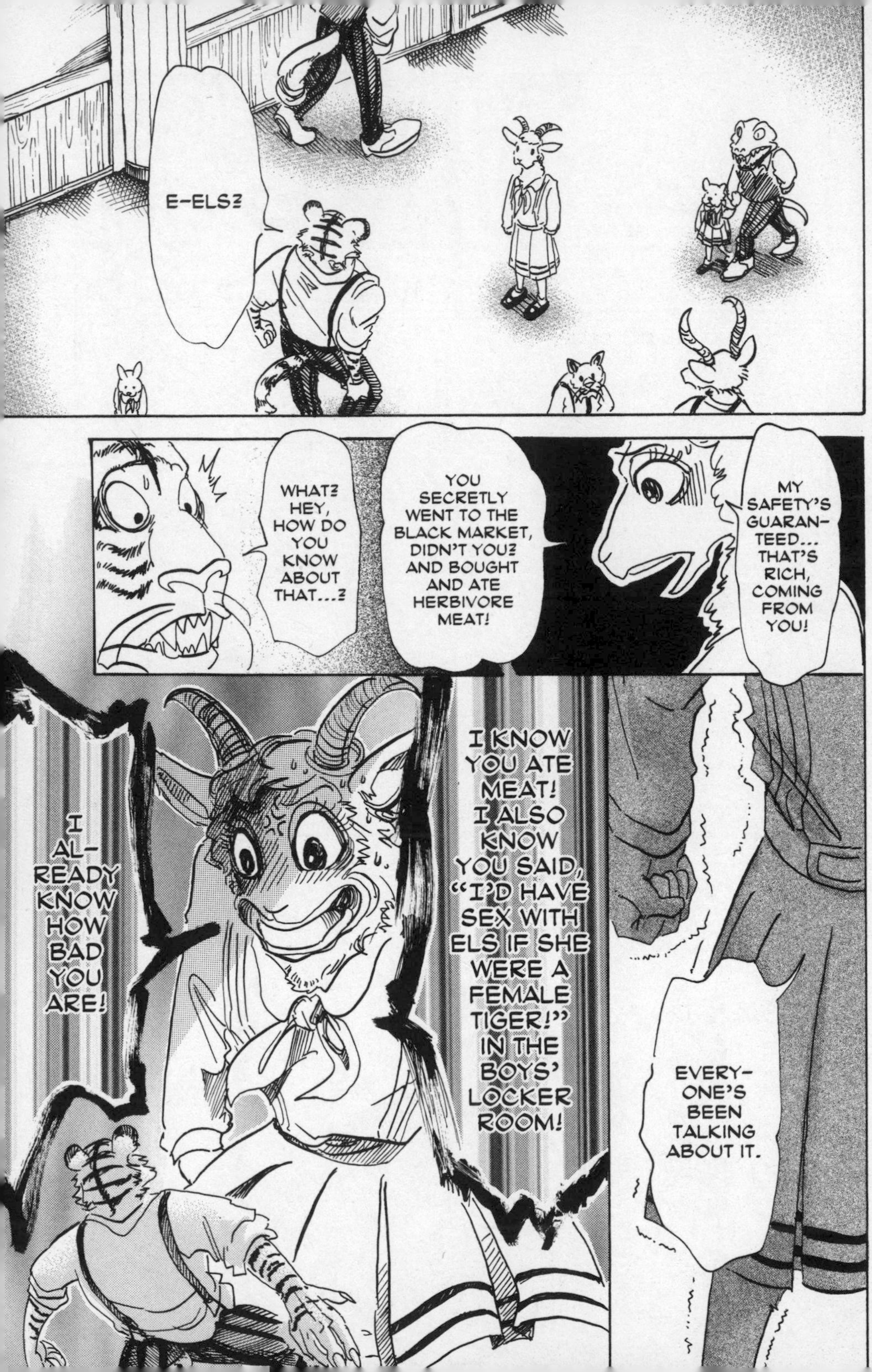
E-ELS?
MY SAFETY'S GUARANTEED... THAT'S RICH, COMING FROM YOU!
YOU SECRETLY WENT TO THE BLACK MARKET, DIDN'T YOU? AND BOUGHT AND ATE HERBIVORE MEAT!
WHAT? HEY, HOW DO YOU KNOW ABOUT THAT...?
EVERYONE'S BEEN TALKING ABOUT IT.
I KNOW YOU ATE MEAT! I ALSO KNOW YOU SAID, "I'D HAVE SEX WITH ELS IF SHE WERE A FEMALE TIGER!" IN THE BOYS' LOCKER ROOM!
I ALREADY KNOW HOW BAD YOU ARE!

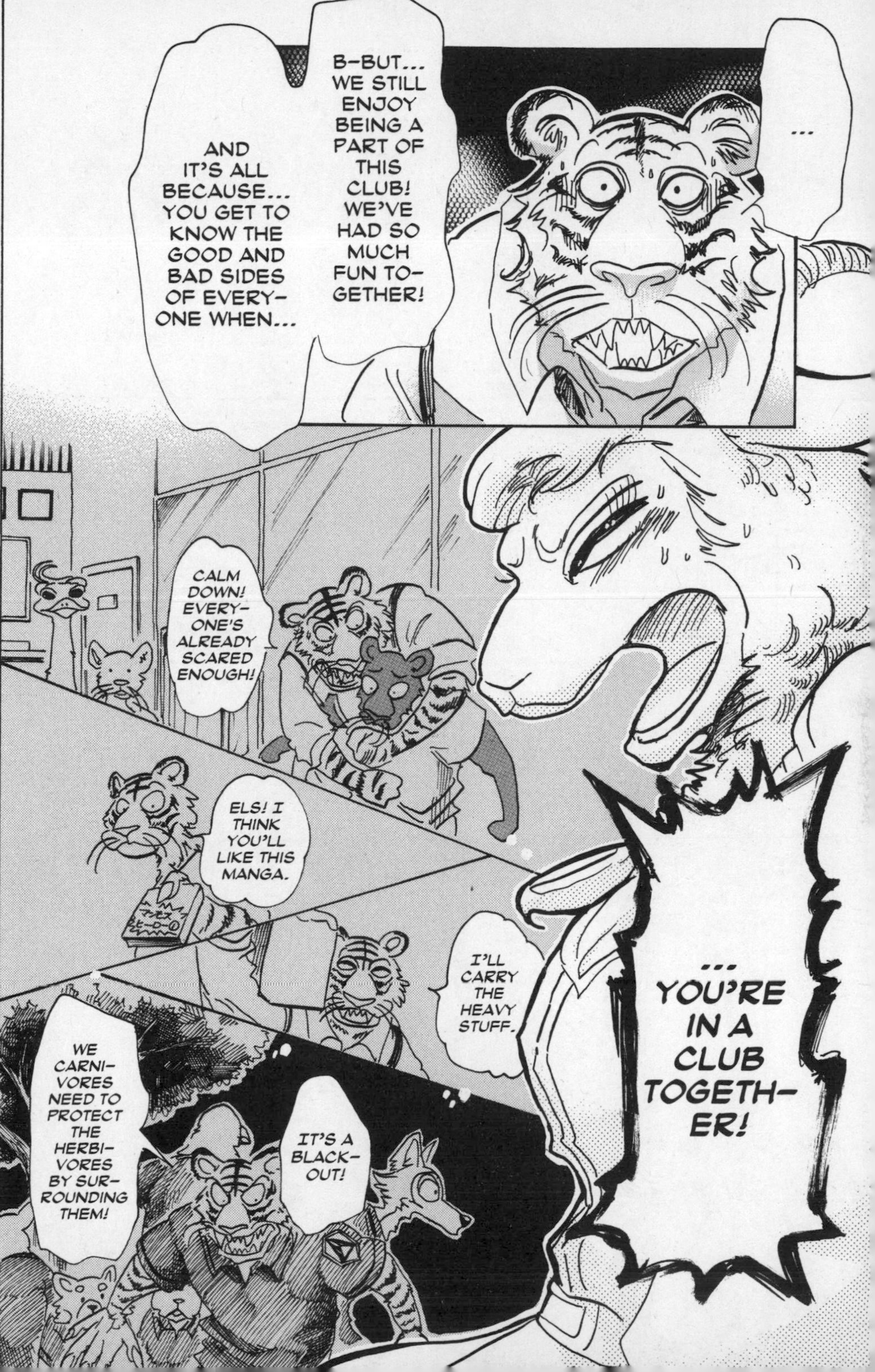
...
B-BUT... WE STILL ENJOY BEING A PART OF THIS CLUB! WE'VE HAD SO MUCH FUN TO-GETHER!
AND IT'S ALL BECAUSE... YOU GET TO KNOW THE GOOD AND BAD SIDES OF EVERY-ONE WHEN...
...YOU'RE IN A CLUB TOGETH-ER!
CALM DOWN! EVERY-ONE'S ALREADY SCARED ENOUGH!
ELS! I THINK YOU'LL LIKE THIS MANGA.
I'LL CARRY THE HEAVY STUFF.
IT'S A BLACK-OUT!
WE CARNI-VORES NEED TO PROTECT THE HERBI-VORES BY SUR-ROUNDING THEM!

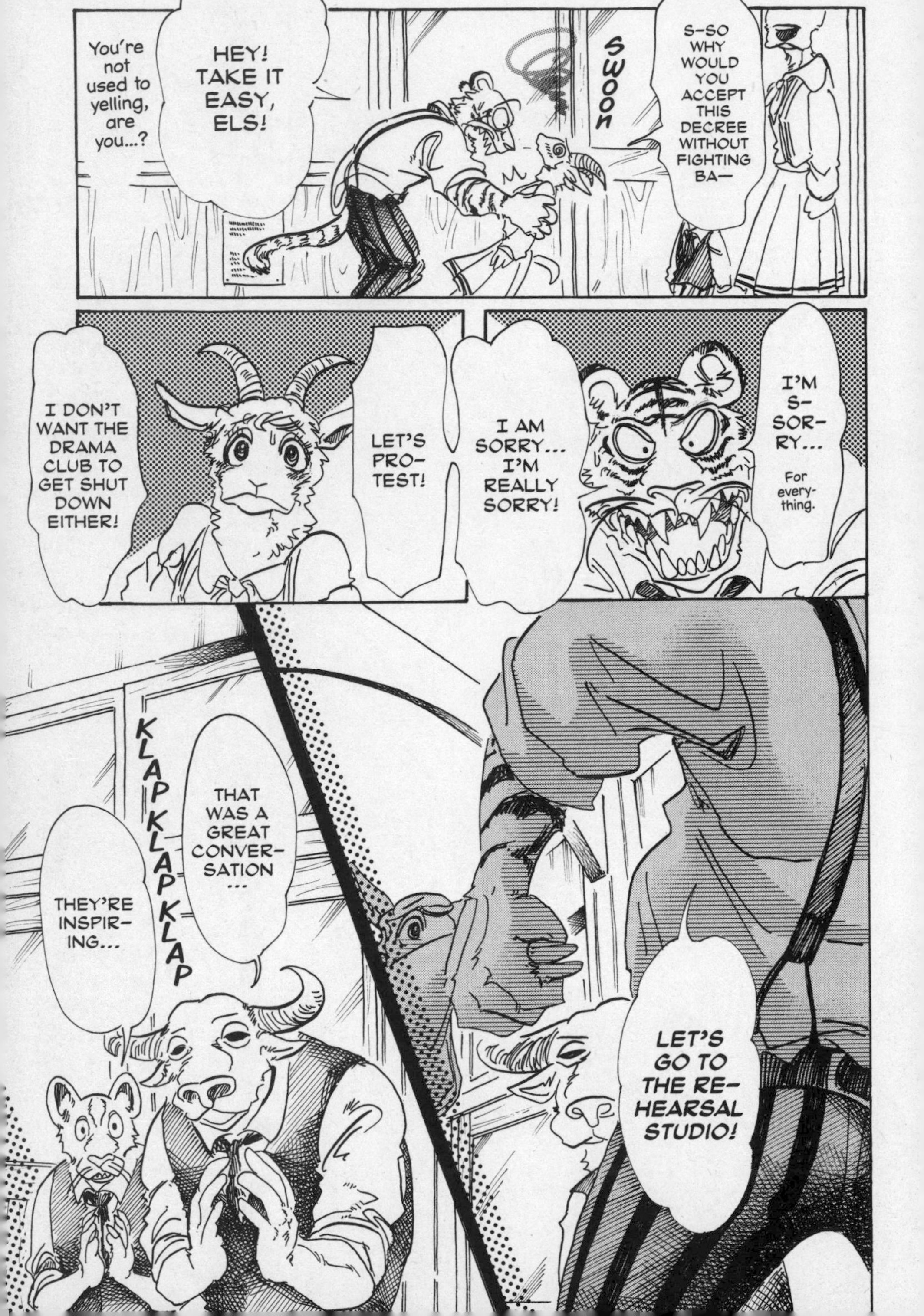
S-SO WHY WOULD YOU ACCEPT THIS DECREE WITHOUT FIGHTING BA—
SWOON
HEY! TAKE IT EASY, ELS!
You're not used to yelling, are you...?
I'M S-SORRY...
For everything.
I AM SORRY... I'M REALLY SORRY!
LET'S PROTEST!
I DON'T WANT THE DRAMA CLUB TO GET SHUT DOWN EITHER!
LET'S GO TO THE REHEARSAL STUDIO!
KLAP KLAP KLAP KLAP
THAT WAS A GREAT CONVERSATION...
THEY'RE INSPIRING...

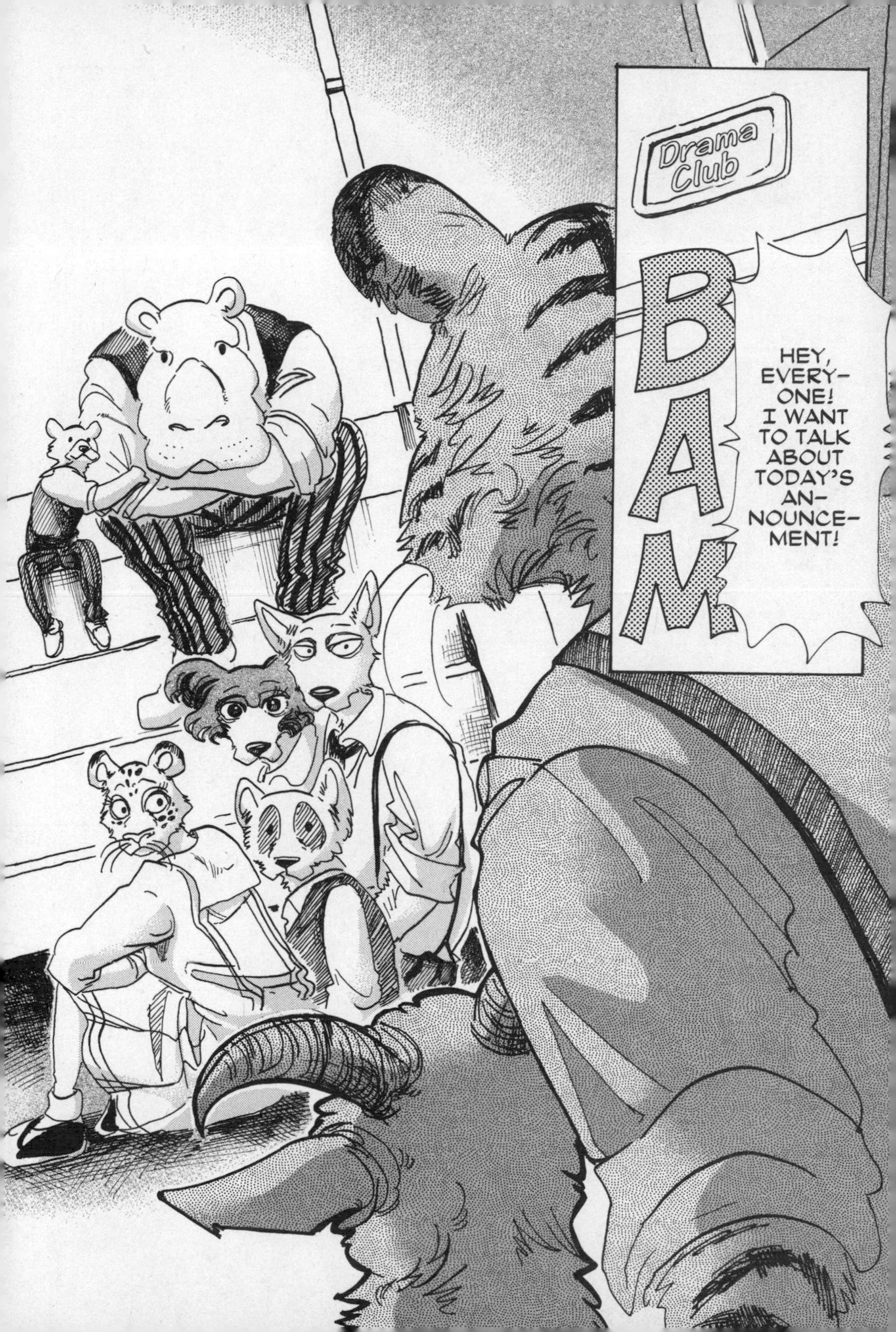
Drama Club
BAM
HEY, EVERY-ONE! I WANT TO TALK ABOUT TODAY'S AN-NOUNCE-MENT!

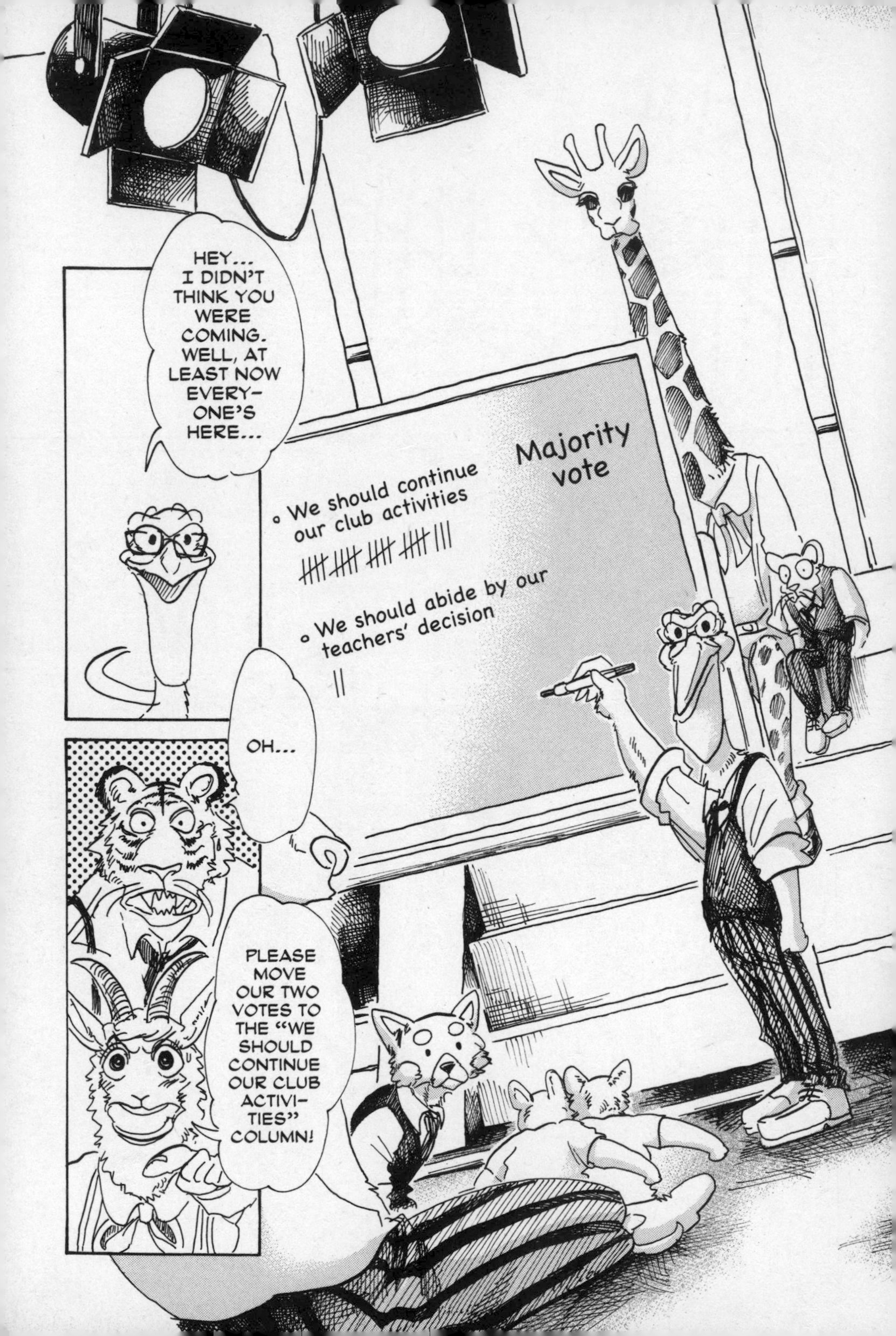
Majority vote
We should continue our club activities
We should abide by our teachers' decision
HEY... I DIDN'T THINK YOU WERE COMING. WELL, AT LEAST NOW EVERYONE'S HERE...
OH...
PLEASE MOVE OUR TWO VOTES TO THE "WE SHOULD CONTINUE OUR CLUB ACTIVITIES" COLUMN!

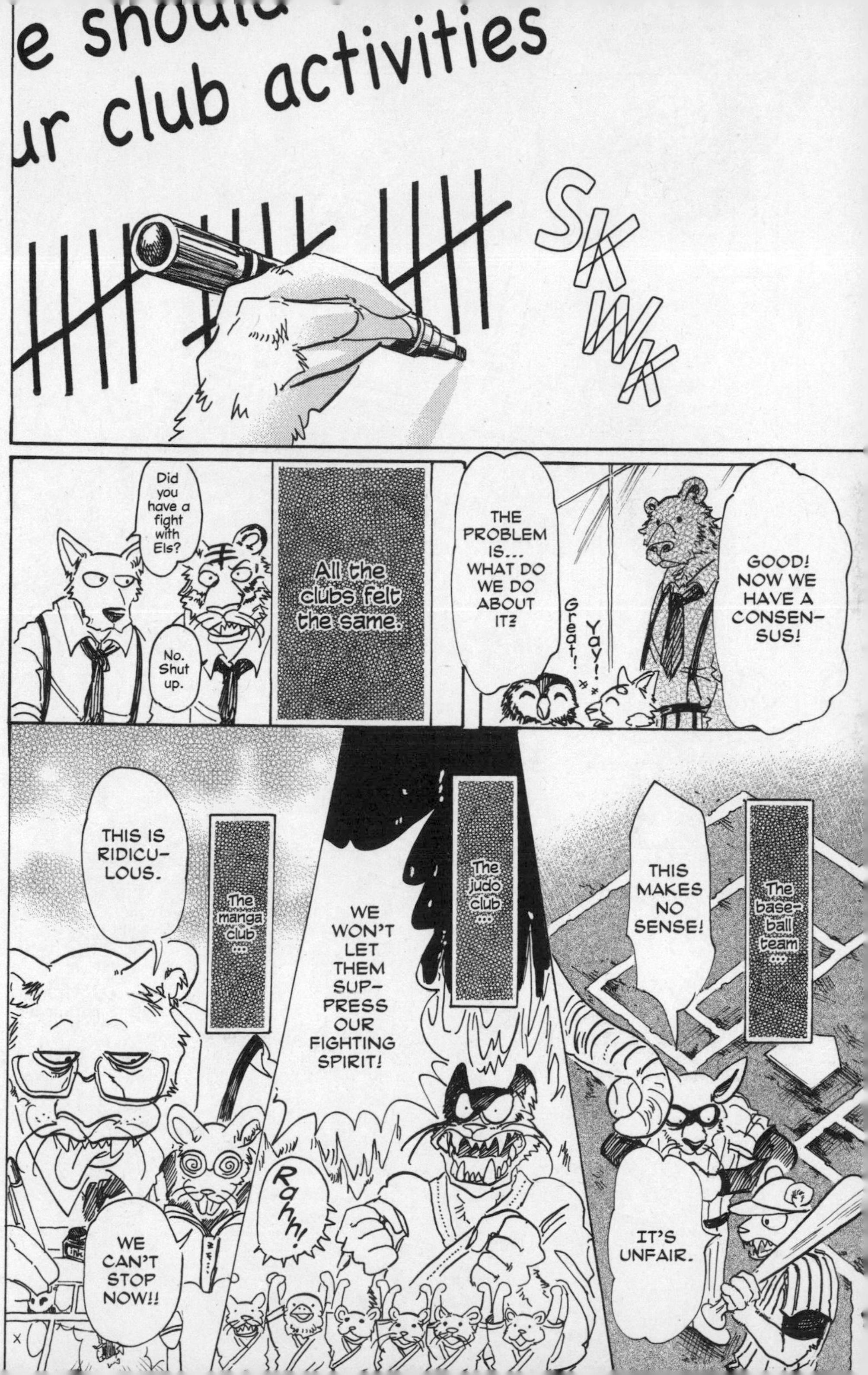
e should
ur club activities
SKWK
GOOD! NOW WE HAVE A CONSEN-SUS!
Yay!
Great!
THE PROBLEM IS... WHAT DO WE DO ABOUT IT?
All the clubs felt the same.
Did you have a fight with Els?
No. Shut up.
The base-ball team...
THIS MAKES NO SENSE!
IT'S UNFAIR.
The judo club...
WE WON'T LET THEM SUP-PRESS OUR FIGHTING SPIRIT!
Rahh!
The manga club...
THIS IS RIDICU-LOUS.
WE CAN'T STOP NOW!!

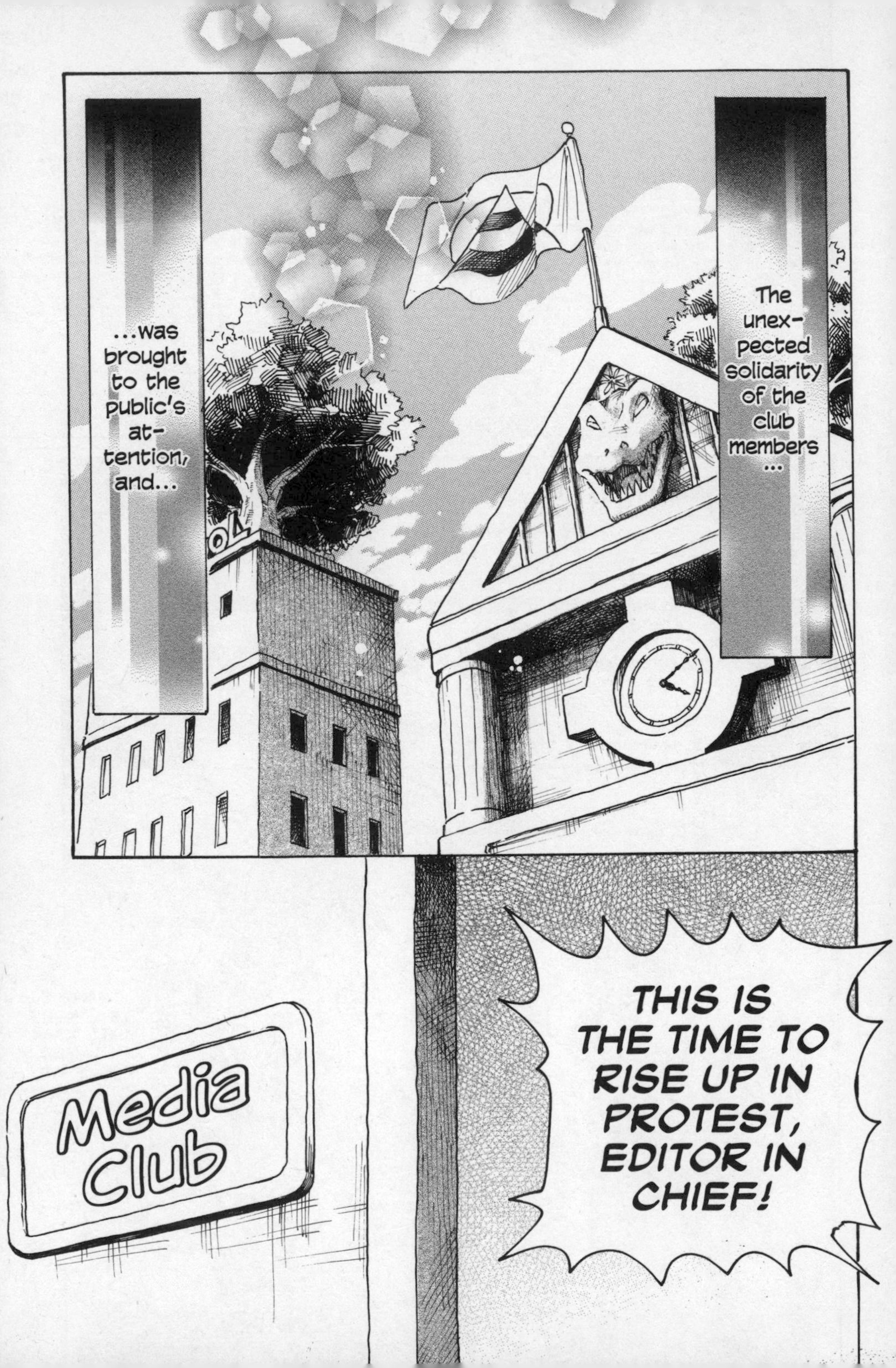
The unexpected solidarity of the club members...
...was brought to the public's attention, and...
THIS IS THE TIME TO RISE UP IN PROTEST, EDITOR IN CHIEF!
Media Club

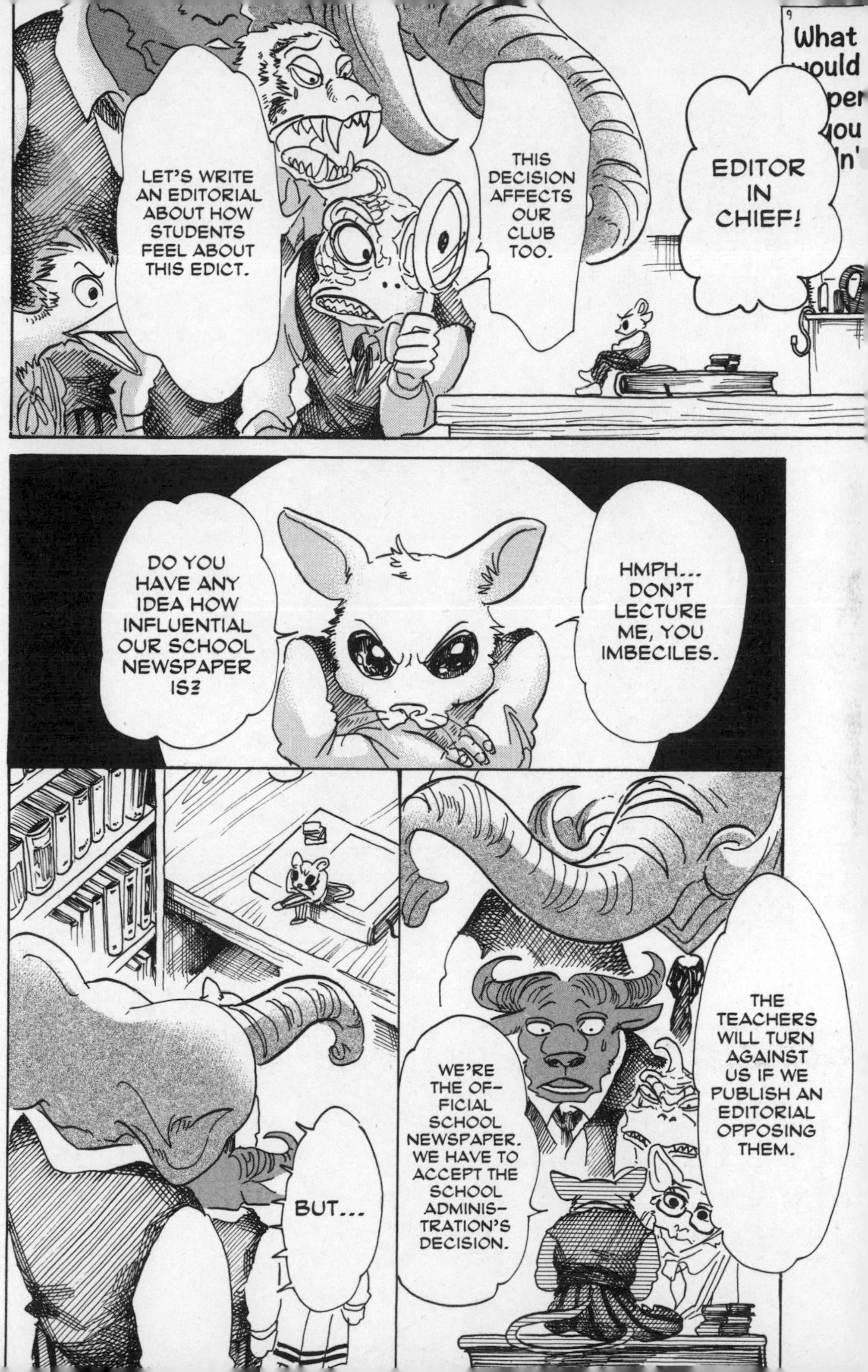
EDITOR IN CHIEF!
THIS DECISION AFFECTS OUR CLUB TOO.
LET'S WRITE AN EDITORIAL ABOUT HOW STUDENTS FEEL ABOUT THIS EDICT.
HMPH... DON'T LECTURE ME, YOU IMBECILES.
DO YOU HAVE ANY IDEA HOW INFLUENTIAL OUR SCHOOL NEWSPAPER IS?
THE TEACHERS WILL TURN AGAINST US IF WE PUBLISH AN EDITORIAL OPPOSING THEM.
WE'RE THE OF-FICIAL SCHOOL NEWSPAPER. WE HAVE TO ACCEPT THE SCHOOL ADMINIS-TRATION'S DECISION.
BUT...

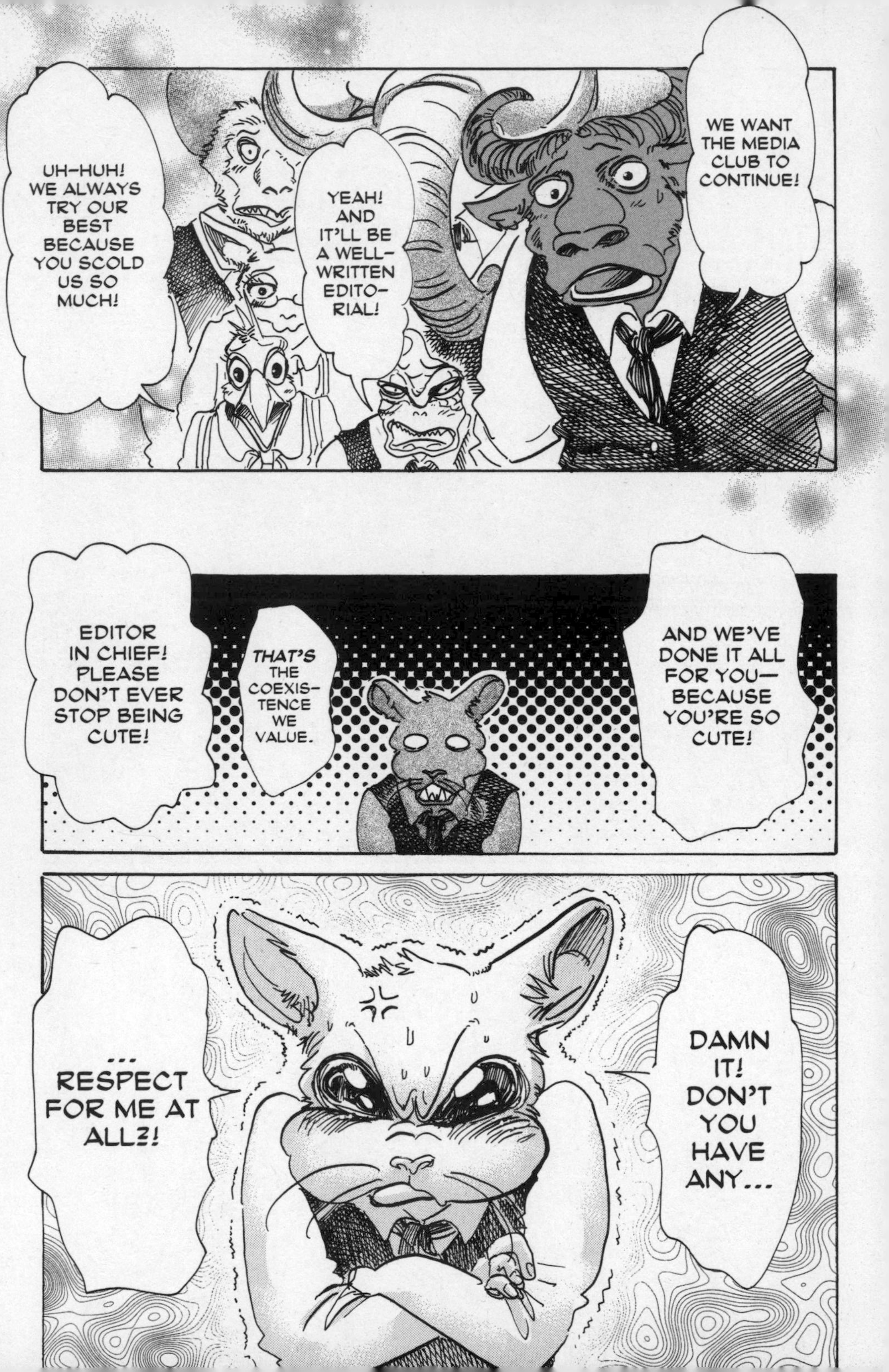
WE WANT THE MEDIA CLUB TO CONTINUE!
YEAH! AND IT'LL BE A WELL-WRITTEN EDITORIAL!
UH-HUH! WE ALWAYS TRY OUR BEST BECAUSE YOU SCOLD US SO MUCH!
AND WE'VE DONE IT ALL FOR YOU—BECAUSE YOU'RE SO CUTE!
THAT'S THE COEXISTENCE WE VALUE.
EDITOR IN CHIEF! PLEASE DON'T EVER STOP BEING CUTE!
DAMN IT! DON'T YOU HAVE ANY...
...RESPECT FOR ME AT ALL?!

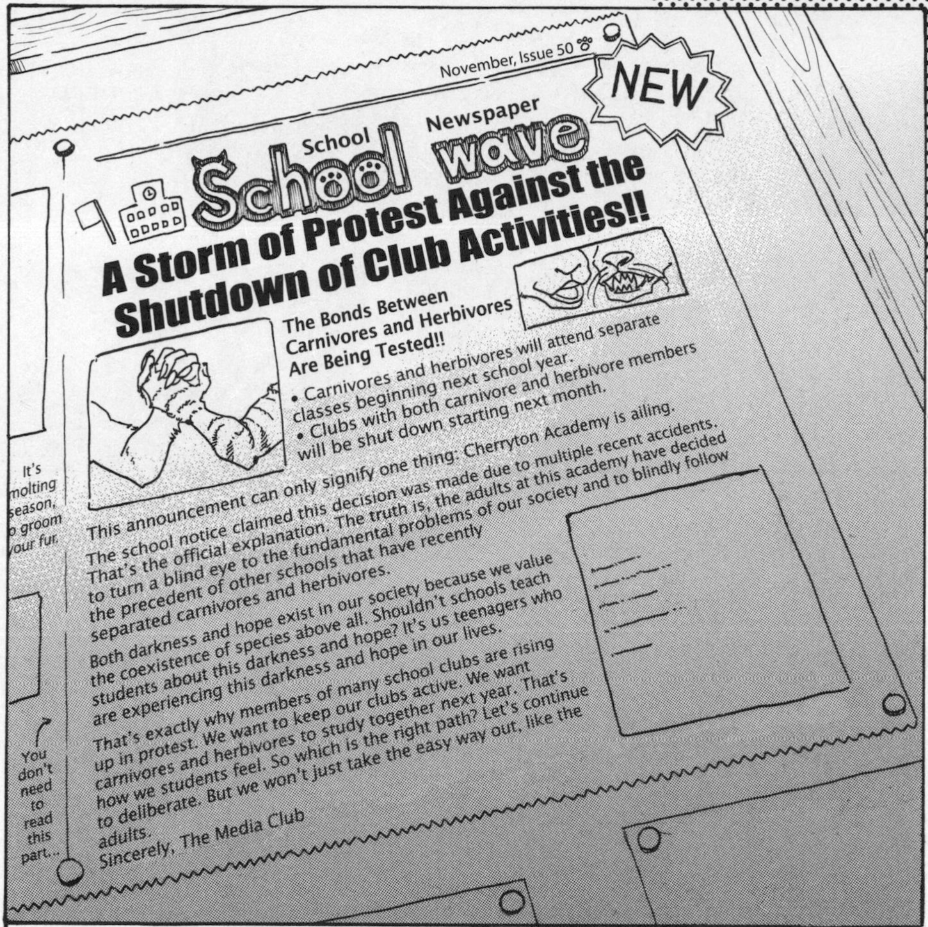
November, Issue 50
NEW
School Newspaper
School wave
A Storm of Protest Against the Shutdown of Club Activities!!
The Bonds Between Carnivores and Herbivores Are Being Tested!!
• Carnivores and herbivores will attend separate classes beginning next school year.
• Clubs with both carnivore and herbivore members will be shut down starting next month.
This announcement can only signify one thing: Cherryton Academy is ailing.
The school notice claimed this decision was made due to multiple recent accidents. That's the official explanation. The truth is, the adults at this academy have decided to turn a blind eye to the fundamental problems of our society and to blindly follow the precedent of other schools that have recently separated carnivores and herbivores.
Both darkness and hope exist in our society because we value the coexistence of species above all. Shouldn't schools teach students about this darkness and hope? It's us teenagers who are experiencing this darkness and hope in our lives.
That's exactly why members of many school clubs are rising up in protest. We want to keep our clubs active. We want carnivores and herbivores to study together next year. That's how we students feel. So which is the right path? Let's continue to deliberate. But we won't just take the easy way out, like the adults.
Sincerely, The Media Club
It's molting season,
groom your fur.
You don't need to read this part...
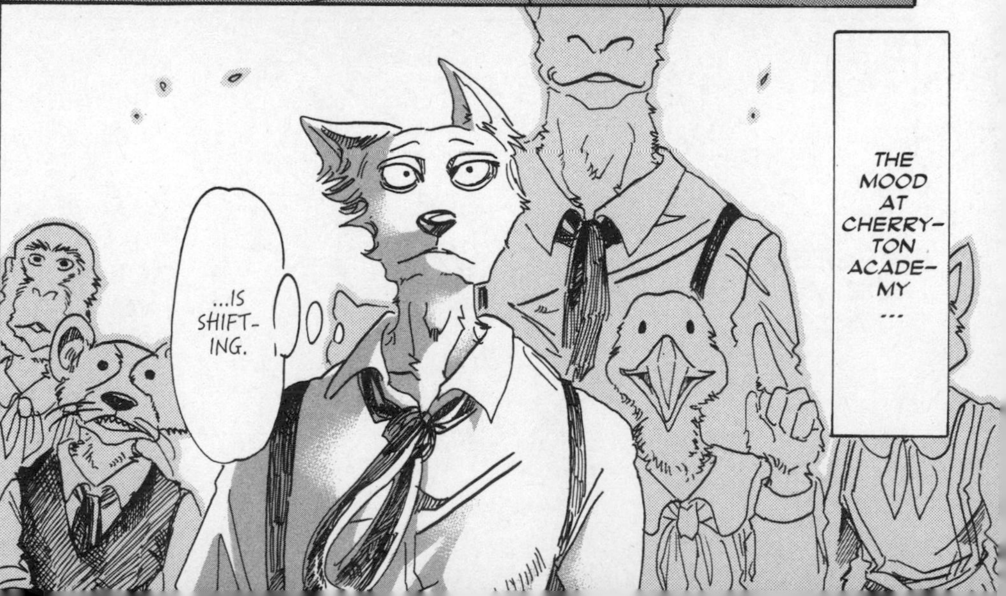
THE MOOD AT CHERRYTON ACADEMY...
...IS SHIFTING.

Chapter 79: Secret Encounter with Lingerie

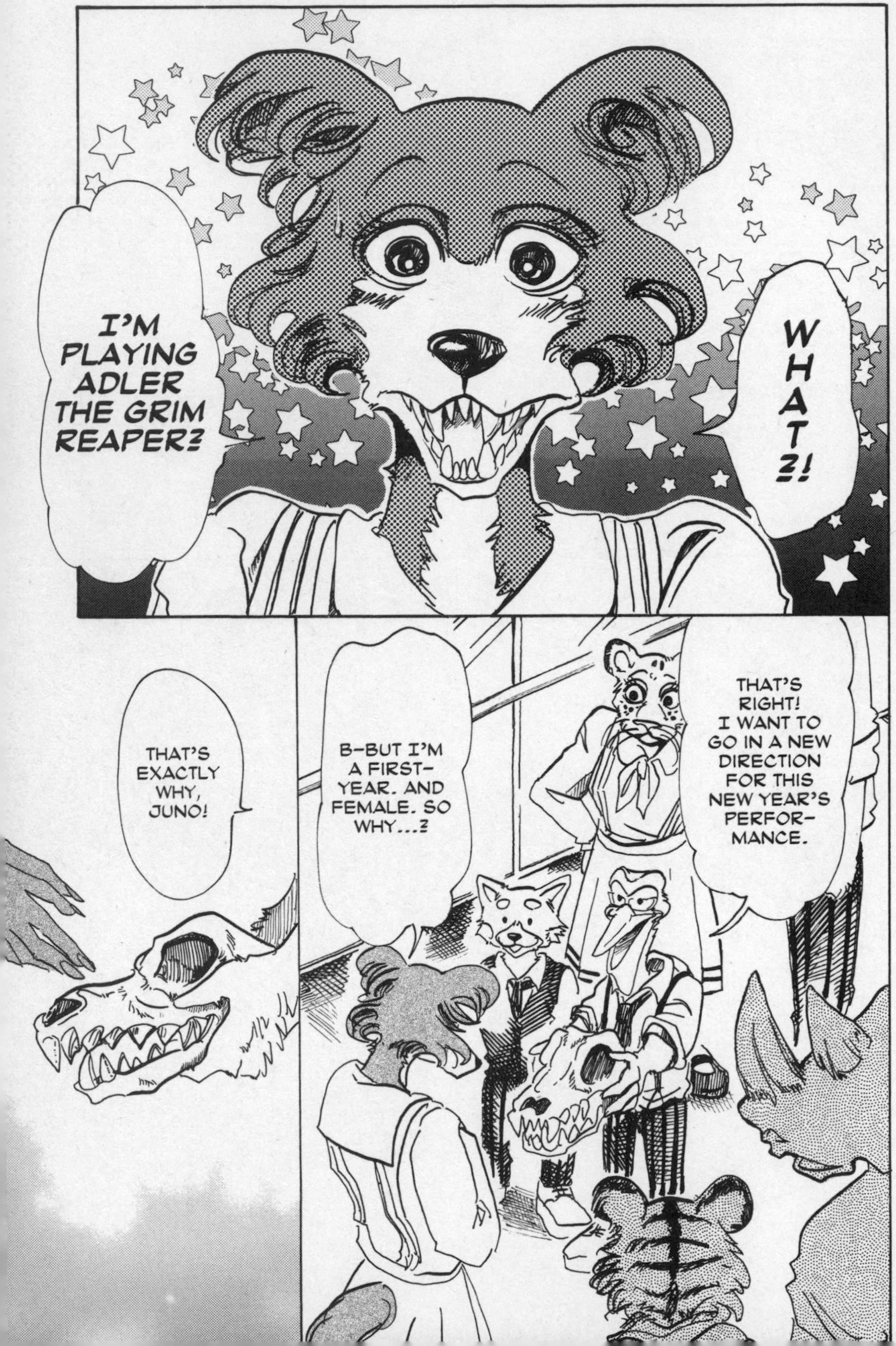
WHAT?!
I'M PLAYING ADLER THE GRIM REAPER?
THAT'S RIGHT! I WANT TO GO IN A NEW DIRECTION FOR THIS NEW YEAR'S PERFORMANCE.
B-BUT I'M A FIRST-YEAR. AND FEMALE. SO WHY...?
THAT'S EXACTLY WHY, JUNO!

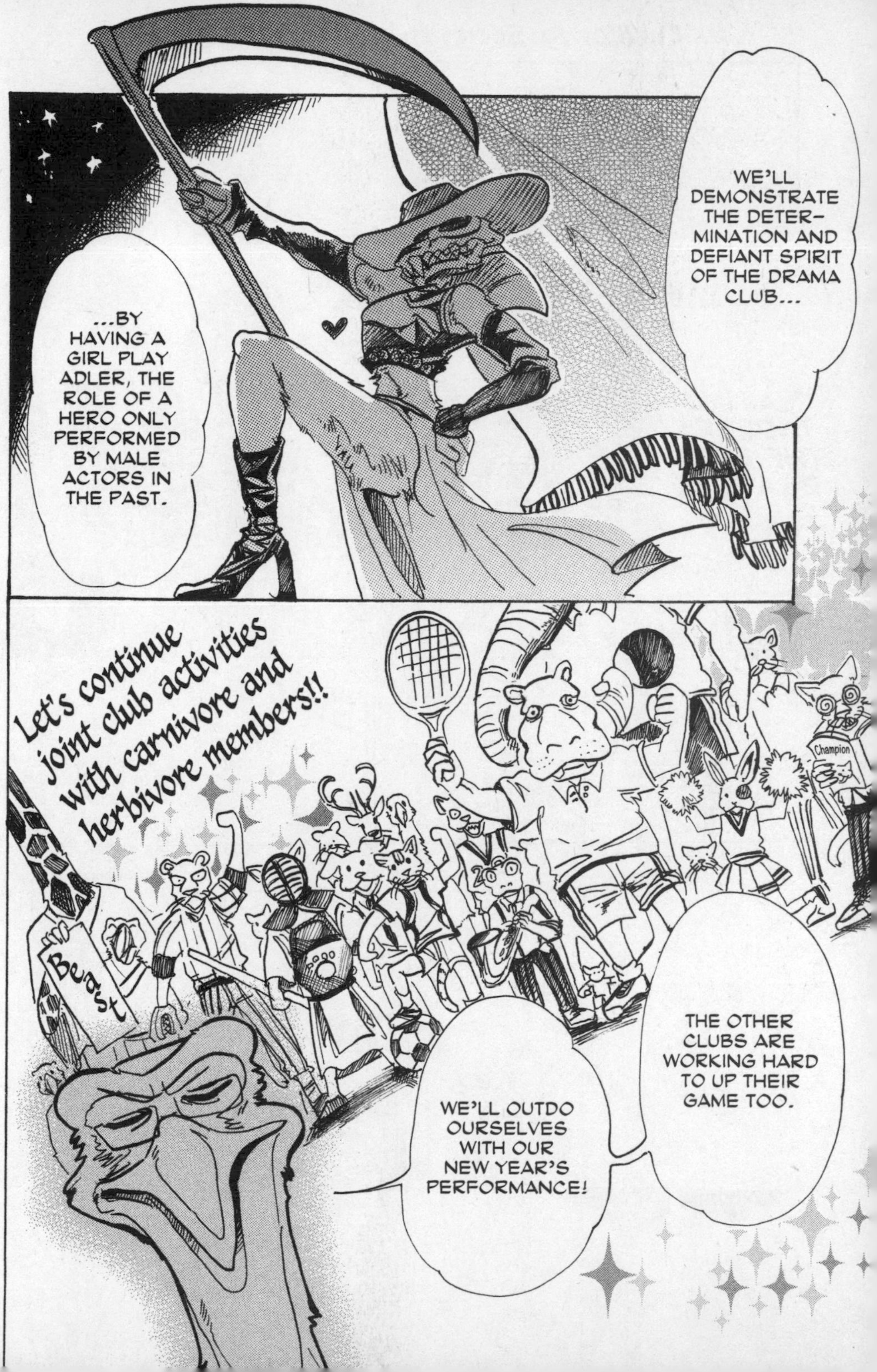
WE'LL DEMONSTRATE THE DETER-MINATION AND DEFIANT SPIRIT OF THE DRAMA CLUB...
...BY HAVING A GIRL PLAY ADLER, THE ROLE OF A HERO ONLY PERFORMED BY MALE ACTORS IN THE PAST.
Let's continue joint club activities with carnivore and herbivore members!!
Champion
Beast
THE OTHER CLUBS ARE WORKING HARD TO UP THEIR GAME TOO.
WE'LL OUTDO OURSELVES WITH OUR NEW YEAR'S PERFORMANCE!

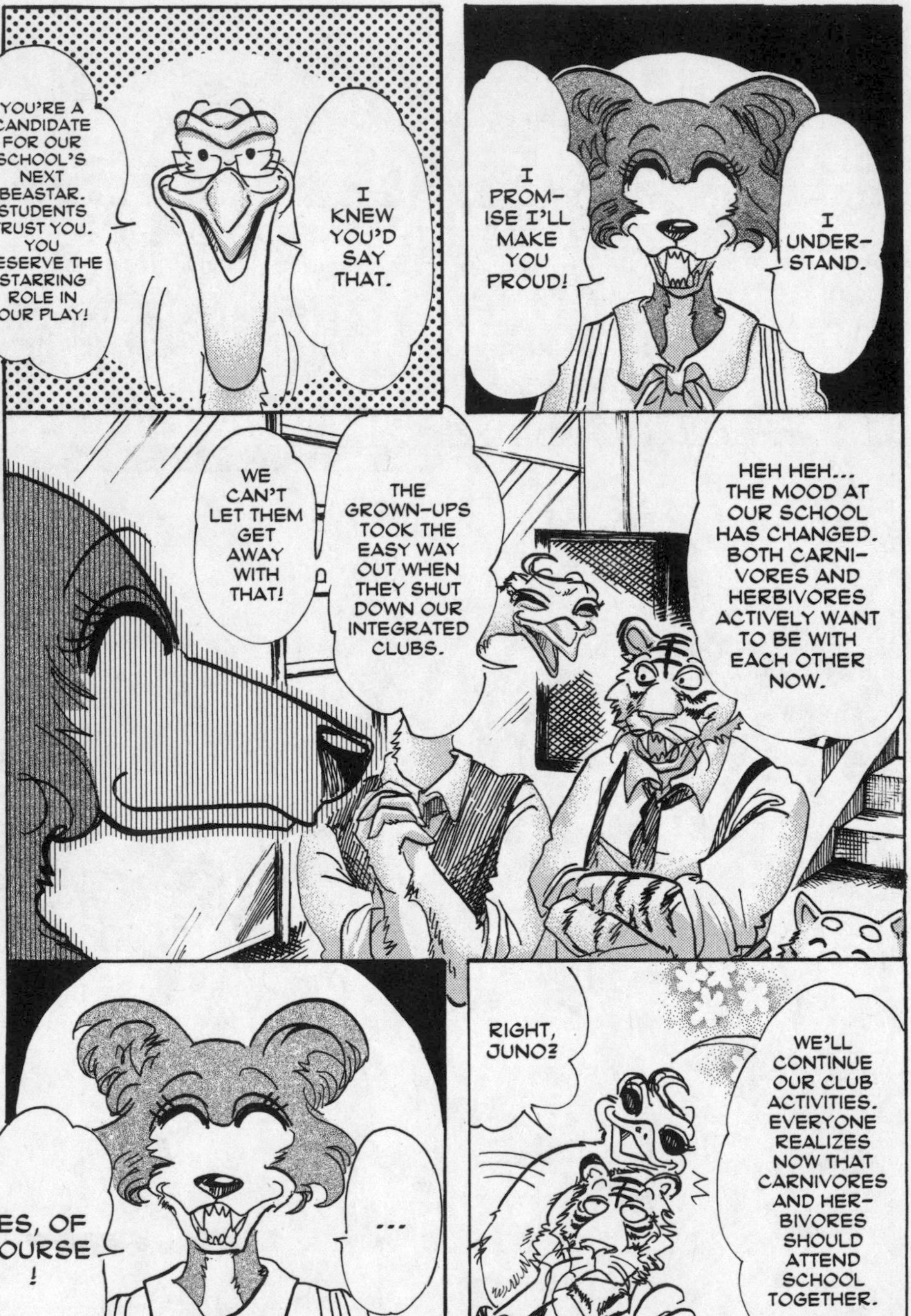
I UNDER-STAND.
I PROMISE I'LL MAKE YOU PROUD!
I KNEW YOU'D SAY THAT.
YOU'RE A CANDIDATE FOR OUR SCHOOL'S NEXT BEASTAR. STUDENTS TRUST YOU. YOU DESERVE THE STARRING ROLE IN OUR PLAY!
HEH HEH... THE MOOD AT OUR SCHOOL HAS CHANGED. BOTH CARNIVORES AND HERBIVORES ACTIVELY WANT TO BE WITH EACH OTHER NOW.
THE GROWN-UPS TOOK THE EASY WAY OUT WHEN THEY SHUT DOWN OUR INTEGRATED CLUBS.
WE CAN'T LET THEM GET AWAY WITH THAT!
WE'LL CONTINUE OUR CLUB ACTIVITIES. EVERYONE REALIZES NOW THAT CARNIVORES AND HER-BIVORES SHOULD ATTEND SCHOOL TOGETHER.
RIGHT, JUNO?
...
YES, OF COURSE!

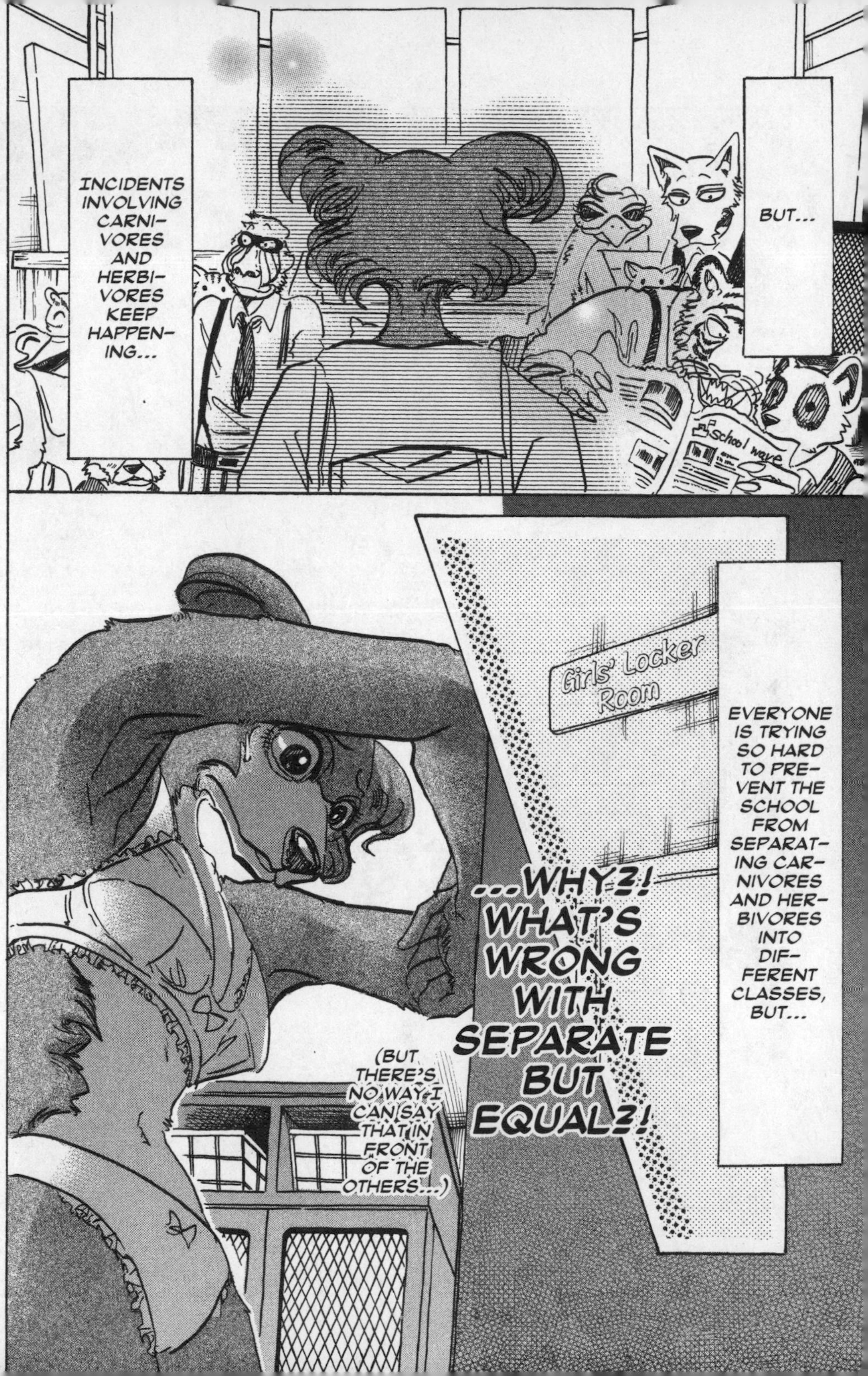
INCIDENTS INVOLVING CARNIVORES AND HERBIVORES KEEP HAPPENING...
BUT...
School wave
EVERYONE IS TRYING SO HARD TO PREVENT THE SCHOOL FROM SEPARATING CARNIVORES AND HERBIVORES INTO DIFFERENT CLASSES, BUT...
Girls' Locker Room
...WHY?! WHAT'S WRONG WITH SEPARATE BUT EQUAL?!
(BUT THERE'S NO WAY I CAN SAY THAT IN FRONT OF THE OTHERS...)

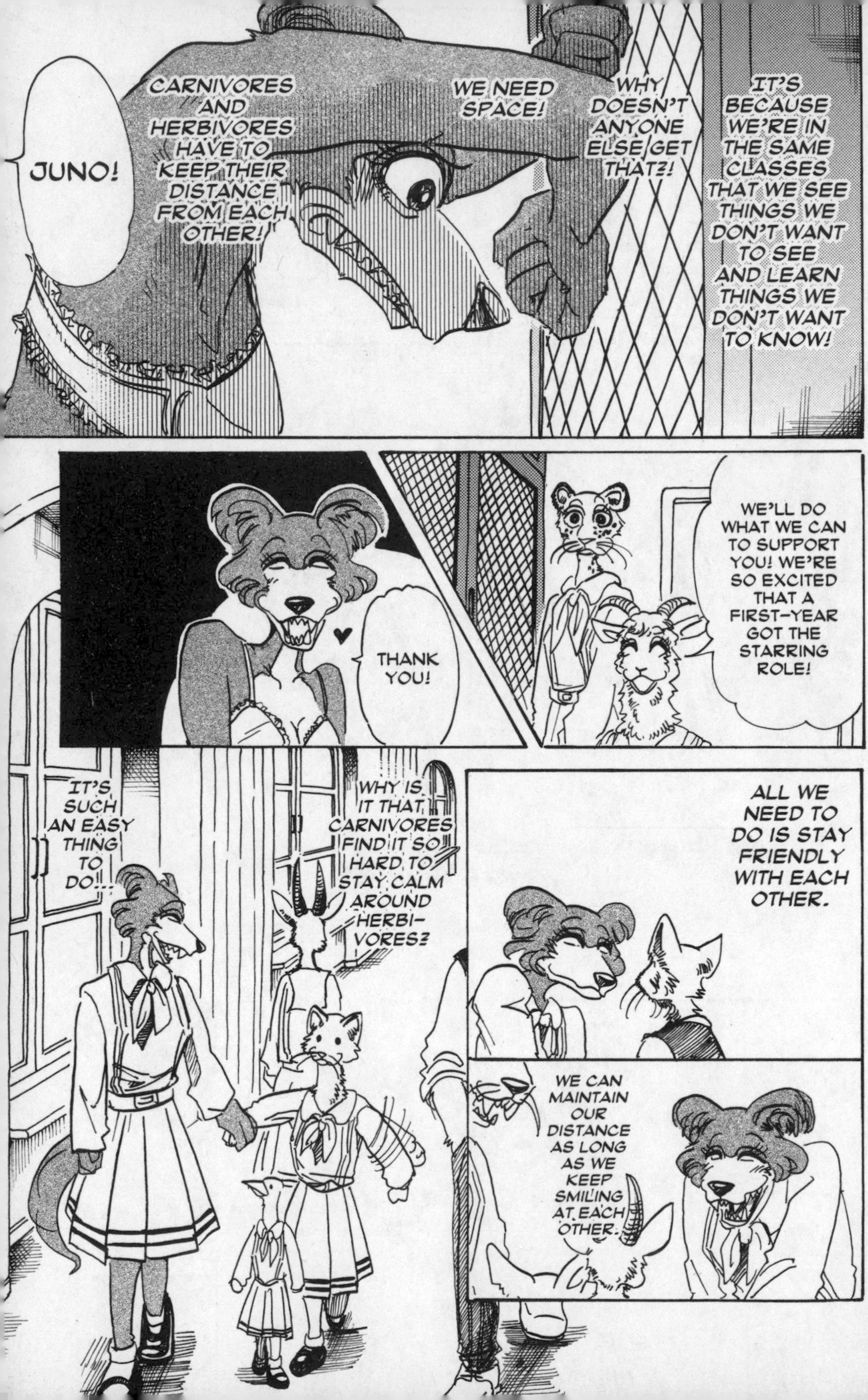
IT'S BECAUSE WE'RE IN THE SAME CLASSES THAT WE SEE THINGS WE DON'T WANT TO SEE AND LEARN THINGS WE DON'T WANT TO KNOW!
WHY DOESN'T ANYONE ELSE GET THAT?!
WE NEED SPACE!
CARNIVORES AND HERBIVORES HAVE TO KEEP THEIR DISTANCE FROM EACH OTHER!
JUNO!
WE'LL DO WHAT WE CAN TO SUPPORT YOU! WE'RE SO EXCITED THAT A FIRST-YEAR GOT THE STARRING ROLE!
THANK YOU!
ALL WE NEED TO DO IS STAY FRIENDLY WITH EACH OTHER.
WE CAN MAINTAIN OUR DISTANCE AS LONG AS WE KEEP SMILING AT EACH OTHER.
WHY IS IT THAT CARNIVORES FIND IT SO HARD TO STAY CALM AROUND HERBIVORES?
IT'S SUCH AN EASY THING TO DO...

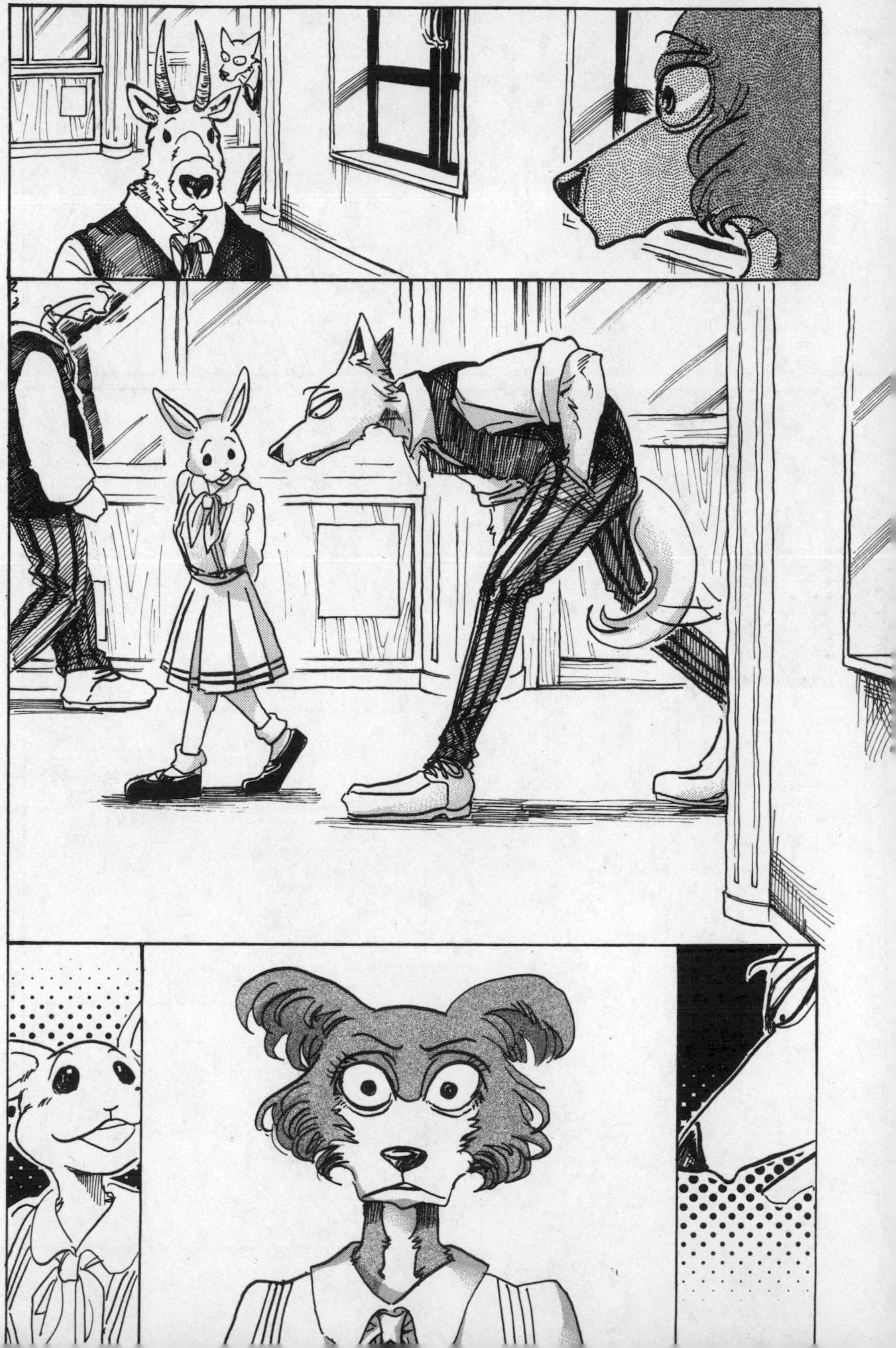

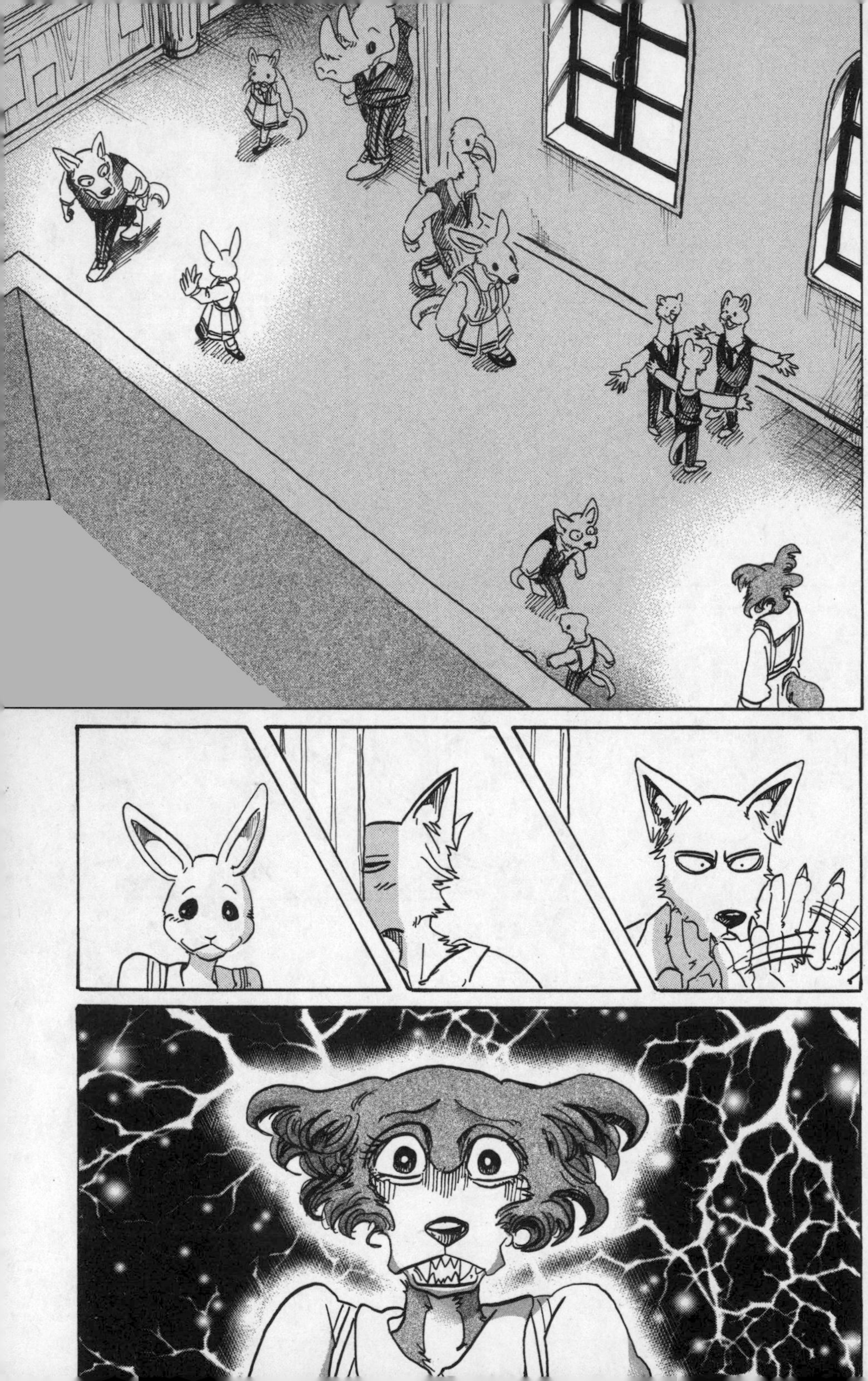

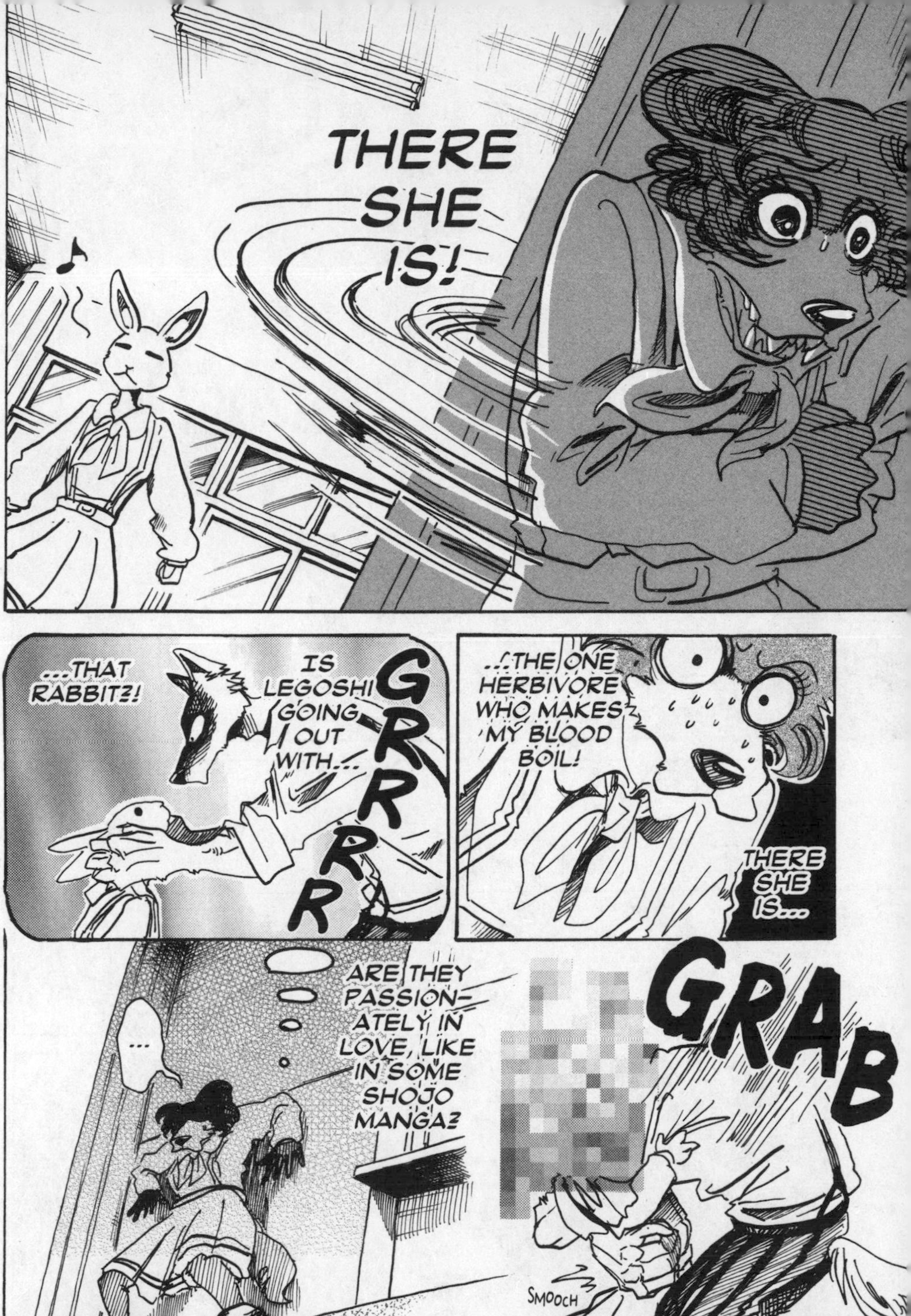
THERE SHE IS!
...THE ONE HERBIVORE WHO MAKES MY BLOOD BOIL!
THERE SHE IS...
GRRRR
IS LEGOSHI GOING OUT WITH...
...THAT RABBIT?!
GRAB
SMOOCH
ARE THEY PASSIONATELY IN LOVE, LIKE IN SOME SHOJO MANGA?
...

*What Juno is imagining.

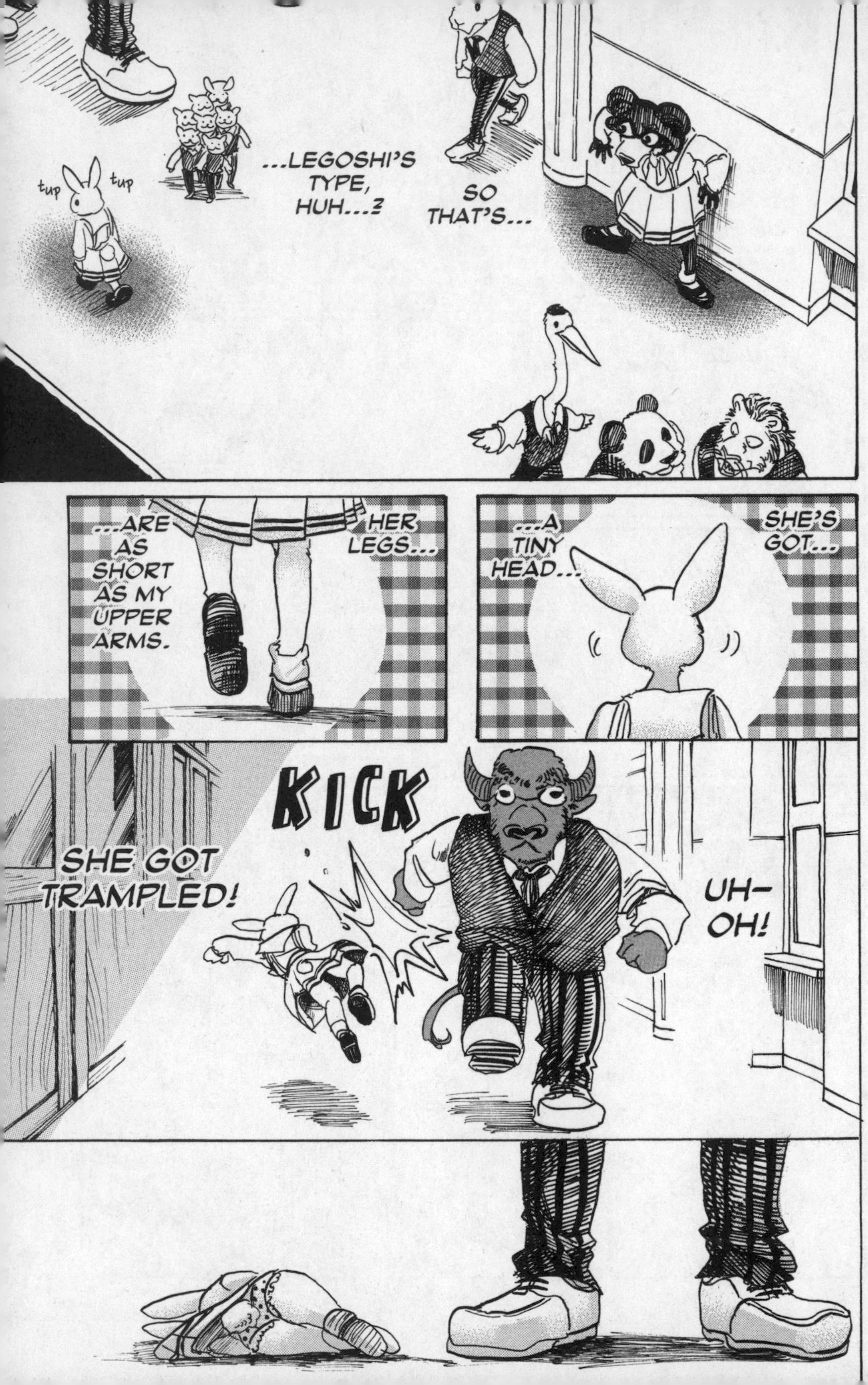
SO THAT'S...
...LEGOSHI'S TYPE, HUH...?
tup tup
SHE'S GOT...
...A TINY HEAD...
HER LEGS...
...ARE AS SHORT AS MY UPPER ARMS.
UH-OH!
KICK
SHE GOT TRAMPLED!

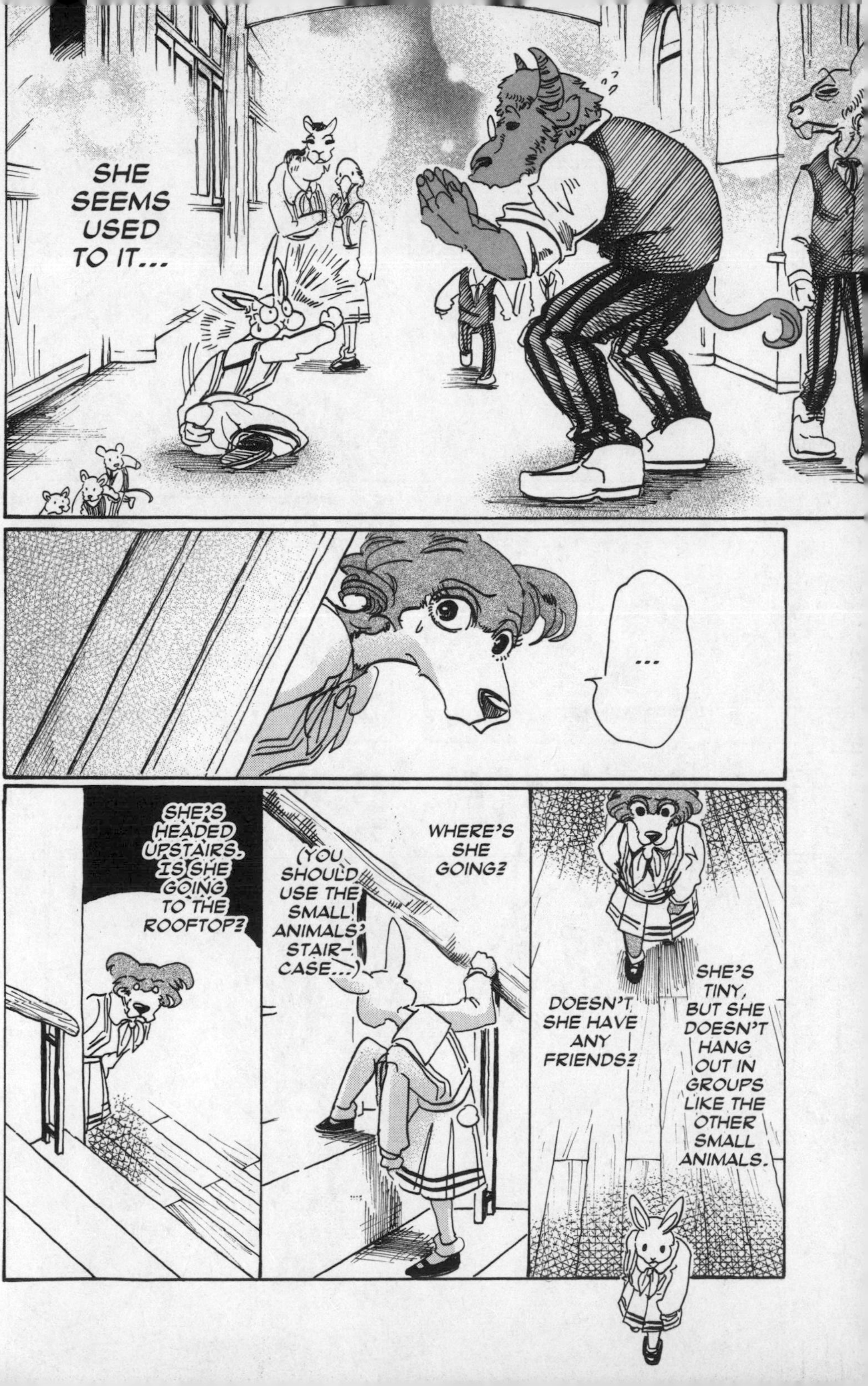
SHE SEEMS USED TO IT...
...
SHE'S TINY, BUT SHE DOESN'T HANG OUT IN GROUPS LIKE THE OTHER SMALL ANIMALS.
DOESN'T SHE HAVE ANY FRIENDS?
WHERE'S SHE GOING?
(YOU SHOULD USE THE SMALL ANIMALS' STAIRCASE...)
SHE'S HEADED UPSTAIRS. IS SHE GOING TO THE ROOFTOP?

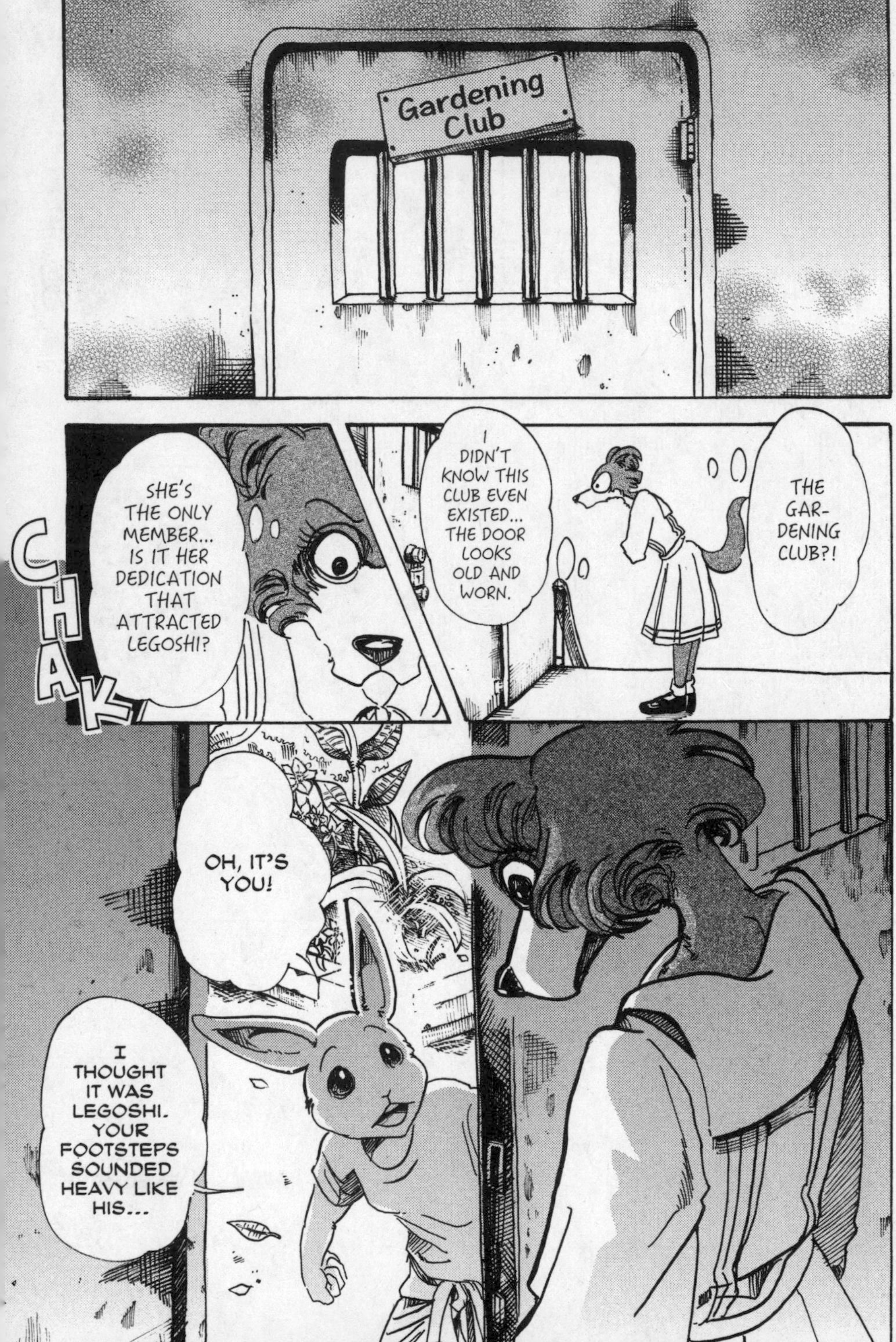
Gardening Club
THE GAR-DENING CLUB?!
I DIDN'T KNOW THIS CLUB EVEN EXISTED... THE DOOR LOOKS OLD AND WORN.
SHE'S THE ONLY MEMBER... IS IT HER DEDICATION THAT ATTRACTED LEGOSHI?
CHAK!
OH, IT'S YOU!
I THOUGHT IT WAS LEGOSHI. YOUR FOOTSTEPS SOUNDED HEAVY LIKE HIS...

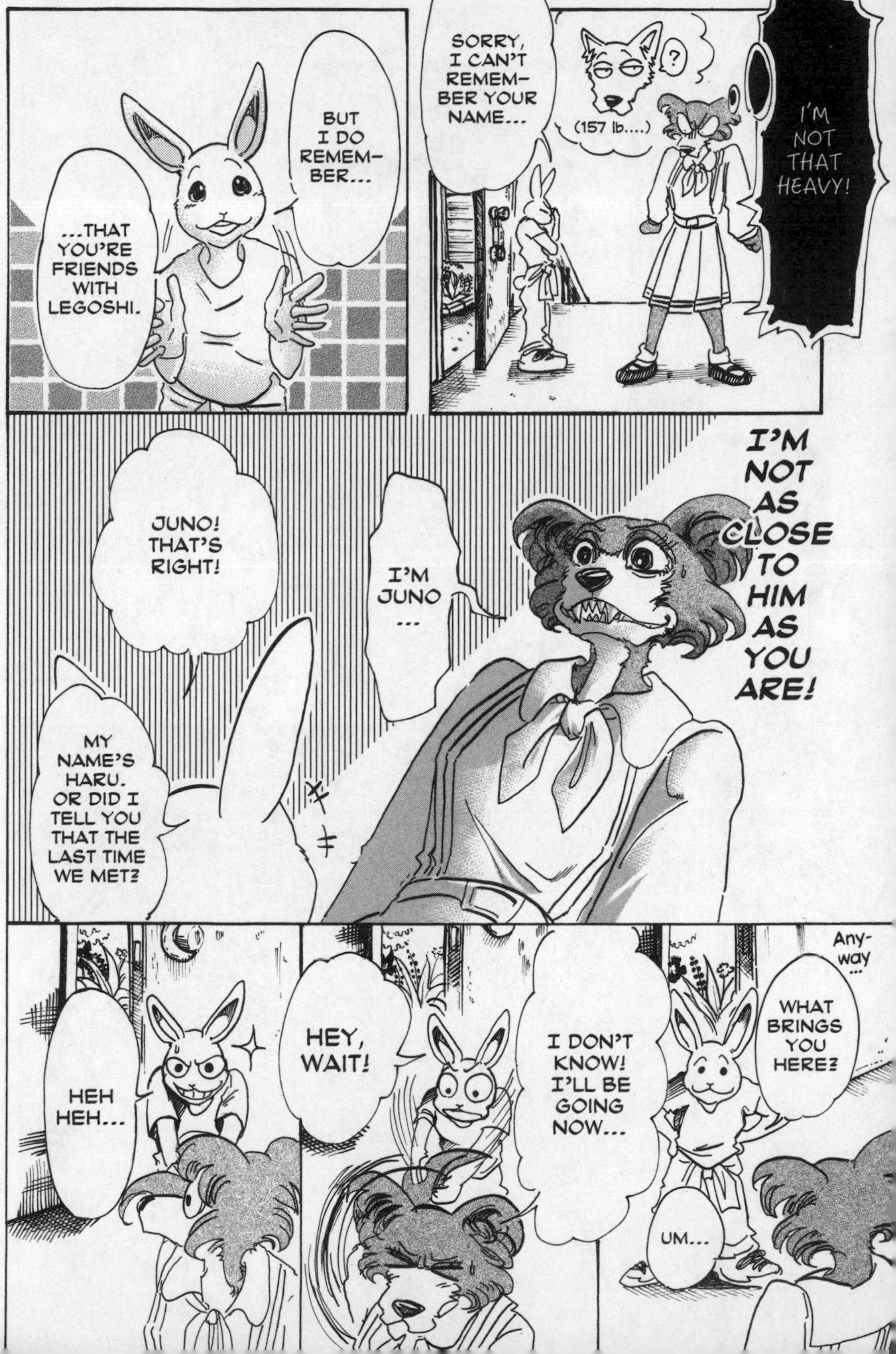
SORRY, I CAN'T REMEMBER YOUR NAME...
?
(157 lb....)
I'M NOT THAT HEAVY!
BUT I DO REMEMBER...
...THAT YOU'RE FRIENDS WITH LEGOSHI.
I'M NOT AS CLOSE TO HIM AS YOU ARE!
I'M JUNO...
JUNO! THAT'S RIGHT!
MY NAME'S HARU. OR DID I TELL YOU THAT THE LAST TIME WE MET?
Anyway...
WHAT BRINGS YOU HERE?
UM...
I DON'T KNOW! I'LL BE GOING NOW...
HEY, WAIT!
HEH HEH...

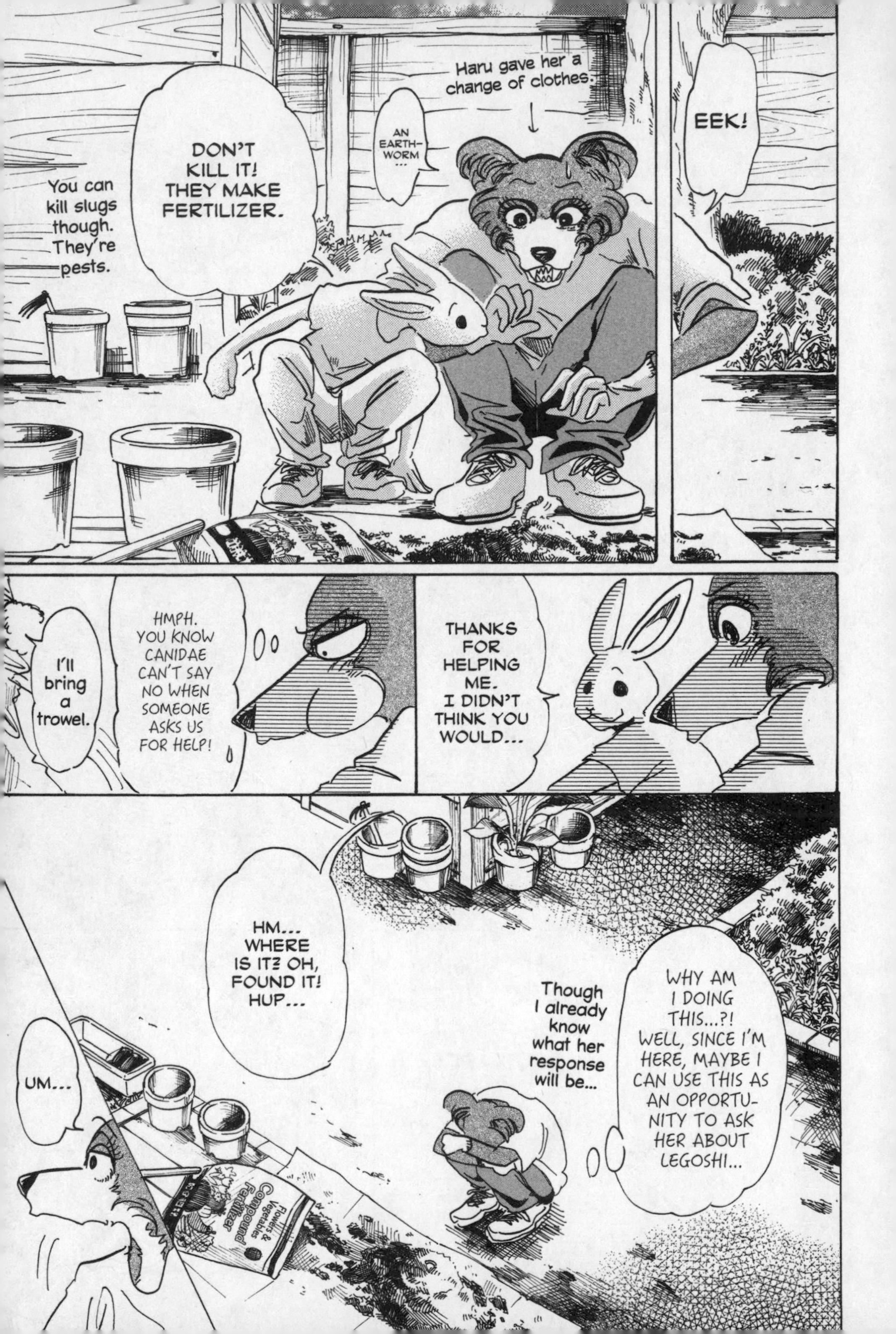
EEK!
Haru gave her a change of clothes.
AN EARTH-WORM...
DON'T KILL IT! THEY MAKE FERTILIZER.
You can kill slugs though. They're pests.
THANKS FOR HELPING ME. I DIDN'T THINK YOU WOULD...
HMPH. YOU KNOW CANIDAE CAN'T SAY NO WHEN SOMEONE ASKS US FOR HELP!
I'll bring a trowel.
WHY AM I DOING THIS...?! WELL, SINCE I'M HERE, MAYBE I CAN USE THIS AS AN OPPORTU-NITY TO ASK HER ABOUT LEGOSHI...
Though I already know what her response will be...
HM... WHERE IS IT? OH, FOUND IT! HUP...
UM...
Compound Fertilizer
Flowers & Vegetables

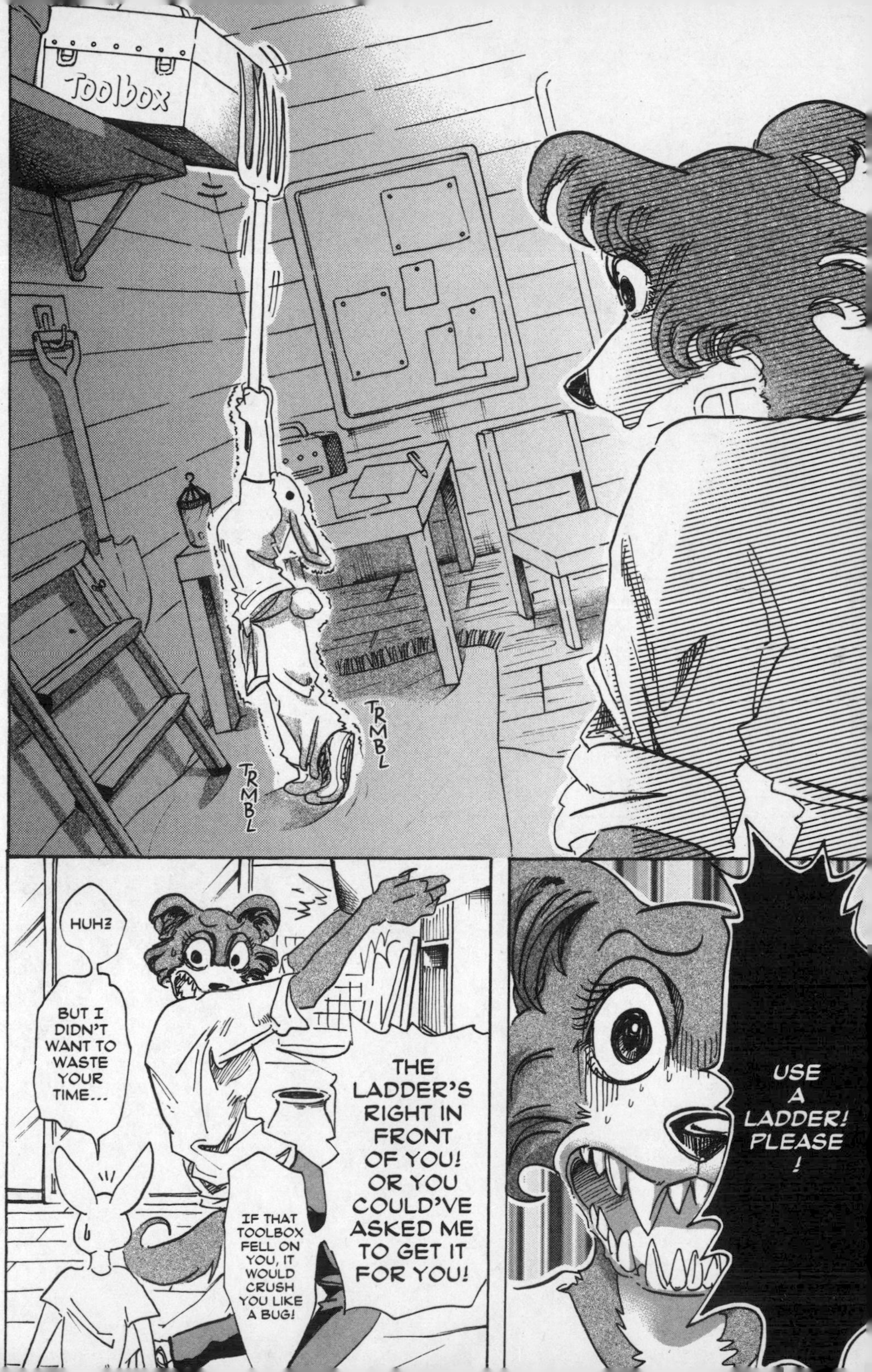

Toolbox
TRMBL
TRMBL
USE A LADDER! PLEASE!
THE LADDER'S RIGHT IN FRONT OF YOU! OR YOU COULD'VE ASKED ME TO GET IT FOR YOU!
IF THAT TOOLBOX FELL ON YOU, IT WOULD CRUSH YOU LIKE A BUG!
HUH?
BUT I DIDN'T WANT TO WASTE YOUR TIME...

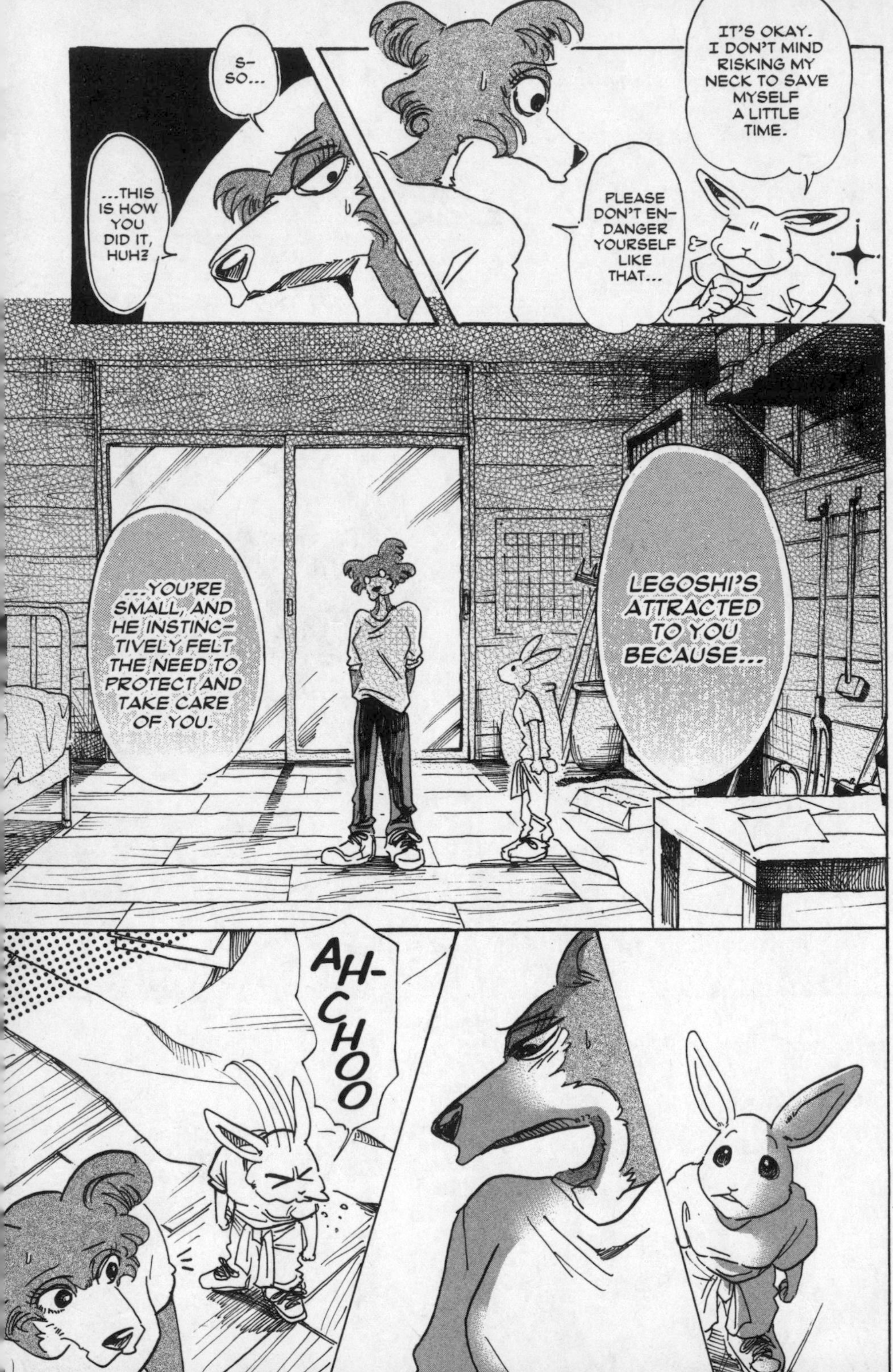
IT'S OKAY. I DON'T MIND RISKING MY NECK TO SAVE MYSELF A LITTLE TIME.
PLEASE DON'T EN-DANGER YOURSELF LIKE THAT...
S-SO...
...THIS IS HOW YOU DID IT, HUH?
LEGOSHI'S ATTRACTED TO YOU BECAUSE...
...YOU'RE SMALL, AND HE INSTINC-TIVELY FELT THE NEED TO PROTECT AND TAKE CARE OF YOU.
AH-CHOO

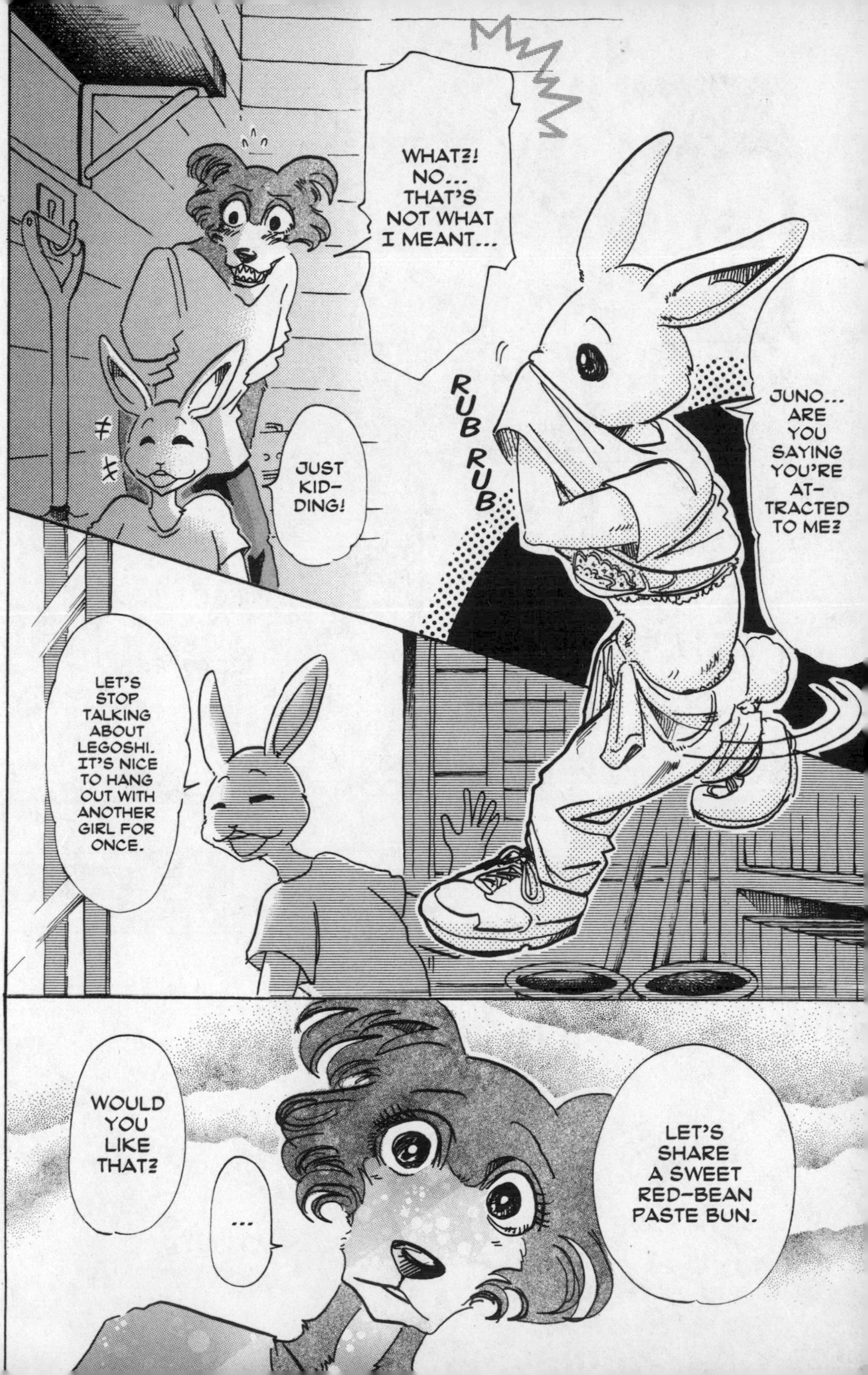
JUNO... ARE YOU SAYING YOU'RE AT-TRACTED TO ME?
RUB RUB
WHAT?! NO... THAT'S NOT WHAT I MEANT...
JUST KID-DING!
LET'S STOP TALKING ABOUT LEGOSHI. IT'S NICE TO HANG OUT WITH ANOTHER GIRL FOR ONCE.
LET'S SHARE A SWEET RED-BEAN PASTE BUN.
...
WOULD YOU LIKE THAT?

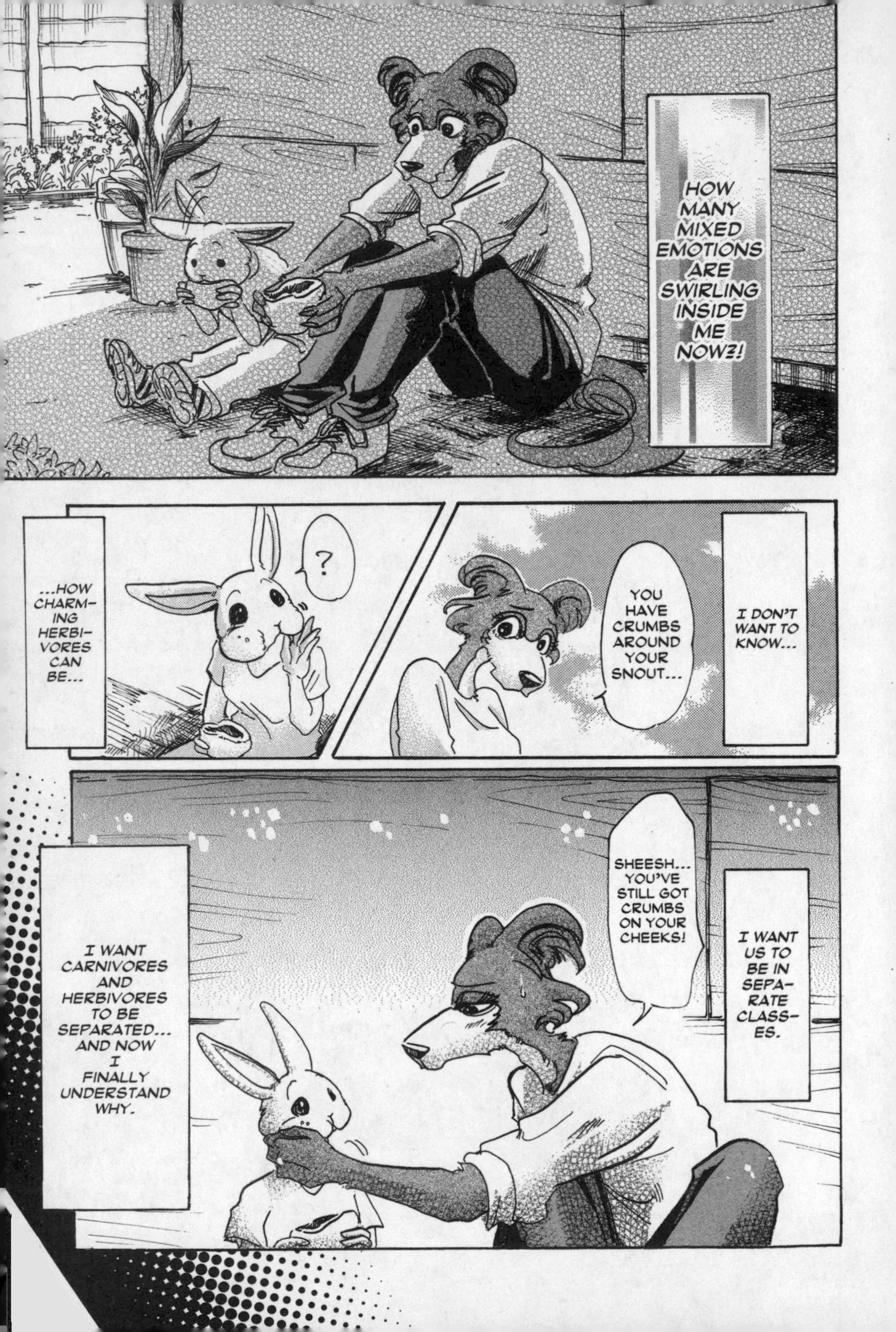
HOW MANY MIXED EMOTIONS ARE SWIRLING INSIDE ME NOW?!
I DON'T WANT TO KNOW...
YOU HAVE CRUMBS AROUND YOUR SNOUT...
?
...HOW CHARMING HERBIVORES CAN BE...
I WANT US TO BE IN SEPARATE CLASSES.
SHEESH... YOU'VE STILL GOT CRUMBS ON YOUR CHEEKS!
I WANT CARNIVORES AND HERBIVORES TO BE SEPARATED... AND NOW I FINALLY UNDERSTAND WHY.

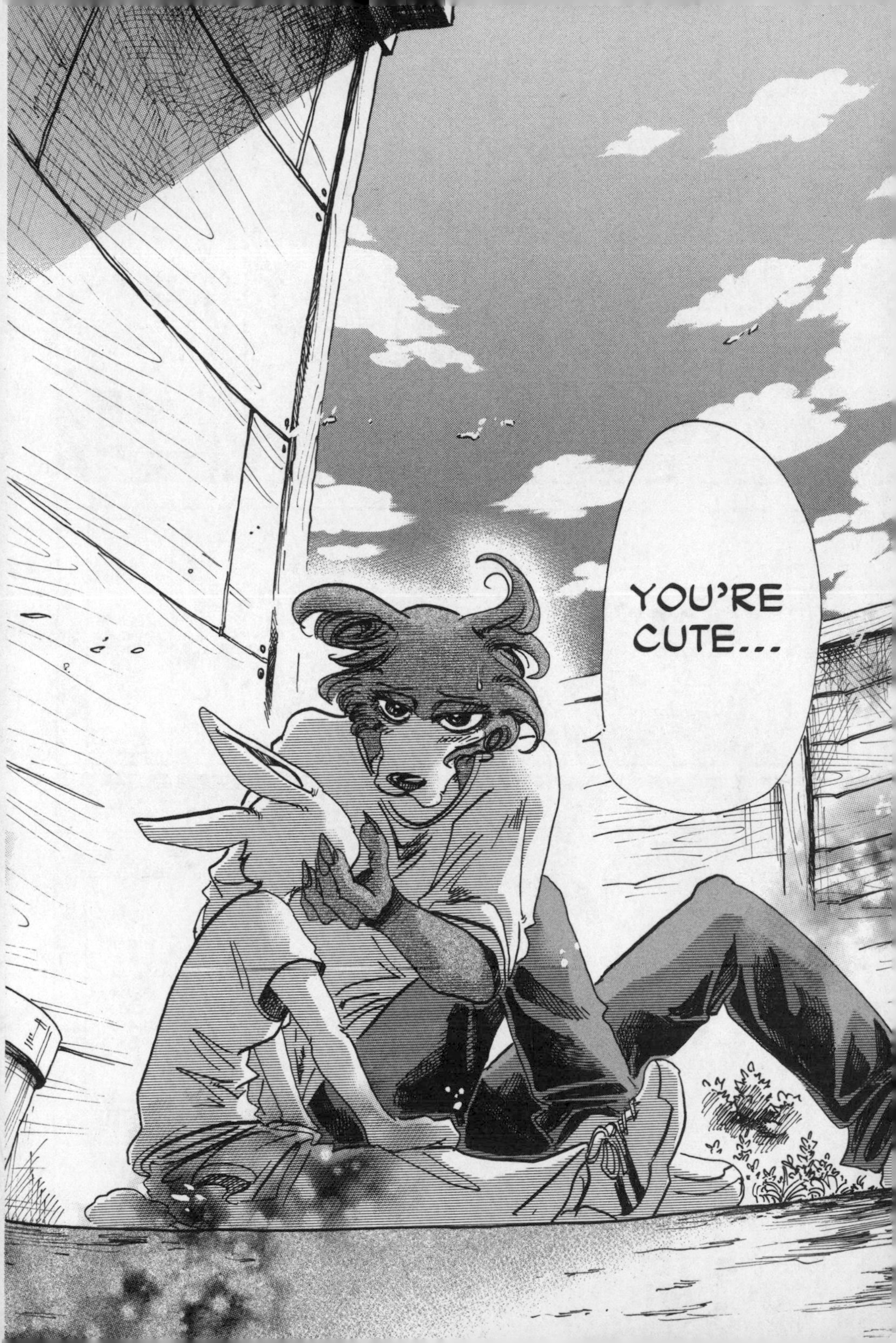
YOU'RE CUTE...

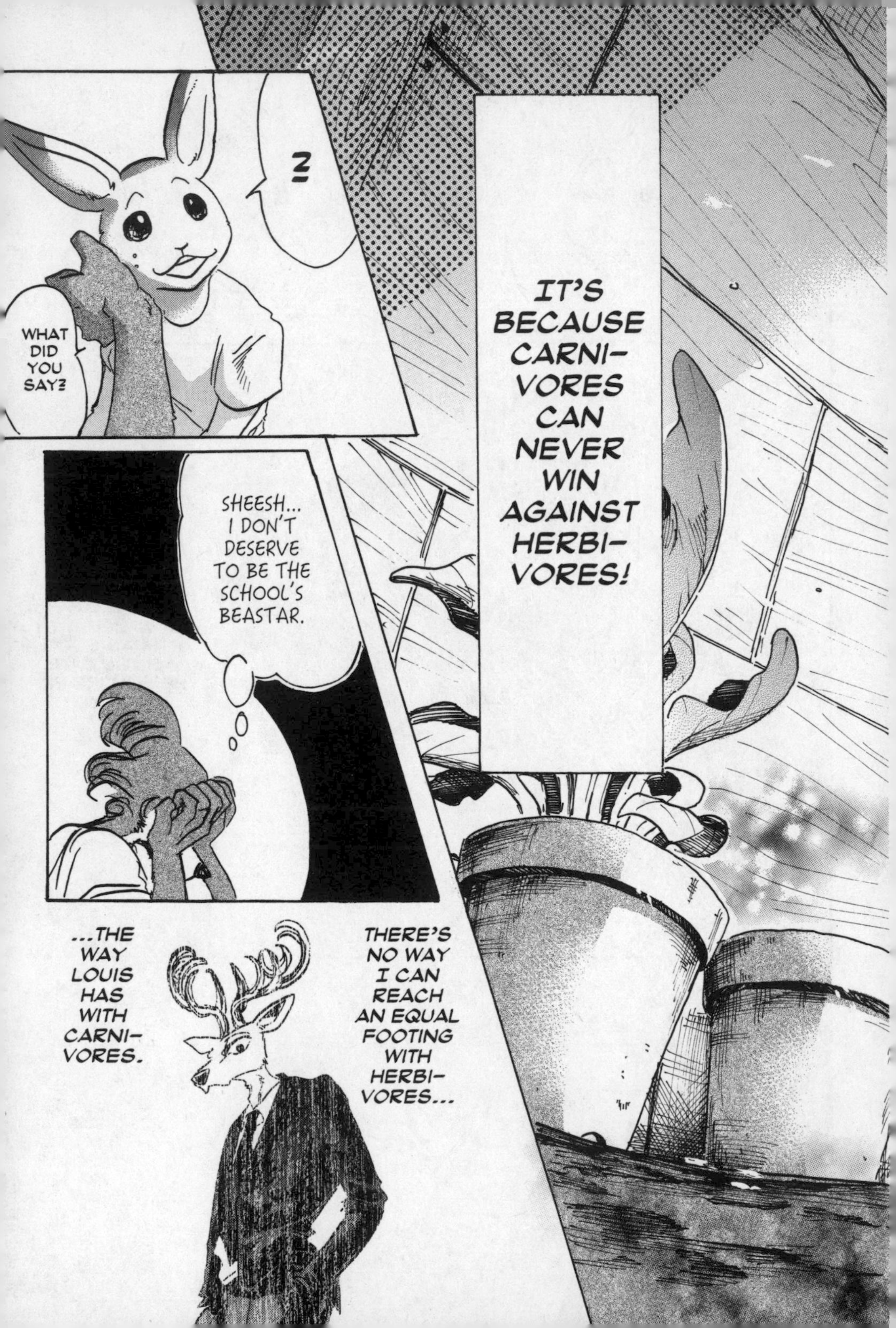
IT'S BECAUSE CARNIVORES CAN NEVER WIN AGAINST HERBIVORES!
WHAT DID YOU SAY?
SHEESH... I DON'T DESERVE TO BE THE SCHOOL'S BEASTAR.
THERE'S NO WAY I CAN REACH AN EQUAL FOOTING WITH HERBIVORES...
...THE WAY LOUIS HAS WITH CARNIVORES.

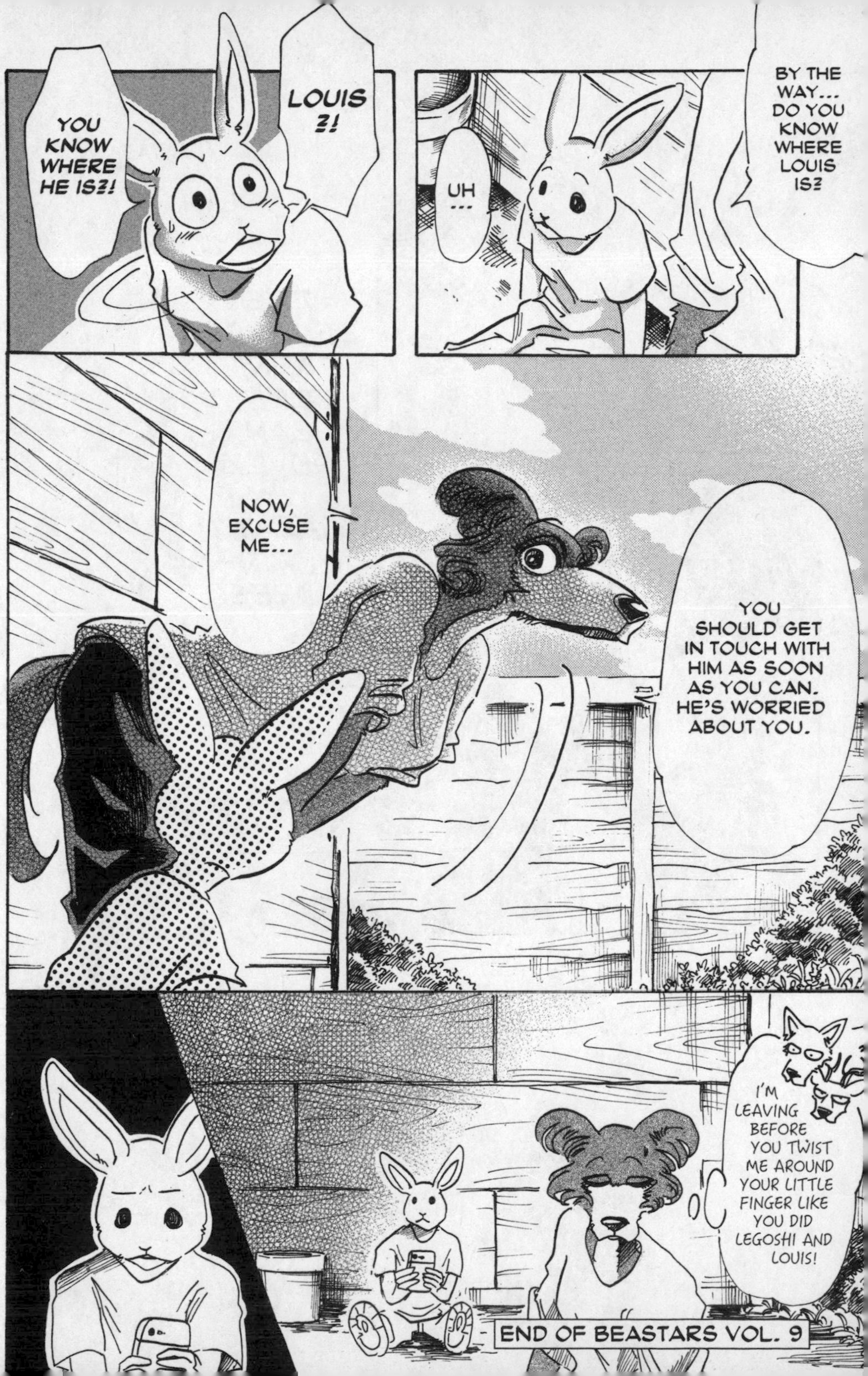
BY THE WAY... DO YOU KNOW WHERE LOUIS IS?
UH...
LOUIS?!
YOU KNOW WHERE HE IS?!
YOU SHOULD GET IN TOUCH WITH HIM AS SOON AS YOU CAN. HE'S WORRIED ABOUT YOU.
NOW, EXCUSE ME...
I'M LEAVING BEFORE YOU TWIST ME AROUND YOUR LITTLE FINGER LIKE YOU DID LEGOSHI AND LOUIS!
END OF BEASTARS VOL. 9

Pina Character Design Notes

Pina's appearance

If you look at the cover of this volume, Pina looks more beautiful than handsome, doesn't he?

When I add a new character to the story, I usually spend several months creating and refining them and eagerly await the right moment for their first appearance. However, with Pina it was different. The story had been kind of gloomy for a while, and I thought, "This is no good! The story needs a cheerful boy with charm and a commanding presence!" Pina was created out of a sense of urgency. And it only took me about three days.

Once Pina entered the story, he became more annoying than I expected. That was a surprise.

PROFILE

PINA (AGE 16)
MALE
BOVIDAE
(DALL BIGHORN SHEEP)
BIRTHDAY: DECEMBER 27
BLOOD TYPE: B
HEIGHT: 5 FT., 7 IN.
WEIGHT: 121 LB. (EXCLUDING HORNS)
LOVES GIRLS AND HIS OWN HORNS

Fooling around with girls

This is Pina's hobby. I suppose girls are his source of emotional support. Pina loves all kinds of females. "I love any girl, as long as she's a species with horns!" Horns are important to him. He must be proud to be an Artiodactyla. But because he loves all kinds of girls, he's currently going out with five of them at once.

How did you come up with his name?

I took it from a German dancer named Pina Bausch. I love the way German words sound because they're so different from Japanese.

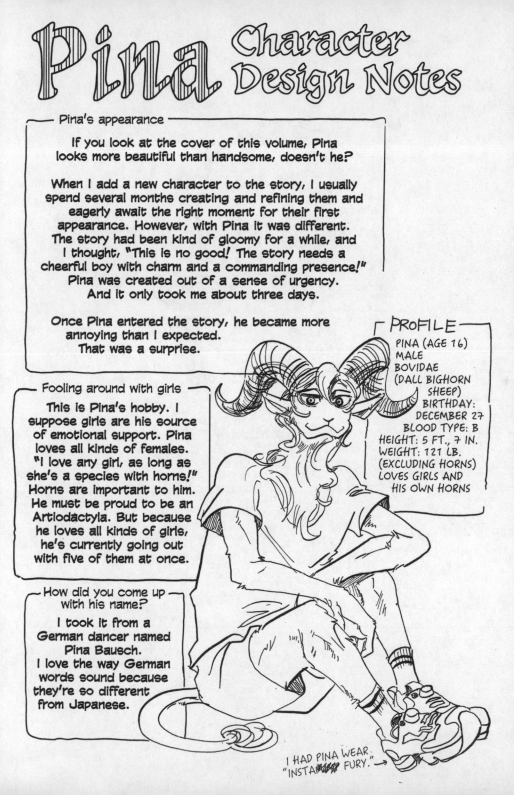

I HAD PINA WEAR "INSTA~~×××~~ FURY." →

The Covers of BEASTARS

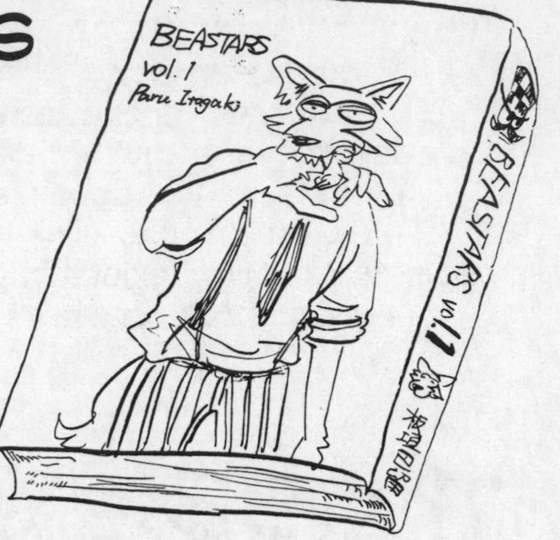
BEASTARS
vol. 1
Paru Itagaki
BEASTARS vol. 1

THE COVER DESIGN IS THE SAME FOR EVERY VOLUME. THE TITLE IS IN THE BACKGROUND. ONE OR TWO CHARACTERS POSE IN THE FOREGROUND.

THE "*B*" OF BEASTARS IS HUGE. I HAVE TO POSE THE CHARACTERS SO THERE'S ENOUGH SPACE ON THE TOP LEFT FOR THE "B."

Please read... ...the panels in this order (follow the arrows).

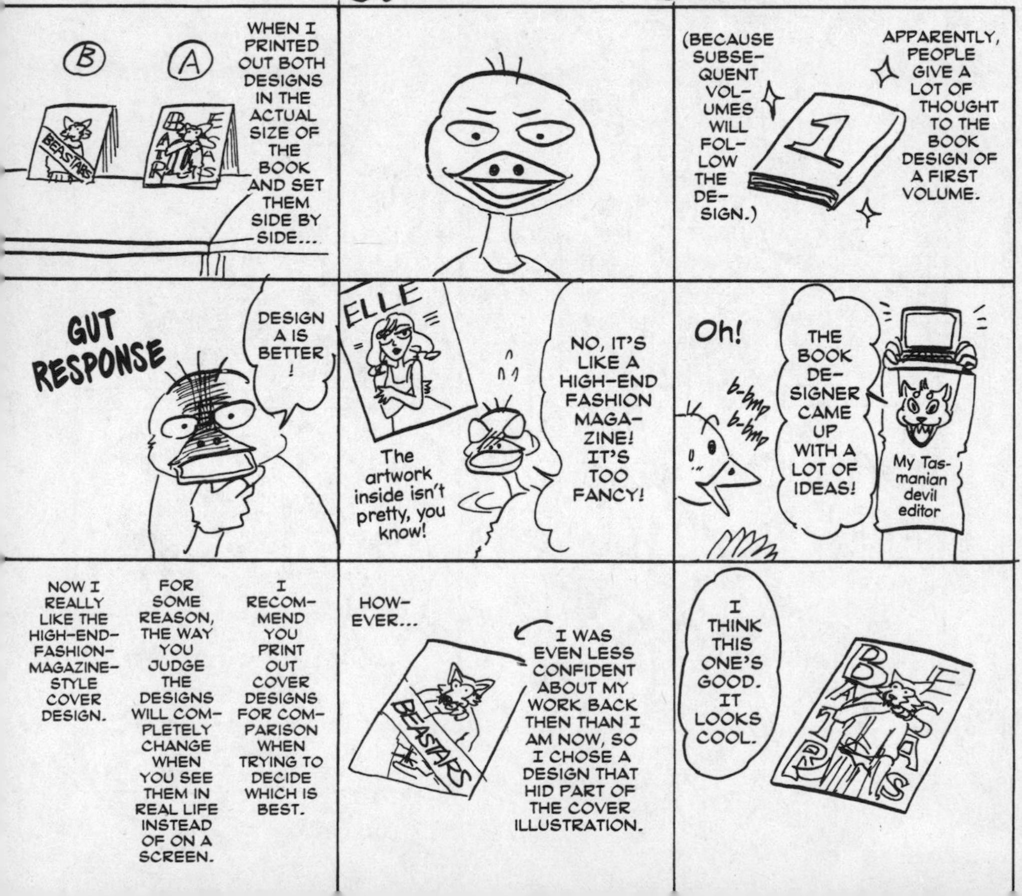
APPARENTLY, PEOPLE GIVE A LOT OF THOUGHT TO THE BOOK DESIGN OF A FIRST VOLUME.
(BECAUSE SUBSEQUENT VOLUMES WILL FOLLOW THE DESIGN.)
1
WHEN I PRINTED OUT BOTH DESIGNS IN THE ACTUAL SIZE OF THE BOOK AND SET THEM SIDE BY SIDE...
B
A
BEASTARS
Oh!
THE BOOK DESIGNER CAME UP WITH A LOT OF IDEAS!
b-bmp b-bmp
My Tasmanian devil editor
NO, IT'S LIKE A HIGH-END FASHION MAGAZINE! IT'S TOO FANCY!
ELLE
The artwork inside isn't pretty, you know!
DESIGN A IS BETTER!
GUT RESPONSE
I THINK THIS ONE'S GOOD. IT LOOKS COOL.
HOWEVER...
I WAS EVEN LESS CONFIDENT ABOUT MY WORK BACK THEN THAN I AM NOW, SO I CHOSE A DESIGN THAT HID PART OF THE COVER ILLUSTRATION.
BEASTARS
I RECOMMEND YOU PRINT OUT COVER DESIGNS FOR COMPARISON WHEN TRYING TO DECIDE WHICH IS BEST.
FOR SOME REASON, THE WAY YOU JUDGE THE DESIGNS WILL COMPLETELY CHANGE WHEN YOU SEE THEM IN REAL LIFE INSTEAD OF ON A SCREEN.
NOW I REALLY LIKE THE HIGH-END-FASHION-MAGAZINE-STYLE COVER DESIGN.

~ The Dangerous 30 ~

In our human world, there's the so-called
3B's a woman should beware of when dating:
boy hairdressers, bartenders, and band musicians.
Maybe it's because people think
they're too slick with women?
Something similar exists in the BEASTARS world!
Watch out for these types of guys!

The 3B's (beasts)!!

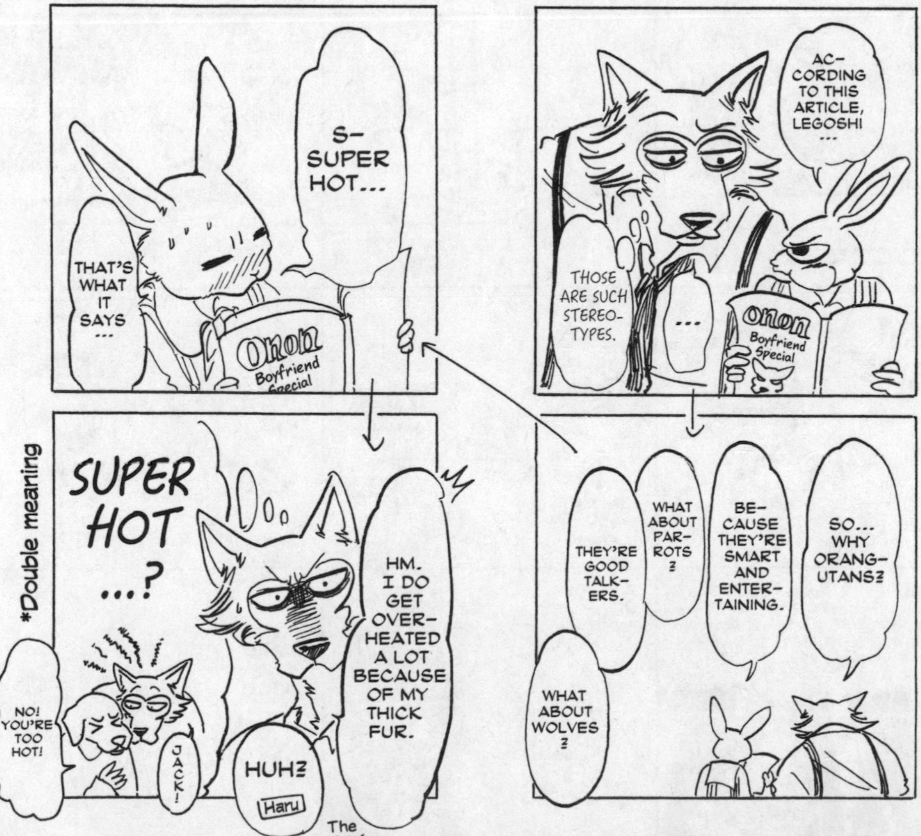
ACCORDING TO THIS ARTICLE, LEGOSHI...
THOSE ARE SUCH STEREOTYPES.
...
onon
Boyfriend Special
S-SUPER HOT...
THAT'S WHAT IT SAYS...
onon
Boyfriend Special
SO... WHY ORANGUTANS?
BECAUSE THEY'RE SMART AND ENTERTAINING.
WHAT ABOUT PARROTS?
THEY'RE GOOD TALKERS.
WHAT ABOUT WOLVES?
HM. I DO GET OVERHEATED A LOT BECAUSE OF MY THICK FUR.
SUPER HOT ...?
*Double meaning
HUH?
Haru
The article's correct!
JACK!
NO! YOU'RE TOO HOT!

We are shishi-GUMI

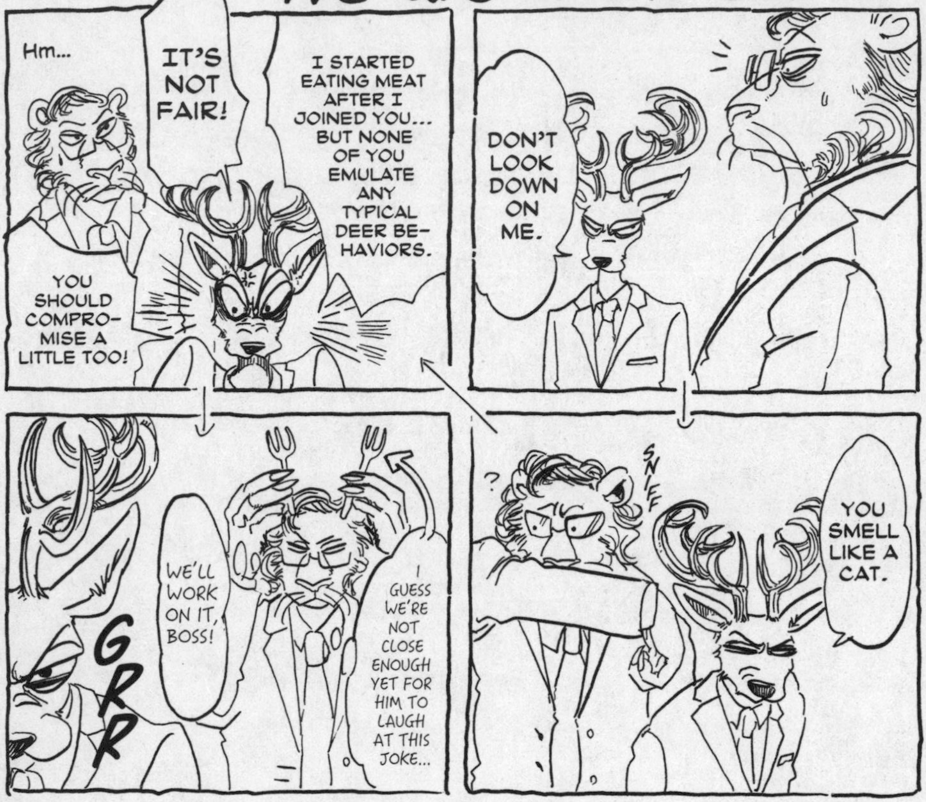
DON'T LOOK DOWN ON ME.
SNIFF
YOU SMELL LIKE A CAT.
I STARTED EATING MEAT AFTER I JOINED YOU... BUT NONE OF YOU EMULATE ANY TYPICAL DEER BEHAVIORS.
IT'S NOT FAIR!
Hm...
YOU SHOULD COMPROMISE A LITTLE TOO!
I GUESS WE'RE NOT CLOSE ENOUGH YET FOR HIM TO LAUGH AT THIS JOKE...
WE'LL WORK ON IT, BOSS!
GRR

~Shishi-gumi's New Rules~

(*Top secret. Don't let the boss find out.)

1. Wear low-heeled shoes.
2. Don't use perfume designed for felines.
3. Shower if you get wet in the rain.
4. Wear a black suit (except for the boss).
5. When you talk to the boss, make sure your field of vision is level with his. (Bend over slowly. He won't notice.)
6. Never serve venison at the table.

Ibuki wrote these up. →

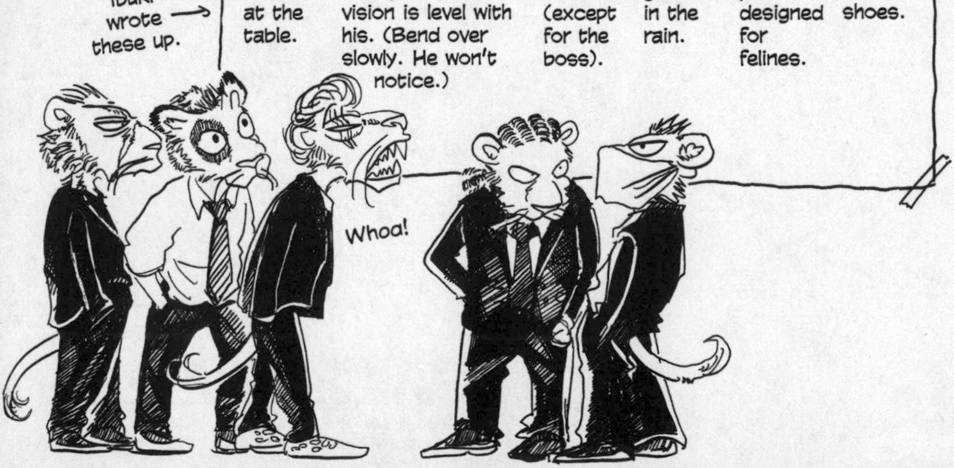
Whoa!

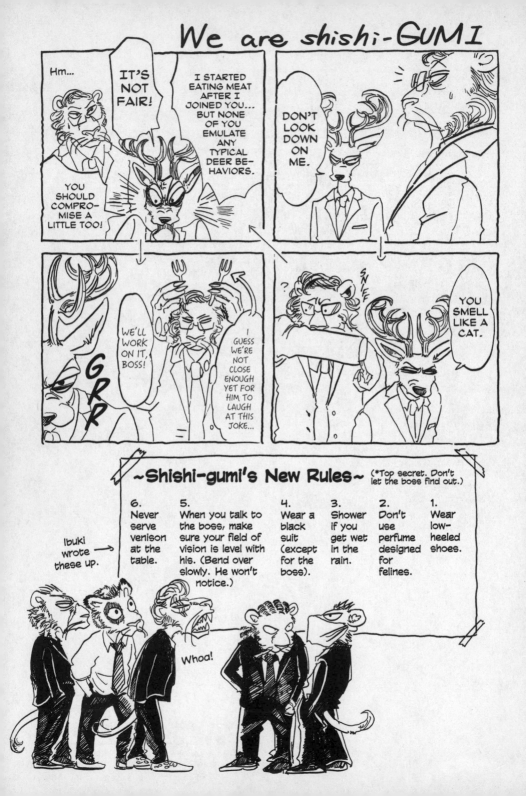

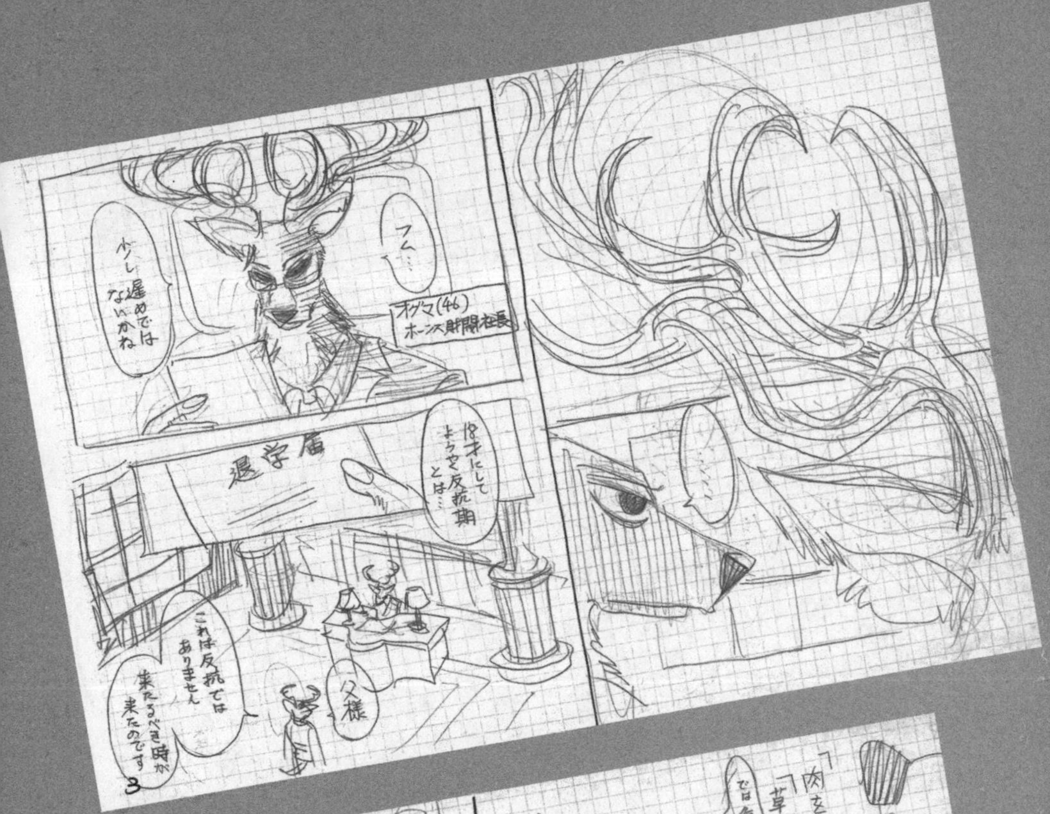
……
フム……
オグマ(46)
ホーンズ財閥社長
少し遅めではないかね
18才にしてようやく反抗期とは……
退学届
父様
これは反抗ではありません 来たるべき時が来たのです
3

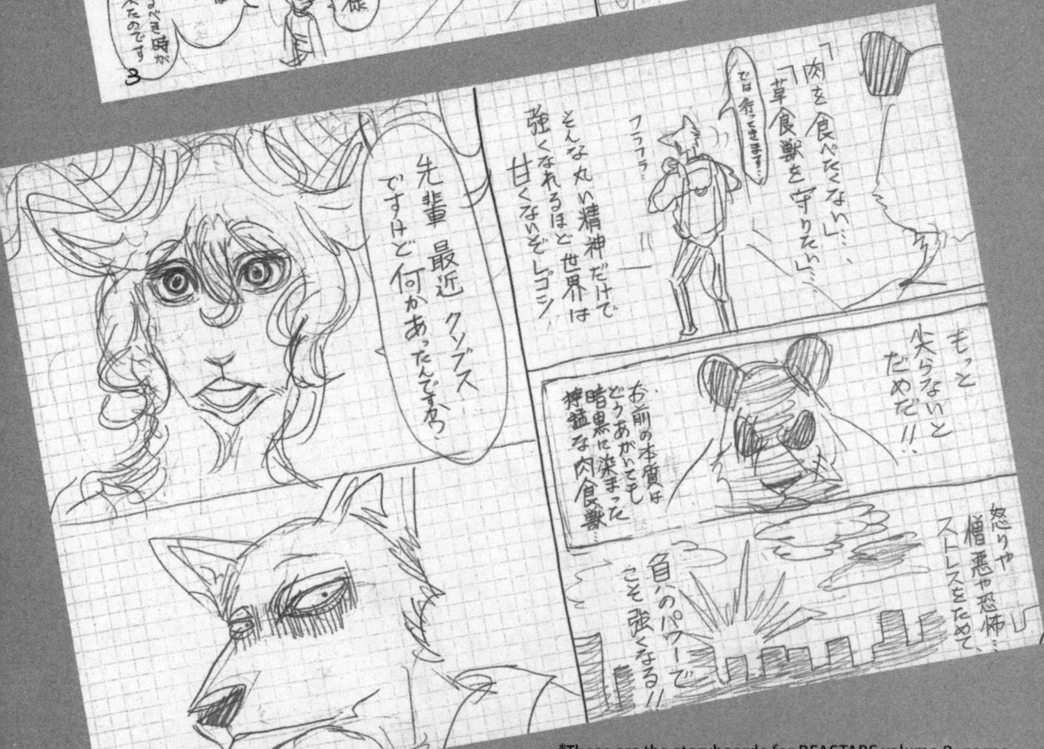
「肉を食べたくない」……
「草食獣を守りたい」……
では行ってきます……
フラフラ
そんな丸い精神だけで強くなれるほど世界は甘くないぞレゴシ
もっと尖らないとだめだ!!
お前の本質はどうあがいても暗黒に染まった獰猛な肉食獣……
怒りや憎悪や恐怖……ストレスをためて
こそ自分のパワーで強くなる!!
先輩 最近 クソブスですけど何かあったんですか?
11

*These are the storyboards for BEASTARS volume 8, pages 70–71, 38–39, 104–105 and 196–197. Manga artists show storyboards to their editor to communicate what they have in mind for upcoming chapters.

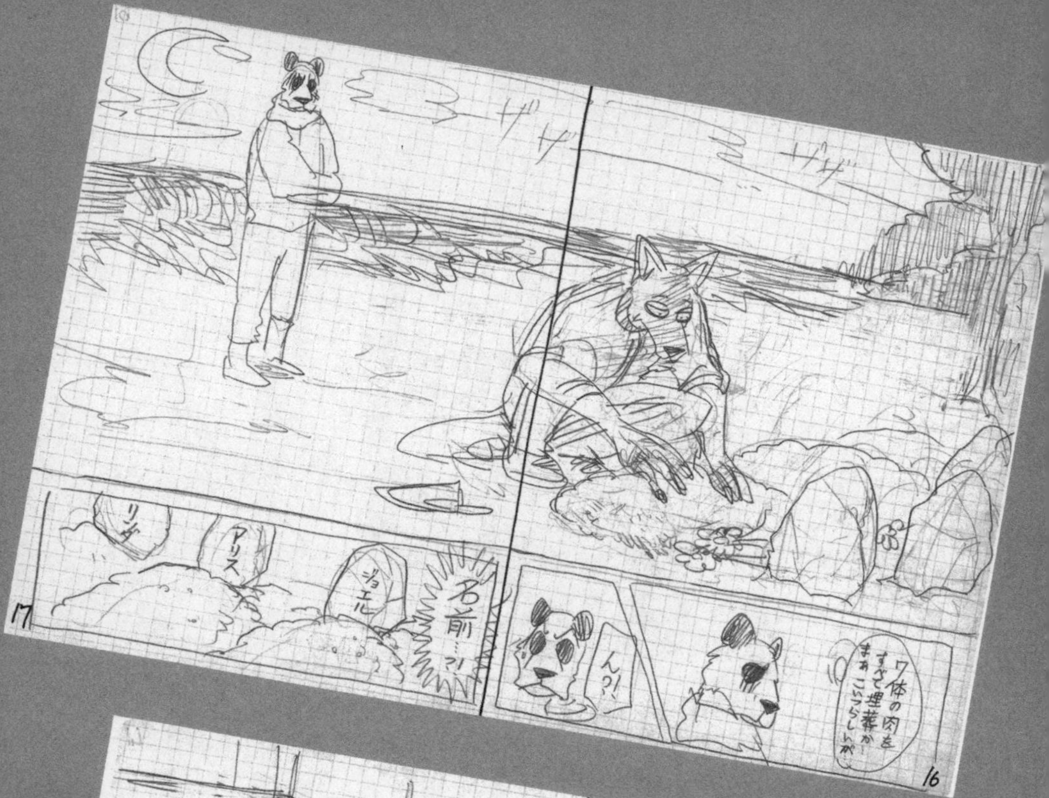
ザザ
ザザ
7体の肉をすべて埋葬か！ まぁこいつらしいが
ん?!
名前…?!
ジョエル
アリス
リンダ
16
17

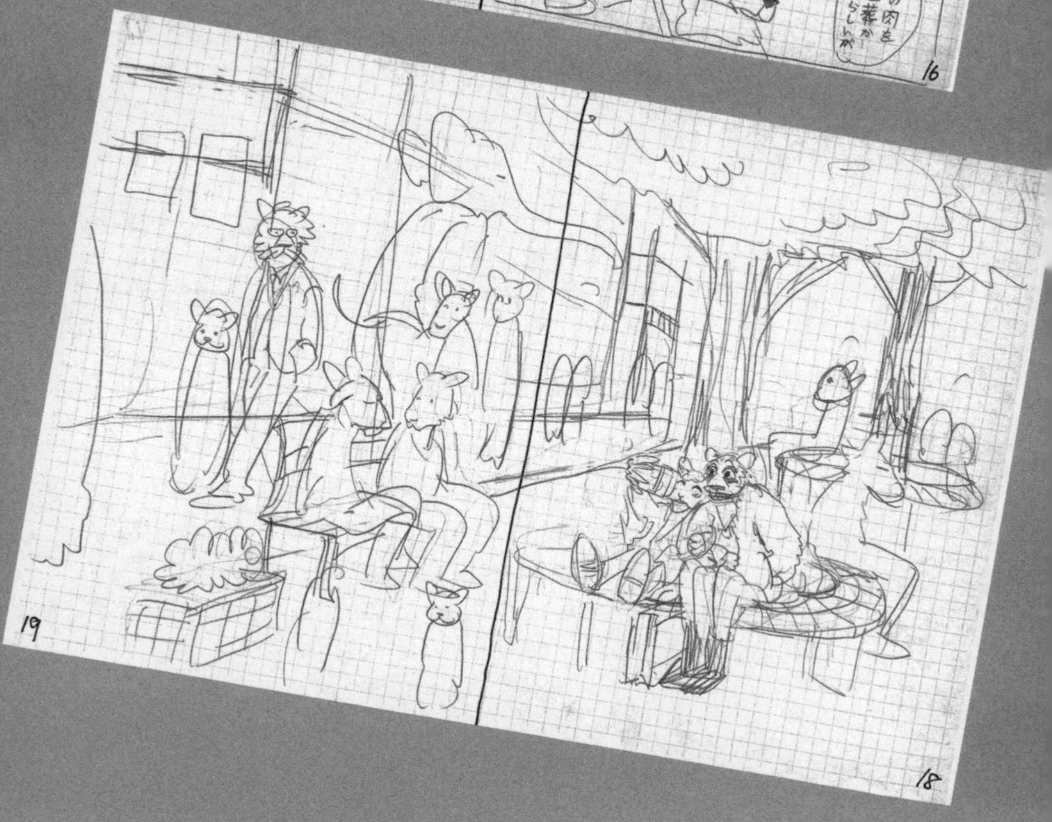
18
19

I'M GOING BACK TO BEING A BABY
CHICK. I'LL HIDE MY ADULT CHICKEN
COMB INSIDE MY HEART!

PARU ITAGAKI

Paru Itagaki began her professional
career as a manga author in 2016 with the
short story collection **BEAST COMPLEX**.
BEASTARS is her first serialization.
BEASTARS has won multiple awards in
Japan, including the prestigious 2018
Manga Taisho Award.